Civil Society Activism under Authoritarian Rule

This book examines how civil society actors operate under authoritarian constraints, and examines how this is linked to regime change.

This book moves beyond traditional notions of civil society and explains the complexity of state–society relations in authoritarian contexts outside the framework of democratization. Rejecting a wholly normative approach, the contributors focus on the whole range of civic activism under authoritarianism, from resistance to support for the political system in place. They explain how activism under authoritarianism is subject to different structures, and demonstrate how active citizens have tried to claw back powers of expression and contestation, but also sought to create a voice for themselves as privileged interlocutors of authoritarian regimes.

With a strong empirical focus on a wide range of countries and authoritarian regimes, this book presents cross-country comparisons on Spain, Portugal, Romania, Czechoslovakia, Poland, Hungary, Russia, Kyrgyzstan, Tajikistan, Cuba, Chile, Tunisia, Yemen, Jordan, Afghanistan and Burma.

Civil Society Activism under Authoritarian Rule will be of interest to students and scholars of international politics, comparative politics, civil society, authoritarianism and regime change.

Francesco Cavatorta is Senior Lecturer in the School of Law and Government at Dublin City University, Ireland.

Routledge/ECPR studies in European political science
Edited by Thomas Poguntke
Ruhr University Bochum, Germany on behalf of the European Consortium for Political Research

The Routledge/ECPR Studies in European Political Science series is published in association with the European Consortium for Political Research – the leading organization concerned with the growth and development of political science in Europe. The series presents high-quality edited volumes on topics at the leading edge of current interest in political science and related fields, with contributions from European scholars and others who have presented work at ECPR workshops or research groups.

1 **Regionalist Parties in Western Europe**
 Edited by Lieven de Winter and Huri Türsan

2 **Comparing Party System Change**
 Edited by Jan-Erik Lane and Paul Pennings

3 **Political Theory and European Union**
 Edited by Albert Weale and Michael Nentwich

4 **Politics of Sexuality**
 Edited by Terrell Carver and Véronique Mottier

5 **Autonomous Policy Making by International Organizations**
 Edited by Bob Reinalda and Bertjan Verbeek

6 **Social Capital and European Democracy**
 Edited by Jan van Deth, Marco Maraffi, Ken Newton and Paul Whiteley

7 **Party Elites in Divided Societies**
 Edited by Kurt Richard Luther and Kris Deschouwer

8 **Citizenship and Welfare State Reform in Europe**
 Edited by Jet Bussemaker

9 **Democratic Governance and New Technology**
 Technologically mediated innovations in political practice in Western Europe
 Edited by Ivan Horrocks, Jens Hoff and Pieter Tops

10 **Democracy without Borders**
 Transnationalisation and conditionality in new democracies
 Edited by Jean Grugel

11 **Cultural Theory as Political Science**
Edited by Michael Thompson, Gunnar Grendstad and Per Selle

12 **The Transformation of Governance in the European Union**
Edited by Beate Kohler-Koch and Rainer Eising

13 **Parliamentary Party Groups in European Democracies**
Political parties behind closed doors
Edited by Knut Heidar and Ruud Koole

14 **Survival of the European Welfare State**
Edited by Stein Kuhnle

15 **Private Organisations in Global Politics**
Edited by Karsten Ronit and Volker Schneider

16 **Federalism and Political Performance**
Edited by Ute Wachendorfer-Schmidt

17 **Democratic Innovation**
Deliberation, representation and association
Edited by Michael Saward

18 **Public Opinion and the International Use of Force**
Edited by Philip Everts and Pierangelo Isernia

19 **Religion and Mass Electoral Behaviour in Europe**
Edited by David Broughton and Hans-Martien ten Napel

20 **Estimating the Policy Position of Political Actors**
Edited by Michael Laver

21 **Democracy and Political Change in the 'Third World'**
Edited by Jeff Haynes

22 **Politicians, Bureaucrats and Administrative Reform**
Edited by B. Guy Peters and Jon Pierre

23 **Social Capital and Participation in Everyday Life**
Edited by Paul Dekker and Eric M. Uslaner

24 **Development and Democracy**
What do we know and how?
Edited by Ole Elgström and Goran Hyden

25 **Do Political Campaigns Matter?**
Campaign effects in elections and referendums
Edited by David M. Farrell and Rüdiger Schmitt-Beck

26 **Political Journalism**
New challenges, new practices
Edited by Raymond Kuhn and Erik Neveu

27 **Economic Voting**
Edited by Han Dorussen and Michael Taylor

28 **Organized Crime and the Challenge to Democracy**
Edited by Felia Allum and Renate Siebert

29 **Understanding the European Union's External Relations**
Edited by Michèle Knodt and Sebastiaan Princen

30 **Social Democratic Party Policies in Contemporary Europe**
Edited by Giuliano Bonoli and Martin Powell

31 **Decision Making Within International Organisations**
Edited by Bob Reinalda and Bertjan Verbeek

32 **Comparative Biomedical Policy**
Governing assisted reproductive technologies
Edited by Ivar Bleiklie, Malcolm L. Goggin and Christine Rothmayr

33 **Electronic Democracy**
Mobilisation, organisation and participation via new ICTs
Edited by Rachel K. Gibson, Andrea Römmele and Stephen J. Ward

34 **Liberal Democracy and Environmentalism**
The end of environmentalism?
Edited by Marcel Wissenburg and Yoram Levy

35 **Political Theory and the European Constitution**
Edited by Lynn Dobson and Andreas Follesdal

36 **Politics and the European Commission**
Actors, interdependence, legitimacy
Edited by Andy Smith

37 **Metropolitan Governance**
Capacity, democracy and the dynamics of place
Edited by Hubert Heinelt and Daniel Kübler

38 **Democracy and the Role of Associations**
Political, organizational and social contexts
Edited by Sigrid Roßteutscher

39 **The Territorial Politics of Welfare**
Edited by Nicola McEwen and Luis Moreno

40 **Health Governance in Europe**
Issues, challenges and theories
Edited by Monika Steffen

41 **Republicanism in Theory and Practice**
Edited by Iseult Honohan and Jeremy Jennings

42 **Mass Media and Political Communication in New Democracies**
Edited by Katrin Voltmer

43 **Delegation in Contemporary Democracies**
Edited by Dietmar Braun and Fabrizio Gilardi

44 **Governance and Democracy**
Comparing national, European and international experiences
Edited by Yannis Papadopoulos and Arthur Benz

45 **The European Union's Roles in International Politics**
Concepts and analysis
Edited by Ole Elgström and Michael Smith

46 **Policy-making Processes and the European Constitution**
A comparative study of member states and accession countries
Edited by Thomas König and Simon Hug

47 **Democratic Politics and Party Competition**
Edited by Judith Bara and Albert Weale

48 **Participatory Democracy and Political Participation**
Can participatory engineering bring citizens back in?
Edited by Thomas Zittel and Dieter Fuchs

49 **Civil Societies and Social Movements**
Potentials and problems
Edited by Derrick Purdue

50 **Resources, Governance and Civil Conflict**
Edited by Magnus Öberg and Kaare Strøm

51 **Transnational Private Governance and its Limits**
Edited by Jean-Christophe Graz and Andreas Nölke

52 **International Organizations and Implementation**
Enforcers, managers, authorities?
Edited by Jutta Joachim, Bob Reinalda and Bertjan Verbeek

53 **New Parties in Government**
Edited by Kris Deschouwer

54 **In Pursuit of Sustainable Development**
New governance practices at the sub-national level in Europe
Edited by Susan Baker and Katarina Eckerberg

55 **Governments, NGOs and Anti-Corruption**
The new integrity warriors
Edited by Luís de Sousa, Barry Hindess and Peter Larmour

56 **Intra-Party Politics and Coalition Governments**
Edited by Daniela Giannetti and Kenneth Benoit

57 **Political Parties and Partisanship**
Social identity and individual attitudes
Edited by John Bartle and Paolo Belucci

58 **The Future of Political Community**
Edited by Gideon Baker and Jens Bartelson

59 **The Discursive Politics of Gender Equality**
Stretching, bending and policy making
Edited by Emanuela Lombardo, Petra Meier and Mieke Verloo

60 **Another Europe**
Conceptions and practices of democracy in the European social forums
Edited by Donatella Della Porta

61 **European and North American Policy Change**
Drivers and dynamics
Edited by Giliberto Capano and Michael Howlett

62 **Referendums and Representative Democracy**
Responsiveness, accountability and deliberation
Edited by Maija Setälä and Theo Schiller

63 **Education in Political Science**
Discovering a neglected field
Edited by Anja P. Jakobi, Kerstin Martens and Klaus Dieter Wolf

64 **Religion and Politics in Europe, the Middle East and North Africa**
Edited by Jeffrey Haynes

65 **New Directions in Federalism Studies**
Edited by Jan Erk and Wilfried Swenden

66 **Public Policy and the Media**
The interplay of mass communication and political decision making
Edited by Sigrid Koch-Baumgarten and Katrin Voltmer

67 **Changing Government Relations in Europe**
From localism to intergovernmentalism
Edited by Michael J. Goldsmith and Edward C. Page

68 **Political Discussion in Modern Democracies**
A comparative perspective
Edited by Michael R. Wolf, Laura Morales and Ken'ichi Ikeda

69 **Dominant Political Parties and Democracy**
Concepts, measures, cases and comparisons
Edited by Matthjis Bogaards and Françoise Boucek

70 **The Political Representation of Immigrants and Minorities**
Voters, parties and parliaments in liberal democracies
Edited by Karen Bird, Thomas Saalfeld and Andreas M. Wüst

71 **The Role of Governments in Legislative Agenda Setting**
Edited by Bjørn Erik Rasch and George Tsebelis

72 **Administrative Reforms and Democratic Governance**
Edited by Jean-Michel Eymeri-Douzans and Jon Pierre

73 **Puzzles of Government Formation**
Coalition theory and deviant cases
Edited by Rudy B. Andeweg, Lieven De Winter and Patrick Dumont

74 **New Regionalism and the European Union**
Dialogues, comparisons and new research directions
Edited by Alex Warleigh-Lack, Nick Robinson and Ben Rosamond

75 **Politics of Religion in Western Europe**
Edited by François Foret and Xabier Itcaina

76 **Ageing Populations in Post-industrial Democracies**
Comparative studies of policies and politics
Edited by Pieter Vanhuysse and Achim Goerres

77 **New Participatory Dimensions in Civil Society**
Professionalization and individualized collective action
Edited by Jan W. Van Deth and William A. Maloney

78 **Parliamentary Roles in Modern Legislatures**
Edited by Magnus Blomgren and Olivier Rozenberg

79 **Party Government in the New Europe**
Hans Keman and Ferdinand Muller-Rommel

80 **Migration and Organized Civil Society**
Rethinking national policy
Edited by Dirk Halm and Zeynep Sezgin

81 **Civil Society Activism under Authoritarian Rule**
A comparative perspective
Edited by Francesco Cavatorta

Also available from Routledge in association with the ECPR:
Sex Equality Policy in Western Europe, *Edited by Frances Gardiner*; **Democracy and Green Political Thought**, *Edited by Brian Doherty & Marius de Geus*; **The New Politics of Unemployment**, *Edited by Hugh Compston*; **Citizenship, Democracy and Justice in the New Europe**, *Edited by Percy B. Lehning & Albert Weale*; **Private Groups and Public Life**, *Edited by Jan W. van Deth*; **The Political Context of Collective Action**, *Edited by Ricca Edmondson*; **Theories of Secession**, *Edited by Percy Lehning*; **Regionalism Across the North/South Divide**, *Edited by Jean Grugel & Wil Hout.*

Civil Society Activism under Authoritarian Rule

A comparative perspective

Edited by Francesco Cavatorta

LONDON AND NEW YORK

First published 2013
by Routledge
2 Park Square, Milton Park, Abingdon, Oxfordshire OX14 4RN

Simultaneously published in the USA and Canada
by Routledge
711 Third Avenue, New York, NY 10017

First issued in paperback 2014

Routledge is an imprint of the Taylor & Francis Group, an informa business.

© 2013 Francesco Cavatorta for selection and editorial matter; individual contributors their contribution.

The right of Francesco Cavatorta to be identified as the author of the editorial material, and of the authors for their individual chapters, has been asserted in accordance with sections 77 and 78 of the Copyright, Designs and Patents Act 1988.

All rights reserved. No part of this book may be reprinted or reproduced or utilized in any form or by any electronic, mechanical, or other means, now known or hereafter invented, including photocopying and recording, or in any information storage or retrieval system, without permission in writing from the publishers.

Trademark notice: Product or corporate names may be trademarks or registered trademarks, and are used only for identification and explanation without intent to infringe.

British Library Cataloguing in Publication Data
A catalogue record for this book is available from the British Library

Library of Congress Cataloging in Publication Data
Civil society activism under authoritarian rule : a comparative perspective / edited by Francesco Cavatorta.
   p. cm. – (Routledge/ECPR studies in European political science ; 80)
   Includes bibliographical references and index.
   1. Civil society–Case studies. 2. Political participation–Case studies.
   3. Authoritarianism. 4. Regime change. 5. Comparative government.
   I. Cavatorta, Francesco.
   JC337.C5342 2012
   322.4–dc23

                                          2012012754

ISBN 13: 978-0-415-69264-9 (hbk)
ISBN 13: 978-1-138-82594-9 (pbk)

Typeset in Times New Roman
by Wearset Ltd, Boldon, Tyne and Wear

Contents

List of illustrations	xiii
List of contributors	xiv
Acknowledgments	xv

1 Civil society activism under authoritarian constraints   1
FRANCESCO CAVATORTA

**2 'Everyday citizenship' under authoritarianism: the cases of
Spain and Portugal**   13
PEDRO RAMOS PINTO

**3 Dissident writings as political theory on civil society and
democracy**   34
MARLIES GLASIUS

**4 Civil society activism and authoritarian rule in Romania
and Chile: evidence for the role played by art(ists)**   57
CATERINA PREDA

5 Contesting order in Tunisia: crafting political identity   73
LARYSSA CHOMIAK AND JOHN P. ENTELIS

**6 Voice, not democracy: civil society, ethnic politics, and the
search for political space in Central Asia**   94
MATTEO FUMAGALLI

**7 The influence of civil society activism on regional
governance structures in the Russian Federation:
cross-regional and policy comparisons**   111
KARINA MIKIROVA, KATHRIN MUELLER AND
JOHANNES SCHUHMANN

xii *Contents*

8 **Entrenching authoritarianism or promoting reform? Civil society in contemporary Yemen** 135
VINCENT DURAC

9 **Relations between professional associations and the state in Jordan** 158
JANINE A. CLARK

10 **An 'activist diaspora' as a response to authoritarianism in Myanmar: the role of transnational activism in promoting political reform** 181
ADAM SIMPSON

11 **Civil society in the digital age: how the Internet changes state–society relations in authoritarian regimes: the case of Cuba** 219
BERT HOFFMANN

12 **Reconsidering two myths about civil society: evidence from Afghanistan** 245
KEVIN W. GRAY

13 **Conclusion** 261
FRANCESCO CAVATORTA

Index 265

Illustrations

Figures

10.1	Proposed dam sites on the Salween River	191
10.2	The Salween River in the dry season between the Wei Gyi and Dar Gwin Dam Sites	194
10.3	Anti-dam poster by Karen River Watch at Ei Tu Hta IDP Camp in KNU-held Myanmar	196

Tables

6.1	How effective is the UNCC in dealing with Uzbek-related issues?	103
6.2	How effective is the Society of Uzbeks in dealing with Uzbek-related issues (Kyrgyzstan only)?	103

Contributors

Francesco Cavatorta, Senior Lecturer, School of Law and Government, Dublin City University.

Laryssa Chomiak, Director, Centre d'Etudes Maghrebines à Tunis (CEMAT).

Janine A. Clark, Associate Professor, Department of Political Science, University of Guelph.

Vincent Durac, Lecturer, School of Politics and International Relations, University College Dublin.

John P. Entelis, Professor, Department of Political Science, Fordham University.

Matteo Fumagalli, Associate Professor, Department of International Relations and European Studies, Central European University.

Marlies Glasius, Senior Lecturer, Department of Political Science, University of Amsterdam.

Kevin W. Gray, Assistant Professor, American University of Sharjah.

Bert Hoffmann, Director, Institute of Latin American Studies, German Institute of Global and Area Studies (GIGA).

Karina Mikirova, PhD Candidate, Heinrich Heine University Düsseldorf.

Kathrin Mueller, PhD Candidate, Heinrich Heine University Düsseldorf.

Caterina Preda, Assistant Professor, Department of Political Science, University of Bucharest.

Pedro Ramos Pinto, Lecturer, School of Arts, Histories and Cultures, University of Manchester.

Johannes Schuhmann, PhD Candidate, Heinrich Heine University Düsseldorf.

Adam Simpson, Lecturer, School of Communication, International Studies and Languages, University of South Australia.

Acknowledgments

This book is based on the workshop 'Civil society dynamics under authoritarian rule' held at the ECPR Joint Sessions in Lisbon on April 14–19, 2009 and co-directed by Ellen Lust and Francesco Cavatorta.

I warmly acknowledge the invaluable work of all the contributors to this edited collection who were both patient and responsive to all the requests I made. I have a huge debt of gratitude to Ellen Lust at Yale University who contributed enormously to the success of the workshop and to the publication of this book. She is a tremendous scholar and an inspirational colleague.

I would also like to thank the referees and editors of the ECPR/Routledge series whose comments and suggestions contributed to clarifying and strengthening the arguments made.

Finally I would like to acknowledge the support of the editorial team at Routledge and in particular Alexander Quayle.

1 Civil society activism under authoritarian constraints

Francesco Cavatorta

Introduction

In 2000, Laith Kubba proclaimed that the 'awakening of civil society' in the Arab world would be the decisive factor in challenging the authoritarian regimes in the region and eventually lead Arabs to the 'promised land' of democratisation. This belief in the positive and pro-democratic role of civil society activism has characterised much of the scholarship on civic activism. There are two main factors that contribute to explain how Kubba framed the rise of civil society activism in the Arab world. First, is the widespread acceptance of the theoretical assumption that civil society activism is per se conducive to democratisation where authoritarianism exists and to the maintenance of democracy where democracy already is in place (Rau, 1991; Putnam, 2000). Second, the historical experience of the 1980s and early 1990s processes of democratisation seemed to prove the assumption correct, as a number of cases in Eastern Europe and Latin America indicated. The belief in the emancipatory and democratising power of civil society activism is however not limited solely to the Arab world, with scholars of authoritarianism in other contexts such as China, Burma, Cuba, Vietnam and Central Asia also emphasising the importance of 'growing' a local civil society in order to weaken authoritarianism. There is no doubt that the attachment to the notion of civil society as both a concept and tool of change is significant in the context of Eastern Europe and Latin America, but even in these seemingly clear-cut cases the notion that civil society was the instrument of democratic change has been contested (Tempest, 1997).

Building on this earlier critique, the theoretical conceptualisations and practical achievements of civil activism and its relationship to democratisation have more recently been contested. To begin with, a number of studies (Encarnacion, 2006; Jamal, 2007) argue that civil society activism is not directly related to democratisation and that in fact such activism can be detrimental to democracy and can contribute to strengthening authoritarian practices. While the critique of the assumptions of how civil society activism actually functions under authoritarian constraints has contributed to shed some of the normative bias inherent in the understanding of civil society, such critiques are still framed around the assumptions of democratisation. From this it follows that the debate on the role

2   F. Cavatorta

of civil society in authoritarian systems, its perceived normative value and the still problematic nature of its definition are still central to academic and policy-making discussions. Building on the literature contesting the inevitability of the linkage between civic activism and democratisation, this edited book moves beyond traditional notions of civil society and explains the complexity of state–society relations in authoritarian contexts outside the democratisation framework through the use of the concept of 'activated citizenship'.

On the one hand the notion of activated citizenship highlights the fact that classic civil society activism with its emphasis on formal organisations and structures is unable to capture the complexity of how society 'expresses' itself in authoritarian regimes where other modes of engagement exist, from individual writings to mass participation to non-political events to artistic expression. On the other, it is recognised that authoritarian systems, while sharing a number of traits, differ from one another in terms of survival strategies, institutions and legitimising ideologies. The number of countries that can be defined as totalitarian has progressively shrunk over time and today many forms of authoritarianism exist. What is both paradoxical and interesting about the majority of political systems where decision-making is not in the hands of citizens through free and fair elections for meaningful offices is that such systems have over the last two decades introduced a number of democratic and liberal reforms. However, such reforms do not reflect any significant change in the authoritarian nature of the system and are simply a facade reformism emptied of any significant substance.

The holding of regular elections, the creation of seemingly independent authorities, the loosening of restrictions of freedom of expression and the introduction of human rights legislation do not necessarily indicate the democratisation of such political systems. Quite the opposite seems in fact to be true, as all these reforms are designed to deflect attention away from the fact that through informal channels and linkages real decision-making power remains in the hands of unelected and unaccountable ruling elites. The emergence of semi-democracies is one powerful indication of the renewal of authoritarian rule. Thus, the way that authoritarianism is upgraded (Heydemann, 2007) has significant repercussions on how society then organises itself and relates back to the state because through the upgrading process new social actors and new demands are formed, activating citizens in different ways. It follows that the varied forms of authoritarianism have a profound impact on how society is structured and responds to the constraints that authoritarian regimes put in place. At the same time, in a sort of feedback loop, the regime responds to social transformations in different ways. State and society are therefore not conceived as separate and in opposition, but on a sort of continuum where the two meet to cooperate or to come into conflict. This edited volume attempts to analyse the conditions under which such dynamics take effect and hopes to contribute to the strengthening of an emerging research agenda, which focuses more on variations of civil society activism *within* authoritarian regimes than on the extent to which they promote or thwart democratisation. This shift in attention mirrors two developments in the broader literature: first, a move away from the transition paradigm and

Civil society activism 3

toward an understanding that liberalised authoritarian regimes, or 'hybrid regimes', may be a relatively stable equilibrium (Hinnebusch, 2006; Carothers, 2007; Volpi, 2007), and second, a recognition that civil society is neither 'good nor bad' and it should be treated as a neutral variable (Browers, 2006). This has opened the door for a more nuanced exploration of the variations in civil society activism under authoritarian rule. Drawing from extensive fieldwork in a wide range of regimes the chapters collected here provide important theoretical insights into the conditions and roles that civil society activism plays in authoritarian regimes. In conclusion, this edited volume moves beyond the traditional conceptualisation of civil society both theoretically and in its organisational forms in order to understand how abandoning the belief that the expansion of civil society and democratisation are inherently linked contributes to a clearer understanding of how civil society dynamics occur in practice on the ground. By doing so, they not only contribute to a better understanding of civil society activism, but of authoritarian politics as well. The volume covers a number of countries across both time and space in order to illustrate the diversity of civil society activisms in radically different authoritarian contexts. We thus have cases ranging from the 1970s Iberian peninsula to 1980s Eastern Europe and Latina America and from the contemporary Arab world where authoritarian forms of government still prevail to the new republics of Central Asia and, finally, from South-East Asia to Russia.

Civil society and democratisation

The assumption that civil society activism is per se conducive to democratisation seemed borne out by the historical experience of the 1980s and early 1990s when democratisation processes in Eastern Europe and Latin America were very rarely discussed without referring to the importance of civil society. The rapid rise of civil society organizations, promoting diverse issues – ranging from human rights to governmental accountability and from business transparency to environmental protection – and supported in part by the international donor community following the fall of the Soviet Union, seemed a propitious omen. Indeed, the belief that civil society fostered democratisation was so firmly engrained that 'building a robust civil society [was] … postulated as a precondition for democracy and democratization' (Sardamov, 2005: 379).

However, this assumption that civil society per se promotes democratic governance came under criticism by the mid-1990s (Ndegwa, 1996; Berman, 1997). Experiences of Eastern Europe and Latin America have been empirically re-evaluated, and a degree of scepticism has emerged regarding the actual importance of civil society activism in the transitions to democracy in both regions. Indeed, as mentioned, some went so far as to argue that civil society activism in authoritarian settings may in fact reinforce authoritarian practices rather than promote the development of pro-democracy social capital (Cavatorta and Durac, 2010). Enduring authoritarianism in the Arab world, China, Central Asia, East Asia and parts of Africa, despite their burgeoning civil society, has led many to

4   *F. Cavatorta*

argue that civil society activism allows regimes to satisfy the international community's demands for liberalisation, de-politicises important issues and grants limited space for liberal activists who remain marginalised in the wider society.

State–society relations in authoritarian contexts

The problematic linkage between civil society activism and democratisation is partly the function of the theoretical constraints of the paradigm of transition to democracy, which had always an in-built teleology based on a list of preconditions. More recently however the scholarship on democratisation has begun to re-consider many of the assumptions of the transition paradigm. Critics of it concentrated their attention on the reality of world politics and began to argue that when one applies 'democratic criteria' in a strict manner, it becomes evident that only a handful of countries actually managed to make a successful transition to a system of government that is truly liberal and democratic over the last three decades. As Carothers (2007: 7) put it, 'by far the majority of the third wave countries have not achieved a relatively well functioning democracy or do not seem to be deepening or advancing whatever democratic progress they have made'. Accordingly, on an imagined continuum, the vast majority of countries are stuck between rigid authoritarianism on the one hand and democracy on the other. The 'Arab Spring' further confirms this in so far as the uprisings in Tunisia, Egypt or Syria were neither predicted nor led by traditional groups and associations, but are more the product of mass dissatisfaction and loose horizontal networks (Challand, 2011). If anything, far from being the triumph of civil society activism, the Arab Spring seems to be the product of mass revolutionary fervour.

The novelty of a number of recent analyses (Brumberg, 2002) is that liberalised authoritarian political systems, rather than being transient, are examined as if they were permanent arrangements. Thus, there is today a literature arguing that the whole transition paradigm should be abandoned because its assumptions are no longer valid in interpreting the current reality. The re-evaluation of the transition paradigm in terms of the sequence that supposedly characterises transitions has an impact not only on the stages and outcome of processes of democratisation, but has profound implications for political actors central to such processes, including civil society groups and their role. It is therefore unsurprising that the whole concept and practical application of civil society in the context of democratisation has also undergone a profound re-examination. From a theoretical point of view, the most significant contribution has come from those scholars (Berman, 2003; Encarnacion, 2006) questioning the positive normative traits of civil society activism and by implication the positive mechanism whereby a stronger civil society leads inevitably to demands for more democratic participation in authoritarian settings. Once the positive normative liberal connotation of the concept is shed, its usefulness in examining the reality of civic life in any given context re-emerges because it is no longer linked to what is a partisan interpretation of the concept, albeit the dominant one. Their contribution is important because the notion that civil society should shed its normative character facilitates the analysis, as the focus of investigation is the nature and objectives of the associations and groups constituting civil society and not on civil society as a normative whole. The premise of these new studies is that it is methodologically unsound to attach normative value to concepts and notions that are utilised as causal mechanisms to explain political phenomena. Thus, when dealing with the concept of civil society, no positive normative traits should be attached to it because they would inevitably bias it as an explanatory variable. Their argument is that civil society is neither 'good nor bad' and it should be treated as a neutral variable. Neutrality of values ensures that therefore one should analyse the component parts of civil society (groups and organisations) by highlighting their ethos, their activities and their commitment, or lack of, to democratic practices. In addition, this approach permits to avoid the hotly debated topic of 'exporting' the concept to non-Western contexts because it becomes then important to look at the many facets of how the concept is translated, integrated and subsumed into non-Western political theories (Browers, 2006).

In addition to the theoretical criticism, a re-evaluation of the empirical evidence linking civil society activism to democratisation in both Eastern Europe and Latin America has provided the confirmation that previous enthusiasm had been partially misplaced. According to Tempest (1997) and Grugel (2000) for example the role assigned to civil society in undermining the regimes of Eastern Europe has been greatly exaggerated. The existence of such empirical evidence does not automatically disqualify those who provide an alternative view or different empirical findings from the cases they studied, but it certainly undermines the previous consensus about civil society's role in the processes of transition of the 1980s and 1990s.

All this has repercussions on the linkage between democratisation and civil society, rendering it much more complex in so far as a transition to democracy is no longer the central element framing the debate. There is one significant shortcoming however in the scholarly debate outlined above: its polarisation around the dichotomy of civil society as 'promoter' of democratisation and, conversely, of civil society as 'enhancer' of authoritarianism. While it is certainly necessary to examine the validity of both sides of the debate through a careful theoretical discussion and the provision of empirical evidence for one of the two positions, the polarisation created in the literature fails to capture the complexity of both authoritarian rule and civil society activism in authoritarian contexts because it leaves little room for nuance. For instance, when it comes to authoritarianism, it should be noted that this comes in many forms, and authoritarian elites, while learning from each other, deal with challenges in very different manners exploiting material and legitimacy resources that vary across regime types. Thus, for example, some regimes, such as the one in Myanmar, rely very heavily on military repression of internal dissent and operate almost exclusively in isolation from the domestic population, whereby the latter lives in near enslavement and almost entirely cut off from international linkages.

6   F. Cavatorta

Other regimes, such as the Moroccan one, do not rely so excessively on repression and tend to survive by using a plethora of different strategies including co-optation and divide and rule. This is possible because different authoritarian regimes rely on different types of legitimacy, which vary considerably across regime types, and utilise different instruments to deal with the social transformations they face. The differences that exist between authoritarian regimes imply that the 'societies' they face are also very different from one another and it becomes therefore impossible to generalise whether civil activism in authoritarian contexts weakens or strengthens the regime, as it might be responsible for the latter in one case and for the former in another. More generally, it follows that social transformations and social changes might not have the same impact in different authoritarian regimes and that there might be in fact a range of civic 'activisms' under authoritarian rule. This also has implications for the degree of 'structuration' civil activism possesses, as it might vary widely ranging from formal traditional non-governmental organisations to individual dissent through the cyber-sphere.

Thus, the dichotomy generated in earlier studies needs to be problematised in so far as democratisation might not be the 'name of the game' and civil activism might come in very different guises that go beyond the traditional notions of civil society. State–society relations under authoritarian constraints have become very complex and if we are to explain the different outcomes we see across different authoritarian regimes when it comes to their interactions with their respective societies, we have to drop many of the assumptions that underpin studies of civil society, including their almost exclusive focus on traditional non-governmental organisations as the channels through which society expresses itself and relates to the state.

As the 'demo-crazy' (Valbjørn and Bank, 2010) years of the 1990s faded, there has been a renewed scholarly interest for the way in which authoritarian regimes operate and a significant amount of attention has been paid to the changing coalitions supporting authoritarian rule and to the institutions that underpin authoritarianism, including elections and parliaments. Such studies have provided a wealth of information and insights on how authoritarian regimes operate and have managed to survive the third wave of democratisation. Building on this, it is possible to look at authoritarian regimes on a number of dimensions whereby significant differences emerge between them. These differences in turn affect the way in which each authoritarian regime deals and engages with social transformations that might challenge the nature of governance. These dimensions include legitimacy, degree of integration into the world economy, ethnic or religious composition and survival strategies.

- Legitimacy is quite a difficult concept to define with a degree of precision, but there are a number of forms of legitimacy upon which different authoritarian regimes rest, ranging from historical legitimacy to economic ones and from traditional to ideological. Different authoritarian states fall in different categories when it comes to how they legitimise their rule and while discourse should not be taken at face value it is still an important part of how socialisation occurs in a regime and therefore attention should be paid to it. Different types of legitimacy present a range of opportunities and constraints that influence the manner in which the state relates to its citizens and social life more broadly. It could be conceived for instance that traditional legitimacy, as in long-standing monarchies, is more difficult to challenge as the ruling elite has had a significant amount of time to consolidate alliances and coalitions with broad social groups, as the case of Morocco might indicate. Economic legitimacy is much less stable as it is contingent upon the delivery of material goods, which is difficult to achieve on a consistent basis over a long period of time. This type of legitimacy might rest on much more contingent alliances with different social groups, which might find it easier to mount a challenge to the ruling elites, as the Chilean dictatorship under Pinochet demonstrated. Ideological legitimacy might be on the wane, but it might still be an important factor in a number of authoritarian regimes, although in the daily practice of governance such ideological legitimacy does not find concrete application. It might nevertheless shape how society responds, as the case of China illustrates.

- The degree of integration into the world economy of any state fundamentally shapes governance and social relations. As globalisation progresses, there is convergence of economic policy-making governance occurring at many levels with spill-over effects in the political and social realms. The way in which the regime integrates with and opens up to global forces strongly influences how it relates to domestic society and provides different constraints and opportunities for social actors. In more closed political systems such as Burma or North Korea, the regime can resort very quickly to repression without suffering too many external costs for its actions, which is an aspect that domestic social actors are aware of. Conversely more open and penetrated regimes incur more external costs when cracking down on opposition civil society actors, leading them to diversify their responses to social transformation and new demands emerging from society.

- Studies of civil society in democracies tend to focus their attention on formal and informal associations 'fighting' for equality and recognition of minority groups, be they ethnic or religious. In democratic contexts they have the advantage of equal citizenship in order to meet their objectives and democratic governments are more responsive. In authoritarian governments ethnic and religious divisions are a double-edged sword in so far as such divisions can be manipulated by the regime and by social actors alike. Thus profound ethnic and religious divisions can be further deepened and exploited because of the absence of liberal citizenship. Authoritarian systems where such divisions are minor or non-existent might have a shorter menu of choices when it comes to respond to social transformations.

- Finally, authoritarian regimes differ in the way in which they attempt to survive because they tend to adopt a variety of means and strategies to deal with changes within society. The way in which a regime responds has

8   F. Cavatorta

repercussions on how then society organises itself. Over-reliance of repression has both costs and benefits as do other strategies including cooptation and they trigger a different response from the groups that are targeted.

A better specification of how different authoritarian systems legitimise their existence and the denial of key democratic and liberal rights should also be accompanied by a better understanding of social transformations that have occurred under authoritarianism and how this influences the organisation of the demands of society whatever they might be. It should be recognised that just like autocratic regimes have not remained static over time (Albrecht and Schlumberger, 2004), the same can be said of the societies they rule over.

Rethinking civil society

The contributions in this volume take a variety of approaches to examining civil society. Some focus attention on formal associations, following along the lines of scholars such as Larry Diamond (1994: 5), who defined civil society as 'the realm of organised social life that is voluntary, self-generating, (largely) self-supporting, autonomous from the state and bound by a legal order or set of shared rules'. Janine Clark's study of professional associations in Jordan, Vincent Durac's analysis of associational life in Yemen, and Matteo Fumagalli's focus on ethnic associations fit within this framework. Others, however, have expanded the focus, considering more amorphous groups, as seen in Adam Simpson's study of environmental activists in the Burmese diaspora or Bert Hoffman's analysis of activists engaged on the Cuban internet. Others still have focused on individuals and their activism, as in the case of Marlies Glasius on dissidents in Eastern Europe or Caterina Preda on artists. In any case, all the contributions focus on the way in which activism has changed when confronted with specific types of authoritarianism.

Activated citizenship

Collectively, these chapters thus attempt to articulate what we call 'activated or activist citizenship'. This notion reflects the fact that classic civil society activism with its emphasis on formal organisations and structures is unable to capture the complexity of how society 'expresses' itself in authoritarian regimes. In addition to traditional organisations, other modes of engagement exist, from individual writings to mass participation, from seemingly non-political events to political engagement. These modes have important implications for the nature of civil society, as well as for politics within these regimes, particularly because some of their attempts at upgrading their authoritarianism may spur civil society to counter-act such efforts through innovative ways of organising as outlined in the historical study of Spain and Portugal by Ramos Pinto.

Technological changes have spurred some of these new forms of activism. For example, Bert Hoffman examines how the Internet has made horizontal

Civil society activism 9

voice possible in Cuba, creating a broader, leveller activist community that is more capable of withstanding government pressure. Comparing the repression on Cuban opposition in the 1990s and 2000s, he argues that the distribution of information and ideas through the Internet, and particularly the blogosphere, created a more 'self-assertive' 'citizenship from below' which demands, and to some degree enacts (empowered by digital and web-based technologies) a widening of the public sphere, and a greater degree of citizen autonomy from the state, leading to a different type of civil society activity.

Similarly, Adam Simpson's study of the Burmese diaspora demonstrates how the relatively safe spaces of border regions, combined with increased interactions between global environmental groups facilitated by technological changes, have bolstered the activist community. This has not only facilitated the community's ability to challenge the Burmese regime on both environmental and wider political issues, but it has also altered ethnic relations within the Diaspora community.

This does not mean that hierarchical associations and organised social movements have disappeared. Janine Clark's study of professional associations in Jordan reminds us not only of the importance of associational hierarchies, but also emphasises how organisational imperatives affect the relations between opposition and the state. The leaders' duty to fulfil professional obligations and meet members' needs partially constrains their opposition to the regime. Similarly, Matteo Fumagalli and Vincent Durac explore the implications of hierarchical associations in their contributions on Central Asia and Yemen respectively. For them, the formal hierarchical nature of associations shapes the set of strategies these movements use when they find themselves losing public support.

Fuzzy boundaries

The collection also re-examines the relationship between apparently distinct social and political arenas. Literature on civil society has long recognised that the skills obtained in apparently non-political arenas can provide important building blocks for democratic processes. Yet, less attention has been given to the ways in which engagement in one arena, or issue area, is equally intended, and better understood, as an effort to affect policies and processes in other arenas. Fault-lines between issue areas, as well as between the political and social spheres, are overdrawn.

In this vein, Adam Simpson's discussion of environmental activism in Burma's diaspora powerfully demonstrates that what may appear at first to be purely environmental demands are, at heart, far more political. Given the concentration of the environmental degradation in the homelands of historically repressed minority groups, attempts to undermine the dam-building projects are not only linked to environmental concerns but also issues of redistribution, equity and minority rights. The 'political' aspect of activism does not disappear simply because the social issue at stake seems a-political or because activists themselves claim to be a-political.

Voice, not choice

Third, the collection reflects what we term 'voice and not choice', meaning that civil society can be seen as a competitive arena where organisations and activated citizens have different and at times potentially conflicting objectives. On the one hand, we find activated citizenship is directed towards expanding societal space per se with a focus on clawing back powers of expression and contestation from the authoritarian regimes. Entelis and Chomiak's study on Tunisia argues convincingly that spaces of contestation are not necessarily political, but can challenge received national myths the regime has put in place in settings such as football stadiums. In this case the linkage with traditional conceptualisations of civil society as engines for democratisation re-emerges, although it is based on forms of organisation that do not reflect the way in which, traditionally, hierarchical associations operated. On the other hand, we also find that activated citizenship and citizens aim at creating a space or 'voice' for themselves as privileged interlocutors of the authoritarian regime rather than striving for 'choice' and presenting a case for all voices to be heard. In this case, the strengthening of the authoritarian regime is the outcome.

Janine Clark's study of the professional associations (PAs) and the state in Jordan nicely illustrates this point. She argues that associational leaders as well as their counterparts within the state play dual roles; associational leaders are engaged in both politics and social service provision, while the state needs to maintain itself as an entity as well as to perform organizational tasks. The result is that the state needs the PAs to provide important functions of insurance provision, professional licensing and other factors, otherwise relegated to the state, while activists within these associations rely on the state for their ability to recruit supporters and maintain a platform from which to voice their demands. Consequently, a symbiotic relationship between the activists within the PAs and the state develops, with contradictory incentives for both to cooperate with or contain each other. The result is that PA leaders refrain from pushing the collective demands possible and the state fails to repress the PA as soundly as it might. This otherwise puzzling outcome is best understood by recognising the dual positions played by both sides.

Civil society, activism and the public sphere

Finally, the chapters assembled here shed light on the relationships between the public sphere, civil society and activism. Embedded in much of the discussion on civil society is an assumption that it exists within a healthy public sphere. Indeed, as Bert Hoffman claims, 'a precondition for civil society activism to evolve is some degree of public sphere in which it can "breathe"'. How can we understand the prospects of a healthy public sphere in authoritarian regimes?

Bert Hoffman suggests one answer: technological changes make simultaneously existing, distinct public spheres possible. In his study of Cuban activism, he distinguishes between the 'web-based voice' and the 'non-virtual' public sphere. The first is given relative freedom, while the latter is strictly repressed. He argues that this echoes the state's

> traditional 'under roof, everything – in the street, nothing' approach towards dissenting voices; on the web, as under roof, much may be tolerated, as long as it doesn't take to the street, that is, combine with social action in the physical world.

The jury is still out on the extent to which these pressures may ultimately force changes in the Cuban regime, but the case demonstrates how technological changes shape opportunities, as well as regime responses. Kevin Gray's study of Afghanistan also looks at the boundaries between civil society and public sphere in order to examine the way in which Afghan organisations deal with the issue of regime change in a very volatile environment.

Conclusion

The studies presented in this volume turn our attention to the attributes and choices of civil society in authoritarian regimes. Political liberalisation in the past decades has expanded the sphere of civil society dramatically, even in very closed societies. Yet, it has also become increasingly clear that these liberalised authoritarian regimes are relatively stable systems, not simply way stations on the path to democracy. Consequently, they deserve to be studied 'as is'. This is true still in the wake of the changes taking place in the Arab World, where 'presidents have left, but the regimes are still in place' (Ottaway, 2011).

The same is true of civil society. The past decade has prompted a rethinking of the concept and study of civil society and civil activism, the conditions shaping activism, strategic choices made, and consequences. The chapters in this volume offer a number of theoretical insights and empirical data that can provide a rough map on the role of activism under authoritarian constraints, highlighting how society and the authoritarian state interact where personal freedoms are restricted.

Bibliography

Albrecht, H. and Schlumberger, O. (2004) '"Waiting for Godot": regime change without democratization in the Middle East', *International Political Science Review*, 25: 371–392.

Berman, S. (1997) 'Civil society and the collapse of the Weimar Republic', *World Politics*, 47: 401–429.

Berman, S. (2003) 'Islamism, revolution and civil society', *Perspectives on Politics*, 1: 257–272.

Browers, M. (2006) *Democracy and Civil Society in Arab Political Thought: Transcultural Possibilities*, Syracuse: Syracuse University Press.

Brumberg, D. (2002) 'The trap of liberalised autocracy', *Journal of Democracy*, 13: 56–68.

12   F. Cavatorta

Carothers, T. (2007) 'The sequencing fallacy', *Journal of Democracy*, 18: 12–27.

Cavatorta, F. and V. Durac (2010) *Civil Society and Democratisation in the Arab World*, London: Routledge.

Challand, Benoit (2011) 'The counter-power of civil society in the Middle East', available at: www.deliberatelyconsidered.com/2011/03/the-counter-power-of-civil-society-in-the-middle-east-2/ (last accessed 12 March 2011).

Diamond, L. (1994) 'Toward democratic consolidation', *Journal of Democracy*, 4: 4–17.

Encarnacion, O. (2006) 'Civil society reconsidered', *Comparative Politics*, 38: 357–376.

Grugel, J. (2000) 'Romancing civil society: European NGOs in Latin America', *Journal of Interamerican Studies and World Affairs*, 42: 87–107.

Heydemann, S. (2007) 'Upgrading authoritarianism in the Arab world', The Brookings Institution, *Analysis Paper*, 13, pp. 1–37. Available at www.brookings.edu/~/media/Files/rc/papers/2007/10arabworld/10arabworld.pdf (last accessed 15 April 2010).

Hinnebusch, R. (2006) 'Authoritarian persistence, democratization theory and the Middle East: an overview and critique', *Democratization*, 13: 373–395.

Kubba, L. (2000) 'The awakening of civil society', *Journal of Democracy*, 11: 84–90.

Jamal, A. (2007) *Barriers to Democracy*, Princeton: Princeton University Press.

Ndegwa, S. (1996) *The Two Faces of Civil Society: NGOs and Politics in Africa*, Hartford, CN: Kumarian Press.

Ottaway, M. (2011) 'The Presidents left, the regimes are still there', 14 February. Available at: http://carnegieendowment.org/publications/?fa=42627 (accessed 14 February 2011).

Putnam, R. (2000) *Bowling Alone: The Collapse and Revival of American Community*, New York: Touchstone.

Rau, Z. (ed.) (1991) *The Re-emergence of Civil Society in Eastern Europe and the Soviet Union*, Boulder, CO: Westview Press.

Sardamov, I. (2005) 'Civil Society and the Limits of Democratic Assistance', *Government and Opposition*, 40: 379–402.

Tempest, C. (1997) 'Myths from Eastern Europe and the legends of the West', *Democratization*, 4: 132–144.

Valbjørn, M. and A. Bank (2010) 'Examining the "post" in post-democratization: the future of Middle Eastern political rule through lenses of the past', *Middle East Critique*, 19: 183–200.

Volpi, F. (2007) 'Algeria's pseudo-democratic politics: lessons for democratization in the Middle East' in Frédéric Volpi and Francesco Cavatorta (eds) *Democratization in the Muslim World: Changing Patterns of Power and Authority*, Oxon: Routledge.

2 'Everyday citizenship' under authoritarianism

The cases of Spain and Portugal

Pedro Ramos Pinto

> The Argentine, unlike the Americans of the North and almost all Europeans, does not identify with the state.... One thing is certain: the Argentine is an individual, not a citizen. Aphorisms like Hegel's 'The State is the reality of the moral idea' strike him as sinister jokes. Films made in Hollywood often hold up for admiration the case of a man (usually a journalist) who seeks out the friendship of a criminal in order to hand him over to the police; the Argentine, for whom friendship is a passion and the police a mafia, feels that this 'hero' is an incomprehensible swine.
>
> Jorge Luis Borges 'Our Poor Individualism' (2000[1946])

Borges' image of the baffled Argentine is instantly recognisable for a student of history and politics of the Iberian Peninsula. It is also parallel to Banfield's idea of 'amoral familism', said to be common to the European South, where the concrete bonds of kin and friendship, Borges' 'passions', easily trump the duties of citizenship (Banfield, 1967). Whether these patterns are rooted, as Borges and Banfield would have it, on long-standing cultural traits, or are the result of particular patterns of state–society relations is another matter: it is important not to forget how much the character of citizenship in South America owes to the traditions of statecraft it inherited from its former colonial rulers.

Regardless of its origins, this cleavage between the state and 'civil society' is clearly visible for most of the contemporary history of Portugal and Spain, which can be read as a long-running conflict between the two (Vincent, 2007). The construction of nation-states in the Iberian Peninsula has rarely gone hand in hand with the development of forms of citizenship characterised by a mutually reinforcing relationship between the state and its population. This is evidenced, for instance, by the recurrence of authoritarian government since the early nineteenth century, or the strength of 'excluded ideologies' such as anarchism among the working classes (Mann, 1987). Historically speaking, and through both diktat and choice, the 'civil society' of Iberian countries was largely absent from the process of construction of the modern nation-state.

The transitions to democracy in Portugal and Spain of the 1970s, however, reveal an essentially different dynamic of state–society relations that contradicts

14   *P. Ramos Pinto*

historical tradition. Not only did citizens exercise their citizenship actively by participating fully in the transition, they also voted for moderate political parties promising an extensive social contract. The first post-authoritarian elections in both countries are notable for the remarkable turnouts: over 91 per cent in Portugal in 1975 and nearly 79 per cent in Spain in 1977. Despite the obvious differences in the form of transition – Portugal's was initiated by a military coup and was certainly more radical, while Spain witnessed a process of accommodation and pact-making between the old regime elites and the new democratic parties – it is also clear that neither process would have been successful without the consent and willingness of a large majority of the population to support a democratic regime. Societies that were traditionally unengaged, uninterested, if not downright suspicious of the state, were involved en masse in its transformation. Accounting for democratisation in Spain and Portugal requires that we explain this shift in political beliefs and values.

This transformation of political values and the formation of a broader consensus regarding the need for regime change have often been connected to two processes: that of 'modernisation' and the emergence of a 'civil society'. Yet neither seems sufficient to explain them. Modernisation theories are often invoked to explain the emergence of pro-democratic values, but too often a determinist connection between economic, social and political change is assumed (Lipset, 1959). This removes any of the agency of individuals and groups, underplays the interaction, creativity and serendipity that is possible in the construction of new values, and tends to create a monolithic view of societies that is formulaic and necessarily shallow. Furthermore, the assumption that modernity necessarily breeds democracy has severe limitations and there are many examples of how modernity and authoritarianism can co-exist, as we can read elsewhere in this volume.

The importance of the emergence of a 'civil society' as a prerequisite to democratisation has also been invoked by seminal contributions to the field (e.g. O'Donnell *et al.*, 1986; Pérez Díaz, 1993). However, these accounts suffer from three important shortcomings: a narrow conception of 'civil society', a lack of close attention to the dynamic relationship between civil society and political institutions, and a persistent failure to address the underlying question of changing values and preferences. Most accounts of transition narrowly define 'civil society' as a collection of formally organised groups such as political parties or trade unions. Yet, their success in promoting democracy is judged to be linked to their capacity to appeal to constituencies well beyond their organisational boundaries. How do the pro-democracy claims of 'civil society' organisations come to resonate with broader populations? Finally, in common with modernisation theories, these accounts tend to make the assumption that 'civil societies' will be characterised by pro-democratic values (sometimes through the circular argument that only pro-democratic organisations can be considered as being part of civil society): recent post-colonial critiques of civil society have been considerably successful at puncturing such conceits (Kaviraj and Khilnani, 2001; Chatterjee, 2004).

In sum, neither 'modernisation' nor 'civil society' theories have been sufficient to account for the historical transformation of popular beliefs and values that supported the transitions to democracy in Spain and Portugal. The contention of this chapter is that such a transformation is located in the history of citizenship in the two countries, and that it deserves to be analysed through the lens of what has been called 'everyday citizenship'. This requires dragging our attention away from the concept of 'civil society' as an agent or category of actor, the manner in which it is most often invoked by democratisation theory, and refocusing it on the various actors with multiple beliefs, interests, strategies and capacities that act in a political space we can term 'civil society'. By seeing it as a space, rather than an actor, we can avoid the reification of 'civil society' that troubles so much of the literature, without totally casting off its heuristic and polemical value highlighted by Edwards and Foley (1998).[1]

'Everyday citizenship'

It would be a shame if we were to jump out of the frying pan of a chronically ill-defined concept such as 'civil society' only to fall into the fire of a similarly fuzzy idea. There is some danger of that in invoking the idea of citizenship, yet there is sufficient consensus surrounding its main elements to make it a useful analytical lever. Citizenship appears in scholarship in several main guises: as a category – to be or not to be a citizen of a given state; as participation; but mainly as a relation between a state and its population, both as individuals and as social groups (Turner, 1990; Tilly, 1995). In Tilly's words, citizenship is

> a continuing series of transactions between persons and agents of a given state in which each has enforceable rights and obligations uniquely by virtue of (1) the person's membership in an exclusive category, the native-born plus the naturalized and (2) the agent's relation to the state rather than any other authority the agent may enjoy.
>
> (Tilly, 1995: 8)

This latter definition encompasses the concept of citizenship as a category (by identifying who is part of that relationship), and qualifies the idea of citizenship as participation: all recognised citizens have some kind of relationship to the state, even if they do not act upon it, or if that relationship is merely formal. Citizenship relations can range from 'thin' to 'thick'; that is, entailing few or many mutual obligations: from simply the duty of obedience to dense interchanges of rights and duties, such as voting and paying taxes, freedom of thought to compulsory participation in state celebrations. It is clear that by using citizenship to describe a relationship we also give it a neutral status: citizenship relations can be unequal and disempowering, depending on the norms that rule the relationship. In this sense citizenship is a feature of all state–society relations, encompassing those adhering to democratic rules and pluralism, but also many other types, including authoritarian citizenship.

16   *P. Ramos Pinto*

Citizenship then exists as de facto relationships between states and citizens, but also exists as an ideal: citizens not only perceive the relationships that bind them to the state and to each other, but they can also imagine alternative blueprints to rule that relationship. Seen in this light, the question posed at the beginning of this chapter is transformed. Explaining the transition to democracy in Portugal and Spain is no longer a question of accounting for an emergence of a 'civil society', but rather to understand how an important and pivotal section of the population went from holding a limited view of citizenship, along the lines of Borges' Argentine, to envisaging a much 'thicker' form of citizenship, which included extensive expectations of rights and widespread political participation. It is, in that sense, a question of transformation of beliefs about citizenship, which then motivated political action.

There are, of course, multiple ways in which such beliefs can change. This chapter, however, focuses on one particular avenue that may be of special relevance in authoritarian states which are able to achieve a degree of hegemony in controlling the means of information and cultural production that could otherwise be sources of that change. It will argue that citizens' beliefs about citizenship can be shaped by their everyday interaction with the state, their experience of 'everyday citizenship'.

The relationship between states and peoples takes place on at least two levels: that of the quotidian or of the extraordinary. Certain types of events where this relationship is experienced occur less regularly and are often endowed with a special symbolism: spectacular displays of union between Nation and State in mass rallies, parades, celebrations or other 'heroic experiences'; national mobilisation for war or service in the military are well-known examples; in democratic states, the highly salient acts of voting, serving jury duty or holding public office, are also examples of this extraordinary citizenship (Holston, 2008).

But attitudes, preferences and values are much more likely to be shaped by mundane encounters with the state, its rules and its agents. While individuals rarely experience the 'heroic' affirmation of citizenship, they are daily reminded of their position vis-à-vis the state through the regulation of their labour, their residence, their consumption, the boundaries of legality; and through interaction with agents of the state such as police officers, taxmen or social workers. It is also at this level that the awareness of commonality is often developed, discovering others who have to pay taxes, use services, wait for buses and are, as such, like us. It is through these day-to-day experiences – beyond the pale of 'ordinary political participation' – that citizens learn the rules of their relationship to the state and come to develop sets of ideas about how these work, why they work as they do and, crucially, how they ought to work. In James Holston's words, such experiences propitiate 'the discursive and contextual construction of the relations called citizenship and that indicate not only particular attitudes of belonging in society, but also the political imagination that both produces and disrupts citizenship' (2008: 13).

Using the concept of 'everyday citizenship' offers us two advantages in analysing the formation of new political values over a focus on modernisation or

'Everyday citizenship' under authoritarianism   17

civil society. Unlike macro approaches to modernisation, by investigating the point at which structural transformation meets individuals and groups, we can question how such changes are interpreted, adapted to or even subverted by individuals endowed with agency, largely absent from macro approaches. Unlike civil society approaches, 'everyday citizenship' is also capable of capturing a much wider array of citizenship practices that, while not outwardly 'political', shape the outlook and values of citizens and have, therefore, important political implications. It shifts our attention from the limited field of oppositionist politics of that of a general public who are ultimately responsible for the success of transition but too often invisible to scholarship. The focus of 'civil society' on formal organisations is a serious handicap, particularly when it comes to the study of political attitudes and beliefs. Authoritarian regimes strictly control formal groups, which makes their actions and membership necessarily limited, while much broader interactions between citizens and state may be responsible for changes in values that make the claims of pro-democracy civil society groups resonate in the first place.

This chapter focuses on a particular type of encounter that makes structural change 'experienceable' and seeks the political beyond traditional definitions of civil society: the encounter between the state and its populations at the level of day-to-day experiences of citizenship. State action, although occurring on a macro level, impacts directly on individuals' everyday lives: economic shifts are experienced by investment in particular industries, changing taxation rules or changes in social transfers; labour laws structure everyday work relations, and other laws even more personal interactions and practices, from divorce to clothing. Migrants experience it in their reception in cities, families through health and education. The main contention of this chapter is that the expansion of governmentality under the Franco and Salazar Dictatorships fundamentally altered the experiences of 'everyday citizenship' of those that came into contact with it. The development of authoritarian welfare as a means of social control, national integration and of regime legitimation, altered the nature of state–society relations. The question of state-provided housing is used as a specific example indicative of the transformation of political values operated in part through the transformation of state–society relations by the dictatorships.

For better or for worse, the process of state strengthening and centralisation operated by both dictatorships and their use of modern technologies of power brought a much greater proportion of the population in contact with the state. This happened at the same time as larger economic processes were transforming traditional forms of social support through large-scale migration, urbanisation and the entry of women into the labour force, and increasing numbers of ordinary citizens became at least partially dependent on the state for their welfare.

In these conditions, the everyday experiences of citizens were changed as they were forced to interact with social workers, doctors, police and municipal authorities. Two processes developed from this contact: (1) an experience of enjoyment of social rights that made the case for their universalisation plausible; however, (2) in their day-to-day experiences, citizens were able to observe the

18 *P. Ramos Pinto*

highly unequal, preferential and segmented nature of the delivery of welfare services. By introducing social rights, the regimes transformed the nature of state legitimation. By failing to deliver them equitably they contributed to their own de-legitimisation. In this way a political space was created where both liberalising and opposition groups could place themselves, arguing that only democratisation would be able to deliver on the new social contract. James Holston has coined this process as the development of an 'insurgent citizenship', the transformation of day-to-day experiences into political action which happens when citizens come into contact with the fragmented and unequal forms of citizenship their states construct (Holston, 2008). Holston's term echoes the idea developed by O'Brien in the context of his research on China, that of rightful resistance: a form of 'politics of the poor' that uses the legitimating discourse of the powerful to achieve concrete gains. As O'Brien writes, 'rightful resistance' is

> a product of state building and of opportunities created by the spread of participatory ideologies and patterns of rule rooted in notions of equality, rights, and rule of law ... and is the sign of growing rights consciousness and a more contractual approach to political life.
>
> (O'Brien, 1996: 34)

'Rightful resistance' and 'insurgent citizenship' can be said to be two phenomena co-existing along the same continuum. Both emerge from citizens' experience of the realities of the social contract but express different strategies of claim-making by populations. These perspectives, alongside Partha Chatterjee's work on the 'politics of the governed', take us beyond the narrow focus of traditional 'civil society' accounts of democratisation in Spain and Portugal, and point to fascinating interaction between state and society in the production of new forms of citizenship (Chatterjee, 2004). By critically engaging with notions of politics and democracy that are notoriously (northern) euro-centric, these global perspectives open up interesting possibilities in exploring the recent history of Southern Europe.

However, two notes of caution must be introduced. First, this interpretation of the connection between state power, 'everyday citizenship' and democratisation in Spain and Portugal can be no more than tentative. The historiography of the Iberian Dictatorships is still largely restricted to the dichotomy repression/overt resistance. In-depth studies of its institutions and, in particular, how these interacted with the population, are still relatively rare. But by drawing on existing research, it is possible to formulate a hypothesis to inform further questioning and research. A second caveat regards the scope of the process under investigation: the growing intervention of the state in welfare was by no means the only process through which political beliefs about citizenship were transformed and the de-legitimisation of the dictatorships occurred. But it is an important and neglected part of a story that also includes rising education levels, a growing middle class, economic crisis, international pressures and, in Portugal, the failure of the long-drawn African wars.

The changing nature of citizenship in the Iberian Peninsula

The transition of Spain and Portugal from imperial global powers to peripheral European nation-states was painful and convoluted. For centuries the monarchy and its system of rule had been geared towards imperial dominance, with national integration as a secondary objective. Flush with imperial revenue, the crown felt less acutely the need to challenge aristocratic privilege and bolster commercial and industrial investment. As a result, once truly national projects aiming at developing a nation-state emerged with nineteenth century liberalism, they followed particular trajectories influenced by the weakness of the state, the strength of agrarian interests and the low level of integration of popular and national politics. As a result, the forms of citizenship developed by the liberal regimes that emerged from a succession of civil wars were highly exclusionary: civic and political rights, although formally accessible to all males, were in reality highly developed systems for the reproduction of inequality, using education, property and gender to exclude citizens from access to and participation in the state (Ramos, 2004; Vincent, 2007). The development of social rights by the Iberian states throughout the nineteenth century and until emergence of the dictatorships in the 1930s, was even more limited than the construction of civic and political rights. Certainly hygienist concerns prompted urban legislation and, despite fairly limited industrial sectors, legislation regulating hours of work, accidents and female and child labour was passed, if not always rigidly enforced. Yet, these policies never went beyond the limits imposed by the dominant liberal order in its various guises and were extremely limited in scope. In both countries, church-led assistance to the poor remained the principal form of social provision, followed by a growing mutualist movement of workers' cooperatives providing health, life and funeral insurance for their members.[2]

The process of urbanisation and transformation that the two countries began to experience at the end of the nineteenth century brought the 'social question' into focus without being able to generate a consensus. Urban intellectual and political elites arguing for an extension of state welfare were hampered by their own small base of support and powerful opposition from different quarters: a Church jealous of its monopoly over assistance, and powerful agrarian landed interests unwilling to contribute to urban relief, least of all agree to the kind of agrarian restructuring that would deprive them of a virtual monopoly on land and a cheap labour force. It is also important not to forget the opposition of a greater part of the organised working class, tendentiously anti-state and anarchist. For instance, attempts to organise compulsory social insurance schemes, repeatedly essayed in the first quarter of the twentieth century, were boycotted by anarchist organisations in both countries. Spanish anarchists refused to participate in both the Institute of Social Reforms and its successor the Institute of Social Security, which aimed at regulating the voluntary insurance sector (Moreno and Sarasa, 1992; Mangen, 2001). In 1930, even as the Salazar Dictatorship was being built around them, the Portuguese anarchist trade union CGT was attacking Communist proposals for a state unemployment subsidy on the

20   *P. Ramos Pinto*

grounds that it could only work on the back of higher taxes for workers or increased production costs (Patriarca, 1995). Even the most progressive of the regimes that preceded the dictatorships, the Spanish Second Republic, was unable to generate popular consensus on the role of the state on welfare, which greatly limited the impact of its legislative programme as successive Republican governments were unable to swing the anarchist unions to back their reforms (Moreno and Sarasa, 1992).

On the whole, notwithstanding the particularities of Spain as a country of nations, as opposed to Portugal where the question of national identity played a less prominent political role, there are considerable similarities between the trajectories of the two countries. In terms of substantive relations of citizenship the Iberian countries were, until the 1930s, characterised by weak, non-hegemonic states with low governmental capacity, and 'thin' forms of citizenship: categorically or formally, citizenship was an expansive category, yet it was translated into very limited political or social rights. Consequently, as Malefakis argues, 'the political realm had not been truly integrated with society but had stayed isolated from it, operating to its own rules' with the population continuing to see the state in the terms of Borges' Argentine (Malefakis, 1995: 59).

The Franco (1939–1976) and Salazar (1928–1974) Dictatorships were long-lived, repressive and deeply transforming.[3] One of their key, but neglected, characteristics was their remaking of the peninsular states. Both men were able to gain the support of key groups and institutions, such as the Church, agrarian landowners and monopolist capital, to centralise power in a manner no regime had been able to since the heyday of the absolutist monarchies. Their ability to do so rested, in great part, in the anti-liberal (and of course, anti-communist), catholic and social conservative coalition they were able to build. The Franco and Salazar Dictatorships were violent – Franco's regime was established by a civil bloodbath. However, the declining resort to force as a means of power experienced in both countries (except in specific, selected circumstances, against troublesome oppositionists) is testament to the strengthening of the central state they achieved. In Salazar's chilling words, 'the state should be strong, ... so strong that it does not need to be violent' (Salazar, 1989).

This extension of state power was used by both regimes to transform the traditional relationship between state and citizens, a process driven by the twin objectives of social engineering and self-legitimation. Despite their socially conservative ideology and political use of the past, both the dictatorships were also essentially modern projects, in so far as they saw state power as an instrument to be deployed in the moral and political shaping of their countries and citizens. The aim of transcending class conflict through the creation of a corporatist society of orders, based on Christian morals and on the imagined 'ideal' family, was no less a social utopia than the Bolshevik Dictatorship of the proletariat. Alongside this ideological aim, both dictators also realised the need to achieve a degree of legitimation for their regimes. Both had come to power on the back of anti-liberal and anti-communist agendas, but were conscious of the need to aggregate a degree of support and ensure, if not the loyalty, at least the

'*Everyday citizenship' under authoritarianism* 21

compliance of their population. Alongside the use of repression, the development of sophisticated propaganda machines, and the careful construction of a national mythology through education, welfare services were part of the panoply of technologies of power put to use to achieve these ends.

While historiography of authoritarian welfare in both countries is significantly underdeveloped, it is possible to distinguish two phases of the development of state provision of social rights under the dictatorships, which followed very similar trajectories.[4] An initial phase, from the inception of the regimes in the 1930s to the 1950s, was characterised by a high degree of social conservatism, and attempts to construct a more or less corporatist structure of welfare. During this period, corporatist ideology saw the state as the organiser, although not necessarily the provider of welfare: both countries witnessed a flurry of legislation aimed at stepping up the provision of social insurance, affordable housing or accessible health care, yet these were to be delivered by non-state or at best semi-public institutions, wherever possible through contributions from employers and employees. While the Catholic Church took for itself a large chunk of the delivery (and was heavily subsidised for doing so) it also became painfully clear there was little capacity outside the state for the financing of such ambitious schemes. The case of the 'family wage complement' (*abono de família*) instituted by the Portuguese *Estado Novo* in 1942 shows how such forays into welfare created a momentum for increasing state intervention. Initially intended to be financed solely by contributions from workers and employers and administered by autonomous institutions, Pereirinha *et al.* have shown how, shortly after its creation, the administration of this social benefit was gradually integrated into the state-run social insurance, revealing a 'statisation of the system' (2009). Despite their limitation in terms of coverage and biases created by political favouritism and social control, these initiatives had a double effect: they signalled the state's first significant commitment to the delivery of public welfare and were responsible for the creation of extensive professional bureaucracies dedicated to them – both were to have a significant influence in the development of social rights in the ensuing decades.

From the 1950s, social welfare was part of a wider refashioning of state policies undertaken by the dictatorships towards what has been called the years of 'developmentalism'. A growing army of state technicians and bureaucrats aided by large business interests began pushing an agenda of modernisation and state-driven development, borrowing heavily from the economic policies of other European nations which were beginning to experience the benefits of the post-war economic boom. This entailed seeing aspects of social welfare as contributors to economic growth and increased productivity, and the recognition of the limitations of contributor-funded social welfare in significantly underdeveloped economies. On the back of these changes, Spain would see the creation of a minimum wage and a new Law of Social Security (1963) 'with universalist intentions' seeking to standardise and systematise existing corporate welfare arrangements (Moreno and Sarasa, 1992). A reorganisation of welfare with similar intentions was legislated in Portugal in 1962, although the process of

22   P. Ramos Pinto

reform it initiated would only gather significant pace after Marcello Caetano's coming to power in 1968 (Lucena, 2000). The testimony of one high-ranking official in the Portuguese regime's welfare bureaucracy on the changes of this period is telling. Writing in 1983, António da Silva Leal attributed these changes not just to an 'authoritarian tendency', but also to the exposure of bureaucrats to the Beveridge Plan and to 'new ideas on social security coming from the International Labour Organisation' advocating the creation of 'universal or quasi-universal' welfare regimes (Leal, 1998: 116).

The receptivity of the higher echelons of the dictatorships to these innovations had political as well as economic roots. The longevity of the dictatorships depended on their ability to recast their legitimation frames: the anti-communist, defensive model of the 1930s would not survive as a new generation who had not lived through the civil war in Spain or the turmoil of the First Republic in Portugal came of age, while both regimes were confronted with challenges to their hegemony, even if these were limited to minorities such as university students. By embracing developmentalism, both sought to secure their legitimacy by claiming to be able to deliver security and prosperity (Rosas and Oliveira, 2004; Townson, 2007b). Salazar's successor, Marcello Caetano, summarised this strategy when he dismissed the need for democratisation, stating publicly that:

> what is asked of leaders is not more freedom – rather prices that match salaries, decent houses, accessible education, efficient social insurance, good medical assistance and guaranteed pensions in old age and incapacity. What good is it to ensure in the Constitution civic rights if citizens do not have the economic and moral conditions of exercising them? ... The State can no longer distance itself from the function of ensuring the services that allow all citizens access to the fundamental commodities and guarantees of civilization.
>
> (Caetano, 1971: xxxiii)

The traditional view of authoritarian welfare, forged during the process of democratisation as a response to the inflated claims of regime supporters, tends to underplay the extension of social rights under the dictatorships, dismissing it as little more than public facades – a sort of Potemkin village used by the dictators to cover their project of domination (e.g. Sevilla-Guzmán et al., 1978). Even those authors who recognise the historical originality of the dictatorships' welfare regimes tend to underplay their political effect, and Garcia reflects the dominant interpretation when she writes that:

> The marginal social policies pursued by the Old Regime failed to encourage the idea of citizenship, since civic and political rights were restricted. Aspirations to universal rights came from heterogeneous opposition, often at the grassroots level, while the structures of welfare were designed by the regime.
>
> (Garcia, 1994: 263)

'Everyday citizenship' under authoritarianism   23

Yet the transformation of state welfare provision in the dictatorships' developmentalist phase, while certainly not achieving universality, was nevertheless an extraordinary step change. Starting from scratch, by 1960 social security covered 35.5 per cent of the active population in Portugal, but by 1970 the proportion reached 60 per cent. Similarly, medical services, which reached only 335,000 users in 1951, were by 1965 accessible to 2.3 million and to 7.3 million ten years later, in a total population of roughly eight million (Carreira, 2000). In Spain, welfare expenditure and coverage also rose considerably and by 1975, the year of Franco's death, almost 90 per cent of the population had some kind of social protection (Mangen, 2001). Such coverage was well beyond anything that had previously been achieved in either country, although, as we shall see, it was also a highly segmented and inequitable system that left many if not completely uncovered, at least only able to draw on the most meagre of benefits.

To argue that the Salazar and Franco Dictatorships were responsible for an unprecedented expansion of the role of the state in supporting citizens' life-chances does not lead in any way to creating an excuse for authoritarianism. These were clearly projects that had their roots in totalitarian tendencies of social control, as well as in self-interested survival objectives. Instead, it is suggesting that their actions were responsible for a social transformation with important political consequences, exactly because of their failure to deliver equitably the very social rights they proclaimed.

Despite its expansion, the Iberian authoritarian welfare regimes created what have been called 'insider' or 'segmented' systems (Mangen, 2001; García and Karakatsanis, 2006). This was a result of reforms that built on an existing framework of corporatist welfare which privileged male heads of household in full-time employment, creating a dual system to the detriment of a large proportion of the population that did not fit into these categories because of gender or reliance on more causal or part-time forms of employment. Even protected workers inside the system enjoyed very different levels of entitlement according to status or sector of employment.

In principle, the social security schemes set up by the dictatorships linked benefits to the contributions of workers and employers, meaning that payments on retirement, illness or incapacity were limited by the level of deductions made to the system according to a 'base salary' calculation. However, not only was this rate gradually decoupled from real wages by inflation, but the dictatorships oversaw the proliferation of 'special regimes' where payments were not linked to individual contributions but guaranteed over and above those by the social security budget. These 'special regimes' were mostly political sweeteners targeted at key constituencies the dictatorships sought to keep on their side: armed forces personnel, liberal professionals and civil servants, whose social security was, in effect, subsidised by blue collar workers whose benefits were limited by contributions (Moreno and Sarasa, 1992).

The establishment of widespread welfare systems redefined, as the dictatorships had hoped for, the basis of the social contract. Using the strength of a virtually unchallenged state apparatus, they were able to do what previous regimes, monarchical, liberal and republican, had failed to achieve either through ideological choice or political weakness. However, in doing so, they also contributed to changing the political values of large sectors of the population who had before been on the margins of the state (Ramos Pinto, 2008). Charles Tilly has argued that one of the key aspects of state development of the modern era is the integration of what he terms 'trust networks' – interpersonal networks used to guarantee prosperity and security through bonds of kin and community – into public politics. Where the state is not a significant part of individuals' survival strategies, there is little incentive for them to invest significant time and resources in exercising their citizenship through the state, which is a good description of popular politics in Spain and Portugal throughout most of the modern period. However, as economic and social transformations such as migration and industrialisation whittle away the capacity of 'trust networks' to ensure prosperity, and the state takes upon itself (or claims it will do so) to assume responsibility over individual life-chances, a political space is created for such groups to exercise voice on the terms of such a relationship (Tilly, 2005).[5] Using the terms referred to earlier, the creation of such a political space created the conditions for 'rightful resistance'. Yet, rather than serving to secure their rule, the inherent inequalities in the system they created contributed to their de-legitimisation and the formation of an 'insurgent citizenship' that was expressed in the creation of grassroots movements directed at demanding the delivery of social rights in a more universal and equitable manner.

Housing, citizenship and democratisation

One particular example of how authoritarian welfare transformed the terms of debate and political action regarding citizenship is the question of state-provided housing in both Portugal and Spain. In both countries the processes of migration and urbanisation brought millions from the countryside to the cities throughout the twentieth century, and particularly in the boom years from the 1950s. Between 1950 and 1970 Madrid doubled in size to almost four million inhabitants, while in the same period greater Lisbon grew almost three-fold to near one million (Naylon, 1986; Baptista and Rodrigues, 1996). Both the Franco and Salazar regimes were the first in these countries' histories to attempt the de-commodification of housing in any meaningful scale. Despite their limited achievements in this field, their interventions contributed greatly to the transformation of popular political values – whereas until the 1930s housing was rarely regarded by working class organisations as social right to be provided by the state, by the late 1960s, urban welfare was a key issue of political contention that motivated widespread mobilisations, contributing to the de-legitimisation of the dictatorships and the transition to democracy itself.

Despite the fact that the poverty of urban housing and conditions in the main cities of Iberia were well documented and widely discussed, it is striking that throughout the first third of the twentieth century, even as other European governments were investing directly and heavily in workers' habitations, the issue

'Everyday citizenship' under authoritarianism 25

remained largely marginal in Spain and Portugal. The issue of housing was almost exclusively debated in terms of the relation between wages and rents, of the need to legislate obligations for landlords to provide minimum hygienic conditions or, at best, in terms of subsidies for workers' building cooperatives. This was the case even when the political parties closest to the urban working classes were in power, as was the case with the Spanish socialists in the Second Republic. Revealingly, the only schemes of direct state building prior to the Franco and Salazar Dictatorships were experimental programmes undertaken by dictatorial governments that were the ideological forerunners of authoritarian corporatism: the rule of Sidónio Pais in Portugal (1918) and of Primo de Rivera in Spain between 1923 and 1930 (Silva, 1994; Calleja, 2005). These experiments, just as the later more extensive house building programmes of the Salazar and Franco Dictatorships, were driven by a desire to control and subdue what Pais called 'citizen Lenin' and were, unsurprisingly, viewed with great suspicion and opposed by many workers' organisations (Samara, 2002).

The corporatist dictatorships of Salazar and Franco counted housing among their first welfarist initiatives: in Spain the creation of the *Instituto Nacional de Vivienda* and its programme of 'protected housing' was created in 1939, while Salazar had created the 'Economic Houses' scheme in 1933, to which the 'Housing for Poor Families' programme was added in 1945 (Gros, 1982; Carbajal, 2003). Housing was regarded as a central instrument for the disciplining of workers, imbued with moral content and aimed at the creation of good Christian families, as evidenced by the emphasis on the terms 'hearth' or 'household' (*lar* and *hogar*) over the more utilitarian terms 'house' or 'habitation' (*casa* or *vivienda*) in propaganda (Baptista, 1998; Díaz, 2003). As Salazar's minister for corporations and welfare, Pedro Teotónio Pereira stated, the aim was to build 'proper homes, around whose hearth familial love is warmed and the bonds of moral life strengthened' (Gros, 1994).

The bias towards a particular kind of family was reproduced in the allocation rules, which often specified that state-provided housing could only be accessed by married couples of child bearing age, while tenure and property rights were conditional on the maintenance of the family unit: separation (divorce was illegal) could mean the forfeiture of the home. Like other forms of social provision in the initial phase of the dictatorships, housing was rolled out on a limited scale and in forms that differed according to the status of the recipient. In both countries it was used extensively to reward loyalty to the regime, with preference being given to soldiers, policemen and members of the approved 'trade unions'. Award of houses was also conditional on references of good moral standing from persons in authority such as policemen or union officials (Carbajal, 2003; Ramos Pinto, 2009).

As was the case with social security, the arrival of developmentalism and the emergence of technocratic modernisers within the state apparatus led to a massification of delivery and the setting of increasingly ambitious targets from the late 1950s onwards. Housing targets in the hundreds of thousands were included in bold national plans and collective apartment blocks replaced single-family houses as the main form of state-provided housing. There had been almost no public housing built before the arrival of the Franco and Salazar Dictatorships; in the 1940s and 1950s their number reached tens of thousands, but it was the last two decades of the dictatorships that witnessed the boom: between 1961 and 1975 the Spanish state was responsible for the construction of over 350,000 social housing units (Carbajal, 2003). By 1970, 18.1 per cent of the housing stock in Lisbon had been built by the state – nearly double the proportion of a decade earlier (Gros, 1994).

It is also significant that the state agencies responsible for housing also began formulating its delivery in terms of social rights. The introduction to the first major conference on housing in Portugal, organised by the ministry responsible, boldly stated the principle that

> the responsibility of the State in the satisfaction of fundamental rights ... covers equally health, education, the supply of jobs, and finally the creation of the living environment, of which housing is a key component.
>
> (Ministério das Obras Públicas, 1969: II–4)

In Spain, a new law granting extensive powers to public authorities over private urban land justified this measure by the saying that 'urbanism is an unavoidable public duty' (Carbajal, 2003: 645).

However, the lived realities of the populations of Iberian cities jarred with statements of housing as a public good equally available to all. Despite the unprecedented scale of the programmes rolled out by the dictatorships, their delivery was just as segmented and inequitable as that of other welfare services. The ambitious targets advertised in the national plans of the 1950s were never met. The number of units built by the Spanish state between 1961 and 1975 was in reality only 44 per cent of what had been programmed. Underinvestment and escalating costs often led to large proportions of the units built being either sold off or let to middle class tenants who could afford higher payments, rather than those most in need. There was also continued favouring of regime insiders that reinforced the inequities in housing allocation. Further exercises in cost-cutting or sheer negligence meant that many social neighbourhoods for the poorest were very low quality, deficiently maintained, and lacking in essential support infra-structure such as transport links, schools, medical centres or even paved roads. In addition, many migrants from the countryside unable to access scarce social housing and unable to afford private rents swelled shantytowns or illegally built neighbourhoods in the peripheries.

With housing, as with other forms of welfare, the dictatorships created a new category of social right, without heeding to Tocqueville's words about the right to work in *Ancién Regime* France: 'it was indiscreet enough to utter such words, but positively dangerous to utter them in vain' (Tocqueville, 1983: 181). In a short period of time, housing was to become a central feature of the develop-ment of the type of 'insurgent citizenship' that contributed to the fall of the regimes.

'Everyday citizenship' under authoritarianism   27

In both countries initial mobilisations on the housing issue, although directed at the state (in itself a novelty), took place well within the boundaries allowed by the regime, that is, they were more examples of 'rightful resistance' which only later would become insurgent exercises of citizenship. The Spanish 'Law of Associations' of 1964 permitted the constitution of neighbourhood associations. These were duly formed, but initially they framed their petitions in the formal terms of an appeal to the grace and favour of the officials responsible – the normal form of address for petitions in such cases (Caprarella and Brotons, 2008). Similarly, in Portugal there is little sign of transgressive insurgency in the petitions handed by shantytown residents to deputies to single-party National Parliament (Ramos Pinto, 2009).

However, by the mid-1970s in Spain, and immediately following the 1974 military coup that overthrew the dictatorship in Portugal, neighbourhood organisations sprang up across the peninsula's major cities, organising demonstrations, convoking local assemblies and generally forcefully demanding housing as a right of citizenship. The resentment generated by the inequitable distribution of housing is apparent in the actions of the urban poor in Lisbon – thousands of unfinished social housing units were seized by groups from shantytowns, who argued that the corruption of housing services meant that houses were being given to the undeserving. One woman argued that an occupation had been decided after the residents of a nearby shantytown had seen how they had been bypassed in the housing waiting list by Américo Tomás' driver, 'engineers' and city council employees.[6] In other neighbourhoods there were protests demanding the removal of social workers accused of taking bribes or tampering with waiting lists in favour of some applicants. The Lisbon municipal police, who patrolled social housing neighbourhoods and whose references for good conduct could guarantee a house (or conversely, whose displeasure could mean immediate eviction), were also a common target of the ire of neighbourhood committees (Ramos Pinto, 2009).

Although they have received much less attention than the labour mobilisations of the transition, the fact that hundreds of urban areas organised their own committees and involved many thousands of ordinary citizens in recurring political participation (as opposed to one-off demonstrations), makes the urban movements one of the key forms of political expression or active citizenship of the period.[7]

Owing to different political circumstances, the mobilisation of the urban poor witnessed a different trajectory in each country. The first difference is one of timing: the legal reforms that permitted the formation of neighbourhood groups in Spain meant that the movement was able to take shape earlier than in Portugal, where formal organisations only appeared after the 1974 coup had removed the old regime. Both movements, however, accompanied the process of transition and would only die away as political forces when electoral politics replaced popular mobilisation as the key form of political expression in the late 1970s.

A second and more substantial difference is the apparent greater degree of autonomy of neighbourhood organisations in Portugal and their more radical

28   P. Ramos Pinto

repertoires of action, which included housing seizures. These differences can be explained by context. In Portugal, the fragmentation of state power that followed the April 1974 coup created the opportunity for much more transgressive forms of protest, a process which was further exacerbated by the competition between the different political forces in play to win the movement over to their side (Cerezales, 2003; Ramos Pinto, 2008). On the other hand, the existence of a more organised political opposition in Spain in the late 1960s and early 1970s led to a closer relationship between the opposition political parties and the urban movement in that country when compared to Portugal. In addition, the fact that state power and its repressive capacity remained more or less intact, certainly contributed to more contained, yet nevertheless forceful, strategies employed by the Spanish movement. In addition, in both cases, recent research suggests that the urban movements were considerably more autonomous from organised political forces than previously thought. In Portugal, the organisation of neighbourhood movements in cities like Lisbon, Oporto or Setúbal during the revolutionary period happened, in many cases, independently of political parties, who only later attempted to capitalise on their energy and commitment. In Spain, despite the more active involvement of opposition activists in the leadership of the movement, the presence of a common enemy in the form of the dictatorship encouraged a 'fragile equilibrium' between movement supporters and party leaderships, who had a greater incentive to focus on the concrete demands of urban dwellers instead of promoting broader political agendas within the movement (Castells, 2008; Ramos Pinto, 2008).

But most importantly, even in different circumstances, both movements won major concessions for urban residents and contributed to their countries' democratisation. In Spain, this was the result of the movement's interclass appeal and the recognised legitimacy of its claims on citizenship rights. As Castells argues, the urban movement was 'essential in the conversion to the idea of democracy of those people still afraid of withdrawing their support from Franquism' (Castells, 1983: 261). In Portugal, where the dictatorship had been swept away following the coup, political competition was not between supporters of the dictatorship and the opposition, but between groups seeking to control the destinies of the country, ranging from supporters of parliamentary democracy to those of radical 'popular democracies'. In a first phase of the Portuguese revolutionary period, the urban movement was part of the wave of popular mobilisation that took the political process beyond what was sought by the minimalist liberalisation advocated by the right, represented by General Spínola. Later on, as the country polarised and came near to civil war, the ordinary citizens that composed the urban movement rejected the attempts of radicals to co-opt them to their project and sided with the moderates and their democratising project. Overall, the movement was able to produce a consensus throughout the political spectrum for a commitment to state-provided housing (Ramos Pinto, 2008).

In wider terms, the question of housing as a right of citizenship, and the mobilisations it motivated, can be construed as evidence of deeper changes in the relations between society and the state that were to a large extent the unintended

'Everyday citizenship' under authoritarianism 29

consequence of the dictatorship's own transformation of the existing social contract. Of course, the broader process of integration of rural migrants and their 'trust networks' into public politics, of which the neighbourhood movements are an expression, is not simply a result of the housing and urban policies of the regime – it is also to an extent the result of the process of migration which brought millions into a sphere of closer government contact. Nevertheless, the political context into which they migrated had a significant influence in the formation of new values of citizenship.

Conclusion

This chapter has argued for a broadening of our understanding of the concept of civil society under dictatorship and a reconsideration of its relationship with the state. It sought to argue that the transformations in the terms of citizenship operated by the dictatorships was, paradoxically, responsible for the transformation of popular political beliefs that motivated growing political engagement before and during the transitions to democracy in both Spain and Portugal. In doing so, it aims to place state policy, and the way it affects populations, as a crucial contextualising and mediating factor between broader structural transformation and democratisation. As Skocpol and Amenta stated,

> Not only does politics create social policies, social policies also create politics. That is, once policies are enacted and implemented, they change the public agendas and the patterns of group conflict through which subsequent policy changes occur.
>
> (Skocpol and Amenta, 1986: 149)

What can the case of the Iberian Dictatorship tell us about the prospects of contemporary 'civil societies' under authoritarianism? While it would be wrong to attribute determinant causality to the role of the state in shaping wider citizenship values, it must be admitted that authoritarian states tend to have an extensive capacity to shape (even unintentionally) the syntax of the public sphere, notwithstanding the growth of globalised media and information sources. The mechanisms of production of new values and beliefs that sustain transitions, not just to democracy, but also to other types of regime, are often located in sites and experiences of 'civil society organisations'. Everyday interactions with other citizens, the state and its agents may not necessarily be 'schools of democracy', but they can play a highly significant role that should not be neglected.

Notes

1 I do not intend to embark on (yet another) revision of the concept of civil society, but would argue that its value is mostly heuristic – drawing our attention to actors and politics beyond the state and 'high politics' – and immediately recognisable to non-experts. Yet analytically, I believe it to be more profitable to use a relational concept such as citizenship to understand what goes on under the bonnet of 'civil society'.

30   P. Ramos Pinto

2 For instance, in 1921 it has been estimated that 44 per cent of the population of Lisbon (57 per cent in Oporto) was a member of a mutualist society. This is a remarkable level of participation, especially if we consider that the great majority of members were male: if these figures are correct, the great majority of male workers belonged to such an organisation. While this suggests a more vibrant urban 'civil society' than Iberian countries are given credit for, it also reveals how little integrated it was into public policy (Pereira, 1999). On Spanish welfare prior to the Franco regime, the overview by Mangen provides a good English-language summary (Mangen, 2001).

3 Franco came to power after leading the reactionary rebellion against the Spanish Second Republic through the Civil War (1936–1939) – the regime did not long outlast his death in 1975. Salazar gained dictatorial powers in 1928 from the military *junta* that had ruled Portugal from 1926. By 1933 he had established himself at the head of the 'New State' and forged a new constitution. Although he was incapacitated in 1968 and died in 1970, the Portuguese Dictatorship lasted until the 1974 coup under his successor, Marcello Caetano.

4 In general, there is marked bias towards political, rather than social history in the historiography of both countries, as noted by Townson for the Spanish case (2007a), and Lopes and Roque for Portugal (2000). A small but growing literature is beginning to address the history of welfare in both countries: Esping-Andersen, 1990; Díaz, 2003; Molinero, 2005; Tatjer, 2005; Cenarro Lagunas, 2006. Another notable contribution to the Portuguese context is the project directed by José António Pereirinha at ISEG, in the Technical University of Lisbon, which is reconstructing important data series on social expenditure during the *Estado Novo* (Carolo, 2006; Pereirinha and Carolo, 2009; Pereirinha *et al.*, 2009).

5 Although I find Tilly's framework a persuasive and useful one, I also find that his analysis of Spain's democratisation using these concepts ignores the role of the state in actively (if unevenly) integrating these 'trust networks'.

6 Américo Tomás was President of the Republic between 1958 and the fall of the Dictatorship. *Luta Popular*, 25 March 1975, p. 10.

7 There is a small, but growing literature focusing on the urban movements in both countries, with the best known work being that of Castells on Madrid. See: Borja, 1977; Ferreira, 1982; Castells, 1983; Downs, 1989; Cerezales, 2003; Quintana and León, 2008.

References

Banfield, Edward C. (1967) *The Moral Basis of a Backward Society*, New York, Free Press.

Baptista, Luís Vicente (1998) 'Casa, família, ideologia; a emergência da política de "moradias unifamiliares" em Portugal nos anos 30', *Ler História*, 34, 137–164.

Baptista, Luís and Rodrigues, Teresa (1996) 'Population and urban density: Lisbon in the 19th and 20th centuries', in Pereira, Pedro Telhado and Mata, Maria Eugénia (eds) *Urban Dominance and Labour Market Differentiation of a European Capital City – Lisbon 1890–1990*, Boston, Kluwer.

Borges, Jorge Luis (2000) *The Total Library: Non-fiction 1922–1986*, London, Allen Lane.

Borja, Jordi (1977) 'Urban movements in Spain', in Harloe, Michael (ed.) *Captive Cities: Studies in the Political Economy of Cities and Regions*, London, John Wiley and Sons.

Caetano, Marcello (1971) *Renovação na Continuidade*, Lisboa, Verbo.

Calleja, Eduardo González (2005) *La España de Primo de Rivera: La Modernización Autoritaria, 1923–1930*, Madrid, Alianza Editorial.

'Everyday citizenship' under authoritarianism 31

Caprarella, Marcello and Brotons, Fanny Hernández (2008) 'La lucha por la ciudad: vecinos-trabajadores en las periferias de Madrid, 1968–1982', in Quintana, Vicente Pérez and León, Pablo Sanchéz (eds) *Memoria Ciudadana y Movimiento Vecinal: Madrid, 1968–2008*, Madrid, Catarata.

Carbajal, Alfonso Fernández (2003) 'La política de vivienda en España durante el Franquismo', *Ciudad y Territorio: Estudos Territoriales*, XXXV, 639–653.

Carolo, Daniel Fernando (2006) 'A institucionalização do estado providência em Portugal: da reforma da previdência social de 1962 à actual reforma da segurança social', *XXVI Encontro da Associação Portuguesa de História Económica e Social*. Ponta Delgada.

Carreira, Henrique Medina (2000) 'Protecção social', in Barreto, António and Mónica, Maria Filomena (eds) *Dicionário de História de Portugal, Volume IX*, Lisboa, Figueirinhas.

Castells, Manuel (1983) *The City and the Grassroots: A Cross-cultural Theory of Urban Social Movements*, London, Edward Arnold.

Castells, Manuel (2008) 'Productores de ciudad: el movimiento ciudadano', in Quintana, Vicente Pérez and León, Pablo Sanchéz (eds) *Memoria Ciudadana y Movimiento Vecinal: Madrid, 1968–2008*, Madrid, Catarata.

Cenarro Lagunas, Ángela (2006) *La Sonrisa de Falange: Auxilio Social en la Guerra Civil y en la Posguerra*, Barcelona, Crítica.

Cerezales, Diego Palacios (2003) *O Poder Caiu na Rua – Crise de Estado e Acções Colectivas na Revolução Portuguesa 1974–1975*, Lisboa, Imprensa das Ciências Sociais.

Chatterjee, Partha (2004) *The Politics of the Governed: Reflections on Popular Politics in Most of the World*, New York, Columbia University Press.

Díaz, Jesús López (2003) 'Vivienda social y falange: ideario y construcción en la década de los 40'. Online. Available www.ub.es/geocrit/sn/sn-146(024).htm (last accessed 4 April 2009).

Downs, Charles (1989) *Revolution at the Grassroots: Community Organizations in the Portuguese Revolution*, Albany, SUNY Press.

Edwards, Bob and Foley, Michael W. (1998) 'Civil society and social capital beyond Putnam', *American Behavioral Scientist*, 42, 124–139.

Esping-Andersen, Gøsta (1990) *The Three Worlds of Welfare Capitalism*, Cambridge, Polity Press.

Ferreira, Vitor Matias (1982) 'Os movimentos urbanos e o SAAL: a ambiguidade e os equívocos', *A Ideia*, 24–25, 17–34.

García, Marisol and Karakatsanis, Neovi (2006) 'Social policy, democracy, and citizenship in Southern Europe', in Gunther, Richard, Diamandouros, P. N. and Sotiropoulos, D. A. (eds) *Democracy and the State in the New Southern Europe*, Oxford, Oxford University Press.

Garcia, Soledad (1994) 'The Spanish experience and its implications for a citizen's Europe', in Goddard, Victoria A., Llobera, Josep R. and Shore, Chris (eds) *The Anthropology of Europe: Identity and Boundaries in Conflict*, Oxford, Berg.

Gros, Marielle Christine (1982) *O Alojamento Social sob of Fascismo*, Porto, Afrontamento.

Gros, Marielle Christine (1994) '"Pequena" história do alojamento social em Portugal', *Sociedade e Território*, 80–90.

Holston, James (2008) *Insurgent Citizenship: Disjunctions of Democracy and Modernity in Brazil*, Princeton, NJ; Woodstock, Princeton University Press.

32   P. Ramos Pinto

Kaviraj, Sudipta and Khilnani, Sunil (eds) (2001) *Civil Society: History and Possibilities*, Cambridge, Cambridge University Press.

Leal, António da Silva (1998) *Temas de Segurança Social*, Lisboa, União das Mutualidades Portuguesas.

Lipset, Seymour Martin (1959) 'Some social requisites of democracy: economic development and political legitimacy', *American Political Science Review*, LIII, 69–105.

Lopes, Maria Antónia and Roque, João Lourenço (2000) 'Pobreza, assistência e política social em Portugal nos sécs. XIX e XX – perspectivas historiográficas', in Coelho, Maria Helena da Cruz (ed.) *A Cidade e o Campo: Colectânea de Estudos*, Coimbra, CHSC.

Lucena, Manuel de (2000) 'Previdência social', in Barreto, António and Mónica, Maria Filomena (eds) *Dicionário de História de Portugal, Volume IX*, Lisboa, Figueirinhas.

Malefakis, Edward (1995) 'The political and socioeconomic contours of Southern European history', in Gunther, Richard, Diamandouros, P. Nikiforos and Puhle, Hans-Jürgen (eds) *The Politics of Democratic Consolidation: Southern Europe in Comparative Perspective*, Baltimore, Johns Hopkins University Press.

Mangen, Stephen P. (2001) *Spanish Society After Franco: Regime Transition and the Welfare State*, Basingstoke; New York, Palgrave.

Mann, Michael (1987) 'Ruling class strategies and citizenship', *Sociology*, 21, 339–354.

Ministério das Obras Públicas (1969) *Colóquio Sobre Política de Habitação: Texto de Base*, Lisboa, Ministério das Obras Públicas.

Molinero, Carme (2005) *La Captación de las Masas: Política Social y Propaganda en el Régimen Franquista*, Madrid, Cátedra.

Moreno, Luis and Sarasa, Sebastià (1992) 'Génésis y desarrollo del estado del bienestar en España', *Documentos de Trabajo des Instituto de Estudos Sociales Avanzados, CISC*, 92.

Naylon, John (1986) 'Urban growth under an authoritarian regime, Spain 1939–1975: the case of Madrid', *Iberian Studies*, 15, 3–15.

O'Brien, Kevin J. (1996) 'Rightful resistance', *World Politics*, 49, 31–55.

O'Donnell, Guillermo, Schmitter, Philippe C. and Whitehead, Laurence (eds) (1986) *Transitions from Authoritarian Rule: Southern Europe*, Baltimore and London, The Johns Hopkins University Press.

Patriarca, Fátima (1995) *A Questão Social No Salazarismo*, Lisboa, Imprensa Nacional Casa da Moeda.

Pereira, Miriam Halpern (1999) 'As origens do estado-providência em Portugal: as novas fronteiras entre público e privado', in Teixeira, Nuno Severiano and Costa Pinto, António (eds) *A Primeira Républica Portuguesa – entre o Liberalismo e o Autoritarismo*, Lisboa, Edições Colibri.

Pereirinha, José António and Carolo, Daniel Fernando (2009) 'Construção do estado-providência em Portugal no período do Estado Novo (1935–1974): a evolução da despesa social', *ISEG/GHES Working Paper Series*, 36.

Pereirinha, José António, Arcanjo, Manuela and Carolo, Daniel Fernando (2009) 'Prestações sociais no corporativismo Português: a política de apoio à família no período do estado novo', *ISEG/GHES Working Paper Series*, 35.

Pérez Díaz, Víctor (1993) *The Return of Civil Society: The Emergence of Democratic Spain*, Cambridge, MA, Harvard University Press.

Portugal, Comissão Nacional de Eleições (2007) 'Base de dados de resultados eleitorais'. Online. Available http://eleicoes.cne.pt/cne2005/index.html (last accessed 30 August 2009).

'Everyday citizenship' under authoritarianism   33

Quintana, Vicente Pérez and León, Pablo Sanchéz (eds) (2008) *Memoria Ciudadana y Movimiento Vecinal: Madrid, 1968–2008*, Madrid, Catarata.

Ramos, Rui (2004) 'Portuguese, but not citizens: restricted citizenship in contemporary Portugal', in Bellamy, Richard, Castiglione, Dario and Santoro, Emilio (eds) *Lineages of European Citizenship: Rights, Belonging and Participation in Eleven Nation States*, Basingstoke, Palgrave Macmillan.

Ramos Pinto, Pedro (2008) 'Urban social movements and the transition to democracy in Portugal, 1974–1976', *The Historical Journal*, 51, 1025–1046.

Ramos Pinto, Pedro (2009) 'Housing and citizenship: building social rights in 20th century Portugal', *Contemporary European History*, 18, 199–215.

Rosas, Fernando and Oliveira, Pedro Aires (eds) (2004) *A Transição Falhada: O Marcelismo e o Fim do Estado Novo (1968–1974)*, Lisboa, Notícias.

Salazar, António de Oliveira (1989) 'Discurso de 30 de Julho de 1930', in Henriques, Mendo Castro and Melo, Gonçalo de Sampaio e (eds) *Salazar: Pensamento e Doutrina Poltítica – Textos Antológicos*, Lisboa, Verbo.

Samara, Maria Alice (2002) *Verdes e Vermelhos: Portugal e a Guerra no Ano de Sidónio*, Lisboa, Editorial Notícias.

Sevilla-Guzmán, Eduardo, Yruela, Manuel Pérez and Giner, Salvador (1978) 'Despotismo moderno y dominación de clase: para una sociología del régimen Franquista', *Papers: Revista de Sociologia*, 8, 105–141.

Silva, Carlos Nunes (1994) 'Mercado e políticas de habitação em Portugal: a questão da habitação na primeira metade do século XX', *Análise Social*, XXIX, 665–676.

Skocpol, Theda and Amenta, Edwin (1986) 'States and social policies', *Annual Review of Sociology*, 12, 131–157.

Spain, Direccíon General de Política Interior (2009) 'Base histórica de resultados electorales'. Online. Available at: www.elecciones.mir.es/MIR/jsp/resultados/index.htm (last accessed 30 August 2009).

Tatjer, Mercedes (2005) 'La vivenda obrera en España de los siglos XIX y XX: de la promoción pública (1853–1975)'. Online. Available www.ub.es/geocrit/sn/sn-194–23.htm (last accessed 4 April 2009).

Tilly, Charles (1995) 'Citizenship, identity and social history', *International Review of Social History*, 40, 1–17.

Tilly, Charles (2005) *Trust and Rule*, New York, NY, Cambridge University Press.

Tocqueville, Alexis de (1983) *The Old Regime and the French Revolution*, New York, Anchor Books.

Townson, Nigel (2007a) 'Introduction', in Townson, Nigel (ed.) *Spain Transformed: The Late Franco Dictatorship, 1959–1975*, London, Palgrave Macmillan.

Townson, Nigel (ed.) (2007b) *Spain Transformed: The Late Franco Dictatorship, 1959–1975*, London, Palgrave Macmillan.

Turner, Bryan S. (1990) 'Outline of a theory of citizenship', *Sociology*, 24, 189–217.

Vincent, Mary (2007) *Spain 1833–2002: People and State*, Oxford, Oxford University Press.

3 Dissident writings as political theory on civil society and democracy

Marlies Glasius

Introduction

Civil society re-entered the political lexicon in the early 1990s, precisely because of its apparent capacity, in Eastern Europe and South America, to contribute to 'opening up' and democratizing totalitarian and authoritarian states. Yet subsequent attempts in other contexts to apply the same recipe from the outside, namely strengthening civil society through funding, capacity-building and networking in order to foster a transition to democracy, have often proved less successful.

This chapter will focus on those countries in Eastern Europe and South America where civil society emerged as a cause célèbre in the successful transition to democracy: Czechoslovakia, Hungary and Poland, Argentina, Brazil and Chile.[1] However, it will not attempt comparative case studies or make causal inferences of who did what when and where, and to what extent civil society drove the transition. Much energy has already been devoted to this debate in the years after transition (see for instance Dahrendorf, 1990; Ekiert, 1996; Kubik, 1994; Stepan, 1989). It may not in fact be possible to satisfactorily resolve this question because with hindsight, the transitions are over-determined by numerous factors.

This chapter has a different intention. It will offer a theoretical analysis of precisely how civil society was conceptualized by its protagonists in their pre-democratic contexts. Their writings from the pre-democratic period have been largely ignored in later narratives which chart a linear progression from brave western-oriented dissidents to mass mobilization to liberal democracy. Studying the original documents may provide new clues as to how these activists, for want of a better word,[2] saw the nature of the regime, how they conceptualized civil society and the sources of its power, and what exactly their democratic aspirations were.

The purpose here then is to re-examine what civil society might actually be and how it might function under authoritarian regimes, and to formulate hypotheses about its potential relation to democratization or non-democratization in contemporary settings, on the basis of the writings of the Eastern European and South American 'members' of civil society who re-introduced the term into

Dissident writings as political theory   35

political theory and practice. The underlying assumption is that if commonalities are found in the thinking of activists in these very different regional and ideological contexts, they might also have relevance for yet different contemporary contexts such as the Middle East or China. Thus, the chapter offers building blocks for a political theory of civil society under authoritarian rule, which others may apply and test in contemporary contexts.

Naturally, it must be acknowledged that this cannot be a 'pure' exercise in time-travel, as the author's selection from and analysis of the material is partially determined by her own twenty-first century perspective on civil society and democratization. But this conundrum is really no different from that of any researcher attempting to 'translate' and analyse the perspective of others who are not in direct contact with the reading audience. The author is unavoidably present in the text but attempts to let voices from the past speak for themselves as much as possible through liberal use of literal quotes.

Sources

This study intends to present a reconstruction of socio-political ideas. The intention is not to reconstruct which ideas were 'most representative' of civil society in each country, but instead to look at commonalities and differences in a variety of sources. The following principles guided the search for sources:

1   All the sources are from either before or during democratization, thus lacking the (questionable) benefit of hindsight, which is the usual point of departure for studies of democratization processes.
2   All the sources are from people who lived principally inside the country in question – although circumstances dictated that many spent some time in exile as well.
3   The voices of 'amateurs', i.e. artists, scientists or housewives are privileged over those of professional political scientists. On the one hand, it was usually difficult or impossible for academics who spoke up to become and remain employed as such within the country. On the other hand, the ideas written by non-professionals are most likely to have stayed outside academic consideration, so they may provide fresher views. At the same time, it must be acknowledged that the voice of intellectuals is necessarily somewhat dominant because they tend to write most extensively.
4   The study limits itself to writing, and explicitly political writing at that. Fiction, documentaries or other forms of expression might well hold equally important clues to the nature of regime and civil society, but they would require a rather different analytical treatment.
5   Finally, but this is a limitation rather than a principle, the study focuses primarily on documents that have been translated into English. A few documents considered key were read in Spanish, but the bulk of the materials used has been published in English. This of course puts a clear limit on the range of possible documents that can be studied. For each of the six

36   *M. Glasius*

countries, there is presumably much more literature in the national language than in translation; moreover there may be certain biases in what has been translated.

Nonetheless, it has turned out to be possible to select a wide variety of sources just from the translated materials. They include collective declarations, newspaper articles, *samizdat* essays, diaries, letters from prison, books written in exile, academic articles and acceptance speeches for prizes.

The remainder of the chapter has organized the ideas found in the source material into three main sections: the first on their understanding of the nature of the regime, its aims and its relation to society; the second on the features of the emergent civil society the writers of these documents desired, observed and helped to create; and a final section on their strategies and aspirations in relation to 'democratization'.

Understanding the regime and its aims

The nature of the regime: not the strong man

Vaclav Havel and Fernando Henrique Cardoso express most clearly and in similar terms what the regime they live under is *not*. Havel argues that 'the term "dictatorship", regardless of how intelligible it may otherwise be, tends to obscure rather than clarify the real nature of power in this system' (Havel, 1979/1985: 24). Whereas classical dictatorships have been temporary, local, ideologically shallow and built on brute force, the 'post-totalitarian' system of the Eastern bloc is lasting, goes beyond national boundaries and is built on ideology itself. Cardoso too points out that while authoritarianism is not new to the South American continent, the authoritarianism of the 1970s and 1980s is no longer the personality-based *caudillismo* of an earlier era (Cardoso, 1979: 32). Its resurgence must instead be understood in a context of modernization. It is 'bureaucratic', and emphatically based on 'the military institution as an organisation' (Cardoso, 1979: 35).

However – and here he seems to make an explicit comparison with Eastern Europe – South American authoritarianism is 'underdeveloped': 'It may kill and torture, but it does not exercise complete control over everyday life.' It has been strong enough in its dealings with so-called subversive groups, 'but it is not as efficient when it comes to controlling the universities, for example, or even bureaucracy itself' (Cardoso, 1979: 48). This difference between the relatively young and spectacularly brutal regimes of South America and the more entrenched and subtle workings of the communist regimes of Eastern Europe is of course generally recognized. But speculations by activists as to who exactly is in power, and for whose benefit, can be divided into two groups that do not follow regional lines.

Dissident writings as political theory 37

Realists: hunger for power

The first, typified by both Cardoso and the Hungarian novelist Gyorgy Konrad, could broadly be called 'realist'. They largely maintain that an elite is in power for its own sake. Cardoso is at pains to explain that the interests of the transnational capitalist class do *not* sufficiently explain the resurgence of authoritarianism. Liberal democracy is quite adequate to their needs, and in some respects gives them better opportunities, than a strong authoritarian state provided that the political clout of the workforce is kept in check. Instead, difficult though this is to accept for the Marxist-oriented South American left, 'bureaucratic authoritarianism is politically profitable for the civilian and military bureaucrats that hold state office' (Cardoso, 1979: 51). The expression 'politically profitable' here would seem to suggest that Cardoso thought not just in terms of private gain, but also and perhaps more in terms of perpetuation in power. This explains why, contrary to what one would expect of a 'dependent capitalist' state, state involvement in the economy, already large in Brazil, only grew during the military dictatorship. Konrad, devoid of illusions about ideology, puts it even more starkly. Politicians, whether East or West, are 'professionals of power', he argues:

> if we don't believe that a great painter paints because it's the way to God or riches, then why should we think that the great born politicians want power for some ulterior reason, good or bad, rather than for the sake of power itself?
>
> (Konrad, 1984: 94)

Constructivists: ideology

Others believe that it is in fact the ideology that rules, and those in power serve it. Argentine journalist Jacobo Timerman deviates from most other South American commentators in characterizing the Argentine *junta* as not only fascist and anti-Semitic, but also as 'totalitarian'. He locates the roots of this totalitarian worldview in a military class that has long been separated from civilian life and increasingly cultivated a series of 'fantasies' based on fear rather than on a utopia of a desirable society (Timerman, 1980/1981: 94). Timerman's claim is well substantiated. He documents how, in its relatively short rule (1976–1983), the Argentine *junta* not only killed large numbers of social scientists and psychiatrists suspected of left-wing sympathies, but attempted to eliminate the suspect disciplines of sociology, philosophy and psychiatry altogether (Timerman, 1980/1981: 93–99). Michnik (1976/1985: xix) also follows Arendt in the belief that the greatest source of totalitarian power lay in 'their ability to infect us with their own hatred and contempt' rather than in the force of jail and jackboot.

These accounts emphasize the destructive aspirations of early authoritarian rule. In order to consolidate, they must stop the natural flow of social change. Chilean writer Ariel Dorfman imputes to the Pinochet regime nothing less than

38   *M. Glasius*

the ambition to 'abolish time, freeze history, colonize space' (Dorfman, 1989: 121). Polish writer Kazimierz Brandys also uses an icy metaphor: 'A totalitarian state frozen in terror gleams like a glacier from the distance' (Brandys, 1983: 118).

This the totalitarian state cannot do over time, and the initial passionate agents of ideology evolve into a post-totalitarian universe where everyone serves ideology *without* being genuine believers. Havel's post-totalitarian system is a self-propelling machine, in which even political leaders are just cogs:

> Western Sovietologists often exaggerate the role of individuals in the post-totalitarian system and overlook the fact that the ruling figures, despite the immense power they possess through the centralized structure of power, are often no more than blind executors of the system's own internal laws – laws they themselves never can, and never do, reflect upon. In any case experience has taught us again and again that this automatism is far more powerful than the will of any individual; and should someone possess a more independent will, he or she must conceal it behind a ritually anonymous mask in order to have an opportunity to enter the power hierarchy at all.

> (Havel, 1979/1985: 34)

Brandys expresses the manner which the system is maintained by the people themselves in a similar way: 'it may be that the most essential mechanism in the system known as communism is this curious twofold one: the counterfeiting and the denying of the self' (1983: 94). In this analysis, collective self-limitation has taken the place of Timerman's ideology of hatred and Konrad and Cardoso's will to power.

Atomization

The differences between the East European and the South American writers are much more a matter of atmosphere than of analysis. In Eastern Europe, the symbol of repression is the tank, in South America it is the torture chamber. At the level of personal reflection, South Americans express a bodily fear of pain, whereas the East European nightmare is more one of mental claustrophobia.

However, when they express their fears not on a personal but on a societal level, it is the same: of atomization, of each individual being isolated from all his peers through the machinations of the regime. The Czech Catholic mathematician Vaclav Benda expresses it in the following terms:

> The Iron Curtain does not just exist between the East and the West: it also separates individual nations in the East, individual regions, individual towns and villages, individual factories, individual families, and even the individuals within those entities from each other.

> (Benda, 1988: 218)

Konrad too, speaks of the Iron Curtain as being 'in our heads' (Konrad, 1984: 112). Havel puts it in more existential terms: 'The post-totalitarian system is mounting a total assault on humans and humans stand against it alone, abandoned and isolated' (Havel, 1979/1985: 67). Ariel Dorfman describes Chileans under Pinochet in very similar words: 'isolated from each other, their means of communicating suppressed, their connections cut off, their senses blocked by fear' (Dorfman, 1985a).

Both Havel and Dorfman, while sharing the more general assumption that it is the 'regime' or 'system' that wills atomization, also connect it to the passive consumerism of modern man. Thus, in the Frankfurter School tradition, they see their own societies as especially morbid varieties of a more general phenomenon. 'There is obviously in modern humanity a certain tendency towards the creation of such a system ... some connection with the general unwillingness of consumption-oriented people to sacrifice material certainties.' Eastern Europe (or indeed South America) can then be seen as standing as 'a kind of warning to the West, revealing to it its own latent tendencies' (Havel, 1979/1985: 38–39).

Jacobo Timerman captures the atomization in the very title of his book *Prisoner Without a Name, Cell Without a Number*. In reality, Timerman was one of the most high-profile Argentine prisoners of conscience, and his international fame may have contributed to his eventual release. Yet he felt the isolation equally in the early days of his arrest. He opens the book with the pivotal experience of a night during which he and an anonymous fellow prisoner had eye-contact for hours because the tiny peepholes of their opposing cells were left open:

> you were my brother, my father, my son, my friend. Or are you a woman? If so, we passed that night as lovers ... that flutter of movement proved conclusively that I was not the last human survivor on earth amid this universe of torturing custodians.
>
> (Timerman, 1980/1981: 5–6)

Features of a proto-civil society

Solidarity

In less poetic terms, many documents emphasize the importance of friendship and communication as a last line of defence and first point of departure for a civil society, before and beyond the emergence of any more overtly political formation.

According to Brazilian political scientist Francisco Weffort, the

> discovery that there was something more to politics than the State began with the simplest facts of life of the persecuted. In the most difficult moments, they had to make use of what they found around them. There were no parties to go to or courts in which they could have confidence. At a

40   *M. Glasius*

difficult time, the primary recourse was the family, friends, and in some cases fellow workers. If there was a legal chance of defence, they had to look for a courageous lawyer. And, above all, someone who is persecuted can always, as an old Brazilian proverb says, 'complain to the bishop'. What are we talking about if not civil society, though still at the molecular level of interpersonal relations?

(Weffort, 1983/1989: 347)

Konrad too writes,

(w)ithdrawal into our huddled private circles enabled us to survive even the grimmest years of the dictatorship. We didn't really live in a state of constant tension because every evening we could be with one another. We talked a great deal; congregated in our lairs, we experienced a kind of campfire warmth.

(Konrad, 1984: 203)

He further points out that it was not by accident that the largest East European democracy movement was called 'Solidarity' (Konrad, 1984: 195).

Living in the truth

However, there is more to this molecular civil society than solidarity or 'campfire warmth'. Another key element repeated by many sources is that of communication, beginning more or less underground but reaching ever wider circles. This has two aspects. The first is the assertion of 'truth' unacceptable to the regime.

It is in these terms that Polish writer Kazimierz Brandys explains switching from trying to slip writings past censors to writing openly for the new independent magazine *Zapis*:

[A]re we deceiving the tyrant or is he deceiving us? Is it not true that in exchange for the chance to publish poetry, we give up on stating the values that that poetry conceals, from which it arose, and to which it makes reference.... If that is the case, then one may suspect that we are paying too high a price.

(Brandys, 1983: 43)

It was also along this path that the Madres de la Plaza de Mayo evolved, first searching for their children each on their own, then 'all for all the children' (Diago, 1988: 119). In the early years they wrote information about their missing children on banknotes in order to achieve maximum circulation (Diago, 1988: 122). After the disappearance and presumed death of their first leader, Azucena de Villaflor, the Madres took the difficult decision to remain out in the open, continuing to congregate on the Plaza de Mayo and other town squares (Gorini,

Dissident writings as political theory 41

2006: 186–187). This was both a strategic decision, calculating that in a fundamentally unsafe situation, publicity might actually provide more security than secrecy, and a principled decision that a just cause should not have to go underground (Diago, 1988: 123; Madres, 2006: 31–32). Vaclav Havel asserts an unambiguous belief in 'living in the truth', i.e. openly asserting one's lack of belief in the official ideology. Havel and other members of Charter 77 emphasize time and again that the force of the Chartists lay not in their (small) number, but in the fact that they asserted themselves at all and communicated their heretic beliefs to others. Anyone who refuses to acknowledge the system 'denies it in principle and threatens it in its entirety' (Havel, 1979/1985: 40).

Jacobo Timerman, too, kept his newspaper *La Opinion* open, and continued to print information about disappeared people, on this basis:

> I know that I saved the lives of some, and believe others were killed merely because *La Opinion* demanded knowledge of their whereabouts. But in the long run the battle, it seems to me, had to be fought, so that at least there *was* a battle, embryonic as it might be.
>
> (Timerman, 1980/1981: 28)

Ariel Dorfman, while admiring the bravery and stamina of those who kept confronting the regime, comments a little more wearily that for many years the frequent but small protests had the 'ritualistic, circular quality' of a 'morality play directed at bystanders that were too scared to join or at the armed forces who were too walled-in to listen' (Dorfman, 1988).

Plurality

While voices emphasize the open expression of dissent, others are less focused on the publicity and more on the re-assertion of plurality and exchange of ideas as a value. Charter 77 characterizes itself as an 'open community of people of different convictions, different faiths and different opinions' (Charter 77 Declaration, 1977). Their numbers included proponents of pop culture, people of Catholic and protestant backgrounds, and ex-Marxist intellectuals. Nonetheless, the shades of difference between Czechoslovak dissidents in their conceptualization of a 'parallel polis', 'second culture' or 'civil society' (Benda *et al.*, 1988) appear to the contemporary reader as very small. It seems as if they discuss and analyse these differences almost for the pleasure of disagreeing with each other, relishing them as in themselves an exercise in opposing the monolithic official ideology. Their Hungarian counterpart Konrad appears to suggest as much: 'Theoretical discussion is inherently more dignified than power struggle. We can become an adult nation if we introduce ideological pluralism in preparation for the political pluralism that will come in due time' (Konrad, 1984: 182). This creates an 'uncontrollable sea of private conversations' regardless of state or government (Konrad, 1984: 198). It is worth recognizing of course that this idealized version of pluralism may not always have reflected the realities in civil

42   *M. Glasius*

society. Moreover, the experience in Poland, where internal democracy and debate within Solidarity were curtailed precisely when it began to engage in serious negotiations with the government (Staniszkis, 1984: 50) may reflect a wider phenomenon.

In South America with its much shorter history of less perfect totalitarianism, pluralism tends to be perceived as a practical problem as much as a value in itself (Dorfman, 1987: 113; Garreton, 1987/1989: 275). Yet it could be argued that it is asserted indirectly through the rejection of violence.

Non-violence

Violence is uppermost in the reflections of many South American writers. Timerman describes Argentina, not just during the *junta* but historically, as possessing an infinite capacity for violence in combination with a political incapacity for pluralism. He calls terrorism and violence 'the sole creative potential, the sole imaginative, emotional, erotic expression' of the Argentine nation (Timerman, 1980/1981: 17). He then asks the following question, which can be considered as one of the lead questions for this chapter: 'Can the community alone, without outside intervention, prevent either of the two fascisms from winding up with Argentina's corpse?' (Timerman, 1980/1981: 21).

Francisco Weffort, writing in Brazil after the ruling military had begun to 'open up', answers this question definitively in the affirmative. He describes a recent history of Brazil where, similar to pre-junta Argentina, the main expression of politics, right or left, was in terms of violence. But under the military regime 'right-wing violence took on industrial proportions' (Weffort, 1983/1989: 341), the destructive potential of which frightened the government itself almost as much as it frightened the opposition, to the point that 'an area of consensus has been created around the elimination of terror' (Weffort, 1983/1989: 340). It was this insight, according to Weffort, which produced in a wide variety of political actors 'the discovery of civil society as a political space' (Weffort, 1983/1989: 345). The Madres of the Plaza del Mayo too, affirm in their declaration of principles that 'we stand against violence and against every type of terrorism, private or state' (Madres, 1979), a statement that at least some of their children might not have agreed with prior to their disappearance.

In Konrad, even more than in Weffort, civil society is not just a choice for non-violence, it is the very antithesis of violence: 'military society is the reality, civil society is the utopia' (Konrad, 1984: 92). Unlike other sources, and much more like western peace activists of the same era, his nightmares are less of the gun, prison camp or torture chamber than of the 'global Auschwitz' of nuclear annihilation (Konrad, 1984: 96). Reflections on violence play a much smaller role in the work of other East Europeans, but their conclusions are largely the same: they too have opted for non-violent resistance for both 'realistic' and ethical reasons. Havel echoes the Gandhian sentiment that 'a future secured by violence might actually be worse than what exists now; in other words, the future would be fatally stigmatized by the very means used to secure it' (Havel, 1979/1985: 71).

Dissident writings as political theory   43

It is necessary, however, to recognize that this widespread revulsion is by no means the inevitable response to a surfeit of violence. Ariel Dorfman describes how 'our hands are clean' has become a dominant slogan in anti-Pinochet demonstrations in 1985. He speculates that most Chileans reject a violent solution, both 'out of realism' and for 'deeper moral reasons'. However, he ends the piece by saying 'there is a limit to our patience. Let it be remembered, in the future, that if we are forced to resort to other methods to liberate ourselves, we wanted our hands to remain clean' (Dorfman, 1985b). Less than a year later, after a failed attempt on Pinochet's life, he writes that 'the hopes for a peaceful transition to democracy seem to have been dashed', and that whereas the Chilean Communist Party had traditionally aligned itself with peaceful methods, many on the far left began to believe that armed resistance was the only way to bring the regime down. He ends the article with 'more violence will beget more violence. Is it already too late?' (Dorfman, 1986). As we know, with the benefit of hindsight, the transition in Chile was largely peaceful, but Dorfman's words should remind us that there was no inevitable path-dependency here, but perhaps rather an agency of restraint.

On 'independence' and organizational forms

The East European and South American activists have sometimes been seen by later generations of scholars as responsible for a 'purist' view of civil society free from the pathologies of state and market (Chandhoke, 2002: 36–37; Keane, 2005: 26). A closer consideration of the actual ideas they had on the topic turns out to belie this claim.

In 1987, a western social scientist asked a number of Czechoslovak dissidents whether they thought the term 'independent society' was relevant and meaningful to their conditions. They reacted to the proposition with great caution. Vaclav Benda held that what he conceptualized as a parallel polis 'cannot completely ignore the official social structures' and that the parallel concept instead 'stresses variety, but not complete independence' (Benda, 1988: 217). Political theorist Milan Simecka held that one could speak of 'independent thinking', but certainly not yet independent society (Simecka, 1988: 222). Former journalist Jiri Dienstbier held that the term 'independent society', unlike civil society, contained an unrealistic and indeed undesirable implication that the state could and should 'wither away' (Dienstbier, 1988, 230). Vaclav Havel pointed out that there are only relative gradations of dependence and independence, but that the 'relatively independent enclave' enriches society as a whole (Havel, 1979/1985: 237). Chilean psychiatrist and playwright Marco Antonio de la Parra describes the same relative contamination and regeneration more poetically in his introduction to a photo album on the Pinochet years:

> We were irresolute, oblique; we hid our hands, lowered our eyes. Those who spoke up, stood up straight, were few. But at the same time these photographs show the country did not submit, we kept life vibrant, our hearts alive.
>
> (Parra, 1990: 14–15)

44   *M. Glasius*

Decisions as to what organizational form the manifestations of civil society should take turn out to have been less a matter of principle and more dictated by pragmatic circumstances. Calling oneself an 'organisation' and registering membership, can increase the risks for members. Registering legally as an organization is sometimes simply not allowed, but when it is it can have practical advantages, such as the possibility to collect and receive money in the name of the organization (Madres, 1979; Vargha, 1985). Although these kinds of decisions can have political implications as well, the issue appears not to have been of fundamental importance to its protagonists. Both the signatories to Charter 77 and the Madres de la Plaza de Mayo placed a high value on the public nature of their activities, on being out in the open and bearing witness. The two organizations, very different in many other ways, both explicitly insist on not being a political opposition movement. The Charter 'does not form the basis for any oppositional political activity' (Charter 77 Declaration, 1977). The Madres are 'not moved by any political objective' (Madres, 1979).

The Madres decided, after more than two years of demonstrations, to register as a civic association. Charter 77 on the other hand insisted that is 'is not an organization; it has no rules, permanent bodies or formal membership. It embraces everyone who agrees with its ideas, participates in its work, and supports it' (Charter 77 Declaration, 1977). But according to one of the Chartists, Vaclav Cerny: 'the considerations about how it is to be run and what form this will take ... may change ... it all depends on considerations of need, suitability and effectiveness' (Cerny, 1985: 133).

Poland's *Solidarity* is a case in point. According to Jadwiga Staniszkis, one of its advisors drawn from the ranks of dissident intellectuals, the circumstances of its development required 'the painful process of cramming that radical wave of protest and class war into a "trade union" formula, when in reality it oscillated being a mass movement and a "political party of activists"' (Staniszkis, 1984: 17–23).

Organizational form, then, would appear to be a matter of expediency, not a fundamental feature of civil society in authoritarian settings.

Strategies and aspirations

Appeal to law and human rights

Practically all activists whose works are examined here appeal to laws, and more generally the 'rule of law', as a principle helpful to them. The Charter 77 Declaration is entirely based on this principle: it begins by stating that the International Covenant of Civil and Political Rights (ICCPR) and the International Covenant on Economic and Social Rights (ICESCR) have been incorporated into Czechoslovak national law in 1976, and then goes on to enumerate at length how some of the rights set forth in these Covenants are in practice violated in Czechoslovakia (Charter 77 Declaration, 1977). The Madres in their Declaration point out that they do not demand freedom for their children but treatment according

Dissident writings as political theory 45

to the law: to know where they are, what they are accused of, to be judged according to legal norms with a right to be defended; to not be tortured; to be held in suitable conditions, etc. (Madres, 1979).

Both were undoubtedly aware that the authorities were not serious about their commitments to these legal norms, but the point that Havel for instance makes is that unlike 'some ephemeral dictatorship run by a Ugandan bandit',[3] bureaucratic authoritarianism needs the 'ritually cohesive force' of legal form: 'it wraps the base exercise of power in the noble apparel of the letter of the law' (Havel, 1979/1985: 75). Dorfman considers the plebiscite announced by Pinochet in the same light: an attempt to achieve the appearance of an endorsement for 'more permanent structures of repression' (Dorfman, 1987: 114). 'What limits', he asks, 'should be placed on one's participation in a legal system which one rejects? Is it better to abstain? Or is it better to uncomfortably sabotage the system from within?'

Havel and the Chartists clearly opted for the second option:

> A persistent and never-ending appeal to the laws – not just the laws concerning human rights, but to all laws – does not mean at all that those who do so have succumbed to the illusion that in our system the law is anything other than what it is. They are well aware of the role it plays. But precisely because they know how desperately the system depends on it, on the 'noble' version of the law, that is – they also know how enormously significant such appeals are.
>
> (Havel, 1979/1985: 76)

The ostensible commitment to predetermined, impersonal rules, based on national and international legal traditions, gives activists some leverage when they express themselves in this language.

Francisco Weffort too sets out to explain how law was gradually perverted in twentieth century Brazil by increasing '*casuismos*': instrumental use of it by whoever is in power. Yet, he says, 'the most constant theme in Brazilian politics since 1968 has been the re-establishment of a State of Law' (Weffort, 1983/1989: 342). He argues that although initially liberals, liberal elements of the regime and leftists meant different things by this term, it was a creative ambiguity that eventually converged into 'shades of the same general democratic aspiration' (Weffort, 1983/1989: 343). Most Chilean groups too, finally did decide to participate in Pinochet's self-endorsement plebiscite, giving it so much reality that Pinochet in the end failed to manipulate or rig it as Dorfman had earlier predicted.

Relation to the 'international community'

Jacobo Timerman asks: 'is collaboration possible among the international community to ... enable Argentina's reincorporation into civilized society?' (Timerman, 1980/1981: 21). This of course is the question most often posed in the West

46 *M. Glasius*

in relation to authoritarian regimes, and accompanied by virulent debate about the historically tainted concept of a 'civilized society', and whose fault it is if certain societies are 'not civilized'. Timerman barely attempts to answer his own question, and most of the sources consulted here are curiously unconcerned with it.

East Europeans, Konrad above all, of course demonstrate an awareness of the relation between their national predicament and the wider context of superpower rivalry. Konrad in fact names the problem not 'communism' or 'totalitarianism', but 'Yalta'. But it is precisely because they perceive this situation as immutable and beyond their control that they turn to the bottom-up reform of their own societies as a priority (Konrad, 1984: 116–124; Havel, 1979/1985, 89). They do not ask either western governments or western publics to 'do' anything in particular. Indeed, when describing the subtly electrifying effect of the visit of John Paul II in 1979 on the Polish public, Brandys writes

> we make ourselves ridiculous when we try the instruct the Americans or the French in how best to act and think. Our past is different from theirs; we have no part in their lives.... But they too have no basis for instructing us in how to think and act, for they know even less about us.
>
> (Brandys, 1983: 83)

South American sources, although placing their countries' trajectory against the background of dependency theory (Cardoso, 1979, 1983; Serra, 1979), and reflecting awareness of US involvement in the Chilean coup in particular, appear to have been even less inclined to have expectations of, or make demands on, European or American publics or governments.

Yet the international does feature in a different way: in the self-identification of many of the actors discussed here. Janos Vargha, a Hungarian environmental activist, begins his acceptance speech for the Right Livelihood Award with a story from *Gulliver's Travels* and goes on to mention deleterious dam projects in Brazil, Egypt, West Germany, New Zealand, Sri Lanka and the USSR, and anti-dam activism in the Philippines, the USSR and Austria before actually describing his own group, the Danube Circle (Vargha, 1985). Thus he places himself and his group in the context of the emerging global anti-dam movement. Jacobo Timerman uses examples from Nazi Germany and the contemporary USSR to analyse the Argentinian situation, and identifies himself (to the confusion of his persecutors) as both an international liberal and an international Zionist (Timerman, 1981). Ariel Dorfman in his many short pieces takes inspiration from the 'I have a dream' speech of Martin Luther King, the novels of Gabriel Garcia Marquez and numerous other literary sources from all over the world as relevant to the Chilean predicament (see for instance Dorfman, 1983, 2003).

Gyorgy Konrad however is the one who gives such identification with like-minded people elsewhere an explicit place in relation to the local reconstitution of civil society: 'the trip abroad, the forming of friendships with others across the frontier – these are some of the elements of the intellectuals' struggle for

Dissident writings as political theory 47

freedom; the international Solidarity of the craft is their mutual defence alliance' (Konrad, 1984: 212). But he does not intend this, as we now tend to do when we invoke 'global civil society', in instrumental terms. On the contrary, he writes,

> we ought to avoid becoming a major theater of operations for the world's communications media.... International public opinion's approval and disapproval are transient things, matters of fashion ... we should accord the foreign media only a limited role, as auxiliaries in our enterprise.
>
> (Konrad, 1984: 164)

Thus, the self-identification as a citizen of the world, against the rigidity and brutality of the state, appears to have primarily a morale-boosting function.

The timing of democratization

While it is rarely possible to pinpoint precisely when a democratization process begins, and when, if ever, it is completed, there is a paradox in comparing the East European experience with that of at least two of the South American countries. The decades-long East European domination by the party-state was abruptly converted into a series of multi-party democracies without any special role for the Communist party, while the much shorter military dictatorships of Brazil and Chile went through a decade or more of managed transition before the military had entirely returned to the barracks.

In both cases, the writings examined reveal on the whole a curious lack of impatience about, or even reflection on, the timing of transition to democracy. There is lots of detailed and dated reflection in these writings on the recent past, but with the exception of one expression of despair by Ariel Dorfman at General Pinochet's 1986 announcement that he would stay in power until 1997 (Dorfman, 1986: 111), reflection on the future does not come with dates. Indeed, Brandys uses the example of India to argue that 'sometimes, a nation wins such battles over two or three generations. ... It is a struggle for oneself. Not only a struggle for freedom. We ourselves are transformed in it' (1983: 256).

Brazilians were convinced that they were on the road to some sort of democratization from at least 1983, while Chileans remained uncertain that there would be a transition until after the 1988 plebiscite. But both were convinced that the transition would be long, and the depth of transformation doubtful. East Europeans were under the impression as late as 1988 that no discernible transition at the top could be expected any time soon.

What emerges is that the focus of their concerns is not on transformation at the top. Poland's leading dissident Adam Michnik was the first to express this lack of faith in transformation at the top in 1976 (Michnik, 1976/1985: 136–138). In many other writings, this is implicit. They are much more interested in transformation at the bottom. Konrad even seems, somewhat disingenuously perhaps, to express a complete lack of interest in a change of system when he says: 'Let the government stay on top, we will live our own lives underneath it' (Konrad, 1984: 198).

48 *M. Glasius*

Most authors did believe that sooner or later the widening and deepening of 'civil society' as discussed above would have consequences for the regime, just not very precisely datable ones. As Havel (1979/1985: 82) puts it, the 'primary purpose of the outward direction of these movements is always, as we have seen, to have an impact on society, not to affect the power structure, at least not directly and immediately'. Benda (1988: 219) expresses himself in Gramscian terms of trench warfare:

> given the time and the means available, only a certain number of trenches can be eliminated. If, at the same time, the parallel polis is able to produce more trenches than it loses, a situation arises that is mortally dangerous for the regime.

Chilean social scientist Manuel Antonio Garreton, more descriptively, writes that 'civil society has reasserted itself to the point where it has room to organize and express itself'. He calls this the 'invisible transition to democracy' which predated the visible transition at the top (Garreton, 1987/1989). Judit Vasxheiyi, a librarian and environmental activist of the Hungarian Danube Circle, also gives the mobilization of 'biologists, architects, artists, historians, lawyers, sociologists and teachers', later joined by 'manual workers and ... non-urban population' to oppose a hydro-electric dam project the extraordinary name 'democratization' (Vasxheiyi, 1985).

What appears to have characterized both the South American and the East European situations is that civil societies of a certain width and depth, manifesting themselves not only in mobilization but also displaying the elements of solidarity, truth-telling and plurality predated the transition at the top by several, sometimes many years.

Aspirations (or what democracy is)

The East European and South American 'civil societies' or 'democratization movements' have gone down in history as desiring, and achieving, democracy, or even more narrowly speaking, 'liberal democracy'. There is no doubt that the six countries under particular consideration here achieved fairly successful liberal democracies. But was this what the activists had aspired to? Why then the emphasis on civil society, which had not been an important characteristic of mainstream political theory in the West (it barely features for instance in Lijphart, 1977 or Dahl, 1982)?

There turns out to be a remarkable resemblance between the ideas East European and South American dissidents formulated as the utopian opposite of the regimes they lived under. What they point to, again, is less a change in government and more a structural change in state–society relations.

Francisco Weffort states in the middle of the long drawn-out democratization process in Brazil in 1983: 'we want a civil society; we need it to defend ourselves from the monstrous state in front of us' (Weffort, 1983/1989: 349). Weffort still

Dissident writings as political theory 49

cautiously suggests that if there is no civil society yet, it has to be invented. Konrad writing in Hungary at almost the same time already saw an 'independent ferment' the success of which 'cannot be measured by the replacement of one government by another, but by the fact that under the same government society is growing stronger, independent people are multiplying, and the network of conversations uncontrollable from above is becoming denser' (Konrad, 1984: 198). Weffort discusses a Brazilian political legacy that, underneath a veneer of liberal democracy, was fundamentally statist and indeed authoritarian:

> The superimposition of democratic forms on authoritarian relations, the prevalence of statist ideology even among those who called themselves anti-statist, and the resulting acceptance of coup-making as an everyday form of political action, are all characteristics which cut across left/right divisions. We are capable of calling authoritarianism democracy, and an act of usurpation is called a revolution.

But in the 1970s and 1980s, on the left *and* the right, a process of abdication of this legacy takes place:

> If the State had formerly been the solution, now it was the problem. If before it had been possible to call 'democracy' what were merely juridico-institutional forms of democracy, it was possible no longer. Out of an ambiguous historical legacy new meanings had to be developed, and, slowly and fearfully, democracy began to be seen not as a means to power but as an end in itself. Yet if politics were to have a new meaning, a new sphere of freedom for political action had to be developed. For political Brazil, civil society, previously either ignored or seen as an inert mass, began to signify that sphere of freedom.
>
> (Weffort, 1983/1989: 329)

If this was only a call for 'less state, more society' it could be read as either an anarchic or a libertarian reaction to statist conditions. But the ideas of Konrad, Havel, Dienstbier, Cardoso and Weffort go further and bear a deeper resemblance to each other than that. The political freedoms of liberal democracy are a necessary but not sufficient condition for their aspirations. Multi-party elections appear to be even less a sufficient condition:

> people ... know ... that the question of whether one or several political parties are in power, and how these parties define and label themselves, is of far less importance than the question of whether or not it is possible to live like a human being.
>
> (Havel, 1979/1985: 52)

According to Konrad, Europe's historical reality deserves richer organizational forms than those offered by the moralistic dichotomy of American capitalism and Russian communism (Konrad, 1984: 34).

50   *M. Glasius*

Democratic practices

What they believe civil society to have begun developing during authoritarian rule, is democratic practices at the levels closest to citizens: among neighbours, between women (Garreton, 1987/1989: 271–272) or in the workplace (Cardoso, 1983: 314). Konrad too points out that:

> workplace and local community self-government, based on personal contact, exercised daily, and always subject to correction, have greater attraction in our part of the world than multiparty representative democracy because, if they have the choice, people are not content with voting once every four years just to choose their deputy or the head of government.
>
> (Konrad, 1984: 137)

Chilean feminists even applied this concept of democracy to the private realm with their slogan 'Democracy in the country and in the home' (Chuchryk, 1989: 182).

Far-reaching consequences are attached to these developments. Havel describes a utopia of a post-democratic system consisting of

> structures [that] should naturally arise from *below* as a consequence of authentic social self-organization; they should derive vital energy from a living dialogue with the genuine needs from which they arise, and when these needs are gone, the structures should also disappear.
>
> (Havel, 1979/1985: 93)

The inspiration for this vision comes from the 'informal, non-bureaucratic, dynamic and open communities that comprise the parallel *polis*' which could be seen as 'a kind of rudimentary prefiguration, a symbolic model of those more meaningful "post-democratic" political structures that might become the foundation of a better society' (Havel, 1979/1985: 95). In Havel, it remains somewhat unclear whether his fluid structures would emerge and shrivel within the context of a parliamentary democracy, or instead of it.

Cardoso is much clearer in this respect. He observes that during the Brazilian *abertura*, three conceptions of democracy live side by side: a statist, a liberal and a grassroots conception of democracy. The statist version, proposed by the regime, is very limited: through cautious management, the state could allow the restitution of mediation between state and civil society, on its own terms. In practice this would feature acting for the public good to be located in the executive, guided by a multi-party parliament which can speak but not act, with limited press freedom and freedom of association. The functionalist or liberal version emphasizes liberal rights and representation in a broader capitalist setting. The third version, that of the 'grassroots democrats', comes very close to Havel's ideal: 'autonomous organization of the population around concrete demands – almost always within the reach of and with direct consequences for the well-being of deprived groups of people' (Cardoso, 1983: 311–314).

Dissident writings as political theory 51

The first version is quickly discarded by Cardoso as a feature of contemporary politics, but not really a democratic theory at all. In terms of 'the utopian-theoretical-ideological foundations of the idea of democracy in a mass society in a country with an associated-dependent economy', in other words in his vision for Brazil, he seeks to combine the second and the third version.

> There is an embryonic democratic thought which is not restricted to accepting the party-parliamentary game (although it remains a fundamental part, just as the defense of the dignity of the person and his or her rights remains fundamental to democratic collectivism) as a form of justifying the democratic worldview. Without greater transparency of information and of the decision-making in the firm (whether private or State) and in the bureaucracy, and without evolving mechanisms for participation and control both through parties and directly by the interested publics, the democratization process will be crippled.
>
> (Cardoso, 1983: 324)

This interaction of the state with a collectively expressed civil society supplementing individual citizenship is similarly prefigured by Jiri Dienstbier, who rejects Havel's hope for the 'withering away' of the state:

> If the state does not perform its function, self-organization becomes necessary. The realization of social interests through the strengths inherent in society weakens the totalizing demands of power, which is no longer the only motive force and must begin responding to the needs all the more, the more advanced the self-organization has become. This produces tension which the state power attempts to neutralize sometimes by force, sometimes by pretending the tension does not exist. But when this happens, society enters into a dialogue.

Both in Eastern Europe and South America, a vision appears to have been developed, based on the functioning of civil society under authoritarian rule, that combined the achievements of liberal democracy (civil and political rights; multi-party representation) with more radical forms of democracy based in civil society, which could regularly interact with the state-based democratic system.

Conclusion

In terms of discussions of the nature of the regimes under consideration here, distinctions between 'totalitarian' and 'authoritarian' appear to have relatively little purchase. Instead, there appears to be one area of division and two points of broad agreement between many of the sources.

The disagreement is on the motivations of those in power. Some attribute this to a naked will to power underneath a veneer of ideology, others attribute it to a passionate belief in a totalizing ideology, and one attributes it to the rule of

52   *M. Glasius*

ideology itself exercised through the disseminating of practices in seeing the emperor's clothes. The choice for one of these analyses over others appears to be as much in the eye of the beholder as in the nature of the regime. The contention here is then that contemporary authoritarian regimes are best 'read' by using these frames in complementarity rather than through classification into one of these types.

There is broad agreement that none of the regimes, not even that of General Pinochet, were mere 'strong-man' dictatorships. Under circumstances of modernity, authoritarian regimes require a bureaucracy, an ideology and a set of legal norms. Each of these elements may at different times have a stabilizing or a destabilizing effect on the regime. The hypothesis then is that, with the possible exception of parts of Africa or Central Asia, personalized dictatorships are no longer a relevant category. The terms 'bureaucratic authoritarianism' (from Cardoso) or 'post-totalitarianism' (from Havel) may be more helpful to capture the nature of contemporary regimes.

Second, there is broad agreement that the main thrust of these regimes, their final if never fully realized aspiration, is to 'atomize' society in order to rule for ever. No accounts were found that suggested, as Hannah Ahrendt (1951/1973) did, that society was to be permanently mobilized. The hypothesis here, and one well worth testing, would be that contemporary authoritarian regimes all aim for atomization.

In counterpoise to the aspiration to atomize, activists try to build 'civil societies' based on the values of solidarity, public truth-telling, ideological plurality and non-violence. Two hypotheses can be formulated here. The first is that a variety of activists in contemporary authoritarian settings continue to emphasize these same values. The second, and undoubtedly more problematic hypothesis, would be that those civil societies we observe in these settings which most clearly resemble these characteristics have the best chance of eventually evolving into sustainable democracies.

The 'independence' of the manifestations of civil society was, according to its protagonists, only relative. Yet they held that the 'relative independence' pursued by some strengthened the capacity for independence in the society as a whole. Hence, the hypothesis would be that the existence of even a small group of activists would have the effect of increasing the space of other citizens for at least 'independent thought' and perhaps 'independent activity'. Against that, and also on the basis of Havel's writing, the hypothesis could be formulated that the existence of a small group of dissidents, as a rather irrelevant 'protected species' can act as a safety valve for the regime while creating the impression that the rest of the population is not dissident.

The widespread appeal to 'the law' by activists, whether it be national law or international human rights standards, combined with the insight that bureaucratic authoritarianism requires ostensible adherence to legal norms, leads to the following hypothesis: Appeal to laws can be a productive strategy for civil society because it is a language to which the regime needs to respond.

The sources consulted demonstrated a vivid awareness of the world beyond their state, but did not request outside actions from either western governments

Dissident writings as political theory 53

or western publics. Perhaps the fact that 'the international' does not feature heavily in the strategic political considerations of East European or South American activists is less surprising than it may seem if we consider that one of the discoveries of this chapter so far has been that they rejected explicit strategic political considerations *tout court* in favour of the 'slow ripening' (Konrad, 1984) of broader social transformations. Nonetheless the outside world had a role to play, but it was constructed as a rather passive one, as an audience, a source of inspiration or at most a source of moral support. The hypothesis here might be that hubristic expectations of being able and perhaps obliged to 'help' should be replaced with a much more limited role of taking a positive interest in the predicament of civil society actors in authoritarian settings.

Probably the most interesting findings of this chapter have been those relating to the strategies and aspirations of East European and Latin American activists. Western audiences love the mythology of a brave, non-violent resistance prevailing over a brutal regime, whether it is the Madres of the Plaza del Mayo or the Velvet Revolution of Czechoslovakia. More recently, they have been prepared to fall in love all over again with the more doubtful 'colour revolutions' in Georgia, Ukraine and Lebanon. But they have not been attentive to the strategy of building up a 'democratic' civil society for its own sake as opposed to trying to initiate transition at the top, nor to the rich conception of democracy as encompassing workplace, neighbourhood or cultural circles practicing democracy alongside, and in dialogue with state-based institutions.

Both of these features may hold clues *less* for the causes of the initial transition to multi-party elections, which are over-determined by economic and international factors, but more for the *sustainability* of democracy long afterwards. Antonio Gramsci, likely to have been read by many of the people cited here, famously said that in the West: 'When the state trembled, a sturdy structure of civil society was at once revealed' (Gramsci, 1927–1937/1971: 238). What the East European and Latin American activists may have achieved is perhaps indeed the 'powerful system of fortresses and earthworks' that Gramsci called civil society, not as a system of bourgeois hegemony but as a system of internalized practices of democracy. The Argentine financial crisis for instance threw the political system into confusion, but it was weathered in civil society.

The final hypothesis then, is that the build-up of civil society for its own sake, predating democratization, combined with the vision of democratic practices entrenched in society supplementing representative democracy are preconditions for the later sustainability of a democratic society.

Notes

1 I will refer to the sources from these regions as 'East European' and 'South American' respectively, even though both of these regions obviously encompass more countries than the six under consideration here.
2 The term 'activists' is used here to cover the diversity of actors who opposed the authoritarian regimes under consideration, while 'dissidents' is reserved for a subgroup of high-profile intellectuals. Some, such as Vaclav Havel, explicitly distanced

54 *M. Glasius*

themselves from the term. But alternatives such as 'opposition figures' or 'human rights defenders' have similar drawbacks, and the nature of civil society is too much the subject of inquiry here to adopt this term for these actors.

3 Havel is referring of course to the brief, brutal and erratic rule of Idi Amin. Interestingly, the 'non-party democracy' of Yoweri Museveni that has been in power in Uganda since 1986 is much closer to the bureaucratic rule described in this chapter, and does show the ostensible regard for law described by Havel.

Bibliography

Arendt, Hannah (1951/1973). *The Origins of Totalitarianism*, New York: Harcourt.

Bates, J.M. (2000). 'The "Second Circulation 1976–1989 Poland"', in Derek Jones, ed. *Censorship: A World Encyclopedia*, London: Fitzroy Dearborn.

Benda, Vaclav (1988) in Vaclav Benda, Milian Simecka, Ivan M. Girous *et al*. 'Parallel Polis, or an Independent Society in Central and Eastern Europe: An Inquiry', *Social Research*, Vol. 55, Nos 1–2, 211–246.

Benda, Vaclav, Milian Simecka, Ivan M. Girous *et al*. (1988). 'Parallel Polis, or an Independent Society in Central and Eastern Europe: An Inquiry', *Social Research*, Vol. 55, Nos 1–2, 211–246.

Brandys, Kazimierz (1983). *A Warsaw Diary 1978–1981*, London: Chatto & Windus.

Cardoso, Fernando Henrique (1979). 'On the Characterization of Authoritarian Regimes in Latin America', in David Collier, ed. *The New Authoritarianism in Latin America*, Princeton: Princeton University Press, 33–57.

Cardoso, Fernando Henrique (1983). 'Associated-Dependent Development and Democratic Theory', in Alfred Stepan, ed. (1989) *Democratizing Brazil: Problems of Transition and Consolidation*, New York: Oxford University Press, 299–326.

Cerny, Vaclav (1985). 'On the Question of Chartism', in Vaclav Havel, Milian Simecka, Ivan M. Girous *et al.*, *The Power of the Powerless: Citizens Against the State in Central-eastern Europe*, Hutchinson: London, 125–133.

Chandhoke, Neera (2002). 'The Limits of Global Civil Society', in Marlies Glasius, Mary Kaldor and Helmut Anheier, eds. *Global Civil Society*, Oxford: Oxford University Press.

Charter 77 Declaration (1977). Available at http://libpro.cts.cuni.cz/charta/docs/declaration_of charter_77.pdf (accessed 18 May 2012).

Chuchryk, Patricia (1989). 'Feminist Anti-Authoritarian Politics: The Role of Women's Organizations and the Chilean Transition to Democracy', in Jane Jaquette, ed. *The Women's Movement in Latin America: Feminism and the Transition to Democracy*, Boston: Unwin Hyman.

Dahl, Robert A. (1982). *Dilemmas of Pluralist Democracy: Autonomy vs. Control*, New Haven: Yale University Press.

Dahrendorf, Ralf Gustav (1990). *Reflections on the Revolution in Europe: in a letter intended to have been sent to a gentleman in Warsaw*, London: Chatto & Windus.

Diago, Alejandro (1988), *Hebe Bonafini. Memoria y esperanza*, Buenos Aires: Ediciones Dialectica.

Dienstbier, Jiri (1988) in Vaclav Benda, Milian Simecka, Ivan M. Girous *et al.*, 'Parallel Polis, or an Independent Society in Central and Eastern Europe: An Inquiry', *Social Research*, Vol. 55, Nos 1–2, 211–246.

Dorfman, Ariel (1983). 'A Hopeful Parable of Doom', *Philadelphia Inquirer*, 13 March, reproduced in Ariel Dorfman (2004), *Other Septembers, Many Americas: Selected Provocations 1980–2004*, New York: Seven Stories Press, 146–150.

Dissident writings as political theory 55

Dorfman, Ariel (1985a). 'A Rural Chilean Legend Comes True', *New York Times*, 18 February, reproduced in Susan Meiselas, ed. (1990), *Chile from Within*, New York, W.W. Norton Company, 105.

Dorfman, Ariel (1985b). 'In Chile, A Show of Hands', *New York Times*, 23 November, reproduced in Susan Meiselas, ed. (1990), *Chile from Within*, New York, W.W. Norton Company, 108–109.

Dorfman, Ariel (1986). 'Pinochet Has Reaped What He Has Sown', *New York Times*, 8 September, reproduced in Susan Meiselas, ed. (1990), *Chile from Within*, New York, W.W. Norton Company, 110–111.

Dorfman, Ariel (1987). 'Exile's Return', *Village Voice*, 6 October, reproduced in Susan Meiselas, ed. (1990), *Chile from Within*, New York, W.W. Norton Company, 112–114.

Dorfman, Ariel (1988). 'Reports from the Heart of the NO', *Village Voice*, 4 October, reproduced in Susan Meiselas, ed. (1990), *Chile from Within*, New York, W.W. Norton Company, 116.

Dorfman, Ariel (1989). 'Epilogue: October 1989', reproduced in Susan Meiselas, ed. (1990), *Chile from Within*, New York, W.W. Norton Company, 121.

Dorfman, Ariel (2003). 'Martin Luther King: A Latin American Perspective', *Irish Times*, 20 August, reproduced in Ariel Dorfman (2004), *Other Septembers, Many Americas; Selected Provocations 1980–2004*, 101–106.

Ekiert, Grzegorz (1996). *The State Against Society: Political Crises and their Aftermath in East Central Europe*, Princeton: Princeton University Press.

Garreton, Manuel Antonio (1987/1989). 'Popular Mobilization and the Military Regime in Chile: The Complexities of the Invisible Transition', in Susan Eckstein, ed. *Power and Popular Protext: Latin American Social Movements*, Berkeley: University of California Press.

Gorini, Ulises (2006). *La rebelión de las Madres. Historia de las Madres de Plaza de ayo. Tomo I (1976–1983)*, Buenos Aires [etc.]: Norma.

Gramsci, Antonio (1927–1937/1971). *Selections from the Prison Notebooks*, ed and transl. by Quintin Hoare and Geoffrey Nowell Smith, London: Lawrence and Wishart.

Havel, Vaclav (1979/1985). 'The Power of the Powerless', in Vaclav Havel, Milian Simecka, Ivan M. Girous *et al.*, *The Power of the Powerless: Citizens Against the State in Central-eastern Europe*, Hutchinson: London, 23–96.

Keane, John (2005). 'Eleven Theses on Markets and Civil Society', *Journal of Civil Society*, Vol. 1, No. 1, 25–34.

Keck, Margaret E. (1992). *The Workers' Party and Democratization in Brazil*, New Haven: Yale University Press.

Konrad, George (1984). *Antipolitics*, London: Quartet Books.

Kubik, Jan (1994). *The Power of Symbols Against the Symbols of Power: The Rise of Solidarity and the Fall of State Socialism in Poland*, University Park: Penn State University Press.

Lijphart, Arend (1977). *Democracy in Plural Societies: A Comparative Exploration*, New Haven: Yale University Press.

Madres de Plaza de Mayo (1979). 'Declaración de Principios', 22 August. Available at: www.madresfundadoras.org.ar/pagina/declaracindeprincipiosao1979/24 (accessed 18 May 2012).

Madres de Plaza de Mayo Línea Fundadora (2006). *Memoria, verdad y justicia, a los 30 años X los treinta mil: voces de la memoria*, Buenos Aires: Baobab.

Michnik, Adam (1976/1985). 'A New Evolutionism' in Adam Michnik, *Letters from Prison and Other Essays*, Berkeley: University of California Press.

56   *M. Glasius*

Parra, Manuel Antonio de la (1990). 'Fragments of a Self-Portrait', in Susan Meiselas, ed. *Chile from Within*, New York, W.W. Norton Company, 13–15.

Serra, Jose (1979). 'Three Mistaken Theses Rgarding the Connection Between Industrialization and Authoritarian Regimes', in David Collier, ed. *The New Authoritarianism in Latin America*, Princeton: Princeton University Press, 99–163.

Simecka, Milan (1988) in Vaclav Benda, Milian Simecka, Ivan M. Girous *et al.*, 'Parallel Polis, or an Independent Society in Central and Eastern Europe: An Inquiry', *Social Research*, Vol. 55, Nos 1–2, 211–246.

Staniszkis, Jadwiga (1984). *Poland's Self-Limiting Revolution*, Princeton: Princeton University Press.

Stepan, Alfred, ed. (1989). *Democratizing Brazil: Problems of Transition and Consolidation*, New York: Oxford University Press.

Timerman, Jacobo (1981). *Prisoner Without a Name: Cell Without a Number*, New York: Alfred A. Knopf.

Vargha, János (1985). 'Acceptance Speech', Right Livelihood Awards, 9 December, available at www.rightlivelihood.org/vargha_speech.html (accessed 18 May 2012).

Vasxheiyi, Judit (1985). 'Acceptance Speech', Right Livelihood Awards, 9 December, available at www.rightlivelihood.org/vargha_speech.html (accessed 18 May 2012).

Weffort, Francisco (1983/1989). 'Why Democracy?' in Alfred Stepan, ed. (1989) *Democratizing Brazil: Problems of Transition and Consolidation*, New York: Oxford University Press, 327–350.

4 Civil society activism and authoritarian rule in Romania and Chile

Evidence for the role played by art(ists)

Caterina Preda

Introduction

Artists are not the "usual suspects" one looks to when discussing civil society under authoritarian regimes. Drawing on Negash (2004), the chapter postulates that artists play an important role in these societies and the aim of this study is to present evidence of their role and their creations in two different contexts. The argument is that through an examination of the relationship between art and politics in Romania and Chile during the dictatorships of Ceauşescu (1965–1989) and Pinochet (1973–1990), we can better understand not only the internal mechanisms of dictatorial power but also engage in the analysis of a new locus where to study civil society in authoritarian settings.

Transition to democracy was very different in the two cases discussed here. In the Romanian case "the events of December 1989" provoked the departure of the communist leader Nicolae Ceauşescu followed by his arrest and rapid execution. In May 1990 a democratic government was elected and the period between these two moments can be considered the transition to democracy of Romania. What followed can be understood as democratic consolidation. Conversely, in Chile, in October 1988 the Pinochet regime organized a referendum asking the citizens if they wished to grant the general a presidential mandate until 1997. The "No" won and the Pinochet regime imposed its terms in the negotiated transition to democracy that ensued. The democratic regime was inaugurated by the investiture of Aylwin as president in March 1990 following the elections of December 1989. However, in order to understand the role played by art and artists in the transition, the period under examination is the one before the breakdown of the dictatorial regime. This relation, between the artist and power, between the state and artists, merits to be evoked so as to shed light on a new space for political learning in non-democratic regimes.

The approach taken for discussing these issues is that of a subfield of political science, that of "**art and politics**" that has developed since the 1980s. In the North American case, attention was drawn to artistic practices in democracies as

58   *C. Preda*

a new space for political theory enrichment. This line is primarily related to the literary field ("the narrative turn" followed by the studies of Alasdair MacIntyre, Richard Rorty and Charles Taylor) only to recently include also visual arts practices. In Europe the subfield has developed also with the aid of the Polarts group within the European Consortium for Political Research (ECPR) since 1995. This chapter analyzes cases "outside Western culture."

Generally speaking, there are a set of **roles performed by art** that will be discussed and that can be useful in the perspective of dictatorial regimes and their demise. As such, art offers alternatives by the mere fact that it shows that other worlds and points of view are possible (Whitebrook, 1992: 7). Moreover, by its autonomous stance, art provides a fictional space where to share views so as to transcend the oppressive surrounding reality. It can also criticize and act as the voice of those without a voice. Art criticizes the regime whether directly or in an allusive manner. The use of allusions and symbols for instance helps create a sense of community with the public, sharing a coded language. This in turn revives the sense of community lost by the discretionary rules imposed by authoritarian regimes. Furthermore, art functions also as a refuge or even a new political space. 'Art instead of politics' is then a characteristic common to authoritarian regimes: art assumes the function of the political and acts as a "substitute for politics" or as a "substitutive public opinion" (Dragomir 2007: 213; Richard 1986: 107); it can also function as a distraction, an escape from the repressive environment. Furthermore, art accomplishes of course – and especially in the Romanian case – an instrumental role bestowed on it by the communist regime: the "artistic reflection of political principles."

The chapter presents thus the roles art played under these two dictatorships: on one side as an instrument of political power and on the other side art as a critique or a replacer of the forbidden political.

Art as an instrument of the political: the regimes' outlook

The Chilean and Romanian regimes were at the antipodes both in what regards the ideological frame in which they developed as well as their behavior toward the artistic field (state versus market models). These are two dissimilar regimes that adopt differing strategies. However, the effects they produce on the artistic sphere are similar: unavoidably, art is created in relation to the political. The Chilean and the Romanian shared similarities insofar as they designed authoritarian political projects, but the strategies they imposed on social and political actors differed.

Political centralization of power meant that Ceaușescu was the sole decision-maker as opposed to Pinochet who acted as the "integrator" of various currents and tendencies inside the regime. This is also true for artistic policies: increasingly Ceaușescu became the emitter of policies and delineated the program to be followed by the art community. Moreover, he considered art as a political instrument and used it as a legitimacy tool (for gaining the artists' support) and as an ideological instrument to enforce his intensely nationalistic political project (his

Civil society activism and the role of art 59

"theses"). This preeminence of Ceaușescu's personal ideas on both state and party programs is largely acknowledged and Trond Gilberg has even advanced a specific term to designate Ceaușescu's political approach: Ceaușescuism. That is at the ideological level "a hybrid of nationalism, chauvinism, Marxism-Leninism, and idiosyncratic elements of Nicolae Ceaușescu's own thought."[1] Ceaușescu's approach to the artistic sphere allowed the imposition of his nationalist artistic policy, openly manifest since 1971 ("July Theses"), reiterated in 1983 ("Mangalia Theses") and maintained until 1989. The 1971 July Theses (Ceaușescu 1971) sketched out in a 17-point program the lines that were to be followed by party activists for the purpose of "ameliorating the political-ideological and cultural-educational" level of all citizens. In so doing, artists were assigned specific tasks: "through different forms and varied styles of expression, art must serve the people, the fatherland, the socialist society" (Ceaușescu 1971). The mandatory political *orientation* of all artistic and media products was also announced as well as the support of national products, especially historical films and patriotic poetry and the endorsement of two mass cultural festivals: *Cântarea României* (Romanian Song) and *Cenaclul Flacăra* (The Flame Cenacle).

In the Chilean case there was also political centralization, but of a different type when it came to the arts. The regime *centralizes so as to delegate* certain tasks to specific agents. The absence of an ideological, political project of the military at the moment of the *coup d'état* led to different right-wing groups supporting this intervention. Accordingly, the approach of the Pinochet regime was not a cohesive, clearly articulated and linear one, but a *composite and dynamic* approach subject to different centers of influence. The approach of the regime is articulated in the nationalistic-authoritarian axis, which is traditionalist and Catholic, and the neo-liberal one, which imposes the market model. Two paradoxical directions resulted from this: elitist manifestations (opera and ballet, classical music and theater) and mass-culture, especially in the audiovisual sector but also books. The Chilean model was largely based on private initiative and private patronage, but also on a direct and active state support undertaken specifically by the "Departamento de Extensión Cultural" of the Ministry of Education starting in 1977.

Positive and negative mechanisms: institutions, policies and repressive tools

Similarly to the array of policies that can be applied in a democratic regime, policies in a dictatorship can be found to vary between these two poles represented by Chile and Romania. They match, for dictatorial regimes, the paradigmatic models of democratic institutionalism: the French state dominated model and the United States market articulated model.

Concerning the roles the state plays in the articulation of cultural policies, there can be several. The state regulates (laws and regulations[2]), administrates and promotes public institutions (from theaters to museums), safeguards the

60   C. Preda

national patrimony and encourages artistic creations. Totalitarian regimes in their role of engineers of cultural policies extend to the maximum the role the state has in cultural affairs by monopolizing artistic means of production and constructing an all-encompassing apparatus. The Ceauşescu model was one in which the power held by the state over art was complete. Official art, following the principles announced by party programs, was increasingly encomiastic art portraying the dictator. Institutional centralization was joined by a diffusion of tasks between multiple overlapping state structures, and carried out repression (of artists) and censorship, thereby ensuring the superiority of the regime's vision. At the opposite end, the Pinochet model imposed the supremacy of the market; no official art was created but certain art was officialized. Moreover, at the institutional level there was a process of de-institutionalization or a dismantlement of previous institutions although intentions to centralize and to create a unique center of power over culture existed. In this context repression and censorship, less refined than in the case of the Ceauşescu regime, were also activated. A paradox is found in the Chilean case in the sense that the regime decentralizes and privatizes but in fact all is politically controlled and sanctioned and thus all messages become politicized.

Dictatorial regimes use not only positive mechanisms such as the enforcement of specific policies and the creation of comprehensive institutions, but they also recur to negative mechanisms that encompass an entire range of repressive measures. Upon the establishment of dictatorial regimes, repression meant primarily exclusion – negation of what was there before. Artists and intellectuals were eliminated physically and institutionally through persecution. This series of eliminations aimed at individuals was accompanied by the imposition of censorship of their works which differed accordingly to each artistic expression. In Chile, while only literary and cinematographic censorship were codified, political control was carried out through strong disincentives such as imposition of high taxes – around 20 percent for books, theater shows and cinema. Several other measures aimed at establishing well-disciplined societies molded the outlook of the two regimes. Romania, especially in the 1980s, appeared as a world in which one only had to survive/get by. In this context one can observe the creation of alternative private spaces in which people would exchange information, music, books (the Shogun phenomena), would reunite to watch video films – this also explains the nostalgia of nowadays for the good old times when culture was reuniting people. The quasi permanent maintenance of the nocturnal curfew during the 17 years of the Pinochet regime also affected the way in which lives were privatized and thus controlled by the regime in Chile.

Thus, these were two inward-looking countries (Neustadt, 2001: 23; Tismăneanu, 2003: 216) and which **demobilized, depoliticized and privatized their societies**. These atomized societies were also the result of economic policies: the imposition of the market ideology by the Pinochet regime openly declared this objective of controlling, while the way the Ceauşescu regime, in the 1980s, maintained the population in a constant search for basic survival products can be considered as a method to keep control upon society. The

Civil society activism and the role of art 61

closure of the public space is seen in the two cases, as only the official vision of reality is tolerated. The difference between the two is that the political and societal project of the Pinochet regime does not allow in theory any opposition to its vision or any alternative voice, but in practice it tolerates it so far as it is not contagious and thus controllable (marginal and marginalized art). We could even argue for an absence of a public space, discernable in the privatization of life and its articulation around private homes; in Romania the population was focused on physical survival especially in the 1980s so no interest whatsoever was given to a public space, while in Chile, people were confined to their homes by the curfew. The *omnipresent terror* is a further characteristic of the way these two regimes control their societies. Fear, suspicion, terror, the maintenance of a "war state" in Chile and the permanent threat are seen in both cases. As Moulian (1998: 187–193) wrote, "terror needs that its presence be remembered. Repression is punctual, terror must be permanent, [it] is omnipowerful because it has no brakes, so much that it acts through the double way of action and presence, of its simple enunciation."

It is in this context that mass culture (the theory of kitsch of Clement Greenberg) infiltrates the two societies in opposing forms: television entertainment culture in Chile and "popular amateur culture" in Romania. Culture *becomes* a refuge, a way to escape reality.

Art as a reflection of the political

Art as a reflection means the mirroring of official artistic principles. The two conceptions of art by the two regimes are ideologically driven: art must reflect politics (politicized art) and art must only pursue artistic purposes (apolitical art). These standpoints are translated in an encouragement of artistic expressions that portray them and a dissuasion of artistic practices that infringe on them.

If the theoretical basis for a "politics of the art" ("within liberal culture") as they are laid down by Whitebrook – through an inquiry into literary practices as a site for political understanding – depart from the statement that art does not merely reflect politics but "expresses, reflects and challenges that culture" and acts as a "prism" sending back a distorted image (Whitebrook, 1992: 7–17), this exact supposition is established by modern dictatorships: art *must* reflect politics. For that purpose, the Ceauşescu regime requires a politicized art and the Pinochet regime an apolitical one.

In a nutshell the principles announced and imposed by Ceauşescu were: (1) the glorification of the past (historical figures and cultural heritage); (2) the valorization of the natural talent of the Romanian people (leading to the promotion of amateur/popular culture); (3) the exaltation of the nation and thus of its leader (patriotic poetry, songs, films); (4) the necessary inspiration from the socialist reality. The translation of the ideological principles into an artistic form was then discernible in the Romanian case and was materialized using all creative formats, from visual arts to literature and from film to music. Thus, *art had to portray the dictator* (homage art). Cioroianu (2006: 251) has called this phenomenon the

62   C. Preda

"videology" of Ceauşescu; that is, the "ideology that tends gradually but unavoidably to resume to the exhibition of the same effigies, to the display of an only portrait." This "obsession of the self-portrait" (Cioroianu, 2006: 251) led to the repetition of the same idealized image of the leader. The official iconography has then Ceauşescu at its fore and it has to dominate all public spaces. Besides the obligation of art to portray the leader, *art had also to portray the socialist reality*. One of the privileged means in this sense was cinema. Moreover, the glorification of the past as an instrument in the construction of the socialist reality was also largely seen in the cinematographic productions that increasingly privileged historical dramas portraying the grand leaders of the past and, by association, shining their light on the "Greatest leader"). The educational function of cinema is its primary task according to the Party theses. Furthermore, from an art *for* the masses (socialist realism) art became the privileged product of creation *by* the masses. This was best seen in two mass festivals promoted by the communist regime: Cântarea României (1976–1989) and its precursor Cenaclul Flacăra (1973–1985) which was in fact integrated in the first. The consecration of the privilege accorded by the Ceauşescu regime to amateur cultural expressions was accomplished by the Festival Cântarea României, which was

> a form of cultural enrolment to which theoretically the entire population had to participate and which, in fact, supported primarily, through important official means, amateur art, considered as the true art "of the people" in the detriment of professional, learned art.
>
> (Cârneci, 2000: 133)

When it comes to Chile, there are different tendencies that structure the official approach of the regime and thus there are several artistic expressions that can be catalogued as "mirroring the official precepts." What is common to them all is the affirmation of *apoliticism in artistic endeavors*: art must only look for developing its specific language and must not be tainted by political conceptions. The two poles of action of the Pinochet regime were the "high art" circuit (classical music and theater, academic painting, bourgeois folklore) and the "mass culture" circuit (music, cinema and theater but most importantly television).

Classical music, academic painting, ballet and opera along with classical theater are perhaps the best illustrations of the concept of "high art," anti-foreign, elitist, conservative and traditionalist, addressing a highly educated public. These art forms were promoted especially by private entities such as cultural associations, but also by a state department, the Department of Cultural Extension of the Ministry of Education. For example, aside the forms of music officially promoted, other musical currents were also recuperated by the regime. As Torres (1993: 203) writes, "in the circuit of mass culture, the regime granted special importance to the television, transforming the National Channel in the box of resonance of its cultural policy." This official channel of transmission privileged "the most commercial popular music, especially the romantic ballad and the 'rock-mantic ballad'" (Torres, 1993: 203).

Civil society activism and the role of art 63

Furthermore, the regime encouraged the generalization of television by direct economic stimulus (customs' tariffs were lowered for the imports of TV sets) and discouraged reading by directly punishing the book industry through higher taxes (Brunner, 1982). While a TV set was always ready to broadcast light programs, buying a book became a luxury if not an impossible task. Chilean television was administered by universities and, following direct military intervention, by the state. The military regime transformed it in fact in its privileged medium.

For Brunner the use of television as a privileged medium by the Pinochet regime resides in the "degradation of collective consciousness, destined to maintain the masses in a subordinate level ideologically and a lack of cultural perspectives" (Brunner, 1981: 95). The infusion of "motives and topics pseudo-sentimental, police or fictional" imposed a new type of massive socialization (Brunner, 1981: 94) as there was a television set in 95 percent of Chilean houses by 1983 (Brunner and Catalán, 1987: 19). "The permanent party on the screen is the consolation for an anemic nocturnal life" because if "streets were sad, screens were over-cheerful and wore spangles" (Contardo and García, 2005: 12–15). The reality officially promoted was mandatorily happy and celebrating, obscuring the sadness and truthfulness of repression.

Art against the political

There are **different roles assumed** by art as well as **diverse (artistic) strategies** artists employ in a dictatorial regime. Artistic *strategies* range from the support of the official version of reality briefly outlined above to the alternative discourses presented in what follows. *Art as a* critical *reflection* evokes those approaches that seek to convey an alternative discourse by the detour, twist of the phrase, image or sound. This includes the direct opposition/confrontation ("resistance"), as well as the subversion of the official channels through self-publishing/samizdat, and underground culture. Mockery is also part of this array of strategies as is the complete dismissal of the political (get past it,[3] act as if it was not there) translating into aestheticism or art for art's sake. As to the *roles* art performs, especially in a dictatorship, these are also varied. Negash (2004: 191–192) puts it: "without a doubt artists and intellectuals have always been in an advantageous and privileged position to chronicle events, preserve the collective memory, perform the role of teacher and seer, and become social critics."

But the artist cannot be considered a pure mirror of what surrounds him/her, but rather as a "prism" (Sigelman, 1992: 155); reality is registered and transformed through artistic imagination. Thus the artist is "a privileged witness" (Gleizal), an "*alter deus* who creates new worlds" (Esquível, 2008: 109) and provides a "virtual experience" (Kassiola, 1992: 53) to the public. *Art as a critical reflection* states that art, by its intrinsic autonomy, can also accomplish a critique of its environment. For example, in Romania people expected both to find answers and a critique, allusions in a work of art, to find the fine connection to the surrounding reality, but not as an optimistic officially portrayed reality rather as a way to *escape* – through the means of the evocation of another space

64   *C. Preda*

opposed to the "officialized reality." Art in dictatorships is then a means to *deconstruct the officially constructed reality*. This is perhaps the perceived "danger" the dictatorships detect as, "art visibly constructs realities and so demonstrates how easily that can be done" (Edelman, 1995: 68).[4]

Furthermore, art is also found to replace the missing political arena and recreate a space of sociability through "imagined worlds." Art establishes then a sense of community with the public in an alternative space where the political power cannot intervene – imagination. By the use of allegory, metaphor and a coded language, complicity with the public is created. Art can also be a *refuge*, a means of survival, because it recreates a forbidden, lost past as well as projecting a missing future.

Art as a critical *reflection*

Art can be critical of the dictatorship both in a direct manner, through its message, and indirectly through its form or its disguised message. On one hand, the artist confronts the political power and decries repression and oppression and states it directly, in an easy to grasp language and format. On the other, the artist tackles the political by a disguised critique using symbols and an encrypted idiom based on his/her dialogue with a limited public. Decrypting these artistic discourses could help us better understand the way in which modern dictatorships were constructed and some still are. Discerning the different tonalities artistic imaginaries adopt so as to *re*act to oppression and repression could complete our understanding of dictatorial regimes. The sense of artistic resistance to the oppressing dictatorial environment is best expressed by the Chilean novelist Diamela Eltit:

> The really hard thing was living under dictatorship ... but writing and thinking in the midst of that situation was a form of self-rescue.... Learning to coexist with powerlessness; putting up with a state of daily humiliations ... in a territory where history mingled with hysteria, crime coupled with sales. ... When my freedom was threatened, then I took the liberty of writing freely.... Writing in that space was something passional and personal. My secret political resistance. When one lives in a world that is collapsing, constructing a book perhaps may be one of the few survival tactics.
>
> (Eltit, 1997: 4–5)

Direct artistic confrontation of the dictatorial regime is a characteristic of the left/militant/activist art in Chile – and especially the art of the exile. It is found to gain a form in such different expressions as music in *peñas* (folk clubs) or inside Church spaces and shantytowns (*poblaciónes*) or the continuation by the Brigada Muralista Ramona Parra of the painting of murals displaying images of social critique. The series of works encompassed in this varied panorama are confrontational as they oppose to the dictatorship a distorted mirror that seeks to decry and scream the injustice, the horror and repression, while also attempting

Civil society activism and the role of art   65

to "preserve a cultural patrimony denied by the public sphere" (Rivera, 1983: 115), but still safeguarding an unchanged repertory of references and representations.

In some quarters, representation itself was criticized by several other visual artists that resorted to new supports and mediums – the body, the city, intermedial/experimental art – as an intrinsic critique of the "impossible representation." In fact, as several Chilean artists of the "Avanzada" argue, criticizing directly the regime was not possible and that is why they resorted to a different indirect critique. The "Escena de Avanzada" is a concept forged a posteriori by Nelly Richard in her seminal book of 1986 *Margins and Institutions* that delineates "one of the many dimensions" of "unofficial works produced under the military regime" (Richard, 1986: 17). It does not constitute a group or movement in itself but rather regroups "a spectrum of artistic and political strategies" (Neustadt, 2001: 21) common to visual arts and literature. Inside the *Escena de Avanzada*, CADA (Actions for Art Collective) represented a new-vanguard movement sustaining "the militancy of an art socially committed" and the integrating concept of *"intervention in everyday life* by means of 'art actions'" (Richard, 2000a: 48; Richard, 1986, 107). CADA was an artistic group formed in 1979 by two visual artists, Juan Castillo and Lotty Rosenfeld, a sociologist, Fernando Balcello, the writer Diamela Eltit and the poet Raúl Zurita (Neustadt, 2001: 13). The most important action of CADA was "No+" (1983–1984).[5] This action, whose name translates as "No more," saw CADA artists accompanied by many others going out at night and writing this sign on the walls of Santiago. Soon after, the sign was completed by other anonyms with an image or a word "No+ dictatorship, No+ torture, No+ guns, No+ disappeared, No+ death, No+ and the image of a revolver" (Neustadt, 2001: 36). There is a degree of truth in Robert Neustadt's statement that this action is one that best asserts the principle of the group, of missing an author, while putting forward the idea of anonymity. Thus "the work was led to pertain to the entire community as an anti-dictatorial slogan" and, a few years later, "all the manifestations against the dictatorship were led by the 'No+' watchword" (Neustadt, 2001: 37).

Exposing violence (repression and oppression)

Artists also deployed a rhetoric of the violence imposed on them through their works but using mostly a symbolic and metaphorical repertory. Artistically evoking **fear** can be seen in a work by the Chilean artist Juan Downey, entitled "Map of Chile" (1975) and which functioned as a "metaphor of fear and of the constant menace in which … Chileans lived" (Mellado, 2000: 28). Suggesting the **wound** is Catalina Parra's "Imbunches" (1977). "Imbunche refers to the Araucanian Indian practice of sewing a baby's orifices shut, either to prevent the escape of evil from the body or to ward it off" (Barnitz, 2001: 289). Parra "sews so as to enclose and oppress and feverishly sews also so as to suture, close the edges of a wound' (Valdés, 1990: 34) and it's even more evoking "when a map of Chile is made up of fragments of kodalith hand sewed as if the representation

66   C. Preda

of the country wasn't but the exhibition of some sutures that validate themselves" (Mellado, 2000: 20). **Death** is **quoted** in CADA's last action: "Viuda" of 1985 which consisted in the publication in important periodicals (the magazines *Apsi* and *Cauce* and the newspaper *La Epoca*) of the photo of a grieving woman with the tag "VIUDA" (Neustadt, 2001: 37). As Eltit explains: "We wanted to invert the funerary parameters that had been in art works (faces of dead, of disappeared) by bringing the face of a woman alive. Quote the death, but through life."

Immobile silence: body expressions of exasperation

The disciplined bodies of dictatorship are used as a tool by the artists that wish to suggest pain and grief, exasperation and their incapacities as communities. The forbidden body considered as taboo by the dictatorships is invoked. Because "representation is insufficient" (Valdés, 1990: 35) the **body** becomes **a canvas for pain** as a manner to make violence present. Violence is realized by the artwork which presents it as such, "the artwork as victim." "One no longer speaks about it, but does it." The works of Carlos Leppe such as *Reconstitución de escena* (Scene of the crime), *Cuerpo correccional* and *Sala de espera* don't show violence but do it. In Leppe's works violence is not alluded to but realized (Valdés, 1990: 34).

Romanian artists also resort to self-infliction of pain, using one's body to transmit the surrounding hurt.

> The mutilating effect of the surrounding framework which became hyperpoliticized reflects on the state of spirit of artists that **self-mutilate**, marking on their body the psychic trauma produced by society (Lászlo Újvárossy – Autoportret înainte de defilare, 1983) or on the body of a model staging a possible situation for the epoch, as incarceration or hospitalization in psychiatric hospitals (Baász Imre – Mi se întâmplă un necaz, 1985).
>
> (Pintilie, 2000: 83–84)

"Autoportret înainte de defilare" (Self-portrait before the parade) by Lászlo Újvárossy, an artist member of the "Oradea group" evokes the "state of degradation to which man arrived in the years of communism" by gradually cutting "his hair as a recruit [and] photographing gradually until the phase of boldness underlining [thus] the condition of [being] 'enrolled' in a determined way" (Pintilie, 2000: 70).

The **incapacity to speak** or communicate as well as the deluge of repetitive speech is evoked by the works of Ion Grigorescu and Rudolf Bone. In "Exercițiu de vorbire/Gura mea" (Speaking exercise/My mouth) of 1978 Grigorescu "speaks uninterruptedly and analyzes the action of talking" (Pintilie, 2000: 46). Rudolf Bone's "Autoportret castană" (Self-portrait chestnut) of 1983 transmits this impossibility to communicate. He seems to want to transmit an important message through his concentrated look, but he is incapable of doing it as he has

Civil society activism and the role of art 67

sticks in his moustache and beard (Pintilie, 2000: 69). The **inability to act**, being trapped, enclosed or encircled are seen in many artworks of Romanian artists, especially in the actions of Geta Brătescu and Lia Perjovschi. Geta Brătescu, one of the most important actionist artists of the 1960s and 1970s together with Ion Grigorescu, annuls her body and makes it merge with the environment in two entwined action: "Către alb" (Toward white, 1971) and "Autoportret către alb" (Self portrait toward white, 1975). In the first action, she erases the space of her studio which she covers with white paper and then covers herself with white paper and paints her face and hands as well in white thus annulling herself (Pintilie, 2000: 50).

The **permanent surveillance and the transparent walls** (the control disempowering action) are bluntly quoted in "La închisoare" (In prison, 1978) by Ion Grigorescu. The artist uses a spy-hole with an inward sight as a "surveying eye" and evokes "the docility of the body which, even in its intimate rituals, seems to obey the invisible commands of power [as a rather straightforward] metaphor of daily life during dictatorship" "inside the blocks of apartments, true prisons in freedom" (Pintilie, 2000: 44). **Exasperation** is also discernible in Romanian artists' works, especially in the 1980s. "Exasperation toward political intrusion in the intimate space of the house and private life realized with television" is seen in the work of Constantin Flondor, Anniversary – 26 January[6] "laconically transmitting the state of spirit in front of the unending festive program in flagrant contrast with the poverty of the public" (Pintilie, 2000: 84).

An aesthetics of poverty and marginality can be seen in the works of artists in the two dictatorships. The **penury** of Romanian society could be directly read at the level of the poor quality materials accessible to artists especially in the 1980s. Thus, "the lack of high quality photographic materials on the Romanian market leads to the use of small prints with a bad definition that inherently make the technique look 'modest'" (Balaci, 2003). In Chile, an appropriation of the marginal, the excluded *par excellence* is imagined and re-imagined and used so as to transmit a different image to that of the militant culture (leftist imaginary) especially by those artists included by Richard in the *Escena de Avanzada*. "The margin served as a concept-metaphor so as to render productive the social discard of marginalization and marginality" (Richard, 2000: 67).

The missing public (private art) and the forbidden street as a scene. The closure of the public space in both countries leads *actionist* artists to display their work inside their homes or ateliers/studios (Galaz, Pintilie). Moreover, in the mid- 1980s, as Romanian visual artists were marginalized and could no longer enter the only available professional organization (UAP), they increasingly developed subversive and, at the same time, marginal artistic discourses encompassing body art, performance and post-happening practices (Cârneci, 2001; Pintilie, 2000: 14). Whereas in Chile, the aforementioned actions of CADA best exemplify the "reclaiming [of] the street as the 'true museum'," one of their aims being "to intervene the daily space of Santiago with unusual images so as to interrogate the conditions that had become customary in dictatorial Chile" (Richard, 2000: 43). Lotty Rosenfeld remains a paradigmatic example for

68   C. Preda

art that uses the city, and most specifically the street as a prop. Since 1979, Rosenfeld intervenes in the public space by transforming traffic signs into crosses (or plus signs) "as a way of altering the codes of urban movement" and somehow signaling that "the most inoffensive of signs" can be submitted to inversion (Richard, 1986: 60–61).

Allegories, metaphors, symbols – camouflaged literary practices. Literary practices are also seen to exemplify "the stratification of senses," the "excess of suggestions" and the over-stratified meanings that can also be discerned in the visual arts' discourses (Richard, 1989; Valdés, 1990). The ambiguity[7] (and duplicity) and the multiple, crisscrossed readings that they suggest make the public participate in an open work, becoming "accomplices" of the creation (Brito 1994; Richard, 1986; Runcan, 2003; Valdés, 1990). The open work of art makes the role of the public paramount. Identification is a key concept for these artistic practices. The reader, spectator needs to find him/herself, his/her world in the writings or images displayed in front of him.

Art as a refuge and as a replacer of politics

Confronted with living in the dictatorships, besides exile, Romanians as Chileans had as a solution "in-xile" (Rojo) that is to take refuge inside the country but in a self-designed reality populated by fictional characters found in literature, theater, films and music.

The "virtual experience" (Kassiola, 1992) artistic works provide us with is at the core of the aesthetic research.[8] Artistic autonomy understood as "**art for art's sake**" or **aestheticism,** the development of the artistic discourses for their own sake is another manner of understanding the role art played under the dictatorship (and meets the above mentioned role played by art as a refuge, this time for the artists themselves). By their demand for "internal freedom of creation" Romanian artists infringed the official code that explicitly forbade it and refused to fight it, choosing to ignore it and taking refuge instead in their personal aesthetic quests.

Also, **art instead of politics** can refer to the role of politics in these two societies in which getting together for political purposes was forbidden and in which artistic expressions came to play (though) partially a substitutive role. It must be remarked how the coded language artists and their public spoke formed in a way a new sort of getting together albeit only for the duration of reading/seeing/listening (to) the artistic work. The public played a paramount role in the assembly of the artwork as it participated to its interpretation and as only by this reception did this find its final form. Lucia Dragomir (2007: 187) writes even about "a new literature that grants to the reader the role of accomplice of the author in the deciphering of the text through 'the reading through the lines'" that characterized all the literary spaces in Eastern Europe and that characterizes all literatures written under dictatorships.

Then, at least in a first phase, in Chile, art served as a means of expression in a space where communication was forbidden by the authorities. "Art was

Civil society activism and the role of art 69

without a doubt the first visible expression that emerges from the groups that opposed the authoritarian order" because of two factors. "The artistic was in a first moment one of the few alternative discourses to the official one that could be emitted as the political discourse is excluded" and "the artistic one played from the beginning a major role in the re-establishment of a common language, of collective identities [through] folk music, theater and critical poetry"; "the artistic practice is transformed, for thousands of persons in a basic form of expression, of saying what they cannot express in other languages" (Rivera, 1983: 109–110, 114). Even more, as Carlos Ochsenius (1991: 179) shows, popular theater developing in shantytowns and all throughout Chile during the entire period of the dictatorship (but especially after 1983), indicates "the tendency to search for means of using any public place or event so that people there have the opportunity to become involved; to express themselves; to participate, communicate, act, and reflect." "Everything [in this type of artistic expression] is done with the intention that the **audience** participate actively" and thus, "from the political point of view, it helps create active citizens [and] from the cultural point of view it promotes a sense of belonging" (Ochsenius, 1991: 180). In sum, for Ochsenius, grassroots theater has as a message "the ritual of rediscovery (who are we), of reexamination (what are we doing), and of projection (what do we want)" (Ochsenius, 1991: 184).

Art as an alternative to politics encapsulates both "art for art's sake" – outside any reference to the role art should play in relation to society and the politics – and art as a replacing arena for the forbidden political one. Creating outside of political references is – at least in these cases – still an activity that refers, through their absence, to these references.

Conclusion

The main argument for the study of art under modern dictatorships is that this tells us how dictatorships function. It does this by first highlighting the limits of domination; the discourse on authority (against it, deconstructing it so as to understand how it functions in accordance with the theories on literature as another place to understand how the political functions) illustrates this in the best manner. It also realizes this through an evocation of *le vécu*, of personal experiences that achieved a universal sense by having passed through an artistic lens (prism of realities). Additionally, the creation of alternative artistic worlds helps people survive the "reality" and comforts them. The contours of the shared reality are thus manifest in artistic works; duplicity, ambiguity and marginality are all characteristics of the art produced during the dictatorships reflecting also the way societies perceived this experience.

At the moment of transition to democracy, in 1989 and in 1990 respectively, the artistic discourses that developed during the dictatorships were also important for several reasons. First, by the sense of community established with the public/readers, artists were in a privileged position early on and participated in the process of transition/and or the first stage of power-sharing. An example in

70   *C. Preda*

this sense is that of Romanian poets Mircea Dinescu and Ana Blandiana joining the ranks of the revolutionaries and helping legitimate the new power arrangements. In the Chilean case, artists collaborated with the political movement against the "yes" to the 1988 plebiscite by bringing their "expertise" (i.e., creating the video campaign under the slogan "La alegría ya viene"/Happiness is coming) that influenced the electorate and also helped turn the tables on the Pinochet regime. Second, and aside the symbolic capital and the direct participation of artists to the transition processes, one could argue also for the permanence of artists in the public space as continuators of the previous regimes. As such, artistic institutions in Romania are still (today) dominated by artists that were both used by the Ceaușescu regime and profited from this such as Verdery and Barbu. One example in this sense is the maintenance of professional union of artists Union of Visual Artists dominated by the same pre-1989 figures and the influence of the previous ideological stances visible for example in the case of the ICR scandals of 2008.[9] At the same time one could perceive the artistic discourses that developed after 1990 in Romania and Chile and that evoke themes of the "before" still unresolved and still questioning the recent past, as exemplified by Carlos Altamirano's *Retratos* in Chile or Dan Perjovschi's works in Romania.

Notes

1 Gilberg (1990: 56) defines Ceaușescuism as a style of operation and a set of parameters for acceptable behavior by subelites.

2 Garretón makes a distinction between two aspects of cultural institutionalism: the organizational (structures and apparatus of the state) and normative (laws and dispositions including budgetary allocations). See Garretón (1992: 67).

3 For example, the Romanian writer Ana Blandiana who was forbidden to publish, would read her writings in the scheduled meetings with readers and says that: "And there I would read everything" (Dragomir, 2007: 291).

4 Whitebrook (1992: 7) also observes how "Because art offers alternatives, it questions the status quo; simply by being apprehended at all, it allows the recognition that 'the existence of one subjectivity makes possible other subjectivities'."

5 CADA realized five art actions: "Para no morir de hambre en el arte" (1979); "Inversión de escena" (17 1979); "¡Ay Sudamérica!" (12 July 1981); "Residuos americanos" (18 March and 23 April 1983); "No+" (end of 1983–1984) and "Viuda" (1985) (Neustadt, 2001).

6 26 January was the birthday of Nicolae Ceaușescu and it was intensively celebrated.

7 "Hybridity, double-codedness, and ambiguity were ingredients of everyday life under the Ceaușescu regime, when experience was double-coded from the earliest age" (Oțoiu, 2003: 93).

8 The concept of "virtual experience" is borrowed by Kassiola from Susanne Langer (*Feeling and Form: a theory of art developed from philosophy in a new key*, 1953) that had introduced the idea of virtual experience in her discussion of the visual arts referring to what is depicted in a painting as a "virtual space." Kassiola uses it to highlight the enlargement of human experience as "the major contribution of literature to the quintessential normative political question of how we ought to act politically" (Kassiola, 1992: 54, 58).

9 The Romanian Institute of Culture is an institution attached to the Ministry of Foreign Affairs and which coordinates the activities of the institutes in foreign countries.

Civil society activism and the role of art 71

Bibliography

Balaci, R. (2003), "Photography – a Proposed Chronology of an Experimental Epoch". *I-can*. www.c3.hu/ican.artnet.org/ican/text1c91.html?id_text=20 (accessed on 16 May 2012).

Barbu, D. (2002), "The Burden of Politics. Public Space, Political Participation and State Socialism," *Studia Politica Romanian Political Science Review*, 2(2), pp. 329–346.

Barnitz, J. (2001), *Twentieth Century Art of Latin America*, Austin: University of Texas Press.

Brito, E. (1994), *Campos minados. Literatura post-golpe en Chile*, Santiago: Ed. Cuarto Propio.

Brunner, J. J. (1981), *La cultura autoritaria en Chile*, Santiago: FLACSO.

Brunner, J. J. (1982), *Vida cotidiana, sociedad y cultura: Chile 1973–82*, Documento de Trabajo Programa FLACSO-Santiago de Chile, 151, July.

Brunner, J. J. and Catalán, C. (1987), *Industria y Mercado Culturales en Chile: Descripción y cuantificación*, Documento de Trabajo, Programa FLACSO-Santiago de Chile, 359, November.

Cârneci, M. (2001), *Artele plastice în România 1945–1989*, Bucureşti: Editura Meridiane.

Ceauşescu, N. (1971), *Propuneri de măsuri pentru îmbunătăţirea activităţii politico-ideologice, de educare marxist-leninistă a membrilor de partid, a tuturor oamenilor muncii, 6 iulie 1971*, Bucureşti: Editura Politică.

Cioroianu, A. (2006), "'Videologia' lui Nicolae Ceauşescu. Conducătorul şi obsesia autoportretului," in *Comunism şi represiune în România*, ed. Ruxandra Cesereanu, pp. 251–265, Iaşi: Polirom.

Contardo, O. and García, M. (2005), *La era ochentera. Tevé, pop y under en el Chile de los ochenta*, Santiago: Ediciones B.

Dragomir, L. (2007), *L'Union des Ecrivains. Une institution transnationale à l'Est*, Paris: Belin.

Edelman, M. (1995), *From Art to Politics: How Artistic Creations Shape Political Conceptions*, Chicago and London: The University of Chicago Press.

Eltit, D. (1997), *E. Luminata*, Santa Fe: Lumen Inc. Translated by Ronald Christ.

Esquível, P. (2008), *L'autonomie de l'art en question. L'art en tant qu'Art*, Paris: L'Harmattan.

Garretón, M. A. (1992), "Estado y política cultural. Fundamentos de una nueva institucionalidad", in *Seminario sobre políticas culturales en Chile*, pp. 65–75, Santiago: División de Cultura Ministerio de Educación.

Gilberg, T. (1990), *Nationalism and Communism in Romania: The Rise and Fall of Nicolae Ceauşescu's Personal Dictatorship*, Boulder, San Francisco, Oxford: Westview.

Golomstock, I. (1990), *Totalitarian Art in the Soviet Union, the Third Reich, Fascist Italy and the People's Republic of China*, London: Collins Harvill.

Kassiola, J. (1992), "Political Values and Literature: The Contribution of Virtual Experience," in *Reading Political Stories. Representations of Politics in Novels and Pictures*, ed. Maureen Whitebrook, pp. 53–72, Boston: Rowman & Littlefield Publishers.

Mellado, J. P. (2000), "Historias de transferencias y densidad en el campo plastico chileno (1973–2000)," in *1973–2000 Transferencia y densidad. Octubre – diciembre 2000*, ed. Museo Nacional de Bellas Artes, pp. 8–23, Santiago: Museo Nacional de Bellas Artes.

Moulian, T. (1998), *Chile Actual. Anatomía de un mito*, Santiago de Chile: LOM-Arcis.

72   C. Preda

Negash, G. (2004), "Art Invoked: A Mode of Understanding and Shaping the Political," *International Political Science Review*, 25(2), pp. 185–201.

Neustadt, R. (2001), *CADA día: la creación de un arte social*, Santiago: Editorial Cuarto Propio.

Ochsenius, C. (1991), "Popular Theater and Popular Movements," in *Popular Culture in Chile: Resistance and Survival*, ed. Kenneth Aman and Cristián Parker, pp. 173–188, Boulder, San Francisco, Oxford: Westview Special Studies on Latin America and the Caribbean.

Oprea, M. (2006), "L'Héritage de la Securitate: Terreur en Roumanie 1952–2002," in *Le Jour se lève. L'héritage du totalitarisme en Europe 1953–2005*, ed. Stéphane Curtois, pp. 240–253, Paris: Editions du Rocher.

Oțoiu, A. (2003), "An Exercise in Fictional Liminality: The Postcolonial, the Postcommunist and Romania's Threshold Generation", *Comparative Studies of South Asia, Africa and the Middle East*, 23: 1 & 2, pp. 87–105.

Pintilie, I. (2000), *Acționismul în România în timpul comunismului*, Cluj: Idea Design & Print.

Pintilie, I. (2007), "The Public and the Private Body in Contemporary Romanian Art," *Art Margins* (June). www.artmargins.com.

Richard, N. (1986), "Margins and Institutions: Art in Chile since 1973," *Art & Text*, 21, Special Issue.

Richard, N. (1989), *La estratificación de los margenes. Sobre arte, cultura y politica*, Santiago: Francisco Zegers Editor.

Richard, N. (2000), *La insubordinación de los signos*, Santiago: Editorial Cuarto Propio.

Rivera, A. (1983), *Transformaciones culturales y movimiento artístico en el orden autoritario*, Santiago: CENECA.

Runcan, M. (2003), "Teatrul față cu cenzura. Motivații, mecanisme, strategii de atac și apărare," *Caietele Echinox*, 4, pp. 182–192.

Sigelman, L. (1992), "Taking Popular Fiction Seriously," in *Reading Political Stories. Representations of Politics in Novels and Pictures*, ed. Maureen Whitebrook, pp. 149–163, Boston: Rowman & Littlefield Publishers.

Tismăneanu, V. (2003), *Stalinism for All Seasons. A Political History of Romanian Communism*, Berkeley, Los Angeles and London: University of California Press.

Titu, A. (2003), *Experimentul în arta românească după 1960*, București: Ed. Meridiane.

Torres, R. (1993), "Música en el Chile autoritario (1973–1990): Crónica de una convivencia conflictiva," in *Cultura, autoritarismo y redemocratización en Chile*, ed. Manuel Antonio Garretón, Saúl Sosnowski and Bernardo Subercaseaux, pp. 197–220, Santiago: Fondo de Cultura Económica.

Valdés, A. (1990), "Una historia de miedo," in *Museo Abierto* (6–30 Sept. 1990), ed. Museo Nacional de Bellas Artes, pp. 32–35, Museo Nacional de Bellas Artes: Santiago.

Verdery, K. (1991), *National Ideology Under Socialism*, Berkeley, Los Angeles and London: University of California Press.

Whitebrook, M. (1992) (ed.), *Reading Political Stories. Representations of Politics in Novels and Pictures*, Boston: Rowman & Littlefield Publishers.

5 Contesting order in Tunisia
Crafting political identity

Laryssa Chomiak and John P. Entelis

> I really do inhabit a system in which words are capable of shaking the entire structure of government, where words can prove mightier than ten military divisions.
>
> Vaclav Havel (1989)

> The subconscious is ceaselessly murmuring, and it is by listening to these murmurs that one hears the truth.
>
> Gaston Bachelard (1884–1962)

> Ideas are refined and multiplied in the commerce of minds. In their splendor, images effect a very simple communion of souls.
>
> Gaston Bachelard (1884–1962)

Introduction

Since 1987 and until the 2011 uprising, the Republic of Tunisia under the leadership of Zine El Abidine Ben Ali dignified itself, primarily to an international audience, for ushering in democracy, expanding political and individual rights, encouraging the growth of civil society, and accelerating the country's already impressive economic development. With a population of just over ten million, the regime boasted more than eight thousand functioning civil society organizations as well as its hosting of the second phase of the World Summit on the Information Society (WSIS) in November 2005. While the holding of the Summit meeting in a dictatorial police state was met with criticism by local and international civil society actors, the Tunisian regime strategically used the event to solidify its international image as a liberal and progressive Arab state, a blatantly transparent effort to mask its authoritarian expansion.

This chapter will map the channels through which ordinary Tunisians expand spaces for expression and contestation under the constraints of authoritarian rule and the way in which such expansion might have fueled popular and widespread anti-regime sentiments that eventually found a collective and public voice. We argue that in expanding public space, Tunisians are developing

74   *L. Chomiak and J.P. Entelis*

alternative political identities alongside or in opposition to the dominant political narrative constructed by the regime. Contrary to the growing body of work on authoritarianism in the Middle East and North, we contend that public space in Tunisia is both contested and formed through competing visions of the social order, an order imposed by the state and challenged by citizens as well as among citizens themselves. Accordingly, the intensification of authoritarianism in Tunisia has not gone uncontested. In disciplines outside of political science, scholars have written of the ways in which state and non-state actors envision and contest public spaces, how their respective visions are at times irreconcilable and at other times complementary. Susan Slyomovics (2005) and Don Mitchell (1995), for instance, examine public performances by state and society and write of the ways in which public space is defined and contested by both actors. Slyomovics examines the "performance of human rights" in Morocco arguing that the Moroccan state successfully co-opted a public human rights discourse and subsequently engaged itself in "performing human rights" through the establishment of reconciliatory institutions. Mitchell, on the other hand, writes of the irreconcilable visions of the nature of public space by activists and city authorities in Berkeley, California. He shows how official authorities view public space as "a controlled and orderly *retreat* where a properly behaved public might experience the spectacle of the city" (1995: 115, original emphasis). Non-state actors, on the other hand, understand public space as "marked by free interaction and the absence of coercion by powerful institutions ... an unconstrained space within which political movements can organize" (1995: 115).[1]

By examining competing visions of the public order through the lens of space, this chapter offers a critique[2] to the now well-established neo-Tocquevillian civil society literature inspired by Robert Putnam in 1993, arguing that the fetishizing of organizational activities has clouded ordinary practices that "do" the work of civil society, especially in closed regimes. Unlike neo-Tocquevillian studies of civil society, we do not seek to hypothesize the effects of organizational activity on regime performance and responsiveness, nor the effects of associational membership on conceptions of citizenship and civic-ness (Cohen and Arato, 1992; Diamond, 1999; Putnam, 1993; Seligman, 1992; Shils, 1997). Instead, we identify practices and spaces of contention among everyday Tunisians that imbue the population with an alternative political, national, if not civic identity, in the absence of representative institutions and independent civil society organizations. As in other authoritarian contexts, such a popularly constructed identity stands opposite dominant nationalist and more recently neo-liberal discourses produced by the state, and is constituted by practices and activities that are not necessarily overtly political. Evidence from comparative experiences (i.e., Colored Revolutions in Eastern Europe beginning in 2000) shows that political identity formation resisting a dominant state narrative can significantly shift power relations and redefine the rules of the game, once a political opportunity presents itself, as the 2010–2011 events in Tunisia exemplify.

The Tunisian paradox

The Tunisian paradox refers to the country's comparatively high level of economic development with a robust middle class existing within a closed, illiberal political system. Unlike the experience of other transitioning countries, where steady economic growth has contributed to political liberalization (Di Palma, 1990; Haggard and Kaufman, 1995; Karl, 1990; Karl and Schmitter, 1991; Przeworski, 1991; Rustow, 1970; O'Donnell *et al.*, 1986), Tunisia has not only failed to liberalize politically but has instead stalled on the democracy continuum (Bellin, 2002) reverting to an even more robust form of authoritarianism (Bellin, 2004; Brownlee, 2007; Entelis, 2004a, 2005; Penner-Angrist, 2006) that seemed unshakable. The paradox is the inability of a relatively large, educated middle class to press for political change that would result in greater regime responsiveness to middle class interests. Explanations for this impasse vary widely, from an ever-expanding security apparatus (Bellin, 2004), to a state-led development program (Bellin, 2002) or controlled privatization and liberalization (Cammett, 2007), to an ineffective, controlled, and dysfunctional civil society (Redissi, 2007), or to popular political apathy as witnessed through Tunisia's bogus elections (Entelis, 2005; Schwedler and Chomiak, 2006).

The Ben Ali regime puzzled analysts and scholars alike in its persistent unwillingness/inability to transform its impressive market-oriented reforms, which have created one of the Arab world's most socioeconomically progressive societies, into a genuine political democracy most often associated with such progress. While Habib Bourguiba (1903–2000), Tunisia's first president, was instrumental in promoting liberal economic reforms through a program of adaptive modernization and a pro-Western foreign policy in the three decades in which he ruled over Tunisia (1956–1987), he was also decisive in institutionalizing authoritarian political processes and practices, or an authoritarian political culture, which his successor nurtured and advanced.

In the name of fighting colonialism, achieving independence, establishing a modern national state, and advancing social and economic reforms, Bourguiba justified a benign form of authoritarian rule as reflected in the monolithic party and state structures he created. His charismatic appeal and populist vision found ready acceptance among his tolerant citizenry, at least in the early years of post-independence rule. Too soon, however, the "supreme combatant" lost his populist touch depending increasingly on the authoritarian state to impose its will on a restive civil society. Yet the authoritarian legacy was already well in place by the time of his ouster by General Zine Abidine Ben Ali on 7 November 1987 in a so-called "constitutional coup."

More than anything else, it is this contradictory legacy – economic liberalism and democratic illiberalism – that Bourguiba has passed on to Ben Ali, which helps explain the latter's ability to sustain an authoritarian political order in the face of populist challenges emerging within local public space including civil society and the international human rights environment. Rather than promoting a successful transition and consolidation of democratic rule, Ben Ali instead

76   *L. Chomiak and J.P. Entelis*

advanced a form of manipulative democracy that uses democratic rhetoric and institutions to hide a more robust version of authoritarianism suggesting a reconfiguration and strengthening of authoritarianism rather than a promotion of political liberalism (Heydeman, 2007).

This authoritarian political culture imposed by Bourguiba and his ruling elite over a three-decade-long period does not by itself, of course, explain the illiberal character of Ben Ali's regime. Important economic forces including cooptation of key classes and groups within civil society of which Chris Alexander, Stephen King,[3] Eva Bellin, Greg White, Melanie Cammett, among others, have written about, also serve to explain the way in which incipient democratic forces have receded from politics under the influence of carrot-and-stick policies of the regime. From this perspective, rather than fostering "third wave" democratization, neoliberal reforms of the kind pursued both by Bourguiba in the 1970s and 1980s and Ben Ali since then have reinforced authoritarian rule. Compared to Bourguiba's benign form of authoritarianism, the Ben Ali regime solidified a so-called corporatist-authoritarian system understood as

> extensive government control over labor through corporatist mechanisms in the new market arrangements. Patron-client ties between rural notables and the small peasantry keep the state anchored in the countryside, civil society is kept on a short leash, and repression is utilized to control subordinate groups when necessary. [An] [e]xceptionally powerful executive that dominates a weak legislature and judiciary characterizes the regime institutionally.
>
> (King, 2003: 5–6)

Corporate-authoritarianism in Tunisia differs from earlier forms of corporatist rule in that the Ben Ali regime utilizes "the rhetoric of liberal democracy, permit[s] a degree of political openness, and hold[s] partially competitive elections in order to appear to be moving towards international norms" (King, 2003: 56). However, in practice the regime created mechanisms that effectively prevent the transfer of power. The most current effort in this regard has been the amending of Article 39 of the Tunisian Constitution, which limits the presidential incumbent to three consecutive terms of five years each. Ben Ali has been in power since 1987 with his rule being given plebiscitary approval in four consecutive uncontested presidential elections in 1989–1994, 1994–1999, 1999–2004, and 2004–2009, although the latter exercise included token "opposition" candidates. He ran once again in October 2009 winning the contest over several government-approved but politically anemic opposing candidates.

A mass-based political culture in the form of political Islam represents a dynamic dimension of pre-1987 responses to western-influenced elite manipulation by Bourguiba and his ruling class. Absent a true expression of populist sentiment in the form of democratic participation, an Islamic "counter-culture" emerged in the late 1970s and early 1980s to inspire large groups of disaffected Tunisians across the spectrum of social classes and economic groups but with a

Contesting order in Tunisia 77

particular concentration on the young urban unemployed male population to turn to more "authentic" representations of Tunisian identity (Entelis, 1974). This challenge to the political status quo was met with a reactionary and, at times, violent response by the Bourguiba regime, which his successor took to extreme levels. The latter has been particularly insistent at equating political Islam with threats to middle class economic and social interests at home and security interests abroad. However, since 2008, the Ben Ali regime put extraordinary efforts into reconciling Tunisia with its Arabo-Islamic identity, including: the creation of an Islam-based radio station, *Radio Zaytouna*, with the slogan "Moderation, Tolerance, Fraternity"; a project to restore many of the country's *zawwiyas* (Sufi gathering places); the declaration of 2009 as the year of Kairouan, the Maghreb's oldest Islamic city; and the financing of mosques across the country. The intent has been to proliferate a Tunisian state-led version of "tolerant" Islam, as a result of popular support for the now-banned Islam-based political movements, increased Arab Gulf-based investment and influence in the country, and also the 2002 terrorist attacks on the isle of Djerba.

In short, a legacy of political illiberalism fastened itself to both economic opportunity and Islamic militancy as the *raison d'être* of national political action. Civil society was sufficiently cowed by the fear that Islamic militancy could upset economic prosperity from which key groups and classes benefited that top-down centralized authority was found acceptable if not mandatory in the face of limited alternatives – stability, prosperity, and political illiberalism versus fear, uncertainty, and political chaos. Bourguiba raised Tunisia's authoritarian scaffold, Ben Ali concretized its structure.

Contesting space, seeking expression

In studies of political transitions and related work on state–society relations and civil society, the Tunisian case either qualifies as an outlier or, in studies of reversals to authoritarianism, represents the status quo. As discussed above, political science work on Tunisia has paid little attention to the underlying practices that reveal political identity formation, public contestation, and other society-level mechanisms that indicate a more vibrant and complex political phenomenon.[4] In fact, the fetishizing of the Tunisian state apparatus has rendered a socio-political image that is virtually devoid of any contentious politics, including co-opted elections, controlled legal opposition, the lack of an independent civil society, the ongoing co-optation of ideas and, most recently, everyday forms of auto-censorship. In the absence of representative institutions so integral to the democratization process as well as its consolidation and sustainability, including an independent parliament, political parties, judicial system, and robust civil society, how are political identities formed? In other words, how can we understand a politically aware citizenry that does not identify with its governing system?[5]

In order to understand Tunisia's alternative political identities, we need to start uncovering political practices that do not take place in direct relation to the

78   *L. Chomiak and J.P. Entelis*

state, or at least not overtly so (Singerman, 1995). Instead, we have to turn to alternative forms of political expression that occur parallel to the state apparatus, practices that do not necessarily address the state but nonetheless produce so-called civic norms,[6] along with national, regional, urban, or sub-urban political identification. A recent study by Lisa Wedeen, for instance, examines the everyday, public practices by Yemeni citizens, including *Q'at* chews,[7] that have contributed to the formation of a Yemeni national-political identity in the absence of representative political institutions (Wedeen, 2008). The discursive interactions in which Yemenis participate habitually, Wedeen argues, resemble elements of Jurgen Habermas' public sphere ([1962] 1989), though, at the same time, offer a critique of his ideal public sphere situation, especially concerning access, social status, and equality. While many public debates occurring within the realm of *Q'at* chews involve routine issues of communal importance, Wedeen also documents the construction and dissemination of resistant and oppositional opinions vis-à-vis a dominant state-led ideology. In particular, she writes of the appearance of oppositional party candidates in promoting their platforms, bolstered by the discrepancy between the regime's dominant political program and ineffective performance, in an effort to increase their constituency.

While Wedeen writes of the public performance of resistant and oppositional acts in her study of Yemen, other studies have examined the more subtle and hidden acts of opposition under systems of domination (Havel, 1978; Kundera, 1967, 1977, 1984; Michnik, 1987, 1998; Scott, 1985, 1990; Wedeen, 1999). James Scott, most notably, writes of the various *Hidden Transcripts* produced and performed by subordinate groups (slaves, serfs, etc.), including mockeries, jokes, masquerades, gestures, gossip, rumors, story-telling, among many others, in locating subversive acts of resistance, those that are not necessarily visible to power holders, and thus more difficult to police (1990: 4). Dissident literature in the Soviet Union has likewise produced accounts of resistant discursive practices.[8] What these essays often stress is that no matter how penetrating the state apparatus, the discursive power of the individual – whether subject or citizen – remains complex even if dominated, functioning within a system of power that is both resisted and encouraged by its participants. As sociologist Hank Johnston argues in his work (2001) scholars seeking to explain oppositional activity and forms of expression under authoritarian systems need to pay special attention to the speech acts, language choices, gestures and movement of individuals, as these very acts might signify ideas, expressions, and opinions that cannot be overtly uttered. Specifically, Johnston contends that in authoritarian systems, "talk" more so than any other action marks the onset of political contention even though such "talk" is forced into a limited number of free spaces.[9] Asef Bayat writes that the mundane activities of millions of citizens under authoritarian rule, the "social non-movements" in other words, constitute "collective actions of noncollective actors" which trigger much social change (Bayat, 2010: 14). "In the Middle East," he contends, "the nonmovements have come to represent the mobilization of millions of subaltern, chiefly the urban poor, Muslim women, and youth," or the underlying politics of the poor (2010: 14–15). Scott (1990) previously wrote of the consequences hidden transcripts present once they are publicly uttered, constituting threats to the legitimacy of domination. The "breaking of a taboo imposed by the dominant," or the "public refusal to reproduce hegemonic appearances," he argues, constitute publicly declarations that rules of subordination are neither legitimate nor set (1990: 215–217). While regimes seek to limit social spaces within which dissident subcultures can emerge, the public declaration of hidden transcripts becomes the first instance in which offstage "talk" defines a public space for expression.

Separating free spaces from systems of domination is nonetheless complicated as every such instance (i.e., oppositional publications, associational formation, jokes, songs, poems, etc.) occurs within intricate power relations. It remains especially difficult to evaluate whether an act or speech is in fact "free" or whether it remains constrained within its own system of power, and thus contributes to its sustainability. In other words, we remain careful in asserting whether certain oppositional or contentious acts occur outside or within a given power structure. An often-cited example is Vaclav Havel's essay "The Power of the Powerless," in which he develops the concept of *auto-totality*, a condition in which individuals who do not believe in Communist ideology nonetheless participate in various acts of legitimizing the system and thus enforce each other's compliance.[10] They do so primarily to proceed with day-to-day activities, to find tranquility in social life, and to escape harassment by the state. Instances of incongruity between practice and belief signify underlying political practices that need to be distinguished from the official political narrative. Take, for instance, the common practice of displaying photos or images of state leaders in shops, coffee houses, restaurants, hotels, and so forth. Like the Syrian case discussed by Wedeen (1999), virtually every public space in Tunisia was "cluttered" with an image of Ben Ali, not to mention the colossal posters of the country's president on principal roads, official buildings, squares, and parks.

The photographic display of the president in his younger and healthier years shows alternate poses from Virgin Mary-like open palms ("for my country") to clasped hands ("my country united") to his right hand covering the heart ("from my heart" or "in my heart"). Despite the smothering of public spaces with presidential images, Tunisians rarely discuss or mention the public display of power or its intended signification. Instead, as one cynical young professional remarked, the image displaying Ben Ali with his hand covering the heart is dismissed by him and his peers as "in my [suit] pocket," (*dans ma poche*) or among the more contemptuous as "genuinely, from his heart, screwing the country."[11] While Tunisians most certainly practice a form of *auto-totality*, such widespread sentiments are testament to more complex political expressions that are not captured in political opinion polling, for instance, and invite further investigation.

As Havel noted in the same essay, political resistance in a country that does provide economic stability becomes even more difficult and can be observed in the average citizen, one who is inscribed with "a divided soul," with loyalties to the regime as well as loyalties to personal opinion. Yet, once the economic stability promised by the regime is questioned, even mocked as in the Tunisian

80 L. Chomiak and J.P. Entelis

case, new areas of contention and resistance become apparent in both popular discourse and practice. Popular reactions in Tunisia signify that imposed compliance not only fails in producing a Tunisian citizen-subject, but instead that forced obedience can impel resistance against state-led projects. Probing a bit deeper, one finds an even more sarcastic and contentious discourse about increased dissatisfaction with the Ben Ali regime, a mockery of the so-called mafia state and its ever-growing practice of silencing dissident voices. Taxi-cabdrivers, for instance, routinely criticized the regime for increasing the prices of staple foods and subsidizing the export of Tunisia's finest agricultural goods, thus providing European markets with cheap goods yet denying basic living standards to Tunisian citizens. The "prostituting" itself to Europe, one cabdriver remarked, provides just one of the many incentives why young Tunisians increasingly yearn to emigrate. Others note that US and EU development programs in Tunisia are primarily interested in expanding foreign investment opportunities, paying lip service to socio-political and economic reform that might benefits others besides the Tunisian regime and foreign investors. "If development programs are willing to pay an additional thirty percent for each micro-business program," one critic noted, "we could actually afford to pay off our pimp [the state], and develop our own industry." Yet, the same critic noted, talking about such issues with international actors is like "performing a striptease to myself."

Another intrepid instance of contentious discourse appeared in a number of articles published in the semi-independent weekly *L'Expression*, under the broad heading of *Liberté d'Expression* ("Freedom of Expression" [*L'Expression* 2009]). The articles directly address censorship and self-censorship in the Arab world, even debating whether an "Arab exception" can be discerned, and criticizing its effects on intellectual thought, societal trust, and political development. In the words of the author, *L'autocensure est plus complexe, ses impacts son néfastes. La rôle de la censure et du censeur disparaitrait s'il y avait democratie et état de droit* ("Self-censorship is more complex with adverse impacts. The role of censorship and those who engage in censoring disappears if there is democracy and a state of law"). Yet the author, a Tunisian journalist who regularly covers Tunisian civil society for the same publication, omitted any mentioning of the state of censorship in Tunisia. In fact, he did not speak of any Arab country in particular but instead presented sweeping facts, including details that seventeen Arab countries practice censorship of intellectual production before publication and another seven countries that censor information technology more generally. Yet among such banal and prosaic statements, the author skillfully integrated information about the blatant ridicule and buffoonery of laws stipulating press freedom and publication of intellectual thought.

The context within which the articles on censorship appeared is likewise insightful in understanding the complexity of subtle contention in Tunisia. *L'Expression* is a sister publication of two major Tunisian daily French and Arabic newspapers, *Le Temps* and *Al-Sabah*, and has been in circulation for just over a year. Initially, *L'Expression* was pulled off the news-stands for its investigative analysis although it was reinstated within just a few weeks. After the

Contesting order in Tunisia 81

publishing of some critical articles in the fall of 2008 questioning the absence of freedom of the press and expression, a controversial debate between the student union UGET (*Union Générale des Etudiants Tunisiens*) and the government and political pluralism more generally, the editor was dismissed and replaced by a more suitable candidate a few weeks before Tunisia's celebration of Ben Ali's 7 November coup. The publication took on a new tone, covering mundane Tunisian matters, profiling the legalized opposition parties, as well as regional North African and global affairs. Yet, during the same week that the capital was preparing for its first 2009 soccer derby in which Tunis' archrival football teams battle for the nation's championship, *L'Expression* published the two articles on censorship. The timing was important in that the entire nation was being consumed with soccer fever at the expense of any other national or international event. While this parallel clash in coverage – that is, the juxtaposition of the country's most vocal form of expression in soccer stadiums versus the virtual absence of expression lamented in the articles on censorship – might be considered coincidental, it can also point to moments when contestation finds its voice in popular discourse.[12]

The debates in *L'Expression* and even more critical calls in *Al-Mouatin*'s[13] column entitled *Citoyens non Sujets* ("Citizens not Subjects") as well as *Al-Mouatin* ("The Citizen") are examples of interventions that seek to expand a space for expression. Journalists, columnists, and contributors often make claims to rights guaranteed by the Tunisian state, including press freedom, freedom of expression, open dialogue with state authorities, freedom of association (including unions), independent judiciary, and competing conceptions of citizenship. While such practices fall short of what O'Brian and Li term "rightful resistance," (2006) – the resistance to a dominant ideology (in their case Chinese villagers) by making claims to rights through the employment of official discourse that defines and guarantees such rights – they nonetheless point to an alternative and oppositional ideology that exists alongside the official narrative of the Tunisian state. In the next section we will turn to a larger public venue – soccer matches – and discuss the formation of political identities in an arena that attracts a significant portion of Tunisia's population. Subtle identity debates in the form of soccer chants and songs functioned as a venue for individuals to debate questions of belonging, substituting the traditional outlets of independent civil society organizations or oppositional groups which were largely absent in Ben Ali's Tunisia. During the Jasmine Revolution in January of 2011, protesters in Tunis would oftentimes switch between anti-Ben Ali chants (especially "Ben Ali Dégage!") and popular soccer songs, a practice that resonated in Cairo's Tahrir square as well.

Producing political identities

Political identity formation in Tunisia is as complex as in any other context and a result of a host of overlapping historical and political experiences and moments. The concept of a Tunisian national identity was initially constructed

82   L. Chomiak and J.P. Entelis

by the Young Tunisians movement of the early twentieth century and later sustained by Habib Bourguiba in response to a weak sense of national identity during the French colonial period (Perkins, 2005). Yet, even Bourguiba recognized that Tunisian identity, rooted as it was in a fragile admixture of Phoenician, Roman, Carthaginian, Berber, Arab, Muslim, Turkish/Ottoman, Maltese, French, Italian, Jewish, and Mediterranean influences, required a more focused modernist-nationalist strategy to buttress his approach. As a consequence, Bourguiba strategically selected glorious historical moments, narrated by commissioned academics and historians, to construct a nationalist project that would resonate among Tunisia's early independent nation and instill each citizen with a new sense of "nation-ness" (Brubaker, 2006).[14] Bourguiba was especially wary of a uniquely Arab-Muslim identity that would possibly alienate Tunisia from its more cosmopolitan Carthaginian past. With the weakening of Bourguiba's political project, his increased usage of authoritarian political practices, and the subsequent bloodless *coup d'état* by Ben Ali, Tunisian political identity has been largely understood to reflect the authoritarian political culture imposed by the state (Alexander, 2010; Entelis, 2004b, 2005). In this section, we problematize this perception and show how alternative political, if not civic, identities are formed in public venues that challenge the dominant narrative of the state.

The ancient Roman slogan *Panem et Circences*[15] ("Give them bread and games") developed by Roman poet Juvenal in the late first and early second century quite accurately captures the Tunisian approach of state-led development, one that provides a comparatively high standard of living and rather broad freedom of expression during public sporting events. As described above, soccer stadiums in particular enjoy a comparatively high level of "free" expression, where fans sing, chant, and shout in support of their respective teams, and where political identities are stimulated and debated, whether purposefully, subversively, or inadvertently.[16] For instance, when Tunis' two teams play, songs and chants not only reflect team rivalry but also represent a dialogue concerning the socio-economic status and residence of team supporters. During the February 2009 soccer match, supporters of *Club Africain*, the team traditionally supported by blue-collar fans residing around *Bab Jedid* in the medina, would sing:

> We come from every place in the medina, Bab Jedid, the Kasbah, and Sabaghrine.[17] Our dream is to win; Club African please fulfill our dream and give us happiness. We are so trashed and ready to fight. White and red, like our hearts, we want the championship.

In their chant, *Club Africain* supporters are claiming crucial areas of the medina that include their traditional home base (*Bab Jedid*, whereas *Esperance* fans traditionally reside by *Bab Souikha*), the Kasbah (the location of governmental power), as well as Sabaghrine (an up-and-coming commercial district). Even though *Club Africain* fans might not directly live in the areas specified in the song, they are, through the vehicle of a soccer team, making claims to areas of Tunis that define changing political as well as economic trends. Fans solidify their commitment by chanting *With our souls and blood, we will always trust you and be faithful to you.* If their team wins, *Club African* supporters will occupy those streets and areas defined in their chants. Besides making claims to physical spaces in Tunis, fans also chose nationalist rhetoric in their chants – we are ready to fight, our hearts, our souls, our blood – a rhetoric that is not found in any other public discourse. The sole other producer of such nationalist concepts remains the Tunisian state, which continuously uses rhetoric such as "faithfulness to the country," "love for this glorious land," "[Tunisian] dignity is indissociable [*sic*] from [the nation's] dignity," as well as "[Tunisia] remains glorious and invulnerable forever."[18]

The proclamation by fans of trust and faithfulness to a soccer team as well as claiming of physical space constitutes an alternative socio-political identity which dismisses an official historical-nationalist narrative that is publicly visible, individually sanctioned, and, at the same time, challenged. We are not arguing that this necessarily constitutes oppositional voices, but rather that fans and spectators dismiss an official narrative and opt to locate their sense of belonging and community elsewhere. Yet, the very act of dismissing a state-imposed narrative may be an act of opposition itself. However, separating opposition or resistance from power may be problematic (Foucault, 1984) as well as deterministic. "Where there is power, there is resistance, and yet, or rather consequently, this resistance is never in a position of exteriority in relation to power" (Foucault, 1984). In cases such as Tunisia, power and opposition are not only contingent but also foment and stimulate each other; alternative and state-sanctioned political practices alike can therefore only be located within the constraints of the power system. It is within this densely interwoven web of power and opposition that political practices have to be uncovered and alternative political identities discerned.

In competing nationalist discourses, for instance, power and opposition or resistance are especially difficult to untangle. We do not know whether such popular rhetoric as exemplified in the chants above is co-opted by the state and reinvented in official declarations, whether the declaration for a love of a team representing sub-national and sub-urban identification supersedes or replaces the love of a nation as defined by the ruling regime, or whether the two narratives co-exist in parallel proximity. Similarly, we cannot confirm whether these narratives are competing or reinforcing. However, we can observe a discernable behavioral difference in the clamorous expression of popular loyalty in stadiums and the silent mockery, if not rejection, of the state and its affected political identity.[19]

Tunisian soccer stadiums have developed into areas of free speech in comparison to other spaces that continue to be controlled by the state, including organizations, associations, and publications. It remains difficult, however, to characterize them as arenas for resistance, as the Tunisian state has always been instrumental in supporting soccer. Following the discussion in the previous section, soccer stadiums are "free" arenas for expression, yet they cannot be fully separated from the power of the state. Historically, the Tunisian state and soccer clubs have always enjoyed a close partnership, in part because the state finances a large percentage of the team's operating expenses and in part because a number of ministers close to Tunisia's first president Habib Bourguiba have served as presidents, managers, or chairmen of the country's major teams. Unlike other public organizations and events supported by the state, soccer games are powerful events that transform public behavior and the general atmosphere of the city. On weekends when the country's two strongest teams play – *Club Africaine* and *Espérance* ("Hope") – downtown Tunis is embellished with club paraphernalia of either team; small newspaper stalls transform into fan shops selling clothing, headbands, stickers, flags, and banners; apartment balconies and windows sport their respective banners and flags; and individuals dressed in either team colors crowd the streets awaiting the game. The spectacle of a soccer derby and its accompanying paraphernalia markedly supersedes the already omnipresent political spectacle of Ben Ali in the city. Those fortunate enough to attend the match in the brand-new *Rades* stadium seating 60,000, leave their homes hours before the game, creating hour-long traffic jams that line the eight kilometer highway from the outskirts of downtown to the stadium in the south of the city. Most cars and trucks are crammed with fans chanting and singing, drivers honk the distinctive sound of each team, flags flutter from car windows and sun roofs, while children living in the poorer southern outskirts watch and cheer the informal highway parade and excitedly imitate players and moves. While such images might characterize the social environment of any soccer derby in any given country, it is important to note that no other event in Tunis consumes a public of this size.

Though less spectacular, fans living outside the capital even in desert villages will find refuge in small cafés and restaurants, huddling around television screens, gearing up for the game. Even in tourist-populated areas in the South, Tunisians living in small towns and Berber villages usually employed as guides at tourist sites will pay little attention to foreign visitors and head to a nearby café to watch even less significant matches. The café culture in larger cities, including the capital, is similar throughout – men-only as well as mixed cafés are overflowing with fans, leaving the streets empty. Tunisian love for soccer seemingly transcends all other emotions and socio-economic realities; as one *Clubist* (from a working-class background) said, "I could never marry a foreign woman and live in a country where I cannot watch *Club Africain* games every week," or an *Esperance* fan (upper class) who warned his girlfriend before the last February 2009 match that their relationship would seriously suffer should *Esperance* lose. What do such public reactions for a sports team reveal about the political identities of everyday Tunisians?

The linkage between athletic events and political identities is neither unique nor improbable, most visibly present during Olympic Games when sentiments of national belonging are elevated. Even Robert Putnam, in his seminal study on civil society and civic traditions in Italy, cited membership in sports and specifically soccer clubs (along with membership in various other associations and organizations) as a mechanism by which civic norms and interpersonal trust are

Contesting order in Tunisia 85

fostered (Putnam, 1993). Soccer has likewise received recent attention in popular literature, including two books entitled *How Soccer Explains the World: An [Un]likely Theory of Globalization* (Foer, 2004) as well as *Soccer Against the Enemy: How the World's Most Popular Sport Starts and Fuels Revolutions and Keeps Dictators in Power* (Kuper, 2006). In his chapter on soccer in the Arab and Muslim world, Simon Kuper writes:

> For a young man in the Middle East, obliged to spend his leisure time hanging around with other young men, soccer is often the only recreation. That's why in Tripoli, the Libyan capital, games between the two biggest clubs draw crowds of 100,000 – more than anywhere in Europe except occasionally Barcelona or Real Madrid.... Yet the game does help us understand this secretive region. In societies like Libya, Iran, and previously in Saddam Hussein's Iraq, where there is no freedom of press, no legal dissent, and hardly any foreign journalists, soccer can reveal the undercurrents.
>
> (286)

In conversations with Tunisian academics and intellectuals about the location of public spaces in Tunisia, soccer games, along with Facebook,[20] are often cited as the only public arenas in which Tunisians can gather publicly, express themselves openly, and debate national, subnational, urban, regional, as well as economic undercurrents. The level of expression afforded in soccer stadiums allows for the transgression of various social boundaries, whether proper versus vulgar behavior, acceptance versus mockery of the rules of governance, or male-female relations, indicating broader collective behavioral change. For instance, as Kuper finds in his study of soccer in post-revolutionary Iran, women supporters dressed up as men would slip into soccer stadiums, transgressing forced gender boundaries. Women are not a rare sight in Tunisian soccer stadiums, though certain segments of Tunisian society still believe that no respectable woman should witness, or partake, in the vulgar brawl that defines Tunisian soccer games. Even young Tunisian women, including those of upper class backgrounds, enter the stadiums especially during highly contested matches, behaving in the same manner and chanting the same songs as their male counterparts. As chants, songs, and cries are usually more vulgar than the "proclamations" analyzed above, it is significant to observe the stark differences in female public behavior outside the stadium as compared to that within it.[21] Take for instance the chant *You cannot beat my dick, my dick* (meaning that the opposition team has absolutely no chance of winning; the chant usually follows a goal), which women and men supporters cry out alike. Similar public exclamations among men outside of soccer stadiums usually refer to threats of ego, some type of transgression (if someone flirts with a girlfriend or insults a family member), and any type of anger or awe, but are never uttered by women. Yet during soccer games, women also shout *z'bi* (dick) and imitate vulgar hand gestures when signifying dissatisfaction with the opposing team, the fans, or an unpopular referee decision. The point here is that soccer stadiums provide a public venue for all

86　*L. Chomiak and J.P. Entelis*

forms of expression – including vulgarities that are generally excluded from public debate – and that both men and women perform them. Women adopt a masculine temperament that allows for association with their fellow fans – most of whom are men – the soccer team, and the cultural cult that accompanies the spectator sport. The intent here is not so much to analyze shifting gender dynamics but rather to use the examples as indicators of behavior change in a space that is both public and safe for expression.

Political identity debates in soccer derbies are most pronounced during what fans call pre-game "spectacles" or the public contestation of each team's identities as well as the identities of team supporters: their intelligence, socio-economic status as well as degree of team support. Before the March 2009 derby, for instance, *Clubists* unfurled a gigantic cloth with a picture of Mona Lisa with a banner reading *C'est le charme de notre club qui fait sourire la jaconde* ("Our team's charm makes Mona Lisa smile"), and *Espérance* fans answered with a likewise large display of an eagle, reading *L'aigle n'a que deux couleurs* ("The eagle has only two colors," meaning those of *Espérance*). In response, *Clubists* unfolded, one by one, large cloths displaying renowned scientists, including Newton and Einstein. While *Clubists* were utilizing symbols of civility and sophistication, *Espérance* fans dismissed their "weak symbol" with one of strength. Instead of challenging *Espérance*'s strength, *Clubists* opted for symbols of knowledge, intelligence, and progress, contending common prejudices that *Club Africain* supporters are generally less educated, less sophisticated, as well as less successful. This subtle identity contest between team supporters signifies a debate that not only exists among soccer fans ("even though you might be the stronger team, we have the power to make Mona Lisa smile"), but likewise among everyday Tunisians: education versus status (or proximity to the state) as well as intelligence versus professional success.

While journalists and other dissident Tunisian writers challenge the official state narrative through oppositional publications as well as more subversively in the semi-independent press, as the articles on censorship in *L'Expression* indicate, larger masses debate the very meaning of Tunisian identity in soccer stadiums, a debate that is public yet hidden by commotion and vulgarity. In the latter instance, ideas of nationhood or belonging to a group (whether city, region, nation, or economic class) are articulated via references to soccer teams, more so than through homage to the state.[22] These practices and experiences seem to suggest a social connection between elite and mass-based contestatory narratives that find common cause in alternative venues pointing to an emergence of a counter-culture within an authoritarian political environment.

Conclusion

In this chapter, we problematize the assumption that public, contentious activity does not exist under authoritarian regimes, and that all forms of public expression are co-opted by the regime. We do not deny the authoritarian nature of the Tunisian state under Ben Ali, nor its transformation from a nationalist-corporatist

Contesting order in Tunisia 87

style of authoritarianism to a more pervasive neoliberal police state. Instead we find that increased political closeness and the more aggressive construction of a dominant national-political identity do not necessarily impede the formation of alternative political identities. In some cases, more blatant displays of political power and omnipresence in public space invite more widespread public ridicule, and give incentive for the construction of alternative political identities outside the realm of official political discourse.

This chapter identified spaces and locations where political identities are contested, debated, and formed in the absence of autonomous civil society activity. As Tunisia's political landscape under Ben Ali did not allow a space for the growth of independent civil society organizations, or an associational sphere that facilitated a dialogue between state and citizen, we examined other areas that "do" the work of civil society. The political identities that are contested in Tunisia – when the state is held accountable by journalists or writers or when soccer fans debate and redefine their sense of belonging – show that a dynamic citizenry does exist and is willing to engage in vibrant as well as contentious dialogue. This points to a set of practices that are neither captured in scholarly studies on authoritarianism in the Middle East and North Africa, nor in policy-oriented work including opinion-polling to determine a country's "political culture." For this reason, we were previously unable to capture the opinions and voices of those who mobilized a nation-wide resistance movement culminating in the Jasmine Revolution. The quotidian practices, especially, are not intended to provide indicators for potential regime changes, though naturally their effects could, as we witness today, but rather to tell a story of how political identity formation, dialogue, and debate contribute to changing perceptions of state–society relations even in closed, authoritarian contexts.

Notes

1 Mitchell's description of public spaces is influenced by Lefebvre's (1991) distinction between *representational space* and *representations of space*. Representation of space refers to controlled, ordered, and planned space such as monuments, court-house squares, public parks, etc.; however, as people make use of these spaces, or appropriate them, they also become representational spaces.

2 For a comprehensive critique of the neo-Tocquevillian tradition, see Berman (1997, 2001), Chatterjee (2001), Coleman (1988), Comaroff and Comaroff (1999), Edwards and Foley (1997), Edwards *et al.* (2001), Glenn (2003), Howell and Pearce (2002), Kaviraj and Khilani (2001), Migdal (2001), Muller and Seligson (1994), Tarrow (1996), Zubaida (2001).

3 King refers to the neoliberal character of the Tunisian state as "corporate-authoritarianism," rooted in the country's former Import Substituting Industrialization (ISI) populism (2003).

4 Exceptions to this include a study of Tunisian "counter-culture" in the 1970s by Entelis (1974), as well as a recent political economy study by Melanie Cammett (2007) in which she examines contestation among business groups in achieving material incentives.

5 This question is especially pertinent to international organizations and bi-lateral government programs (such as the US-led Middle East Partnership Initiative or the EU

88 L. Chomiak and J.P. Entelis

Neighborhood Policy, among many others) as well as opinion and attitudinal surveys (i.e., Arab Barometer) involved in democracy-promotion and dissemination of "civic norms" in non-democratic countries. Such initiatives are rooted in a scholarly tradition pioneered by Almond and Verba in *The Civic Culture* (1963). For an edifying critique of such programs and categories of political agents (i.e., agents of democratization), see Timothy Mitchell, Keynote Address, "Foucault and Middle East Studies – The Virtues of Recalcitrance: Democracy from Foucault to Latour," UCLA, 29 April 2009.

6 The term "civic" in this study is understood to mean practices that pertain to citizens, and more explicitly, the formation of collective identities through deliberative and communal activities.

7 *Qat* chews are daily practices in Yemen, where individuals chew the leafy stimulant *qat* in groups, providing an opportunity for family, friends, community members, and strangers to discuss various issues, including political matters (Wedeen, 2008: 3).

8 Defining works include, *The Power of the Powerless* by Vaclav Havel (1978); *Letters from Prison and Other Essays* (1986) *and Letters from Freedom: Post-Cold War Realities and Perspectives* (1998) by Adam Michnik; *The Unbearable Lightness of Being* (1984), *The Book of Laughter and Forgetting* (1978), and *The Joke* (1967) by Milan Kundera.

9 Johnston's argument speaks to studies of social movement and collective action, and he contends that mainstream work in this field has not sufficiently considered (if not taken for granted) the constraints within which collective action and oppositional speech function in authoritarian systems. Specifically, he argues that free spaces where such activity does occur are uniquely configured and need to be both theorized and conceptualized (Johnston, 2001). See also Francesca Polletta (1999) who argues that analysis has to be reoriented towards the "performative role of free spaces," in other words what such free spaces "do" rather than their structural contours. The argument follows that by understanding the function of such free spaces in authoritarian conditions, we can likewise improve our knowledge of free spaces in liberal democracies. For a compelling study of "what free spaces of expression and performance do," see Susan Slyomovics, *The Performance of Human Rights in Morocco* (2005).

10 "...by pulling everyone into its power struggle everyone is an instrument of mutual totality, the autototality of society."

11 Both statements refer to the widespread popular sentiment that the regime has not only become a neoliberal state involved in large-scale privatization, but also that the president and his wife's family are running the country as a mafia state. In everyday conversations with Tunisians, it is evident that the neoliberal character of the state is more bothersome on the whole than the absence of political liberalization, even though the two are generally connected.

12 *L'Expression* was shut down after the issue covering autocensorship (March 2009). Explanations vary: some say that the president's son who had recently acquired the publishing house *Al-Sabah* decided to shut down the magazine because of low circulation and loss in revenues, while the opposition newspaper which interviewed the author of the articles on autocensorhip claims that the magazine closed because of its critical coverage, as it has been in the past.

13 *Al-Mouatin* ("The Citizen") is a weekly newspaper published by the opposition party FDTL (The Forum Democratique pour le Travail et les Libertes).

14 The novelist Abdelaziz Belkhodja, for instance, often located Tunisian identity in Carthage's history, especially Hannibal's might. See Belkhodja (2003, 2008).

15 The concept appeared in Juvenal's *Satire X* (10–17–81), where he writes of the Roman populace relinquishing its birth right of political involvement, "...we sold our vote to no man, the people have abdicated our duties...." The satire equally referred to the Roman practice developed under Gaius Sempronis Gracchus (123 BC) of giving free wheat and access to costly circus games, a practice that was upheld by subsequent

Contesting order in Tunisia 89

Roman emperors. Similar concepts were chronicled by German writer and Egyptologist Georg Moritz Ebers (1837–1898) in his *A Thorny Path*, "The louder they shout in the Circus, the quieter they act in the streets…" a phrase that also referred to keeping women quiet; as well as in Franco's Spain, *Pan y Toros* (bread and bullfight); in nineteenth and twentieth century Russia, *Khleb I Zreleshte* (bread and spectacle); and finally in Aldous Huxley's *Brave New World*.

16 For an innovative and compelling discussion of political identity formation through song, chant, and dance during protest moments, see Schwedler (2005). Unlike the case discussed here, Schwedler examines the competing national identities among Jordanian protestors and police during riots and protests. While we are likewise concerned with competing visions of national identity, especially between state and non-state broadly defined, Tunisian national or political identity formation rarely occurs through direct contestation between, say, police and protestors, as discussed in Schwedler's study.

17 Sabaghrine is a quarter in the medina located near the tanneries. The tannery quarter (Rue El Jeld) of the medina has been completely restored by various foundations, and now houses luxurious restaurants such as Dar El-Khayrat and Dar El-Jeld, as well as high-end galleries, book stores, coffee houses, and boutique hotels or *Maison d'Hautes*. This area of the medina also borders the Kasbah, the seat of the majority of ministries.

18 *Tunisian Youth Pact Declaration*, 7 November 2008 (Tunis, Tunisia). For a discussion of a reproduction of hegemonic discourses under Ben Ali, see Sadiki (2002); for citizenship under Ben Ali, see Powell and Sadiki (2010).

19 In a conversation with a former prime minister under Bourguiba, he stressed his dissatisfaction with the usage of nationalist symbols in soccer stadiums – particularly the parading of flags and performance of national anthems. He maintained that such symbols and practices should not be mixed with soccer games ("flags should not be placed at the same level as feet"), which are usually defined by brawls and vulgarities. He was especially dissatisfied with what he defined as disrespecting important historical and political symbols.

20 The effects of social networking sites on revolts and revolutions continue to be scrutinized and evaluated by scholars, analysts, and journalists. We believe that their contribution to successful mobilization and coordination is central in addition to other factors (i.e., structural shifts and elite defection) that contribute to the culmination of large-scale protests, resistance, and revolt.

21 Here it is likewise important to note that women do use vulgar language among themselves, what is often referred to as "women's curses" in Tunisian Arabic. What is interesting in this case is that women adopt male curses and vulgarities and scream these during soccer games.

22 Exceptions include some popular Facebook pages for Bourguiba, such as "Fans of Bourguiba" (37,000 members) as well as "In Memory of President Habib Bourguiba" (7,000 members) where individuals comment on the independence movement, the first Tunisian party Neo-Destour led by Bourguiba, as well as the progressive and pragmatic character of the nascent Tunisian nation.

Bibliography

Alexander, C. (2010) *Tunisia: Stability and Reform in the Modern Maghreb*, London: Routledge.

Almond, G. and S. Verba (1963) *The Civic Culture: Political Attitudes and Democracy in Five Nations*, Princeton: Princeton University Press.

Ayubi, N. (1995) *Over-Stating the Arab State: Politics and Society in the Middle East*, London: Tauris.

90 L. Chomiak and J.P. Entelis

Bayat, A. (2010) *Life As Politics: How Ordinary People Change the Middle East*, Stanford, CA: Stanford University Press.

Beau, N. and J. P. Tuquoi (1999) *Notre Ami Ben Ali: L'envers du 'miracle tunisien'*, Paris: La Découverte.

Belkhodja, A. (2003) *Le Retour de L'Elephant*, Tunis: Apollonia.

Belkhodja, A. (2008) *Le Signe de Tanit*, Tunis: Apollonia.

Bellin, E. (2002) *Stalled Democracy: Capital, Labor, and the Paradox of State-Sponsored Development*, Ithaca: Cornell University Press.

Bellin, E. (2004) "The Robustness of Authoritarianism in the Middle East: Exceptionalism in Comparative Perspective," *Comparative Politics*, 36: 139–157.

Berman, S. (1997) "Civil Society and the Collapse of the Weimar Republic," *World Politics*, 49(3): 401–429.

Berman, S. (2001) "Ideas, Norms and Culture in Political Analysis," *Comparative Politics*, 33(2): 231–250.

Brownlee, J. (2007) *Authoritarianism in an Age of Democratization*, New York: Cambridge University Press.

Brubaker, R. (2006) *Ethnicity Without Groups*, Cambridge: Harvard University Press.

Camau, M. and V. Geisser (2003) *Le syndrome autoritaire: politique en Tunisie de Bourguiba à Ben Ali*, Paris: Presses de Sciences Po.

Cammett, M. (2007) *Globalization, Business Politics and Development: North Africa in Comparative Perspective*, New York: Cambridge University Press.

Chatterjee, P. (2001) "On Civil and Political Society in Postcolonial Democracies," in S. Kaviraj and S. Khilani (eds.) *Civil Society: History and Possibilities*, New York, NY: Cambridge University Press.

Cohen, J. L. and A. Arato (1992) *Civil Society and Political Theory*, Cambridge: MIT Press.

Coleman, J. S. (1988) "Social Capital in the Creation of Human Capital," *American Journal of Sociology*, 94: 95–120.

Comaroff, J. L. and J. Comaroff (eds.) (1999) *Civil Society and the Political Imagination in Africa: Critical Perspectives*, Chicago: University of Chicago Press.

Diamond, L. (1999) *Developing Democracy: Towards Consolidation*, Baltimore: The Johns Hopkins University Press.

Di Palma, G. (1990) *To Craft Democracies: An Essay on Democratic Transitions*, Berkeley: University of California Press.

Edwards, B. and M. W. Foley (1997) "Social Capital and the Political Economy of Our Discontent," *American Behavioral Scientist*, 40(5): 669–678.

Edwards, B., M. W. Foley and M. Diani (eds.) (2001) *Beyond Tocqueville: Civil Society and the Social Capital Debate in Comparative Perspective*, Hanover, NH: University Press of New England.

Eickelman, D. and J. W. Anderson (1999) *New Media in the Muslim World: The Emerging Public Sphere*, Bloomington: Indiana University Press.

Entelis, J. (1974) "Ideological Change and An Emerging Counter-Culture in Tunisian Politics," *Journal of Modern African Studies*, 2: 543–568.

Entelis, J. (2004a) "The Sad State of Political Reform in Tunisia," *Arab Reform Bulletin*, 2.

Entelis, J. (2004b) "L'héritage contradictoire de Bourguiba: modernisation et intolérance politique," in M. Camau and V. Geisser (eds.) *Habib Bourguiba: La trace et l'héritage*, Paris: Karthala, 223–247.

Entelis, J. (2005) "The Democratic Imperative vs. the Authoritarian Impulse: The

Contesting order in Tunisia 91

Maghrib State Between Transition and Terrorism," *The Middle East Journal*, 59: 537–558.

Entelis, J. (2007) "Republic of Tunisia," in D. Long and B. Reich (eds.) *The Government and Politics of the Middle East and North Africa*, Boulder, CO: Westview Press, 516–548.

Foer, F. (2004) *How Soccer Explains the Word: An [Un]Likely Theory of Globalization*, New York: Harper Collins.

Foucault, M. (1984) *History of Sexuality I: An Introduction*, London: Penguin Books. Cited in: E. W. Mitchell, *Self-Made Madness: Rethinking Illness and Criminal Responsibility*, Burlington, VT: Ashgate Publishing, 2003.

Glenn III., J. K. (2003) *Framing Democracy: Civil Society and Civic Movements in Eastern Europe*, Stanford, CA: Stanford University Press.

Habermas, J. ([1962] 1989) *The Structural Transformation of the Public Sphere: An Inquiry into a Category of Bourgeois Society*, Cambridge: MIT Press (translated by T. Berger).

Haggard, S. and R. Kaufman (1995) *The Political Economy of Democratic Transitions*, Princeton: Princeton University Press.

Hall, J. (ed.) (1995) *Civil Society: Theory, History, Comparison*, New York: Polity Press.

Havel, V. (1978) "The Power of the Powerless," in J. Keane (ed.) *Citizens Against the State in Central-Eastern Europe*, London: Hutchinson, 1985.

Heydeman, S. (2007) "Social Pacts and the Persistence of Authoritarianism in the Middle East," in O. Schlumberger (ed.) *Debating Arab Authoritarianism: Dynamics and Durability in Nondemocratic Regimes*, Stanford, CA: Stanford University Press.

Hirschkind, C. (2006) *The Ethical Soundscape: Cassette Sermons and Islamic Counterpublics*, New York: Columbia University Press.

Howell, J. and J. Pearce (2002) *Civil Society and Development: A Critical Exploration*, Boulder, CO: Lynne Rienner.

Huntington, S. (1991) *The Third Wave: Democratization in the Late Twentieth Century*, Norman: University of Oklahoma Press.

Johnston, H. (2001) "Talking the Walk: Speech Acts and Resistance in Authoritarian Regimes," paper prepared for Workshop on Repression and Mobilization, University of Maryland, 21–23 June.

Karl, T. (1990) "Dilemmas of Democratization in Latin America," *Comparative Politics*, 23(1): 1–21.

Karl, T. and P. Schmitter (1991) "Modes of Transition in Latin America and Eastern Europe," *International Social Science Journal*, 43: 267–282.

Kaviraj, S. and S. Khilani (eds.) (2001) *Civil Society: History and Possibilities*, New York, NY: Cambridge University Press.

King, S. (2003) *Liberalization Against Democracy: The Local Politics of Economic Reform in Tunisia*, Bloomington: Indiana University Press.

Kundera, M. (1967) *The Joke*, New York: Penguin.

Kundera, M. (1977) "Comedy is Everywhere," *Index on Censorship*, 6(6): 307.

Kundera, M. (1978) *The Book of Laughter and Forgetting*, New York: Penguin.

Kundera, M. (1984) *The Unbearable Lightness of Being*, New York: Harper Publishers.

Kuper, S. (2006) *Soccer Against the Enemy: How the World's Most Popular Sport Starts and Fuels Revolutions and Keeps Dictators in Power*, New York: Nation Books.

L'Expression (2009) No. 71, 27 February–5 March, pp. 10–14.

Lefèbvre, H. (1991) *The Production of Space*, Cambridge, MA: Wiley-Blackwell (translated by D. Nicholson-Smith).

92   L. Chomiak and J.P. Entelis

LeVine, M. (2008), *Heavy Metal Islam: Rock, Resistance, and the Struggle for the Soul of Islam*, New York: Three Rivers Press.

Michnik, A. (1987), *Letters from Prison and Other Essays*, Berkeley: University of California Press.

Michnik, A. (1998) *Letters from Freedom: Post-Cold War Realities and Perspectives*, Berkeley: University of California Press (ed. G. Grudzinksa Gross).

Migdal, J. (2001) *State in Society: Studying How States and Societies Transform and Constitute One Another*, New York: Cambridge University Press.

Mitchell, D. (1995) "The End of Public Space? People's Park, Definitions of the Public, and Democracy," *Annals of the Association of American Geographers*, 85: 108–133.

Mitchell, T. (1990) "Everyday Metaphors of Power," *Theory and Society*, 19: 545–577.

Muller, E. N. and M. A. Seligson (1994) "Civic Culture and Democracy: The Question of Causal Relationships," *American Political Science Review*, 88: 635–652.

O'Brien, K. and L. Li (2006) *Rightful Resistance in Rural China*, New York: Cambridge University Press.

O'Donnell, G., P. Schmitter and L. Whitehead (eds.) (1986) *Transitions from Authoritarian Rule: Comparative Perspectives*, Baltimore, MD: Johns Hopkins University Press.

Penner-Angrist, M. (1999) "The Expression of Political Dissent in the Middle East: Turkish Democratization and Authoritarian Continuity in Tunisia," *Comparative Studies in Society and History*, 41: 730–757.

Penner-Angrist, M. (2006) *Party-Building in the Modern Middle East*, Seattle: University of Washington Press.

Perkins, K. (2005) *A History of Modern Tunisia*, New York: Cambridge University Press.

Polletta, F. (1999) "Free Spaces in Collective Action," *Theory and Society*, 28: 1–38.

Posusney, M. P and M. Penner Angrist (eds.) (2005) *Authoritarianism in the Middle East: Regimes and Resistance*, Boulder: Lynne Rienner.

Powell, B. and L. Sadiki (2010) "The Second Republic and Citizenship in Bin Ali's Tunisia: Democracy vs. Unity, 1987–2001," in *Europe and Tunisia: Democracy via Association*, London: Routledge.

Pratt, N. (2006) *Democracy and Authoritarianism in the Arab World*, Boulder: Lynne Rienner.

Przeworski, A. (1991) *Democracy and the Market: Political and Economic Reforms in Eastern Europe and Latin America*, New York: Cambridge University Press.

Putnam, R. (1993) *Making Democracy Work: Civic Traditions in Modern Italy*, Princeton: Princeton University Press.

Redissi, H. (2007) "Etat fort, société civile faible en Tunisie," *Maghreb-Machrek*, 192: 89–118.

Rustow, D. (1970) "Transitions to Democracy: Toward a Dynamic Model," *Comparative Politics*, 2: 337–363.

Sadiki, L. (2002) "Bin Ali's Tunisia: Democracy by Non-democratic Means," *British Journal of Middle Eastern Studies*, 29(1): 43–60.

Schwedler, J. (2005) "Cop Rock: Protest, Identity, and Dancing Riot Police in Jordan," *Social Movement Studies*, 4: 155–175.

Schwedler, J. and L. Chomiak (2006) "And the Winner Is … Authoritarian Elections in the Arab World," *Middle East Report*, 238.

Scott, J. (1985), *Weapons of the Weak: Everyday Forms of Peasant Resistance*, New Haven: Yale University Press.

Scott, J. (1990) *Domination and the Arts of Resistance: Hidden Transcripts*, New Haven: Yale University Press.

Contesting order in Tunisia 93

Seligman, A. (1992) *The Idea of Civil Society*, New York: The Free Press.

Shils, E. (1997) *The Virtue of Civility*, Liberty Fund Press.

Singerman, D. (1995) *Avenues of Participation: Family, Politics, and Networks in Urban Quarters in Cairo*, Princeton: Princeton University Press.

Slyomovics, S. (2005) *The Performance of Human Rights in Morocco*, Philadelphia: University of Pennsylvania Press.

Stone, R. (1982) "Tunisia: A Single Party System Holds Change in Abeyance," in I. W. Zartman (ed.) *Political Elites in Arab North Africa: Morocco, Algeria, Tunisia, Libya, and Egypt*, New York: Longman.

Tarrow, S. (1996) "Making Social Science Work Across Time and Space: A Critical Reflection on Robert Putnam's Making Democracy Work," *American Political Science Review*, 90: 389–397.

Wedeen, L. (1999) *Ambiguities of Domination: Politics, Rhetoric, and Symbols in Contemporary Syria*, Chicago: University of Chicago Press.

Wedeen, L. (2008) *Peripheral Visions: Publics, Power and Performance in Yemen*, Chicago: University of Chicago Press.

Zubaida, S. (2001) "Community and Democracy in the Middle East," in S. Kaviraj and S. Khilnani (eds.) *Civil Society: History and Possibilities*, New York: Cambridge University Press.

6 Voice, not democracy

Civil society, ethnic politics, and the search for political space in Central Asia

Matteo Fumagalli

Introduction

Over the past decade popular uprisings have led to the ousting of authoritarian regimes in post-communist Eurasia and more recently in North Africa and the Middle East. Democratic breakthroughs in Serbia (2000), Georgia (2003), Ukraine (2004), and Kyrgyzstan (2005) were accompanied by an authoritarian backlash in countries such as Russia, Belarus, and Uzbekistan. Kyrgyzstan itself soon turned into a brutal authoritarian regime under Kurmanbek Bakiev, until that regime crumbled in April 2010. The real or exaggerated role played by both domestic and international NGOs in this process has made the study of civil society and its assumed relationship with democratisation timely once again. Authoritarian regimes across the post-Soviet space have responded to the 'revolutions' by cracking down on civil society organisations, leaving an increasingly narrow space for autonomous political action. As a result of these crackdowns, civil society organisations have increasingly turned to less politically sensitive issues, such as health, migration, and poverty reduction. Democracy and overt democracy promotion now appear to be off the agenda for civil society groups in the region.

This chapter examines the case of ethnic minority politics as a vantage point from where to examine the development of state–(civil) society relations in post-Soviet Central Asia. It shows how ethnic minority groups in Central Asia have used the spaces allowed by authoritarian governments to carve themselves a public, though not necessarily political, role. Understanding the interplay between civil society and ethnic politics in Central Asia is important for two reasons. First of all the topic remains an empirically under-researched issue and second and probably more significantly civil society organisations in the region show that what they are after is '*voice, not choice*'.

By focusing on the public engagement of members of the Uzbek community in Kyrgyzstan and Tajikistan, where this forms a sizeable minority, the chapter makes the following contributions to the understanding of civil society under authoritarian rule. First, the chapter shows that a study of civil society in Central Asia should move away from a narrow focus on formal associations and pay

Voice, not democracy 95

more attention to a looser and more individualised participation in other organisations. Second, ethnic minority groups make an instrumental use of the opportunities to engage outside the state, but not against the state. Rather than seeking involvement in official state-sanctioned ethnic cultural organisations, some elements within ethnic communities have sought alternative spaces for becoming publicly engaged without becoming too closely aligned with the state (in fact, trying to retain some autonomy from it).

This largely disorganised, non-institutionalised, and informal galaxy of civil society activism is providing ethnic minority groups with a more complex and nuanced view of state–group and state–society relations, where official organisations claiming to represent the 'authentic voice' of the community are being challenged. Finally, the search for space and voice should not be confused with a search for choice, and therefore earlier assumptions in the literature that greater public engagement would be conducive to democratisation should be carefully reconsidered.

After the 'coloured revolutions': civil society and the authoritarian backlash in post-communist Eurasia

The post-Soviet coloured revolutions that ousted authoritarian regimes on the wave of popular protests against electoral frauds in Georgia, Ukraine, and Kyrgyzstan (and in Serbia before them) brought the question about the role played by civil society organisations in such events to the attention of policymakers, practitioners, and academics. In the spotlight was not just the role that local NGOs[1] may have played in organising and mobilising protesters, but also their ties with western organisations and donors. The 'transnational nexus' behind those events (i.e. the link between local and western NGOs) may have overall been overstated (Herd, 2005); McFaul, for example, does not consider foreign support and funding a precondition of the revolutions (2005, 2007). At the same time the possible link between civil society and democratisation and regime change has not gone unnoticed by the local rulers. For fear of being ousted in the guise of their neighbours, a number of post-Soviet leaders (Belarus's Lukashenko, Uzbekistan's Karimov, and Russia's Putin) swiftly mounted a 'pre-emptive strike', seeking to make the local environment non-conducive to analogous dynamics (Hale, 2005, 2006; D'Anieri, 2006). The case of Uzbekistan is a case in point: despite the fact that no coloured revolution was ever even a remote possibility the government virtually eliminated all civil society, leaving legal space only for GONGOs ('governmental non-governmental organizations') or NGOs created, funded, and controlled by the state.[2]

The authoritarian fight-back that has marked political developments in the region since 2003 has seen not only a crackdown on civil society organisations, but also a decisive shift – imposed by a narrowing opportunity structure and the perceived risks associated with the pursuit of an overtly political agenda – towards less political (and therefore less risky) issues. Civil society organisations have increasingly turned to health, migration, and poverty reduction in order to

96   *M. Fumagalli*

escape government interference and ensure security (even physical) of their members.

The Central Asian republics well illustrate the renewed vigour of authoritarianism, after hopes of reform and liberalisation were dashed at various moments in time during the 1990s and 2000s. At present, the entire region is home to more or less consolidated forms of authoritarianism. More to the point, the regimes all exert increasingly tight controls on the activities of civil society organisations. At the same time there is another, surprising, and thus far neglected aspect of Central Asian civil society, which offers a more nuanced and to some extent less bleak picture of the region: ethnic politics. The story this study tells is not one of organisations working towards the achievement of democratic goals or working by democratic means. Quite the contrary, the ethnic cultural organisations are, in their own ways, 'microcosms of repressions', where different individuals compete for state attention and resources. To this end, they try to marginalise and silence potential challengers and competitors. However, and here lies the 'glimmer of hope', members of ethnic minority groups have become increasingly involved in other (non-state related) civil society organisations in large part because of the narrow spaces available for autonomous voices.

While civil society is also host to opposition politics (Islamist organisations in some particular regions of Central Asia do run schools and hospitals), this phenomenon remains marginal, albeit of growing popularity. What is more evident is the instrumental use that ethnic minority groups make of the opportunities to engage *outside the state, but not against the state*. Rather than seeking involvement in official (state-sanctioned, though not state-supported) ethnic cultural organisations, some elements within ethnic communities have sought alternative spaces for becoming publicly engaged without becoming too closely aligned with the state. In fact, they try to retain some autonomy from it. This has resulted in an intra-community process of contestation of the official organisations. At the same time, and in line with what other contributions in this volume also find, the outcome of greater engagement has often been more a search for voice, rather than choice. The chapter concentrates on the cases of ethnic politics and civil society activism in Kyrgyzstan and Tajikistan as these provide rather similar cases to observe how minority groups in multi-ethnic societies and (soft) authoritarian states carve themselves spaces in the public realm. Data are drawn from several research visits made to those two countries between 2003 and 2009. Methods used to collect data include individual interviews with leaders and ordinary members and activists of ethnic cultural organisations, and 'ordinary citizens' of Uzbek ethnicity, and a small-scale survey of the views of ordinary Uzbeks living in Kyrgyzstan and Tajikistan, conducted in 2003. First the chapter provides some background to ethnopolitics in Central Asia, before turning to the empirical section which provides a nuanced assessment of public engagement and social activism within Kyrgyzstan and Tajikistan's largest non-titular community, the Uzbeks.

Ethnic politics in Central Asia

In the early 1990s the five post-Soviet Central Asian republics (Kazakhstan, Kyrgyzstan, Tajikistan, Turkmenistan, and Uzbekistan) showed a remarkable degree of diversity in terms of the way in which they tackled issues of political and economic transformation in the early post-Soviet period. Turkmenistan showed immediate reluctance to undertake any sort of change, and embarked upon a path of isolationism and neo-Sultanism (Bohr, 2003). Tajikistan soon descended into civil war (1992–97) at the end of which the country existed only on paper (Akiner, 2001). Uzbekistan claimed to follow its own 'Uzbek path', marked by gradualism and obtained alternate success in both political stability and economic development (Ruziev *et al.*, 2007). Kazakhstan and especially Kyrgyzstan embarked on political and economic reforms (Pomfret, 2006). Gradually, however, they all converged towards one kind or another of authoritarianism (Cummings 2002; Collins 2006). Apart from Soviet institutional, cultural, and economic legacies, what the five Central Asian republics shared was a lack of a prior experience of independent statehood, a weak sense of national identity, and the presence of sizeable ethnic minorities. Tajikistan and Kyrgyzstan have been the two Central Asian countries more open, though not necessarily receptive to international action, in the form of aid, democracy assistance, and post-conflict reconstruction/conflict prevention. Thus, if international action were to have any effect on the domestic political system and local society, these are the two countries where we should expect it.

Although authoritarian regimes are often associated with an idea of a strong state because of the regime's hold on the means of coercion and the frequent resort to repression, Kyrgyzstan and Tajikistan have often been referred to as the 'weak(est) links' of Central Asian statehood ('un-integrated states', according to Adamson, 2002). As noted above, Tajikistan resembled a failed state during the civil war which destroyed the country's social fabric, national and local institutions, and killed up to 100,000 people, leaving another million either domestically or internationally displaced. The roots of the civil war are complex and multi-faceted, and a mono-causal explanation fails to capture the different dynamics operating at different levels. Several cleavages divided Tajik society and factions organised around them: regional and geographic, of course, but also ideological, for instance between Islamic and democratic factions, and more Sovietised ones. Though the war never took ethnic tones, it was also about defining what being Tajik meant. A critical reason for the outbreak of hostilities lay in the failure of government and opposition to moderate and accommodate their respective demands following the withdrawal of the external arbiter (Moscow), on whose support the northern Leninabadi faction had relied for ensuring its dominance in local politics since the 1940s.

Kyrgyzstan experienced inter-communal conflict on a smaller scale in June 1990. As Pauline Jones Luong notes, 'regional identities, regionally-based actors, preferences, and conceptualizations of power and power relations' characterised Soviet Kyrgyzstani politics (2002: 2). In Kyrgyzstan two parallel types

98 *M. Fumagalli*

of competition can be identified: inter-regional, between northern and southern factions, and intra-regional, between northern groups (Jones Luong, 2002: 76). Regional divisions were reinforced by Soviet policies of economic specialisation, with an industrial north and an agricultural south, and cadre recruitment policies. This led to competition between regional elites for the control of the centre and in return the dependency of the centre on the periphery. Kyrgyz from various clans and regions 'competed for dominance' (Jones Luong, 2002: 81). Apart from intra-Kyrgyz competition, Kyrgyzstan was also home to dozens of ethnic groups, some of which, like Russians in the north and Uzbeks in the south, were particularly sizeable, and these came to expect shares in political and economic rewards in return for support. Uzbeks, Jones Luong observes, traditionally occupied key places in the agriculture and water ministries. If on the one hand Soviet authorities fostered inter-regional political conflict, they also made regional solidarity possible, particularly in the south where Uzbeks and Kyrgyz shared not only cultural traits, but also political and economic interests, such as limiting the dominance of northern groups. However, these commonalities did not prevent the outbreak of riots between Uzbeks and Kyrgyz in the southern Kyrgyzstani towns of Osh and Uzgen in June 1990. Towards the end of the 1980s a conjuncture of socio-economic crisis, decreasing living standards, and political destabilisation led to the eruption of inter-group tensions over the competition for resources (land lots), lack of housing, and control over power structures (Tishkov, 1995: 135). Mass riots broke out on 4 June and were 'extinguished' on 10 June 1990 only after the armed forces intervened and a state of emergency was declared in the republic. The possible triggering factors of the riot are multiple, including the KGB's covert role, and links between political factions and mafia-like economic groups. Perceptions of losses in both socio-economic status and in political influences resulting from the political changes (related to the distribution of political positions between regional clans) probably played a bigger role as triggers for conflict. What is certain is that, regardless of the real or imagined causes, the Osh conflict left long-lasting scars among the local population. The Osh conflict inevitably brought to the attention of political elites the centrality of inter-ethnic stability for the viability of the country. It also provided a window of opportunity for a political outsider and compromise candidate to emerge as president in October 1990: Askar Akaev.

Akaev managed to defuse tensions and maintained a careful balance between factions, ethnic groups, and clans. A turn to authoritarian practices since 1993 marked the changing of Akaev from an outsider to the system to insider, interested in the consolidation of power and relying on increasingly narrower power bases. Though supportive of the Akaev regime till the very end (Akaev was ousted during the so-called Tulip Revolution in March–April 2005), Uzbeks have grown increasingly discontented with the lack of representation in governing bodies and the lack of response to cultural demands (Spector, 2004: 12).

Voice, not democracy 99

Structuring ethnic politics: an ever smaller space for autonomous action

The party system in both Kyrgyzstan and Tajikistan is under-developed at best. Political parties are formed and disappear regularly, and are typically top-down creatures of a single political leader. Although the president's party (Ak Zhol and the People's Democratic Party of Tajikistan respectively) tends to be present across the country, this is the exception rather than the rule. Political parties appear to be personalised, ideologically vaguely defined, and with a territorially weak presence (Akiner, 2001: 64–72; Abazov, 2003: 559). Similarly to their fellow citizens belonging to the titular group, there seems to be very little inclination among the Uzbek elite to join political parties. Minority groups have progressively been sidelined from political and party life, with political parties and organisations becoming progressively Kyrgyz organisations, that is, with Kyrgyz having the only serious chances to acquire senior positions, thus contributing to Uzbek and Russian frustration. According to Tajikistan's 'National Policy Concept' (2002) the state 'provides the possibility for the national minorities to participate in the public administration', but in the 2000–2005 Majlisi Milli (higher chamber of the parliament) ethnic minorities accounted for 9 per cent of the seats (three seats out of thirty-four, one each for Russians, Uzbeks – from the Nau district, in the northern Sughd province – and Kyrgyz), despite the fact that one in five citizens are not ethnic Tajik. Additionally, in the northern Sughd province non-Tajik presence rises to ca. 40 per cent, of which the near totality is Uzbek. The situation in Kyrgyzstan is analogous. The national parliament (Jogorku Kenesh) during the legislature from 2000 to 2005 included only four Uzbek deputies, down from eight present in the previous legislature. Overall, even the 1995–2000 legislature hardly reflected the country's ethnic composition, where 41 per cent of the population (non-Kyrgyz) won as little as 19 per cent of seats. At local level Uzbek representation appears more problematic than in Tajikistan. In Kyrgyzstan, though there are Uzbek deputies in the city and provincial assemblies, no Uzbeks in senior positions can be found in the southern provinces.[3] By the mid-1990s Uzbeks occupied less than 5 per cent of key posts in provincial administrations (Dave, 2004: 145). At the same time the fact that no Uzbek party exists should not suggest that representation of Uzbek interests is non-existent in those two countries (Fumagalli, 2007).

Uzbek activism and ethno-politics

This section discusses two examples of Uzbek public engagement; in the first case official ethnic cultural organisations are examined. Although these would not fall under the category of civil society according to western understanding of civil society because of their close links with the state, it seems appropriate to look at them because according to local laws these are considered public associations and are not – at least officially – state or state-funded entities. In the second case the Uzbeks who do not wish to be associated with those organisations are examined.

100 M. Fumagalli

This will provide a more diverse and nuanced picture of how Uzbeks become socially active in contemporary Central Asia, despite the presence of strong institutional constraints.

The Uzbek ethnic cultural organisations

Kyrgyzstan is home to two organisations established to promote Uzbek cultural interests: the National-Cultural Centre (*O'zbek Milliy Madaniyat Markazi* in Uzbek, *Uzbekskii Natsional'nyi Kul'turnyi Tsentr'* in Russian) and the Society of Uzbeks (*O'zbeklar Jamiyati*), whereas there is only one cultural organisation among Tajikistan's Uzbeks: the Society of Uzbeks (known by its Russian name, *Obshchestvo Uzbekov*).

The National Cultural Centre (UNCC) is the Uzbek community's official voice in Kyrgyzstan, given the lack of Uzbek political parties and the practical lack of political representation of the Uzbek community in Kyrgyzstani formal politics. It is also the older of the two groups, as it was established in September 1990 in the aftermath of the Osh conflict. It is structured along regional lines and the association is coordinated at a national level in Bishkek. Along with other minority cultural centres it is represented in the Assembly of the People of Kyrgyzstan, the organ set up by former president Askar Akaev as a non-party political institution giving voice to the country's many ethnic minority groups. The Society of Uzbeks was founded in 1996–97 by the Osh-based businessman and politician Davron Sabirov, then leader of the UNCC, in order to create an organisation that would appear less closely associated with state authorities that were perceived as increasingly unresponsive to Uzbek demands. Davron Sabirov is probably the closest Osh has to a media tycoon (he owns a local Uzbek-language Mezon newspaper and, until 2004, Mezon TV, also broadcasting in Uzbek). In 1996 Davron Sabirov was nominated chair of the UNCC, which he intended to rename 'Society of Uzbeks' and re-position it as less openly supportive of state authorities in order to break away from the official denomination and thus broaden the appeal of the organisation and make it more inclusive of the broader Uzbek community.[4]

Even in Tajikistan, the task of promoting and representing Uzbek interests has so far been appropriated by the local national cultural centre. Established in September 1990 under the denomination of 'Cultural Centre of Uzbeks of Tajikistan', it re-named itself in 1992. The Society of Uzbeks has branches in Dushanbe, Khujand, and the Sughd region (established in 1991), Qurghonteppa, Penjikent, and the Khatlon region. The Society of Uzbeks was founded and has been chaired for most of the past decade by Mr Qurbon Sattarov, a former Komsomol' (Communist Youth) and party executive (Asia-Plus, 1996). Similarly to its counterpart in Kyrgyzstan the goals of the organisation are 'to promote the interests of ethnic Uzbeks and [also] to promote ethnic co-operation'. The Society aims primarily at achieving 'political stability, overcoming the effects of the period of stagnation, protection of rights and interests of the Uzbek and Uzbek-speaking population, strengthening the centuries-long friendship between

Voice, not democracy   101

Tajiks and Uzbeks, and other ethnic groups of Tajikistan' (Asia-Plus, 1996). More practically, the Society is mainly concerned with cultural issues, most notably in the educational field (provision of textbooks, literature, and staff for Uzbek pupils). The Society of Uzbeks does not depend on state funding, but derives its budget from individual donations and revenues from events such as music festivals or other public activities.[5] Similarly to other cultural organisations (coordinated at national level by the Congress of the Peoples of Tajikistan), it has very close relations with state authorities. The organisation advocates good relations with the administration and with President Emomali Rahmon in particular. In fact, support for the state administration is among the topics any respondent from the organisation regularly emphasises. 'We do not side with the opposition.' 'We support the administration.'

Differences between the Uzbek ethnic organisations in Kyrgyzstan and Tajikistan exist when it comes to their functioning, organisational isomorphism aside (all ethnic cultural organisations tend to look the same across the former Soviet Union). The UNCC in Kyrgyzstan has a capillary presence throughout most of the country, or at least in those areas where Uzbeks are concentrated. Although the regional branches can organise autonomously, the Bishkek office exercises functions of coordination and leadership, setting the main guidelines and strategy. The occasion for delineating such a strategy is the Kurultai, where representatives from all centres and sections gather in what resembles more a display of loyalty to the administration[6] than a forum for strategic discussions. The other Uzbek organisation, the Society of Uzbeks, is by constrast concentrated in the south only, particularly in the city of Osh, as this is where Davron Sabirov's activities and even business are centred. The Uzbek organisation in Tajikistanhas has gone through a process of fragmentation along regional and sub-regional lines, partly as a consequence of the civil war.

Both organisations claim to be dealing with cultural issues and demands. Members of the UNCC systematically underscore how politics lies beyond the scope of the organisation. These statements are highly problematic, for a number of reasons. First, the leading figures of these groups are also well-known politicians, active at both local and national level. Even those who most vehemently reject any political involvement (i.e. Kadyrjan Batyrov, founder and head of the Batyrov University in Jalalabat and among the wealthiest individuals in the country) find it hard to convincingly portray themselves as non-political. Mr Batyov is a leading figure of the Jalalabat UNCC, has hosted repeated conferences of the UNCC, and has created his own institutions providing higher education to Uzbek students. This is politics in all but name and he was later elected deputy in the 2000 parliamentary elections. The organisation itself (UNCC) is represented in a national institution (Assembly of the People of Kyrgyzstan).

Rather than becoming a locus of 'opposition politics' like civil society organisations in other parts of the world, ethnic cultural organisations have sided with state authorities and maintained this strategy throughout the whole post-independence period. In fact, one of the defining elements of the newly established Uzbek cultural centre was the concern for stability and inter-ethnic

102 M. Fumagalli

harmony. This appeared as a particularly pressing issue in the early 1990s, following the Osh events. Also, this strategy serves the purpose of countering the belief that Uzbeks in the south of the country had an agenda aiming at a land swap or outright defection to neighbouring Uzbekistan. The fear among Kyrgyzstani authorities that Uzbeks in the south might play the role of a 'fifth column' never actually vanished, despite the Uzbek community's commitment to the state-building project of the Kyrgyzstani state under President Akaev. The representatives of the organisation do not conceal that they share and fully support the administration's goal of a stable multi-ethnic state built on peaceful relations between the more than a hundred ethnic groups living in the country. Uzbek leaders appropriate President Akaev's slogan of 'Kyrgyzstan is our common home' and share his concern that 'preserving civic peace is the most important goal, more critical than surviving cold and famine' (Slovo Kyrgyzstana, 2004). Almost every conversation with members of the UNCC starts with the sentence: 'We fully support the goals of the state's leadership.' The next sentence was a statement of self-positioning in the power struggle taking place in Kyrgyzstan since independence: 'We do not have anything to do with the Kyrgyz opposition.' Support for the president has become not a means to achieve a specific objective, but a strategy per se, indeed one of the defining characteristics of the official Uzbek cultural centres. As Eugene Huskey has defined it (2002), this has become an 'act of faith' in the capacity of the Kyrgyzstani leadership to maintain inter-ethnic stability.

Uzbek politics in Kyrgyzstan has traditionally been dominated by the *Oshliklar* (people from Osh). Only since the unfolding of the Tulip Revolution in 2005 has the balance of power been challenged by Jalalabat, also in the south, and located a few hours' drive from Osh. The extent to which the Uzbek population played an active role in the 2005 events is highly disputed (Saipjanov, 2005; Saipov, 2005). The initial involvement of southern political elites, including Kurmanbek Bakiev, then elected president in July 2005, who is originally from the southern village of Suzak, an area of compact Uzbek settlement, and of Uzbek leaders (Anvar Artykov was briefly named governor of the Osh region from March to December 2005) seemed to herald a new era in state–community relations. Soon thereafter, instead, the situation took a turn for the worse. Artykov was forced to leave his post and in January 2006 the Jalalabat Uzbek Cultural Centre (headed by the local businessman, philanthropist, and patron Kadyrjan Batyrov) sent a petition to the state authorities pointing to the rise in anti-Uzbek discrimination following the 2005 events (Rotar, 2007).

A re-alignment of political actors has indeed followed, with older authority figures discredited by their association with the previous regime (Mamasaidov and Alisher Sabirov) and challenged by new competitors for leadership. The fate of yet another Uzbek authority figure epitomises the contradictions that followed the so-called Tulip Revolution as well as the Uzbek population's unease and ambivalence towards it. Despite depicting himself as a 'revolutionary' and heading to Moscow to receive the resignation letter from Askar Akaev, Kadyrjan

Voice, not democracy 103

Batyrov soon 'retreated' to safer patron–client relations with his loyal constituency in the southern city of Jalalabat.

Searching for voice – Uzbeks beyond officialdom

Official Uzbek leaders are seen as too closely cooperative with the state authorities. The perception of state institutions as ineffective and undemocratic tends therefore to extend to whoever is seen as cooperating too closely with them. Leaders and organisations by extension are seen as self-referential power groups, who owe their legitimacy more to the state administration than the community of whose interests they are allegedly representing. What emerges is the impression that ordinary Uzbeks do not feel the need for this type of organisation. This is not so much for its perceived inefficacy (this appears of little relevance, given that all public institutions are seen in the same light), but due to doubts concerning its very use and purpose, as the data from the survey below show.[7]

In the case of Tajikistan only one in three respondents considers the Society of Uzbeks as either effective or very effective (Table 6.1). About two in five respondents consider it 'not very effective'. In the case of Kyrgyzstan perceptions were investigated with respect to the two competing organisations operating in the country (the Society of Uzbeks is based in Osh only, whereas the UNCC has a capillary presence in most provinces). Both organisations are perceived as 'not very effective' by about half the respondents (Tables 6.1 and 6.2).

The impression is that although there is a growing awareness that perhaps alternative means of advancing the community's interests should be researched and developed, for the time being cultural organisations are still very much taken for granted. This also hints at the fact that most people wonder whether there is

Table 6.1 How effective is the UNCC in dealing with Uzbek-related issues?

	Kyrgyzstan	*Tajikistan*
Very effective	4.3	0.8
Effective	20.0	34.2
Not very effective	49.6	41.7
Don't know	26.1	24.2

Table 6.2 How effective is the Society of Uzbeks in dealing with Uzbek-related issues (Kyrgyzstan only)?

	Kyrgyzstan
Very effective	7.1
Effective	27.4
Not very effective	47.8
Don't know	17.7

104 *M. Fumagalli*

any purpose at all in having this type of organisation, particularly given their close ties to state authorities. Uzbek cultural organisations are by no means exhaustive of the positions of the Uzbek community in either state; rather they seem to monopolise the access to state attention and (limited) resources and de facto preventing other actors – potential challengers – from entering the political arena. In both Kyrgyzstan and Tajikistan there are voices which remain unheard, because of lack of means for airing them or because those actors are not keen on becoming more closely involved in and exposed to the political struggle. In the pages below the (com)positions of three groups which tend to dissociate themselves very strongly from the two official organisations are illustrated: Uzbek women, young male intellectuals, and local journalists working as 'local experts' and consultants to NGOs and IGOs.

Uzbek women. Uzbek women appear particularly active in civil society in Kyrgyzstan and less so in Tajikistan, a much more traditional society where women occupy a less public and thus less visible role. By Uzbek women the reference is not to a discrete group: they do not constitute a cohesive social group or coalesce around any one organisation. Many among them work as journalists for independent newspapers, but also occupy leading positions in local NGOs, in the judiciary, or as private businesswomen. The group appears particularly lively, especially when compared with the static male-dominated official organisations. Aziza Yo'ldasheva, a successful businesswoman in Osh, when asked whether she thought Uzbeks were passive or apathetic, replied by emphasising that:

> I do not think Uzbeks are passive. You can find Uzbeks at any level in Osh. Of course, they are not many, but if you think that the chair of the Osh Regional Parliament is Uzbek [Isabaeev], the speaker of the city parliament is Uzbek [Azimov], the rector of the Kyrgyz-Uzbek University is Uzbek, then you see that Uzbeks are more or less everywhere.

However, she added, while representation per se does not constitute a problem, Uzbeks do not occupy key positions endowed with decision-making power:

> Uzbeks are not in positions of power, that is the problem. I do not feel any pressure, though. If you are capable and show initiative, no-one will bother you then, whether you are Uzbek, Kyrgyz, man or woman. If you show initiative, you can succeed.[8]

This is mainly due, she pointed out, to the self-referential nature of Uzbek organisations, who are mainly concerned with showing how close they are to state authorities without actually benefiting from this closeness. Though she made clear that becoming the leader of an Uzbek organisation did not rank high in her priorities and that she was content with her own work at a local NGO alongside her private business, Aziza clearly referred to the more general condition of

Uzbek women, who are often limited by the constraining psychological barriers of traditional Uzbek *mahallas* (neighbourhood communities). Other Uzbek women, like Aziza and Ba'rno, both employed in the local judiciary in Osh as public defendants, share similar views. They note how the number of Uzbeks working in the judiciary is low, but emphasise that no-one has given them any problem, either as women or as Uzbek.

> I am interested in politics and I follow current affairs. I have always done since when I was a leader in the Komsomol. But look at the two organisations in Osh: they talk and talk between themselves, but ... who is listening? They are very far from the community, they do not represent their needs or demands.[9]

In general, this group tends to show more optimism in terms of the prospects for Uzbek involvement in public life. If anything, Uzbek women tend to be more critical of the constraints coming from within the ethnic community. In this regard they frequently note how the current leadership is totally self-referential, with the goal of preserving its privileged status, and subsequently marginalising any possible challengers.

Nationalist intellectuals. A second social group that has had its voice marginalised by the hegemony of the two Uzbek organisations is that comprising 'more nationalist-oriented intellectuals' and includes cultural elites, namely academics and students. In Kyrgyzstan the positions of this group overlapped with those advocated by Mr Davron Sabirov before his election to the Jogorku Kenesh (Parliament) in 2000. Following his moderation, this group has found itself essentially 'without voice'. Although no-one openly goes as far as to advance autonomist or even separatist claims, there seems to be no love lost for either Kyrgyzstan's leadership or Uzbekistan's leadership. Typically this group involves academics and students at Osh State University's Pedagogical and Uzbek Philology Departments, arguably the departments where the number of Uzbek students is highest. The issues on the agenda are generally the same as those of any other 'constituency' referred to above, such as education, representation, language status. The tone, however, is remarkably different and decisively more confrontational: 'Mamasaidov [the UNCC leader] is a Kyrgyz. He is not Uzbek. Why does a Kyrgyz lead an Uzbek organization? Of course we can't expect anything from him.'[10]

This way of dismissing the political opponent by depicting him as the 'ethnic other' is strikingly similar to the approach of an analogously nationalist fringe of intellectuals in northern Tajikistan. This group does not plan to enter the political arena, and given their position it would not be difficult to envisage problems both in registering their candidates and during the electoral campaign (see events during Sabirov's campaign in 2000). However, it would be incorrect to dismiss this group as the typical fifth column of a kin state. Komil, a young graduate from Osh University and local journalist, makes no secret of his distaste for Uzbekistan's president Karimov's policies. It is noteworthy to observe that while

Akaev tends to be referred to as weak, comments are not so magnanimous when it comes to Uzbekistan's president. Despite the frequent reference to the common cultural ties existing between Uzbeks on either side of the border, no sign of separatism or even request for autonomy has emerged.

A similar group of peoples is also present in Tajikistan. This group also comprises members of the local cultural elites. Though it would be incorrect to consider this as a cohesive, let alone organised or institutionalised, group, it resembles a small network of like-minded people who tend to meet regularly and maintain their own internal dynamic. The grouping is informal as there is no official leader or any sign of a structure, making it difficult to assess its size or even its broader impact on Uzbeks settled outside the main urban centre of Khujand.

Local intellectuals are very critical of the current Uzbek leadership and official representatives in general, which they see as 'feeble, weak, and complacent with authorities'. They are seen as 'too loyal and puppets in the hands of the administration' and, above all, 'largely ineffective'.[11] The closeness of 'self-proclaimed Uzbek leaders' to state authorities has brought no benefit to the community, the argument goes. In essence the official representatives of the Uzbek community are regarded as detrimental to Uzbek interests because 'they are not really Uzbek'. Hence they should be replaced. Depicting political opponents in ethnic terms excludes them from the Uzbek community and questions their legitimacy as representatives. What this marginal group seems to be engaged in is building a stereotype of the current Uzbek representatives as 'non Uzbek', 'selling out Uzbek interests to state authorities': '[The current chair of the Sughd branch of the Society of Uzbeks] Pulatov is not really Uzbek, you know. He is Tajik. His sons are all married to Tajik girls.'[12] This type of comment involves even deputies at Parliament in Dushanbe. Asked to comment on the effectiveness of Uzbek deputies: '[Deputy to the Majlisi Oli from the town of Nau] Zulfiya Isakova? We are not going to say anything about her [showing contempt]! Besides, she is not Uzbek at all!'[13]

'Experts'. A third and final group on the fringes of the debate within the Uzbek community is the one situated somewhere in the middle between the members of the official organisation and the radical intellectuals. The dynamics, strategies, and beliefs of this group can be illustrated by referring to the paradigmatic example of (the late) Mirzo Khakim, then editor of the Uzbek newspaper *Tong* (Dawn) in Khujand. Mirzo showed no interest whatsoever in active political life:

> What does the 'Society' do? Nothing. They publish one newspaper [Kadriyat]. And do you know who reads that newspaper? No-one, because it is boring. It has four pages, but there is nothing to read. It is true that there is no information available in Uzbek. But if you want Uzbeks to read, then give them something interesting, at least![14]

Mirzo-aka tended to avoid openly discussing state policy and focuses mostly on the lack of initiative (*inertiya*) shown from the Uzbek community. The case

Voice, not democracy 107

of Mirzo-aka and the Tong newspaper's journalists[15] is also representative of the complexities and contradictions associated with the sudden arrival of NGOs in a society where previously there were none. Conversations with Mirzo Hakim and local journalists highlight rising expectations from international donors, contributing to the blurring of boundaries between donors, local organisations, and entire communities. This sub-group of the Uzbek elite is developing into the closest thing Tajikistani Uzbeks may have to a lobby. While it may not exert direct pressure on the real decision-maker (the Tajikistani authorities), it does have close relations with a wide range of international organisations, which in turn have a certain degree of leverage on the central government.

Conclusion

This chapter has used the case of ethnic minority politics in authoritarian settings to discuss the development of civil society in post-Soviet Central Asia. It has shown that the members of the local Uzbek community are choosing different types of public engagement. Some have become active in official ethnic cultural organisations, actors that are perceived as closely aligned to the authorities, whose support they seek. Although the emphasis is primarily on cultural actors, the politically sensitive nature of some of the issues at stake (language, education, cross-border relations, and transport) means that the lines between cultural activities and political engagement are blurred at best. These actors have performed two critical functions in the post-independence period: they have distributed services and goods in return for political loyalty at election time and have acted as brokers between their clients and state authorities at the centre.

However, the national-cultural centres are clearly not exhaustive of the positions and preferences of the local Uzbek communities. As official organisations have sought closer ties with the state, ordinary citizens have grown increasingly dissatisfied with such organisations and their leaders' self-referential attitude and authoritarian tendencies (just like the state leadership), and they have sought to carve their own space, autonomous from these actors and potentially from the state too. Thus, rather than seeking involvement in official state-sanctioned ethnic cultural organisations, some elements within ethnic communities have sought alternative spaces for becoming publicly engaged without becoming too closely aligned with the state. This largely disorganised, non-institutionalised, and informal galaxy of civil society activism is providing ethnic minority groups and society as a whole with a more complex and nuanced view of state–group and state–society relations, where official organisations claiming to represent the 'authentic voice' of the community are being challenged. While this process of contestation has shown that ethnic groups have made an effective use of patron–client relations, this has not led to ethnic affiliations being transcended or cross-ethnic coalitions being formed.

An important finding concerns the relationship that civil society organisations have developed with the state. The chapter agrees with McMann where she argues in her study of the civic realm in Kyrgyzstan (2004) that public organisations in

108 M. Fumagalli

Central Asia do not seek autonomy from the state. Quite the contrary, they look for state attention, they compete for it outside formal channels, and they expect state support, be it financial and/or political. What the former shows is the instrumental use that ethnic minority groups make of the opportunities to engage outside the state, but not against the state. For some, however, this seems no longer sufficient. In both countries there is an embryonic space outside state reach and control, where individuals – Uzbeks in this case – who do not wish to work within or with the state are trying to carve themselves the space for doing so. There is something beyond officialdom. However, state suspicion of NGO activities during the coloured revolutions meant that new restrictions have been posed on their activities, and some have turned away from politics towards 'safer' issues. Despite the obvious differences between the two cases, what the cases of Uzbek ethnic politics in Kyrgyzstan and Tajikistan show is that democracy appears less a concern than earlier studies of civil society in post-communist Eurasia had envisaged.

Where does all this leave opposition politics, let alone the push for democratisation? The chapter agrees with Jones Luong and Weinthal who have argued in the case of environmental activism in Kazakhstan (1999) that civil society organisations in Central Asia are less concerned with democratic outcomes than with issues of self-preservation and survival. Oppositional political society may on occasion turn into civil society and preferably human rights organisations, but more often than not the two remain competitive rather than complementary (Stevens, 2007). The 'oppositional landscape' has been essentially hollowed out, paving the way for religious organisations and a-political and single-issue organisations to play a more visible, though not necessarily more effective, role.

Notes

1 I obviously do not assume that NGOs are coterminous with civil society as a whole, but this is the way the two terms are understood (as synonymous) in parts of the post-communist world.

2 See Kandiyoti (2007) and McGlinchey (2009) on GONGOs in Uzbekistan.

3 The only exception was Anvar Artykov, an ethnic Uzbek who was named governor of the Osh province for a short period following the Tulip Revolution in 2005, only to be removed by Bakiev in December that year.

4 Conversations with students at the Department of Uzbek Philology at Osh State University, members of the UNCC from Karasuu, Osh, June–July 2003.

5 Interview with Mr Ismatov (Khujand branch of the Society of Uzbeks), August 2003.

6 Conversation with Mr Adiljan Abidov, former head of the UNCC (Osh, 18 July 2003), the correspondent of the Uzbek newspaper *DDD Ba'rno Isakova* (15 July 2003), and the Osh-based journalist Almaz Ismanov (Osh, June 2003).

7 These data draw from a small-scale survey conducted by the author in both countries in 2003. There are several limitations of the survey that should be noted before proceeding. First is the limited size of the sample (136 in Kyrgyzstan and 137 in Tajikistan). Second is the non-random nature thereof (respondents were identified through snowballing). While one may incur the risk of group thinking as respondents may recommend like-minded people this method is particularly suitable to conducting research on politically sensitive topics.

8 Interview.

9 Interview, Osh, 20 July 2003.

Voice, not democracy 109

10 Interview with Davron Sabirov, Osh, 17 July 2003.
11 Interviews with Uzbek intellectuals (August 2003 and August 2008) in Dushanbe and Khujand.
12 Interview held in Khujand, 10 August 2003.
13 Interview held in Khujand, 25 July 2008.
14 Interviews with Mirzo Hakim, Khujand, August 2003.
15 Interviews held at the *Tong* newspaper, Khujand, 24 July 2008.

References

Abazov, R. (2003) 'The parliamentary elections in Kyrgyzstan, February 2000', *Electoral Studies*, 22: 503–559.
Adamson, F. (2002) 'International democracy assistance in Uzbekistan and Kyrgyzstan: building civil society from the outside?', in S.E. Mendelson and J.K. Glenn (eds) *The Power and Limits of NGOs*, New York, Columbia University Press.
Akiner, S. (2001) *Tajikistan. Disintegration or Reconciliation?* London, RIIA.
Asia-Plus (1996) 'The society of Uzbeks of Tajikistan', 3 May.
Bohr, A. (2003) 'Independent Turkmenistan: from post-communism to sultanism', in S.N. Cummings (ed.) *Oil, Transition, and Security in Central Asia*, London, Routledge, 9–24.
Collins, K. (2006) *Clan Politics and Regime Transition in Central Asia*, Cambridge, Cambridge University Press.
Cummings, S.N. (ed.) (2002) *Power and Change in Central Asia*, London, Routledge.
D'Anieri, P. (2006) 'Explaining the success and failure of post-communist revolutions', *Communist and Post-Communist Studies*, 39: 331–350.
Dave, B. (2004) 'A shrinking reach of the state? Language policy and implementation in Kazakhstan and Kyrgyzstan', in P. Jones Luong (ed.) *The Transformation of Central Asia: States and Societies from Soviet Rule to Independence*, Ithaca, Cornell University Press, 120–155.
Fumagalli, M. (2007) 'Informal (ethno-)politics and local authority figures in Osh, Kyrgyzstan', *Ethnopolitics*, 6: 211–233.
Hale, H.E. (2005) 'Regime cycles: democracy, autocracy, and revolution in post-Soviet Eurasia', *World Politics*, 58: 133–165.
Hale, H.E. (2006) 'Democracy or autocracy on the march? The coloured revolutions as normal dynamics of patronal presidentialism', *Communist and Post-Communist Studies*, 39: 305–329.
Herd, G.P. (2005) 'Colorful revolution and the CIS: "Manufactured" versus "managed" democracy?', *Problems of Post-Communism*, 52: 3–18.
Huskey, E. (2002) 'An economy of authoritarianism: Askar Akaev and presidential leadership in Kyrgyzstan', in S. Cummings (ed.) *Power and Change in Central Asia*, London, Routledge, pp. 74–96.
Jones Luong, P. (2002) *Institutional Change and Political Continuity in Post-Soviet Central Asia*, Cambridge, Cambridge University Press.
Jones Luong, P. and E. Weinthal (1999) 'The NGO paradox: democratic goals and non-democratic outcomes in Kazakhstan', *Europe-Asia Studies*, 51: 1267–1284.
Kandiyoti, D. (2007) 'Post-Soviet institutional design and the paradoxes of the "Uzbek path"', *Central Asian Survey*, 26: 31–48.
Khamidov, A. (2002) 'Ethnic Uzbeks store unrest in southern Kyrgyzstan', *Eurasianet*, 26 June.

110   *M. Fumagalli*

McFaul, M. (2005) 'Transitions from postcommunism', *Journal of Democracy*, 16(3): 5–19.

McFaul, M. (2007) 'Ukraine imports democracy', *International Security*, 32(2): 45–83.

McGlinchey, E. (2009) 'Searching for Kamalot: political patronage and youth politics in Uzbekistan', *Europe-Asia Studies*, 61: 1137–1150.

McMann, K.M. (2004) 'The civic realm in Kyrgyzstan: Soviet economic legacies and activists' expectations', in P. Jones Luong (ed.) *The Transformation of Central Asia. States and Societies from Soviet Rule to Independence*, Ithaca, Cornell University Press, 213–245.

Pomfret, R. (2006) *The Central Asian Economies after Independence*, Princeton, Princeton University Press.

Rotar, I. (2007) 'Kyrgyzstan: ethnic tensions simmer'. *Transitions online*, 28 June, available at www.tol.cz/look/TOL/printf.tpl?IdLanguage=1&IdPublication=4&NrIssue=22 4&NrSection=4&NrArticle=18809&ST1=ad&ST_T1=job&ST_AS1=1&ST2=body&ST_T2=letter&ST_AS2=1&ST3=text&ST_T3=aatol&ST_AS3=1&ST_max=3 (accessed 14 November 2009).

Ruziev, K., D. Ghosh and S.C. Dow (2007) 'The Uzbek puzzle revisited: an analysis of economic performance in Uzbekistan since 1991', *Central Asian Survey*, 26: 7–30.

Saipjanov, A. (2005) 'Uzbeks in Kyrgyzstan view the revolution with caution', *Eurasianet*, 31 March.

Saipov, A. (2005) 'Myth of pro-Akaev Uzbeks shattered', *IWPR*, 364, 30 March.

Slovo Kyrgyzstana (2004) Kuda Uzbeki khotiyat videt' na vershine vlasti? 2 July.

Spector, R.A. (2004) *The Transformation of Askar Akaev, President of Kyrgyzstan*, Berkeley Program in Soviet and post-Soviet Studies, Working Papers Series. Available at http://iseees.berkeley.edu/sites/default/files/u4/bps_/publications_/2004_02-spec.pdf (accessed 14 November 2009).

Stevens, D. (2007) 'Political society and civil society in Uzbekistan – never the twain shall meet?', *Central Asian Survey*, 26: 49–64.

Tishkov, V. (1995) ' "Don't kill me, I'm a Kyrgyz!": an anthropological analysis of violence in the Osh ethnic conflict', *Journal of Peace Research*, 32: 133–149.

7 The influence of civil society activism on regional governance structures in the Russian Federation

Cross-regional and policy comparisons[1]

Karina Mikirova, Kathrin Mueller and Johannes Schuhmann

Introduction

Following the Beslan[2] school hostage crisis in September 2004, the President of Russia Vladimir Putin proposed the creation of a Public Chamber, which was intended to function as a public oversight committee with consultation powers. This body, which was established in 2005 with 126 members, analyses draft legislation and monitors the activities of parliament, government and other governmental bodies of Russia and its Federal Subjects. At the same time new laws on non-governmental organizations (NGOs) have been adopted on the federal[3] and regional level,[4] in order to restructure the interaction between state and non-state actors.

According to the government, the new NGO legislation created the legal basis for NGOs as a new type of actor in the policy arena, enabling them to participate in politics.[5] The Public Chamber, in addition, provides a negotiation platform that involves NGOs in problem solving and in bargaining compromises with state actors. Many observers, however, criticized the legislation as it seemed to tighten the control of the state over NGOs and to create obstacles for negotiations between the state and NGOs (Nußberger and Schmidt 2007). These controversial interpretations raise the question whether state actors really involve NGOs in problem solving and bargaining compromises and why state actors negotiate with NGOs.

Analyses of authoritarian corporatism showed that economically and socially complex states cannot be governed only by technocratic-authoritarian means (Stepan 1978) and that under these conditions authoritarian regimes negotiate politics with societal actors. The literature on governance explains in detail that hierarchical steering causes information problems. This means that decision makers often do not have the required information about the object of their

112   *K. Mikirova* et al.

decision. Thus, the capacity of the state to effectively steer and coordinate society is seriously challenged. Negotiations between stakeholders can provide information and knowledge and can thus enhance the state capacity to solve problems (Scharpf 2000). Nowadays the combination of traditional hierarchical governance and network governance with non-state actors becomes ever more necessary in order to provide state functions, because in modern societies the need for sophisticated information and knowledge is growing constantly (Mayntz 1993).

According to Linz, relations between state and non-state actors in authoritarian states differ, however, from those in democratic ones in that they are limited pluralistic (Linz 2000). Thus, the existence and the leeway of political and societal actors in authoritarian states depend on the authoritarian regime. The state dictates the institutions and procedures for negotiations with non-state actors. This forced institutionalized model of solving conflicts allows for the representation of societal interests while at the same time limiting conflicts. Although the theory of authoritarian corporatism seems to be of great use in understanding why and how state actors involve non-state actors in negotiations in Russian politics, we propose that it does not sufficiently correspond to and explain reality. We claim that NGOs in Russia are nowadays sufficiently powerful to influence whether and how state actors involve them in negotiations.

In order to address the question why and how state actors in Russia involve non-state actors in negotiated governance, we analyse and compare interactions between state and non-state actors in five regions and three policy fields. The chosen cases differ in two ways. First, the interest of state actors to cooperate with NGOs differs depending on the policy field. Second, each policy field is analysed in two regions with different resource distributions among involved actors. The cases are ethnic policy in the Krasnodar and Stavropol regions, social policy in the Perm and Nižnij Novgorod regions and environmental policy in the Krasnodar and Irkutsk regions. The cases were chosen in a way that allows for testing whether the theory of authoritarian corporatism sufficiently explains why and how state actors negotiate with NGOs or whether the resources of NGOs to force the state to involve them in negotiations is a necessary additional contributing cause.

The non-state actors we consider are private business actors and non-governmental organizations (NGOs). The term 'non-governmental organization' describes organizations, linked to civil society. The crucial characteristic is that they are independent of the government, which means autonomous from the state and not oriented to profit-making. They can be differentiated from citizen initiatives and social movements, which often follow close or similar interests by their concrete organizational structure (Nohlen 2002: 324ff.). In our analyses we include NGOs that have an independent articulation of interests, possess differentiated financing, are not profit oriented and have concrete organizational structures.

The following section of the chapter will first introduce the issues at stake in the various cases as well as the interests and resources of the main actors. In the

Civil society activism in Russia 113

second section the interactions between state and non-state actors will be analysed. The chapter concludes with a summary of the findings.

Issues and actors' constellations

The issues in the three policy fields are ethnic tensions among youths in the North Caucasus, accessibility to public buildings for people with limited mobility in the Volga district and ecological disasters and environmental impact assessment at the Sea of Azov and Lake Baikal. These cases differ according to the interest of the state in problem solving and according to the distribution of resources among involved actors.

1 Issues

Ethnic policy

Interethnic conflicts put political stability at risk and ethnic policy, which strives for interethnic stability, is therefore seen as crucial.[6] As young people are the most active participants in interethnic conflicts,[7] education for tolerance and the fight against extremism among youths are important pillars of ethnic policy. Survey data and events in the Stavropol[8] and Krasnodar[9] regions, located in the most unstable district of the Russian Federation, the North Caucasus, show the urgency of solving the problem of interethnic relations among youths. The growth of interethnic tensions among youths is dangerous not only for public security, but has also a tendency to erupt into mass unrest and at times terrorism. The issue discussed between state actors and NGOs in this context is how to maintain interethnic stability among youths in both regions.

Social policy

Within social policy the case focuses on the negotiations between state and non-state actors on "accessibility for the handicapped". Accessibility here means the guarantee for citizens with physical limited mobility[10] to enter public buildings without barriers. Guarantee means that regulations are legally defined *and* implemented. Both the Perm and Nižnij Novgorod regions lack accessibility to all kinds of public buildings[11] and at the same time have an active civil society[12] and NGOs that represent the interests of the handicapped and demand legal guarantees and their implementation.

In Perm all the necessary legislation to solve the issue has been passed,[13] but there are no major improvements in implementation. Thus, the core conflict is about the implementation of existing laws. In Nižnij Novgorod some regulations already exist[14] and one crucial law was negotiated in 2008 and passed in February 2009.[15] In this case, the development of a legal basis for accessibility and the implementation of existing laws and regulations are currently the subjects of negotiations between state actors, NGOs and business actors.

114 *K. Mikirova* et al.

Environmental policy

The cases in environmental policy are negotiations between state and non-state actors concerning major investment projects and the solution of environmental problems in the Krasnodar and Irkutsk regions. The investment projects consist of the construction of an oil extraction platform in the Sea of Azov and ports for oil products on the Taman peninsula, both in the Krasnodar region, as well as an oil pipeline close to the coast of Lake Baikal in the Irkutsk region. The major environmental problem in the Irkutsk region is the Baikalsk pulp and paper mill emitting hazardous and poorly treated sewage directly into Lake Baikal. The ecological problem in the Krasnodar region is a major oil pollution in the Kerch strait following the sinking of several oil tankers in late 2007. Both the investment projects and the environmental disasters pose serious threats to the environment because oil leaking from pipelines and extraction facilities as well as the sewage destabilizes the sensitive ecological systems of Lake Baikal and the Sea of Azov. Both bodies of water are regarded as highly important for the regional, national as well as international community.

2 Actors

Ethnic policy

In both regions the main actors involved in ethnic policy are state entities represented by the regional administrations and the law enforcement bodies[16] and non-state actors represented mostly by 'ethnic' NGOs (EthNGOs), regional scientists on ethnology and business. There are around 85 registered EthNGOs in the Stavropol region and over 120 EthNGOs in the Krasnodar region. Regional ethnologists work on that issue within educational centres, EthNGOs or NGOs. Additional key actors are businessmen who are usually members of EthNGOs and, thus, act within and on behalf of these EthNGOs.

Social policy

In Perm, the main state actors are the regional administration[17] and the regional department of public prosecution. NGOs involved in the negotiations are above all the regional department of the Russian Association for the handicapped (RAH Perm) and, in the background, there are other NGOs for the handicapped and human rights groups. An involved private business actor is the airport administration, which has been confronted by NGOs and the prosecutor's office for violations concerning accessibility in their buildings. The actors in Nižnij Novgorod are the regional administration,[18] the regional prosecution and, different to Perm, the regional board of the tax authorities. The involved NGOs are the regional department of the Russian Association for the handicapped (RAH Nižnij Novgorod) and the organization for invalids *Invatur*, a small, young NGO. As private business actors cinemas and banks are involved in the same manner as in Perm.

Civil society activism in Russia 115

Environmental policy

The main actors in environmental policy are the federal executive actors, primarily the Federal Ministry of Natural Resources and Environmental Protection, the regional administrations, business actors and environmental NGOs (EcoNGOs). There are many EcoNGOs registered in both regions, but only a few of them are active in the cases under scrutiny: six in Krasnodar and two in Irkutsk. Society is only of limited importance, because environmental issues are in most cases of low public concern and with a generally low participatory culture (Ânickij 2007), it is usually impossible for EcoNGOs to mobilize people for environmental problems.

3 Interests

Interests of collective actors are generally "conservation of continuity, autonomy and growth" (Scharpf 2000: 117). However, as these interests depend on the institutional surroundings within which the organization acts (ibid.), transferred to single cases, these interests contain a complex set of individual aspects. We will therefore only consider in detail those interests that influence the policy issue.

Ethnic policy

Interethnic instability is dangerous for regional political, social and economic stability. The above mentioned recent youth interethnic conflicts in the regions showed the urgency of dealing with that issue. Both state and non-state actors agree on the necessity of solving the problem of interethnic tensions among youths. The regional authorities are interested in solving the problem because it is not only their legal competence but it also fosters the stability of their position. After the construction of the "power vertical" in the Russian Federation,[19] governors are directly responsible to the federal authorities for their governance failures. EthNGOs also wish to tackle the problem, as a conflict with an ethnic component has a negative impact on the image of ethnic groups and, thus, on their social status in society. Many EthNGOs have officially declared the aims of maintaining interethnic peace and work with ethnic youths as their main function. Thus, actors agree on their policy goals. Moreover, the actors understand that the problem demands cooperation between state actors and NGOs. State actors underline the need for cooperation in their target programmes,[20] non-state actors reflect the aim to interact with state actors in their regulations. Hence, there is a low level of conflict between actors on that issue. In addition, state and non-state actors attach high priority to cooperate in dealing with ethnic tensions.

Social policy

As in ethnic policy, there is no conflict between state and non-state actors concerning the necessity of accessibility. The discussion is about the priority of this

116 *K. Mikirova* et al.

issue among the involved actors. Therefore, there is a conflict about the way in which accessibility should be implemented. This conflict hinders improvements in both regions. Accessibility is not the highest priority among state actors because they also have to consider the interests of private actors and the expenses for the state, while there is almost no interest for private actors because they have to "spend" money. NGOs, instead, rank accessibility as the highest priority because this is the key obstacle to the integration and participation of the handicapped in work and social life.

There is however a major disparity in interests. These lay in the general attitude of state actors towards civil society and their political participation. Perm state actors are more open to and interested in interaction with NGOs than state actors in Nižnij Novgorod. In Nižnij Novgorod the attitude towards civil society participation is more reserved and distrustful. Interaction should take place in a strictly controlled framework. Thus, there are conflicting interests in Nižnij Novgorod concerning the relation towards civil society in general and the interaction for improving accessibility in particular.

Environmental policy

There is a high level of conflict in environmental policy because the concepts of how environmental policy should be formulated and implemented differ widely among the various actors. The administrations of the examined regions, as well as the federal environmental agencies follow the concept of ecological security, which means that environmental policy should not impede economic growth, but only prevent ecological disasters. Thus, they support huge investment projects in order to discover, extract and transport natural resources (Ânickij 2007). Environmental civil organizations, instead, follow the concept of sustainable development, which calls for a balance of the economic, social and environmental interests of today's and future generations. They demand that Russian environmental law be respected. Business actors have opposing interests. On the one hand most companies do not adhere to corporate social responsibility and try to circumvent environmental laws and regulations, when it is economically beneficial. On the other hand business actors can also use environmental laws and regulations as a mean to compete with other business actors. Thus, the interests of business actors sometimes coincide with those of NGOs when environmental concerns weaken their competitors.

The interest of state actors in problem solving differs considerably between the three policy fields. In ethnic policy the state is highly interested in reducing ethnic tensions and they agree with non-state actors on the urgency to address the problem. In social policy state actors are also interested in accessibility for handicapped people, but it is of low priority, which leaves them in disagreement with NGOs on the pace of addressing the problem. In environmental policy, the state actors are not interested in sustainability. The conflict between state actors and NGOs is very high as a result.

4 Resources

The regions of each policy field are chosen according to the differing resource distribution among the involved actors. Resources are regarded as any mean that helps to accomplish an objective now or in the future (Themudo 2000: 6). They may be institutional, material, informational or organizational resources.

According to Russian legislation, all NGOs have basic institutional resources. They have the right to write petitions, to organize meetings, demonstrations and other legal actions in order to be heard by the authorities and influence decision-making processes. NGOs have the right to participate in policy making within negotiation platforms, such as advisory bodies. EcoNGOs possess for example the right to take part in mandatory Environmental Impact Assessment (EIA) of major investment projects and normative acts with ecological relevance.[21] Thus, EcoNGOs can act as veto players, a major difference as compared to the mainly consulting function of other NGOs, including EthNGOs and social NGOs.

NGOs possess considerable informational and knowledge resources. For example many environmental scientists and academics, as well as former state officials, are engaged in EcoNGOs. They dispose of significant expert knowledge in environment-related sciences, from law to natural and social sciences, as well as broad national and international contacts (Wernstedt 2002). EthNGOs have information about internal processes within a particular ethnic group. With the same mentality and cultural identity, they have knowledge of how to satisfy the interests of an ethnic group, how to solve the problems connected with an ethnic group and how to be heard by an ethnic group. The key resources of NGOs for the handicapped and human rights groups also include information and knowledge resources. Professional experts work on a given problem and are endowed with good skills to use this knowledge.

The NGOs under scrutiny possess financial resources, which derive from various international, national and regional grants as well as from their own economic activities. Financial resources are sufficient to provide for low, but stable income and for most essential equipment. EcoNGOs, for example, engage in consulting ecotourism and receive some international funding. RAH Perm and Nižnij Novgorod have their own companies which provide them with enough material resources to act independently. The NGO *Invatur* in the Nižnij Novgorod region has quite successfully won national and international grants for accessibility projects and is therefore acting independently too. EthNGOs have internal financial funding from businessmen of their ethnic group and membership dues, as well as external financial sources from their ethnic mother countries and international and regional grants. In addition, EthNGOs earn money by consulting migrants and organizing language and dance classes.

NGOs unite people based on the same interests or problems, which give NGOs a manpower resource. EcoNGOs usually consist of two to four core members, and several activists. In the case of social policy, about 10 per cent of Russians are handicapped, which constitutes a potentially powerful resource for

NGOs lobbying for their rights. The problem, however, is that the handicapped in Russia are usually very passive, and relevant NGOs are not able to activate them in significant numbers.[22] EthNGOs possess manpower resources based on the identification of the person to his or her ethnic group. After years of interethnic tensions, the population of the Krasnodar and Stavropol regions can be quickly mobilized along ethnic lines. The degree of manpower of an EthNGO significantly correlates with the number of its ethnic group in the regional population. A regional EthNGO unites formally from a dozen to a hundred people and much more informally, including families of members.

One of the most important resources of NGOs is the idiosyncratic resource, specifically, personal characteristics and the abilities of a NGO's leader. The main idiosyncratic resources for NGOs in social policy are their reputation and personal contacts with state actors. In the Perm region NGOs have access to high-ranking state actors and possess a good reputation due to long-lasting professional cooperation. In Nižnij Novgorod the idiosyncratic resource consists of a long-lasting friendship between the leader of the NGO RAH Nižnij Novgorod and the head of a state agency. This leader has, moreover, many personal contacts and a good relationship with all kinds of state actors as a former staff member of the social ministry and member of the city parliament of Nižnij Novgorod. The main idiosyncratic resource for EthNGOs is popularity and authority of a leader of the EthNGO among the ethnic group and the regional population. Usually EthNGOs are headed by a prominent representative of an ethnic group (scientist, sportsman or businessman).

The ability of NGOs to build coalitions with each other as well as with state and private actors can be viewed as an indirect resource of NGOs. This resource opens additional opportunities for forcing NGO's interests into decision making and depends on the economic and political backgrounds of the regions.

The resources of state actors are pretty much the same in all regions and policy fields. Generally, they are much stronger than NGOs when it comes to institutional, organizational and material resources. Having these resources, the state determines the degree of access of NGOs to advisory bodies and funding. In all policy fields, however, state actors lack other necessary resources, first of all, information, knowledge and manpower. In environmental policy the regional and federal administrative capacities are especially weak, because, following the constant downgrading of environmental institutions and state agencies, they lack institutional and financial resources, sufficient staff and sufficient expertise (Kotov and Nikitina 2002; Wernstedt 2002; OECD 2006). In social policy the authorities claim that they have a shortage of financial resources to fully finance measures of accessibility. Moreover, they lack the technical knowledge of how to reconstruct buildings to make them accessible. In ethnic policy state actors lack the information in order to be well aware about internal processes in the corresponding ethnic group, manpower in order to speak with ethnic groups directly as well as the idiosyncratic resources in order to be heard by ethnic groups.

Resources of NGOs differ among the regions within each policy field. The main differences lie in the material and informational resources of NGOs as well

Civil society activism in Russia   119

as in the possibilities to build coalitions with likeminded actors. In environmental policy EcoNGOs in the Krasnodar region are more powerful than those in Irkutsk because they are able to build coalitions with business actors, which hope to use environmental legislation to fight their competitors. The reason for this difference in coalition building can be found in the differing economic structures of both regions. In resource rich Irkutsk region the resource extracting industry is often the only business in town and thus does not meet competition from other industries. In Krasnodar region the economic structure is rather heterogeneous. It consists of many medium enterprises of various branches – logistic, tourism, agriculture and light industry. Those branches are constantly competing over the right to use resources.

In ethnic policy NGOs from Krasnodar are also more powerful than their fellows from Stavropol. First, NGOs from Krasnodar region demonstrated greater ability to build coalitions with each other. In contrast to the EthNGOs from Stavropol they were able to overcome divisions between and inside EthNGOs and establish an umbrella EthNGO "Centre of Ethnic Culture". This NGO is responsible for representing EthNGOs' interests in state bodies and became a negotiation platform between state and non-state actors on ethnic issues. Additionally, due to the more favourable economic situation in the Krasnodar region[23] most EthNGOs dispose of more financial and organizational resources than in the Stavropol region.

In social policy, NGOs in the Perm region have a greater opportunity to get into contact with state actors and to articulate their interests as well as to negotiate its realization. One reason for this is that the Perm region in comparison to other Russian regions is characterized by a different relation between state actors and opposition groups and NGOs in general. In Perm in the 1990s, NGOs, especially human rights NGOs, succeeded in influencing the political process and gained a positive reputation. This legacy structures interactions between state and non-state actors still today. Human rights activists often opened new channels of communication and negotiation with state actors, which can be used also by NGOs for the handicapped. In Nižnij Novgorod, on the contrary, NGOs face suspicious state actors and getting access is rather difficult.[24]

Thus, the two regions of each policy show a considerable variation in the potential resources of NGOs to influence state actors to engage in negotiations. The main differences lie in the material resources and the reputation of NGOs as well as in their ability to build coalitions with other interested parties.

Negotiations between state and non-state actors in ethnic, social and environmental policies

This section analyses whether and how state actors negotiate with non-state actors. Do state and non-state actors negotiate only in cases where the state wants to solve a problem and therefore needs NGO resources? Does the state dictate the way it negotiates with NGOs? Or are NGOs sufficiently powerful to persuade or force state actors to engage in negotiations?

120   *K. Mikirova* et al.

1 Ethnic policy

In ethnic policy the interest of the regional administrations in solving problems is the highest among the policy fields under scrutiny. State actors admit the utility of EthNGOs in decreasing the interethnic conflict potential of youths and therefore state actors have taken the initiative and created regimes[25] for negotiations with NGOs in order to mobilize the necessary resources. However, only NGOs in Krasnodar were able to persuade the state to intensify negotiations and work on the issue systematically.

In order to address the interethnic tensions in the Stavropol region, the regional administration organized two advisory bodies for ethnic affairs, one reporting to the governor and one reporting to the regional department. The advisory body to the governor was re-established in 2005[26] and is ruled by state officials. This means that state actors head the advisory body, invite the members, set the agenda and hold meetings.[27] The body consists of 28 members, with 16 members from state actors, seven EthNGOs, three scientists and two religious leaders. Meetings are held as often as necessary, which ends up being once a year or even less.

According to official documents the regional administration created the advisory body reporting to the governor in order to provide consultation about the most important social, cultural and educational aspects of life for Stavropol ethnic groups and in order to collect NGOs' proposals on how to maintain interethnic stability in the region.[28] In reality, however, the only role of EthNGOs in these meetings is to increase the legitimacy of state actions in the ethnic sphere. As a result, this advisory body showed its ineffectiveness during the conflict between different ethnic youth groups in May and June 2007 in Stavropol. It could not prevent the conflict and did not emerge as an institutional arrangement for negotiations in the aftermath of the conflict, when intensive negotiations between state actors and EthNGOs took place, because many key EthNGOs were not members of this advisory body.

After the conflict the regional administration established a new advisory body on the departmental level in order to provide consultations between state actors and EthNGOs on the harmonization of interethnic relations and the prevention of interethnic conflicts among youths.[29] The regional administration once again heads the advisory body, appoints the members, organizes the meetings and sets the agenda. This body consists, however, mostly of EthNGOs, namely, youth representatives of EthNGOs. Its meetings take place every three months.

At one meeting in autumn 2008, for example, the advisory body addressed the "Russian march" that was planned by Slavic NGOs on the Unity Day of the Russian Federation. The state actors sought to get information about which EthNGOs were going to participate. In order to prevent unrest, state actors asked EthNGOs to persuade ethnic youths, especially the non-Russian youths, not to undertake any opposing action.[30]

The work of the advisory body demonstrates that it concentrates on the consequences of the problem rather than on the reasons. According to the replies to

Civil society activism in Russia   121

a questionnaire issued, the members of the advisory body maintain that the main advantages of the participating EthNGOs consist in getting information from state actors about their priorities in ethnic policy and the possibility of influencing decision making by informing state actors about their interests and views. They, however, remarked that it is still too early to assess the effectiveness of the body. On the one hand decisions made had still not been realized at the time the questionnaire was issued. On the other hand they highlighted the importance of the advisory body as a platform for negotiations not only for state actors and EthNGOs but also for the youths of different ethnic groups.

There are also two negotiation platforms in the Krasnodar region. The main platform for negotiations is meetings organized by the EthNGO "Centre of Ethnic Cultures" (CEC), which unites more than 30 EthNGOs. The CEC regularly organizes, with the support of state actors, discussions about different topics concerning interethnic relations and invites leaders of EthNGOs and state officials from different branches and levels of power. Within this negotiation platform EthNGOs define the problem, set the agenda and propose policies. The status of decisions made is relatively high as state actors mostly attend the meetings. State actors appreciate attending the meetings because the CEC unites almost all influential EthNGOs. Thus, state actors get extensive information about all relevant problems in the ethnic sphere and can discuss solutions. In 2008 the problem of interethnic relations among youths was raised several times. Being an informal body it is difficult to follow the results of such meetings but in interviews conducted with the author, EthNGOs stated that state actors take their information and suggestions into consideration.[31]

Another negotiation platform is an advisory body on the departmental level. The department of the Ministry of the Interior of Russia in the Krasnodar region founded the advisory body in order to increase the legitimacy of its actions and normative acts and to increase its ability to address problems, particularly ethnic tensions. The staff of the body is formed by NGOs after co-ordination with the head of the department that is in charge of the advisory body. All members including the head are members of various NGOs. State actors participate in meetings but do not dispose of the right to vote. The presence of the authorities raises the status of the decisions because consultations between state actors and NGOs increase the feasibility of the decisions. The agenda is coordinated by NGOs and the head of the department and the implementation of decisions is checked during the next meeting.[32] Meetings are held at least twice a year, but the members work permanently according to a plan that is established by the member-NGOs. The problems of interethnic relations in general, education for tolerance and efforts against extremist activities among youths in particular are among the main efforts of the advisory body work.[33] According to the 2009 working plan of the advisory body, which is the result of negotiations on the issue in 2008, several actions are planned to address interethnic tensions among youths such as the study of youth subcultures in the Krasnodar Region, a round table with members of the advisory body and leaders of regional EthNGOs on the formation of interethnic tolerance among youths, meetings with the media on questions of preventing crimes by persons under the age of 18 and the prevention of extremist activities among youths.[34] Besides, one member-organization of the advisory body developed and realizes the programme "How to live in a multiethnic city?". The aim is to educate people in tolerance and respect for the cultures of different ethnic groups. The suggestions at the end of the programme are presented to the state actors, and all these actions are implemented jointly by state actors and NGOs.

Thus, in both regions the regional administrations created institutional arrangements for negotiations with NGOs. The negotiations about the issue, however, differ considerably. In the Krasnodar region NGOs organize and rule most negotiations, and they negotiate with state actors at all steps of the policy cycle from problem definition to implementation of decisions. Moreover, NGOs succeeded in working permanently with state actors on the problem. In the Stavropol region, instead, state actors control the negotiation process with NGOs. Additionally, in most cases both NGOs and state actors are only ready to share information. Thus, NGOs in the Stavropol region play a mere consulting role, which was offered by state officials. They are strong enough to be helpful with solving youth interethnic conflicts,[35] but not strong enough to force the authorities to negotiate permanently and to address the reasons of the problem. The lack of offices and financial resources impede Stavropol EthNGOs from focusing on their professional activities, as, most of the time, they are searching for material and organizational resources in order to support their existence. The weakness of Stavropol EthNGOs also consists in the division between and within the biggest ethnic groups. Competition among the political elites of the region in 2006–2008 hinders cooperation among EthNGOs and weakens their capabilities for problem solving. Under this circumstance it is difficult to form a joint front on the problem to bring it onto the political agenda and initiate negotiations.

In the Krasnodar region, instead, 31 EthNGOs with significant material, organizational and manpower resources united their forces within the NGO "Centre of Ethnic Culture" which was able to engage state actors in systematic negotiations on the issue. In comparison to other ethnic centres around Russia, this organization is unique because it is an NGO and not a municipal organization. In addition, the head and members of the above-mentioned advisory body at the departmental level, who are representatives of the most strong and active regional NGOs, contribute significantly to the permanent work of the advisory body and to the solution of the problem. Thus, in the Krasnodar region, NGOs had resources and were able to pursue permanent and fundamental work on the problem together with state actors.

Concluding, while the high interest of the state in solving interethnic tensions can explain the establishment of the negotiation platforms among state and NGOs in ethnic policy, it can, however, not explain why negotiations in the Krasnodar region are much more intensive. Thus, the resources of NGOs in persuading the state to engage in negotiations are a major contributor to the evolution of negotiations in the Krasnodar and Stavropol regions.

2 Social policy

In social policy, state actors and NGOs agree on the policy goal that access to important buildings has to be barrier-free for handicapped people. In both regions legislation obligating state and business actors to provide accessibility to buildings already exist. State and business actors, however, do not invest serious resources to solve the problem. Thus, state actors initiated regimes for negotiations only after pressure from NGOs. The cases of social policy in the Perm and Nižnij Novgorod regions reveal that negotiations are not as intensive as in ethnic policy, but they do exist on a stable level. More specifically, NGOs in Perm were able to establish access to negotiation regimes for all interested NGOs, loyal and critical ones, contrary to NGOs in Nižnij Novgorod.

There are several institutional arrangements in the Perm region where negotiations between state actors and NGOs take place. One important platform is a round table at the governor's level for cooperation between state and civil society actors.[36] The governor founded it in 2005[37] after NGOs had demanded it for a long time. The members of the round table include prominent politicians, particularly the governor, the human rights representative and the deputy representative of the regional administration. Therefore, the decisions of this institution are taken into account. The round table meets in cases of necessity, but not less than once every three months and with changing NGO staff. The regulation of access to the round table, as well as the modus of agenda-setting is not transparent. Thus, prior to the formal negotiations at the round table, informal negotiations have to be conducted to set the agenda and appoint the participants.

Another important platform for negotiation, which was actively used by NGOs in 2008, is a network between prosecutors, NGOs and business actors. The network evolved after NGOs threatened to bring cases against businesses to court. Within this network the members cooperate in order to solve the problem informally without bringing the issue to court.

As the legislation already exists in Perm, the aim of NGOs in 2008 was to improve its implementation. Therefore RAH Perm has, for example, been trying to use existing regulations, the round table and the network, to improve the situation of handicapped people. In 2008 they worked for the first time with prosecutors, which increased pressure on private business. The NGOs have prepared surveys on the situation of accessibility by using their human, technical and knowledge resources. They took advantage of the negative results in order to increase pressure on state actors. After bringing the issue on the agenda RAH Perm used the round table to present the results of the survey and to elaborate recommendations. As there is no regulation of how to call a round table, this has been organized informally. Personal contacts played an important role. As a result, the round table formulated recommendations for realizing accessibility faster. They demanded the activation of regional and local executive actors as well as of local NGOs.[38] As current improvements show, RAH Perm successfully invested its knowledge, material and idiosyncratic resources in negotiations with high-ranking executive state actors and the prosecution. They have got

124   *K. Mikirova* et al.

promises and even some real investment of material resources. Thus, the airport, some clinics and public buildings will be made accessible.

In Nižnij Novgorod the institutional platforms for negotiations between state and non-state actors differ from Perm. Here the Public Chamber of Nižnij Novgorod region is an important state controlled[39] institutional arrangement for negotiations. The Perm Regional Public Chamber was introduced at the end of 2008.[40] In Nižnij Novgorod, however, the bill for the foundation of the Public Chamber was passed in 2006[41] and the new institution was founded along the lines of the structure of the Federal Public Chamber.[42] It has a permanent staff of mostly loyal NGOs without high-ranking regional representatives, who take part in the discussions, but the regional representatives are informed of the results later.

The other institution in Nižnij Novgorod, which was especially concerned with elaborating the legislation for accessibility in 2008, is a working group under the leadership of the regional administration with members of the regional parliament and NGOs. The third platform is a network of tax authorities, RAH Nižnij Novgorod and the governor, which developed its own accessibility project.

In the development of the legislation, many different state and non-state actors took part. The Public Chamber formulated and published recommendations and appeals following a session, which addressed the problem of accessibility, contributing, thus, to the faster formulation of the law.[43] Invatur and RAH Nižnij Novgorod have been members of the working group for this law within the administration of the governor. Invatur, with its stronger oppositional character, supported the working process with independent controls on buildings and informed the prosecution about violations of the law. Moreover, Invatur contributed to the organization of an informal round table with state actors in order to inform them about the current legal situation. Finally, yet importantly, the regional parliament passed the bill in February 2009. The working group expanded the law of "accessibility for citizens with limited mobility in Nižnij Novgorod". Therefore, the law represents a negotiated agreement between the various interested parties.[44]

The network between tax authorities, RAH Nižnij Novgorod and the governor was based on personal contacts and brought about a project to establish jobs for handicapped people in the regional board of the tax offices and accessibility to all its buildings. The governor supported the project actively, which explains why the necessary financial resources have been provided. Additional partners are educational institutions that are training the handicapped people for their job. It is, however, questionable whether more actors will join this network and expand the project to a broader circle of organizations or whether it is rather meant to calm down critical voices in civil society with one pilot project. Nevertheless, this improvement is an example of how existing resources can be mobilized much easier when trust in mutual cooperation facilitates negotiations.

In both regions NGOs invest their knowledge resources, their manpower and idiosyncratic resources in order to get the promise of executive state actors and

Civil society activism in Russia 125

private actors to invest in accessibility and to get the support of prosecutors, who facilitate the investments by threatening private business actors or taking them to court. However, as the institutional resources of NGOs are not strong enough and material resources are until now not able to bridge this gap, they often exchange all their resources for promises, which are often only partly realized. The cases showed, moreover, that the negotiations between state and non-state actors were initiated only by NGOs with increased strength and activity. They succeeded in allying with important state actors, especially the office of the prosecution.

The analysis of the negotiations on accessibility for the handicapped in the Perm and Nižnij Novgorod regions reveals that professionally working and experienced NGOs in the social sphere, willing to work with state institutions and able to convince state actors of their experience and ability, are generally able to influence regional social policy through a bottom-up-strategy in both regions. This is highlighted by the alliance between RAH Perm and Nižnij Novgorod and the regional prosecution. Despite these similarities, there are also differences in the institutional settings within which state and non-state actors negotiate. While in Nižnij Novgorod state and civil society actors negotiate mainly within the Public Chamber and personal network, they negotiate in Perm at the round table, which was a demand of NGOs and is also open to critical NGOs. A major factor contributing to these differences is the differing political cultures in the regions, which were to a great extent shaped by civil society actors during the 1990s. In the Perm region powerful NGOs with charismatic leaders evolved in the 1990s during the transformation period and were able to acquire a professional reputation in the regional administration. An open relationship between state actors and NGOs evolved and, thus, NGOs succeeded in persuading the state to establish negotiation platforms to which access is formally controlled by the state, but open to all NGOs, critical as well as loyal ones. This institutional legacy still structures negotiations between state and non-state actors today.

In Nižnij Novgorod, networks based on old friendships and loyalty control informally the access to the negotiation platforms, even to the formal ones, like the Public Chamber. Thereby state actors are much more suspicious of NGOs and they use their control to exclude critical NGOs. Thus, although some NGOs, like Invatur for example, found access, such access for critical NGOs is much more difficult in Nižnij Novgorod. While the lower interest of the state in solving problems of accessibility can explain why negotiations in social policy are not as intensive as in ethnic policy, it cannot explain the variance in access to negotiation regimes between the Perm and Nižnij Novgorod regions. For explaining the differences in the negotiations between state actors and NGOs, the various capabilities of the NGOs due to different political cultures is a necessary contributing cause.

126 *K. Mikirova* et al.

3 Environmental policy

The Russian state and business actors are usually not interested in sustainable environmental policy (Ânickij 2007). They do not seek a balance between social, ecological and economic interests and they do not want to take the financial and political responsibility for tremendous ecological disasters. Thus, their interest in solving problems is much lower in environmental policy than in ethnic and social policy. In consequence state actors usually do not negotiate with EcoNGOs, although EcoNGOs try hard to bring environmental problems on the political agenda. State actors prefer not to react to the demands of EcoNGOs and even try to hinder their activities. Instead of cooperating with EcoNGOs in order to enhance their problem-solving capacity, the regional administration in both cases preferred to pretend they had an effective solution to the problem.

Concerning the Baikalsk pulp and paper mill in the Irkutsk region several regional EcoNGOs struggled for years to close the factory and to restructure the entire economy of the city. In order to do so, they wrote petitions to the regional administration and federal environmental agencies and organized pickets and rallies. Moreover, they proposed ways to restructure the factory as well as the economy of the city.

Although the federal and regional state actors discussed the plans several times in various advisory bodies and issued several laws and regulations banning pulp and paper industry at Lake Baikal, they did not undertake any step to implement these plans and did not consult with EcoNGOs.

Concerning the oil disaster on the Taman Peninsula in the Krasnodar region a consortium of several NGOs sent a petition to the regional administration and the federal agencies of the Ministry of Natural Resources and Environmental Protection with an offer for cooperation in dealing with the pollution. The consortium included all major EcoNGOs of the region and it offered to contribute to the clean-up work by providing activists and knowledge of the local geography. The regional administration, however, declined the offer, stating that the state has enough resources and that activists would disturb work at the site.[45] In reality, the regional administration and the federal environmental agencies did not provide sufficient staff for cleaning the coast.[46] After cleaning a few beaches with great publicity, they declared that the oil pollution had been removed.

In addition to the reluctance to solve environmental problems, state and business actors also seek to circumvent the mandatory Environmental Impact Assessment (Ânickij 2007) when their interests are in conflict with those of EcoNGOs. They either use vague regulations or loopholes in the EIA regulations or even violate them. The regulations of the EIA for example do not clearly state whether the project materials and public hearings of major investment projects, like pipelines, which affect several regions, have to be published and held only in one region, in all affected regions or only in Moscow, the federal center (Kovalev *et al.* 2007: 60). Consequently, state and business actors publish project information and organize the public hearing where they will meet less resistance or can mobilize their own staff.[47] In many cases, companies did even not announce the

Civil society activism in Russia 127

public hearing in time, did not publish the needed project documentation and held the public hearings in localities that were not at all affected by the investment projects or were difficult to reach.[48] State actors, organizing the public hearings, distort the EIA by declaring that the decision to realize the project has already been made at the regional or federal level, and that people at the public hearings have to agree with the investment project. Such direct violation of environmental law became much easier in recent years because lobbying weakened environmental institutions. For example the staff in offices responsible for EIA was considerably reduced in all regions. In the Irkutsk regional office for the EIA, staff was reduced after 2000 from 40 to five. As a result state controllers are very often not able to analyse all project materials and to demand rectifications in the prescribed timeframe. Thus, they are not able to secure all the legal requirements of the EIA, including the participation rights of EcoNGOs (Kovalev *et al.* 2007: 66). Also in the EIAs of the ports on the Taman Peninsula, of the oil exploration platform in the Sea of Azov as well as of the oil pipeline close to Lake Baikal, the companies and the state actors used vague regulations or did not comply with environmental laws and regulations and, thus, tried to exclude EcoNGOs from the environmental decision making.[49]

The cases from the Irkutsk and Krasnodar regions show, however, not only that the state is reluctant to address ecological problems and to hold proper EIA and that it is difficult for EcoNGOs to mobilize civil society (Ânickij 2007). They also reveal that EcoNGOs have learnt that they can force state actors to solve ecological problems and to hold proper EIAs and, consequently, start negotiations by allying with other state or business actors that use environmental laws and regulations in order to pursue their own non-ecological interests,[50] such as weakening business competitors.

The extent to which EcoNGOs are able to ally with other stakeholders depends, however, on the regional economic structure. In many regions, especially regions rich in resources such as Irkutsk, the economic structure is homogenous. The resource extraction, processing or transporting industry is often the only business in town and does not meet competition from other industries. In other regions, such as Krasnodar, the economic structure is rather heterogeneous. It consists of many medium enterprises of various branches – logistic, tourism, agriculture and light industry. Those branches are constantly competing over the right to use resources, such as coast and water. While NGOs in the Krasnodar region can often ally with competing regional branches, EcoNGOs in Irkutsk find it much more difficult to ally with business.

Thus, after their unsuccessful attempts to participate in the oil cleanup and the EIA, EcoNGOs in the Krasnodar region were able to ally with local deputies and the tourist industry as well as fishery companies, which were negatively affected by investment projects and the oil pollution. The main source of income for the population of the Taman Peninsula derives from tourism and fishery. Thus, they fear that the construction of the ports and oil exploration platform, as well as environmental pollution, would undermine their livelihood.[51] This alliance provided EcoNGOs with additional institutional, material and knowledge resources.

128   *K. Mikirova* et al.

EcoNGOs, for example, asked local deputies to pursue a survey and attach the results to the minutes of their sessions.[52] In this way, they were able to declare the opposition to the investment projects by the majority of the citizens and provided the declaration with official status. By allying with business actors they enhanced their material and informational resources in order to file suits in court against the violations of the regulations of the EIA. Moreover, influential businessmen provided EcoNGOs with broad media coverage.

Consequently, EcoNGOs succeeded in forcing the companies and respective administrations to repeat the public hearings, comply with the formal requirements and start to negotiate in order to find mutually acceptable solutions. In consequence, the oil company agreed to move the oil platform to another place, to conduct several corporate social responsibility measures and to implement tight ecological security measures.[53] In exchange, the alliance of EcoNGOs, local deputies and business actors gave up their opposition. The companies, which plan to construct the ports, are currently still in negotiations with various stakeholders in order to get the licence for the construction. Concerning the oil pollution the alliance of EcoNGOs, local deputies and business actors succeeded in forcing the state and business actors to reassume and intensify the cleaning effort. In turn, members of the state environmental control agency agreed to visit the polluted sites together with representatives of EcoNGOs and local deputies, because the federal environmental agency did not have enough resources to monitor the site alone.[54]

EcoNGOs in Irkutsk, on the contrary, did not succeed in allying with additional stakeholders, because no rival business actors competed over the resources, which the oil company asked to use. They were not able to pressure the company and the federal environmental agency to repeat the EIA despite significant flaws in the procedure and content of the assessment or to shut down the pulp and paper mill. As a result, the permission to construct the pipeline was issued by the state controlling agency despite serious harm to the ecological stability of one of the world's most important ecosystems.[55] The enormous potential negative impact of this pipeline is highlighted by the fact that, as a rare exception, the public anger at financial industrial groups destroying homelands grew so much that EcoNGOs in Irkutsk succeeded for the first and only time to date in bringing a large amount of the population to the street. For several days more than 6,000 people rallied in Irkutsk against the construction of the pipeline. In consequence, the President changed the investment project by decree.[56] NGOs, however, did not succeed in forcing state and business actors in charge of the EIA to repeat the EIA and engage in negotiations to find a balance between social, ecological and economical interests. Also, concerning the Baikalsk pulp and paper mill, EcoNGOs did not succeed in forcing the state to involve them in negotiations and solve the problem.

These cases of environmental governance in the Krasnodar and Irkutsk regions show that in Russia relations between state and societal actors do not only depend on the will of state actors to engage in negotiations in order to solve problems. It is true that state and business actors, contrary to the cases from

Civil society activism in Russia 129

ethnic and social policy, try to exclude EcoNGOs from environmental decision making and that the support of the society for environmental issues is usually low. However, civil society actors are nonetheless able to force state actors to engage in negotiations when they are able to ally with other stakeholders.

Conclusion

Governance by negotiation between state and non-state actors is said to reduce information problems occurring in hierarchical direction. These problems are especially acute in modern and complex societies. Authoritarian regimes also need societal actors for negotiating in order to steer and coordinate effectively socially and economically complex societies. Authoritarian regimes, however, as opposed to democratic ones, usually determine the leeway of societal actors as well as the way state and non-state actors negotiate. In this paper we analysed whether the state in Russia is indeed able to determine the relations between state and non-state actors. We asked whether state and non-state actors negotiate only in cases where the state wants to solve a problem and therefore needs NGOs' resources and whether the state determines the way it negotiates with NGOs. Or are NGOs powerful enough to persuade or even force state actors to engage in negotiations? Are NGOs, thus, also influencing the relations between state and non-state actors?

The comparison of the various forms of negotiations between state actors and NGOs revealed that the interest of the state in solving a problem is indeed a major contributing factor. When state actors are interested in solving problems, they mobilize the resources of NGOs. In ethnic policy state actors needed EthNGOs to provide information and to influence their constituencies. In social policy, instead, the state did not want to invest major resources, but they at least did not oppose the goals of NGOs. Under this condition NGOs were able to persuade state actors to engage in negotiations. In environmental policy state actors are reluctant to negotiate with NGOs in order to pick up ecological problems and even tried to circumvent obligatory joint decision systems.

The interest of the state in problem solving is, however, not able to explain the regional variances within each policy field. It cannot explain why NGOs in Krasnodar in ethnic policy were able to significantly extend the intensity of negotiations, why NGOs in Perm in social policy were able to establish the access to negotiation regimes for critical NGOs and why NGOs in Krasnodar in environmental policy were able to force state actors to engage in negotiations and to enforce the joint decision systems. In order to understand why state and non-state actors negotiate in Russia one has to consider the resource distribution of NGOs to influence their relation with the state, as well.

Notes

1 This chapter compares the findings of three research projects on Russian regional governance, which are currently realized by the authors within the PhD programme "Political steering through law and social norms in Russia" at Heinrich-Heine University of Dusseldorf (Germany), financed by METRO Foundation.

130 *K. Mikirova* et al.

2 All Russian words follow the transcript system of ISO 9 (International Organization for Standardization, www.aurint.de/Transliterationssysteme_Russisch_Deutsch. htm).

3 Federal Laws of the Russian Federation "Non-Governmental Organizations", 1996, "On Public Organizations", 1995. These laws were amended in 2006. Federal Law "On the Federal Public Chamber in Russia", 2005. Decree No. 842 of the President of Russia "Formation of Public Councils to federal ministries, federal services and federal agencies, ruled by the President of the Russian Federation, and to federal services and the federal agencies subordinated by the federal ministries", 2006.

4 For example, Law of the Krasnodar region "On the Public Chamber in the Krasnodar region", 2008. Law of the Nižnij Novgorod region "On the Public Chamber of the Nižnij Novgorod region", 2006.

5 www.gipp.ru/opennews.php?id=9916.

6 Concept of the State Ethnic Policy of the Russian Federation, 1996.

7 According to Larisa Ruban, Institute of Social Research at the Russian Academy of Sciences, 80–90 per cent of participants are young people.

8 In May 2007 there was a mass fight in the Stavropol region between Slavic and Chechen youths and in June a mass unauthorized demonstration of Slavic youths with the slogan "Russia is for Russians". The surveys in 2007 and 2008 showed that 13 per cent of the youths in this region are ready to join extremist organizations and 62 per cent of young people are ready to participate in conflict situations to protect the interests of their ethnic groups.

9 In the Krasnodar region in 2008 there were four local youth conflicts between different ethnic groups in the region. The survey of the Youth Group for Tolerance "ETnIKA" (a regional NGO) in 2005 shows that 30 per cent of students of high schools prefer radical methods in the fight against terrorism such as an examination of passports of "dangerous ethnic groups", "resettlement of all non-Russians from Russia", "resettlement of all Chechens".

10 Handicapped (in wheelchairs), older citizens, pregnant women and citizens using pushchairs.

11 The survey of the Perm department of the Russian Association for the Handicapped (further RAH Perm) in 2007 shows that 63 per cent of 216 buildings intended for social needs are not, 27 per cent are partly and only 10 per cent are fully accessible. In the Nižnij Novgorod region the situation is at the most slightly better, but there are no overall and official surveys.

12 Most of the interviewed experts ranked Perm, Moscow, St Petersburg as the regions with the most active and influential civil society, but also counted Nižnij Novgorod as part of the group of leaders after these three.

13 The first bill in the Russian Federation "On the guarantee for barrier free access for the handicapped and other citizens with limited mobility to buildings of informational and social importance and transport" was passed in Perm in 2004. Target programme "On rehabilitation and guarantee of vital activity of the handicapped in the Perm region 2006–2011" followed. The regional law "On the regulation of town-planning activity in the Perm region" from 2006 regulates building activity.

14 For example regional target programmes "Formation of accessibility for the handicapped in the Nižnij Novgorod region", 2003–2005; "Social support of the handicapped in the Nižnij Novgorod region", 2006–2008.

15 Regional law "On accessibility for the citizens with limited mobility in the Nižnij Novgorod region".

16 The department of the Ministry of the Interior of Russia in the Krasnodar and Stavropol regions, the Federal Security Service (FSB), the regional department of public prosecution.

17 The governor, the department for political relations in the administration of the governor, the regional commissioner of human rights.

Civil society activism in Russia   131

18 The governor, the vice governor and its department, responsible for the interaction with civil society actors.

19 The construction of the "power vertical" in Russia is the complex of measures conducted from 2000 to 2008 under V.V. Putin in order to strengthen the federal power and weaken the regional power.

20 The regional target programmes "Harmonization of interethnic relationships and the development of ethnic cultures in the Krasnodar region" (2005, 2006, 2007, 2008), "Development of interethnic and interdenominational relationships in the Stavropol region 2007–2009", 2006, recognize that (Eth-)NGOs play a very important role in maintaining interethnic tolerance and stability and underline the necessity of interaction between state and NGOs.

21 Russian environmental institutions oblige state and business actors to involve NGOs in the EIA in two aspects. First, the expert group, which assesses the environmental impact of an investment project and decides by majority vote whether the project can proceed; second, the EIA of more significant investment projects consists of public hearings, where EcoNGOs can publicly issue their concerns and add them to the minutes of the public hearings.

22 Interviews with representatives of NGOs 2008 (RAH Perm and Nižnij Novgorod, Invatur).

23 Investment rating of Russian regions. www.raexpert.ru/ratings/regions/.

24 To make the difference clearer: Human rights activists in Nižnij Novgorod have considerably less of a chance to interact with state actors. One NGO talks about systematic, even illegal restrictions and attempts to destroy the organization (Interview with Nižnij Novgorod regional association of civil-rights activism, November 2008).

25 Regimes are formal institutional arrangements, which facilitate negotiations, but do not oblige actors to engage in negotiations (Scharpf 2000).

26 Stavropol Advisory Body for Interethnic Affairs to the Governor worked from 1993 to 1998.

27 Interviews with members of the Advisory Body for Interethnic Affairs, Stavropol, September 2008 and May 2009.

28 Resolution of the governor of the Stavropol region "On Advisory Body for Interethnic Affairs to the Governor", 2005.

29 Decree of the administration of the Stavropol region "On Youth Advisory Body for Interethnic Affairs to the Committee for Youth Affairs", 2007.

30 Agenda of the meeting, 30 September 2008.

31 Interviews with the members of the EthNGO "Centre of Ethnic Cultures", Krasnodar, May 2009.

32 Interviews with the head and two members of the advisory body, Krasnodar, May 2009.

33 Resolution of the department of the Interior Ministry of Russia in the Krasnodar region "On the advisory body to the department of the Interior Ministry of Russia in the Krasnodar region", April 2008.

34 www.guvd-kuban.ru/index.php?option=com_content&task=view&id=3295&Itemid=36.

35 During the conflict in Stavropol in May and June 2007, state actors asked the leaders of EthNGOs to appeal to their youths not to get involved in the conflict. The leaders signed a common appeal to the population and organized meetings with their youths. As a result ethnic youths did not get involved in the conflict. The positive role of EthNGOs was mentioned in the report of Stavropol administration to the deputy special representative of the president in the Southern Federal District.

36 Round table for interaction between state actors and civil society actors.

37 Law of the Perm region No. 1568–316 "On the basis of interaction of state actors of the Perm region with NGOs", 1 September 2004. Decree No. 476-p on 21 October 2005 by the governor to implement the law "On a constantly acting round table for

132   *K. Mikirova* et al.

questions of interaction between NGOs and state actors of the Perm region reporting to the governor".

38 Minutes of the round table meeting from 15 July 2008.

39 State control is due to the modus of nomination: Only one third of the members are chosen by the civil society, the rest is chosen by state actors. This modus gives reason to see the Public Chamber as very loyal to the state.

40 State actors and NGOs opposed its introduction. They feared that the Public Chamber would disturb existing institutional arrangements and interaction. In 2008 they had to cede to pressure from federal level to found this institution. The platform existed only formally and cannot be seen as an actor in the period under scrutiny.

41 Regional law "On the Public Chamber of the Nižnij Novgorod region", 19 October 2006.

42 www.oprf.ru/ru/about/.

43 www.palata-nn.ru/activity/results/0/4.

44 As the involved actors already had more experience with the difficulties of implementing such a law than in Perm 2004, the bill is more precise in formulating strict responsibilities for the executive organs. However, it is too soon to draw conclusions about its effect on the situation.

45 "Novaya Gazeta", 14 April 2008. Komu načistit' Čušku? www.novayagazeta.ru/data/2008/26/23.html.

46 EWNC: 18 November 2007. Vlasti ne spravlyajutsja s katastrofoij v Kerčenskom prolive. www.ewnc.org/node/276.

47 EWNC: 5 December 2007. Burenie v Azovskom more možet zakončit'sja takže. www.ewnc.org/node/286.

48 EWNC: 4 July 2008. V rossijskoij časti Kerčemskogo proliva ZAO "Evro-Trans" planiruet organizovat' reijdovuju peregrusočnuju stojanku. www.ewnc.org/node/943.

49 "Sibirksie novosti." "Baikal'skaja ėkologičeskaja volna" i rjad graždan podali žalobu na nepravomernye deijstvija Rostechnadzora po projektu VSTO. http://news.babr.ru/?IDE=31132 EWNC: 10 September 2008. Reijdovaja perevalka sery v Kerčenskom prolive nedopustima! www.ewnc.org/node/1424.

50 Interview with a newspaper redactor in Irkutsk in April 2008.

51 Lagunina, Irina. 29 August 2008. Počemu žiteljam Krasnodarskogo kraja ne nravjatsja neftjanye plany vlasteij. www.svobodanews.ru/content/transcript/463167.html.

52 EWNC: 26 August 2008. Deputaty poprosili Putina zaššitit' Kerčenskij proliv. www.ewnc.org/node/1289.

53 Interview with a member of the movement "Save Taman" in October 2008.

54 EWNC: 5 December 2007. Deputaty obespokoeny tem, čro ne čistitsja bereg. www.ewnc.org/node/285.

55 "Sibirskie novosti" Gos. ėkspertiza utverdila stroitel'stvo nefteprovoda VSTO http://news.babr.ru/?IDE=29181.

56 BABR.RU "Putin potrepobval ot Vaijnžtoka perenesti nefteprovod za predely vodosbornoij zony Baijkala." http://news.babr.ru/?IDE=29534.

Bibliography

Ânickij, O.N. (2007) "Aktory i Resursy social'no-Ėkologičeskoj Modernizacii", available at http://2008.isras.ru/files/File/Socis/2007–08/yanicki.pdf (accessed 30 March 2009).

Bähr, H. and O. Treib (2007) "Governing Modes in Social and Environmental Politics. NEWGOV New Modes of Governance", available at www.eu newgov.org/database/DELIV/D01D50_GM_in_Social_&_Environmental_Policies.pdf (accessed 30 March 2009).

Civil society activism in Russia 133

Bähr, H., O. Treib and G. Falkner (2005) "Modes of Governance: A Note Towards Conceptual Clarification", European Governance Papers No. N-05–02, available at www. connexnetwork.org/eurogov/pdf/egp-newgov-N-05–02.pdf (accessed 30 March 2009).

Benz, A. (2004) *Governance – Regieren in komplexen Regelsystemen*, Wiesbaden.

Benz, A., S. Lütz, U. Schimank and G. Simonis (2007) *Handbuch Governance. Theoretische Grundlagen und empirische Anwendungsfelder*, Wiesbaden.

Gornyj, M. and A. Sungurov (2009) *Publičnaâ politica – 2008. Sbornik statej*, Sankt-Peterburg.

Helmke, G. and S. Levitsky (2004) "Informal Institutions and Comparative Politics: A Research Agenda", *Perspectives on Politics*, 2: 725–740.

Heritier, A. (2002) "Modes of Governance in Europe. Policy Making without Legislating?" in Adrienne Heritier (ed.) *Common Goods: Reinventing European and International Governance*, Lanham, MD, 185–206.

Kooiman, J. (2003) *Governing as Governance*, London.

Kotov, V. and E. Nikitina (2002) "Reorganisation of Environmental Policy in Russia: The Decade of Success and Failures in Implementation and Perspective Quests", available at www.feem.it/NR/rdonlyres/59A79BBF-DE58-4819-BC3F-C0FE71384402/346/ 5702.pdf (accessed 30 March 2009).

Kovalev, N., J. Köppel and E. Dittrich (2007) *Demokratie und Umwelt in Russland*, Münster.

Kropp, S. (2009) "Die subversive Kraft des Informalen. Verfassungsdynamik im foederalen System Russlands", *Zeitschrift fuer Staats- und Europawissenschaften*, February.

Linz, J. (2000) *Totalitäre und autoritäre Regime*, Berlin.

Mayntz, R. (1993) "Policy-Netzwerke und die Logik von Verhandlungssystemen", *Politische Vierteljahresschrift*, Sonderheft Policy Analyse, 39–56.

Mayntz, R. and F. Scharpf (eds) (1995) *Gesellschaftliche Selbstregelung und Politische Steuerung*, Frankfurt a.M.

McLean, I. and A. McMillan (eds) (2009) "WG 'non-governmental organization'", in *The Concise Oxford Dictionary of Politics*. Oxford. Oxford Reference, available at www.oxfordreference.com/views/ENTRY.html?subview=Main&entry=t86.e907 (accessed 30 March 2009).

Nohlen, D. (2002) "Kleines Lexikon der Politik", *Zweite Auflage, Lizenzausgabe für die Bundeszentrale für politische Bildung*, München, pp, 324–326.

Nußberger, A. and C. Schmidt (2007) "Vereinsleben auf Russisch oder Don Quichote und die russische Bürokratie", *Russlandanalysen*, 138: 2–6.

OECD (2006) "Environmental Policy and Regulation. The Implementation Challenge", available www.oecd.org/LongAbstract/0,3425,en_33873108_36016497_38117848_1_ 1_1_1,00.html (accessed 30 March 2009).

Ostrom, E. (1986) "A Method of Insititutional Analysis", in F.X. Kaufmann, G. Majone and V. Ostrom (eds) *Guidance and Control in the Public Sector*, The Bielefeld Interdisciplinary Project, Berlin, 459–475.

Provan, K. and P. Kenis (2008) "Modes of Network Governance: Structure, Management, and Effectiveness", *Journal of Public Administration Research and Theory*, 18: 229–252.

Rhodes, R.A.W. and D. Marsh (1992) "New Directions in the Study of Policy Networks", *European Journal of Political Research*, 21: 181–205.

Scharpf, F. (1997) *Games Real Actors Play: Actor Centered Institutionalism in Policy Research*, Boulder, CO.

Scharpf, F. (2000) *Interaktionsformen*, Opladen.

134   *K. Mikirova* et al.

Smismans, S. (2006) "Reviewing Normative Theories on Civil Society Participation: NEW GOV New Modes of Governance", available at: www.eunewgov.org/database/ DELIV/D11D04_Normative_theories.pdf (accessed 30 March 2009).

Stepan, A. (1978) *State and Society: Peru in Comparative Perspective*, Princeton.

Sundstrom, L. (2006) "Funding Civil Society: Foreign Assistance and NGO Development in Russia", www.sup.org/pages.cgi?isbn=0804754438;item=Chapter_1_pages;page=1 (accessed 30 March 2009).

Sungurov, A. (2008a) *Graždanskoe obŝestvj i ego razvitie v Rossii*, Sankt-Peterburg.

Sungurov, A. (2008b) "Modeli vzaimodejstviâ organov gosudarstvennoj vlasti i struktur graždanskogo obŝestva: rossijskij opyt", *Naučno-kul'turologičeskij žurnal*, 9: 172.

Themudo, N. (2000) "NGOs and Resources: Getting a Closer Grip on a Complex Area", Documentos de discusión sobre el Tercer Sector, Núm. 5. Programa Interdisciplinario de Estudios del Tercer Sector, available at: www.cmq.edu.mx/docinvest/document/ DD05197.pdf (accessed 30 March 2009).

Van Waarden, F. (1992) "Dimensions and Types of Policy Networks", *European Journal of Political Research*, 21: 29–52.

Wernstedt, K. (2002) "Environmental Management in the Russian Federation: A Next Generation Enigma", Discussion Paper 02–04, available at http://ideas.repec.org/p/rff/ dpaper/dp-0204.html (accessed 30 March 2009).

8 Entrenching authoritarianism or promoting reform?

Civil society in contemporary Yemen

Vincent Durac

Introduction

In the past, civil society has been seen as key to democratic transition in many political contexts. While the optimism that surrounded the expansion in the scale of civil society activity in the Middle East which characterized the 1990s has given way to more cautious assessments of its possible impact on political change in the region, nonetheless much work remains to be done in scrutinizing the impact of civil society on political dynamics in specific contexts in the region. Undoubtedly, more critical tones have entered the discourse on civil society in the Middle East, but it is still the case that the assumption of a positive correlation between a healthy civil society sector and political reform in the direction of greater levels of pluralism and democracy remains central to much of the commentary on the region and continues to inform policy-making.

This chapter will examine civil society in contemporary Yemen where, perhaps paradoxically, a comparatively open political system and a seemingly vibrant civil society sector co-exist with patterns of authoritarian politics that are familiar from much of the rest of the Middle East. The chapter will consider the impact that civil society in Yemen has, or can have, on Yemeni political dynamics and will argue, in sympathy with recent work on other states in the region, that, far from challenging an entrenched, authoritarian regime, civil society in Yemen as presently configured, almost certainly has the effect of bolstering the grip on power of that regime. The chapter is divided into three main parts. The first examines the concept of civil society and the question of its relationship to democratic political change. The next examines the literature on civil society in the Middle East from two perspectives – first, the debate on whether the concept of civil society has any meaningful application to Middle Eastern contexts; second, what form and character civil society assumes in the contemporary Middle East. The next section critically examines civil society and the state in Yemen and is based, in part, on fieldwork conducted in Sana'a in March 2008. In the Yemeni context, the role that tribes and tribal allegiances play in all aspects of socio-political and economic life is very important and deservedly attracted considerable academic interest. Although this crucial aspect of Yemeni society should not be underestimated, this study examines emerging dynamics of

136   *V. Durac*

activism that are being created outside the tribal framework. The chapter concludes with a brief discussion of the implications of its findings for the broader literature on civil society and the state in the Middle East.

Civil society

While most commentators acknowledge that a particular conception of civil society, as connoting voluntary organizations that operate in a nebulous zone between those of the family and the state, has become dominant in the literature, at least since the end of the Cold War, it is, nonetheless, a truism to observe that there is no consensus on what the term actually refers to. Diversity characterizes the history of thinking on civil society. Rosenblum and Post point out that:

> Civil society is alternately viewed as a source of stability and legitimacy for government and as a source of resistance against arbitrary, oppressive and overweening government. Civil society is sometimes conceived as a spontaneous growth, prior to an independent of government, and sometimes dependent on government for legal structure, robust recognition, or outright fiscal support. Civil society is described as developing in partnership with government and as substituting for the failings of government.
>
> (Rosenblum and Post, 2002: 1)

The absence of conceptual clarity stems from the diversity of theorizing on the subject of civil society. There is no such thing as 'the classical conception of civil society' (Giner, 1995: 302). There is a Lockean interpretation, but there is a Hegelian one, and there are Hobbesian, Marxist and Gramscian theories of civil society. While these share in common the view that civil society refers to a sphere of life outside the state, there remains 'ample room for disagreement between authors and schools' (Giner, 1995: 302).

This theoretical diversity is explored in Edwards' 'whistle-stop' tour of civil society (Edwards, 2004: 9). Edwards suggests that in classical tradition civil society was treated as synonymous with the state – both concepts referred to a type of political association that governed social conflict 'through the imposition of rules that retrained citizens from harming one another' (Edwards, 2004: 8). This tradition was continued in late medieval thought which equated civil society with 'politically organized commonwealths'. However, according to Edwards, this approach took a different turn between 1750 and 1850 in response to a number of developments, in particular, the rise of the market economy and the social fallout from this, as well as the impact of the French and American revolutions on 'traditional paradigms of authority'. In this Enlightenment tradition, civil society was seen, not as indistinguishable from the state, but as a defence against impingement by the state on newly acquired rights and freedoms. Edwards links this approach to James Madison and Alexis de Tocqueville and through them to writers such as Ernest Gellner and James Madison (Edwards, 2004: 8).

Civil society in contemporary Yemen 137

The dominant theme in this debate was the value of voluntary associations in curbing the power of centralizing institutions, protecting pluralism and nurturing constructive social norms.... A highly articulated civil society with overlapping memberships was seen as the foundation of a stable democratic polity, a defence against domination by any one group, and a barrier to anti-democratic forces.

(Edwards, 2004: 7)

However, while this has become the dominant view of civil society, it is not the only tradition in political thought. Others have focused on structural obstacles that prevent some groups from articulating their interests within society. This approach has been associated with Hegel, Marx and Gramsci, in particular (Edwards, 2004: 8–9). Hegel focused on the inequality and conflict that characterized civil society and which required resolution through state intervention. And, as Edwards points out, Gramsci's ideas of civil society were subsequently taken up by theorists such as John Dewey and Hannah Arendt in the United States and by Jurgen Habermas in Europe who developed the idea of the 'public sphere' as an essential component of democracy. Unsurprisingly, Edwards concludes his survey by noting both the many phases through which thinking about civil society has passed, and the absence of consensus on what civil society means (Edwards, 2004: 9).

Edwards offers a historical survey of the evolution of the idea of civil society. A number of other writers have critiqued the idea for its more contemporary ideological connotations and function. For Rahman, civil society actors such as non-governmental organizations (NGOs) are surrounded by an 'almost reverential aura' by those who view civil society as necessarily good (Rahman, 2002). She proposes an alternative view of civil society as ideologically loaded and inextricably linked to the discourse of the Bretton Woods institutions – the World Bank and the International Monetary Fund. For Rahman, the dominant understanding of civil society organizations (CSOs) as agents of empowerment and guarantors of 'democratization' is integral to the 'neo-liberal package' promoted in the last two decades by 'Washington Consensus aficionados' who see in civil society and its organizations a panacea for all the ills of state-led development models.[1] She argues that this understanding of civil society is core to a neo-liberal reform project that advocates the minimization of the role of the state, privatization of the public sector and the abolition of social welfare measures such as food subsidies, health care and labour legislation protecting the interests of workers. In this model of associational life, the relationship between the state and voluntary associations is turned upside down. Self-governing voluntary bodies are treated not as secondary associations, but as the primary means of both democratic governance and the organization of social life while the state is treated as secondary. However, advocates of this model fail to recognize 'enduring conflicts' within society and the prospect that the most powerful interests will dominate. CSOs therefore run the risk of promoting class inequalities and reproducing existing material hierarchies. The 'associative democracy' that

138   *V. Durac*

results from this could then end up merely as democracy for privileged groups 'that possess the resources to make themselves heard' (Rahman, 2002: 24).

Writing in relation to civil society in sub-Saharan Africa, Chabal and Daloz make similar arguments. Like Rahman, they argue that one of the most common usages of civil society is linked to the liberal ideology of the minimal state, as put forward by the Bretton Woods institutions (Chabal and Daloz, 1999: 22). They suggest that Western donors, following the lead of the World Bank and the IMF, have advocated structural adjustment programmes which limit the economic reach of the state because they no longer trust African states to manage their economies and promote growth. The result is a new emphasis on the significance of civil society which, in turn, has led to a shift of resources to NGOS which are seen as the representatives of that civil society. Given this, Chabal and Daloz suggest that the proliferation of CSOs in sub-Saharan Africa in recent years is less a reflection of its innate vibrancy and has more to do with 'successful adaptation to the conditions laid down by foreign donors on the part of local political actors who seek in this way to gain access to new resources' (Chabal and Daloz, 1999: 22).

The view that this dominant understanding of civil society is inextricably linked to a neo-liberal agenda is shared by Allen, who argues that the ideologically laden character of the concept combined with its conceptual elusiveness deprives it of its utility:

> [A]part from the grant-seeking NGOs and the academic, it is proponents of the 'liberal project' who need civil society; western governments, their associated agencies, multinationals, and IFIs ... civil society forms part of a large body of general concepts that have appeared briefly to illuminate analysis but which are too diffuse, inclusive and ideologically laden to sustain illumination
>
> (Allen, 1997: 337)

Civil society and democracy

The lack of consensus on the definition of civil society is echoed in the range of views that exist on the relationship between civil society and democracy. Although there is often an implicit, if not explicit, assumption that civil society and democracy are positively correlated, some writers are more sceptical of its democratizing capacity. Perhaps the most common perspective derives from a purported analysis of the political transformations that took place in Latin America and Eastern Europe in the late 1980s and 1990s, which focuses on the role of civil society in promoting and effecting democratic political change. In this perspective, civic movements, intellectuals, trade unions, student groups and a host of other voluntary associations came together to press their demands on narrowly based authoritarian regimes with considerable success. Based on the experience of Latin America and Eastern Europe, the non-governmental sector

Civil society in contemporary Yemen 139

is seen as a critical counterbalance to the power of the state, representing an autonomous sphere of social engagement, capable of asserting and protecting the interests of civil society.

(Wiktorowicz, 2002: 79)

Rosenblum and Post identify three functions that civil society performs for democracy. First, it can serve as a centre of 'collective political resistance against rapacious and oppressive government'; second, it can organize people for democratic political participation; third, it can perform the function of 'socialization into the political values necessary for self government'. They conclude that while civil society is no guarantee of democracy, it is necessary for democracy and can serve important democratic functions (Rosenblum and Post, 2002: 17–18).

However, others offer a more nuanced account of the relationship. Norton observes in the first instance that civil society did not, in fact, 'topple regimes' in Latin America and Eastern Europe. Rather, their fall was due to internal corruption and their 'hollow claims of legitimacy'. Civil society was 'more the beneficiary than the wrecking ball' (Norton, 1993: 211). Similarly, some writers have cautioned against any assumption that an expansion in the number of CSOs will somehow engender democratic institutions (Wiktorowicz, 2002: 80). Kamrava and Mora suggest that, for CSOs to become agents of democratization, they must possess three additional characteristics: they must themselves operate democratically; they must complement their own agendas with demands for democracy; they must either gather sufficient powers of their own or be complemented by other CSOs 'in a process of horizontal relations within civil society itself' (Kamrava and Mora, 1998: 895). Kamrava insists further on a clear distinction between civil society and civil society organizations. The latter are the constituent members of the former. They are frequently issue-specific and issue-driven and have a strong sense of corporate identity. He notes that civil society does not necessarily follow 'whenever there is a cluster of CSOs' but is contingent on the nature and extent of the relationship between the state and larger society (Kamrava, 2007: 207).

Berman sounds an even more cautionary note, pointing out that civil society is not, in any case, necessarily democratic in orientation. She argues that under certain circumstances, 'a robust civil society' may, in fact, hasten the 'degeneration' of a democratic regime. Rejecting the assumption that civil society activities are good things in, and of, themselves, she suggests that, under certain circumstances, the organizations of civil society may mobilize dissatisfied individuals for political activity that is subversive of democratic systems. Civil society can fragment, as much as unite, a society 'accentuating and deepening existing cleavages', the most dramatic example of this being seen in interwar Germany, where civil society flourished but exacerbated, rather than alleviated, the country's divisions (Berman, 1997: 565). The extent to which civil society is likely to have this effect is dependent on the political context. If a country's political institutions can channel and redress grievances, then civic activism will

140   *V. Durac*

probably have beneficial effects for political stability and democracy. However, if political institutions are weak and the existing regime is seen as 'ineffectual and illegitimate', then civil society activity may have negative consequences for democracy by deepening existing divisions in society and 'providing rich soil for oppositional movements' (Berman, 1997: 569–570).

Civil society and the Middle East

However the relationship between civil society and democracy is conceptualized, there is general agreement that there has been a very significant increase in the scale of civil society activism in the Middle East in recent decades. It follows that the debate continues as to what it means to talk about civil society in the context of Middle Eastern and Islamic societies. For some, the Western origins of the term rid it of any meaningful application in non-Western contexts. Mardin writes of civil society as 'a Western dream' which does not translate into Islamic terms (Mardin, 1995: 278–279). He contrasts the Western dream of civil society, in the form of 'an ideal counterpoise to the state' with the Muslim dream of society which, among other things, was grounded in the idea that Muslims bow only to the political obligations set out in the Qur'an. Mardin's doubts are echoed by Arkoun, who focuses on the historical absence in Muslim societies of the middle classes that have played a crucial role since the eighteenth century in the emergence of 'Euro-American civil society'. Such sociopolitical realities together with authoritarian and unaccountable state institutions render even the development of the rule of law elusive in Islamic contexts (Arkoun, 2004: 36). Arkoun suggests that the 'culture of citizenship' that is central to civil society is emerging too slowly in most Muslim contexts. Kelsay argues that, in Islamic tradition, civil society becomes a discussion of the ways that Muslims have understood the organization of social life so as to protect the relative independence of Islamic values from the authoritarian tendencies of governments. However, he contrasts this 'Muslim' understanding of civil society, which implies some sort of established status for Islam, with Western understandings which legitimate liberty in religious and other civil matters, and concludes that a fully developed civil society has not been, and is not now, an aspect of most Islamic political thinking (Kelsay, 2002: 310).

Others, however, are more hopeful that civil society has resonance in the Middle East and draw on the historical experience of Muslim societies in order to justify this claim. The existence of politically autonomous *ulama* who enjoyed a high degree of autonomy, or the emergence of merchant guilds that acted to protect the interests of their members, have been offered as evidence of a kind of civil society having emerged in Arab history (Ismael and Ismael, 1997; Browers, 2004; Kamrava, 2007). Browers discusses the views of three contemporary Arab thinkers on the subject, who, in different ways, clearly argue for the position that Arab historical tradition supports the claim that civil society can, and has, existed in the Muslim world. One of these, Wajid Kawtharani, argues that society, under the Arab-Islamic state, enjoyed considerable independence from the state, even

Civil society in contemporary Yemen 141

if that state was one of 'power and coercion' (Browers, 2004: 62). She sets out the argument made by Burhan Ghalyun that civil society in the Middle East should not be confined to 'modern organizations and structures' such as parties, trade unions and human rights organizations, but should be understood to encompass all economic, cultural and religious institutions that fall outside the control of the state. Ghalyun argues that civil society should be seen not as 'a reservoir of democratic practices and freedom' but as 'a diversity of groups and individuals, partial and imperfect solidarities and various forms of competition and contradictions' (Browers, 2004: 65). In his view, this must include Islamist social forces.

Regardless of debates on the theoretical application of civil society to the Middle East, there is little doubt that civil society activity now plays a major role in both policy-making and in a great deal of academic and other commentary on the region. Wiktorowicz has pointed out the influence of the view of civil society as empowerment on Middle East studies. In a region dominated by authoritarian regimes, civil society is seen as a possible remedy for political stagnation as specialists emphasize the role civil society might play in mobilizing opposition and dissent (Wiktorowicz, 2000: 45). Women's organizations, human rights groups and organizations supporting media freedoms are often seen as central to efforts to demands for greater democracy and freedom (Alhamad, 2008: 33). This optimism is reinforced by the seeming inexorable growth in numbers of CSOs in the Middle East. According to Yom, the numbers of CSOs in the Arab world have grown from around 20,000 in the 1970s to 70,000 in the mid-1990s. There are 14,000 in Egypt alone and 21,000 more in Morocco, Lebanon, Jordan, Yemen and Tunisia (Yom, 2005: 18). Carapico (2000) has offered a number of factors to explain the growing prominence of NGOs in the region. At national level, these include the suppression or co-optation of opposition political parties and other 'channels for civil energies', as well as social trends, such as urbanization and education, detachment from roots and the encouragement of NGOs by international, especially Western, actors. International factors include the tendency for development aid donors to transfer resources to NGOs, the availability of funds under the 'peace process' for initiatives in Egypt, Jordan and Palestine, and increased consciousness of human rights, environmental and feminist issues.

However, the growth in scale and significance of the civil society sector in the Middle East has not, for the most part, been accompanied by any substantial alteration in the underlying authoritarian character of the politics of the region. This is due to key limitations on Arab civil society which operate on two levels. The first of these has to do with the social and political environment within which CSOs operate. The second has to do with the character of CSOs in the region. A number of writers have argued for the necessary role of the state in regulating civil society. Government sets limits to the authority of associations over their members and protects against the worst oppression by private authorities. It is the duty of government also to provide a legal framework within which civil society actors can operate (Rosenblum and Post, 2002: 9). In this ideal-type

142   *V. Durac*

model, the state is conceived as a neutral, if not benign, actor overseeing civil society, providing a framework for its operation and resolving any difficulties that flow from this.

However, in the context of the modern Middle East, it is clear that no such role for the state can, or should, be assumed. Rather, Middle Eastern states seek to control and co-opt civil society for their own purposes and benefits. Wiktorowicz (2000: 46–47) comments that, whereas elsewhere civil society emerged from below to challenge dictators and military juntas, in the Middle East, the growth of civil society followed regime-led political liberalization. Political elites therefore have shaped and managed the process in order to maximize their own control. As Moore and Salloukh (2007: 69–70) have noted, 'regimes will organize state–society relations to meet a minimum guarantee of their survival'. Middle Eastern states have enmeshed civil society in a web of regulations, bureaucratic practices and legal codes that facilitate the maintenance of state control. Some states outlaw civil society activity altogether. Others permit it under severe restrictions. These may include permitting NGOs to engage only in social welfare or cultural work, excluding political activities. Intimidation, co-optation, the use of emergency laws, harassment and arrest of those who cross the line into unacceptable political activity are other tactics employed by regimes (Hawthorne, 2004: 10; Alhamad, 2008: 38–39). Legal codes and, what Wiktorowicz (2000: 81–85) characterizes as 'administrative repression', create an atmosphere of self-censorship such that Arab CSOs engage only very tentatively with overtly political issues. State penetration of the sector is underlined by the creation of government-controlled NGOs (GONGOs) through which 'a presumably independent space ... is colonized by the regime'. Arab regimes seek to contain and co-opt civil society actors all the more so because they enjoy access to scarce foreign funds. Governments know that defining institutions as NGOs 'helps attract dollars' (Carapico, 2000: 14).

But, the limited impact of Arab civil society in influencing the direction of political life is not solely the consequence of regime attempts to control the sector. CSOs in the Arab world tend to lack autonomy from the state. The service NGO sector is often an extension of the state – service NGOs often receive significant government funding. Other civil society actors, such as labour unions, chambers of commerce and professional associations rely on the state to promote their economic interests. These intertwining relationships between state and civil society are also characteristic of the Islamic sector. In some contexts, Islamic CSOs have been supported by governments as counterweights to secular opposition forces. In others they originate in conservative religious organizations that may have no interest in challenging established governments (Hawthorne, 2004: 12).

Furthermore, CSOs have been critiqued as undemocratic in terms of their own structures and procedures as well as lacking tolerance of competing points of view. Civility, Norton observes, is missing from large parts of the Middle East (Norton, 1993: 214).[2] Finally, as Hawthorne points out, a critical mass of Arab NGOs has not adopted a clear pro-democracy agenda.

Civil society in contemporary Yemen 143

Indeed, when Arab leaders boast of their countries' burgeoning civil societies, as they often do, they are referring to service NGOs and similar groups that carry out their own national development agenda. Thus, regimes view these groups as 'partners' not adversaries.

(Hawthorne, 2004: 12)

A number of things become clear from this survey. If civil society is broadly conceived of in terms of the zone of civic activism that takes place between the spheres of the family and the state, then the Middle East has indeed witnessed a significant increase in civil society activity since the end of the Cold War. However, civil society in the Middle East assumes very different characteristics to those associated with its counterparts in Western contexts. One of these is that religion plays a much greater role in civil society activism in the region and to neglect the role of religious actors would be to exclude a dominant share of civic activism. Above all, the extent to which state–society relations in the Middle East are dominated and interpenetrated by the overweening power of authoritarian regimes has significant implications. These include the lack of autonomy from the state of civil society organizations and the limited potential of civil society in the Middle East to act as an agent of democratic political change. Indeed, one may question whether such a role is, in any case, seen as desirable on the part of most Middle Eastern CSOs.

Civil society and the state in Yemen

Yemen: an overview

The Republic of Yemen is the newest state in the Middle East and North Africa. It emerged in 1990 out of a process of unification of the former Yemen Arab Republic (YAR) with the People's Democratic Republic of Yemen (PDRY). The YAR had been established in northern Yemen in 1962 following the overthrow of the Zaydi Imamate,

The PDRY was the state which emerged in the South following British withdrawal from its colony of Aden in 1967. How the Republic of Yemen came into existence has not only shaped the subsequent (and in terms of the Arab world, atypical) character of political life, but has also determined the context within which Yemeni civil society operates. Because the modern state resulted from the unification of two apparently very different states (conservative and socialist, respectively), a very different political system was established at unification from those found in the rest of the Arabian Gulf or the region more broadly. In particular, a genuinely competitive party political system came into existence, albeit within limits, as well as space for the activities of civil society actors. The substantial economic, demographic and social problems of the newly united state, combined with economic mismanagement and widespread corruption, left Yemen economically dependent on external aid. This too has contributed to the enlargement of the space available for civil society.

144 *V. Durac*

Pre-unification, the two Yemeni states were governed very differently. The YAR was viewed as a 'weak' state, vast tracts of which were effectively independent of Sana'a. The PDRY, on the other hand, was a highly centralized Marxist dictatorship (Blumi, 2009: 3). However, events in the late 1980s produced two weak and vulnerable regimes that saw unification as a means to long-term security (Blumi, 2009: 4). As the end of the Cold War approached, both regimes lacked legitimacy, both faced substantial economic problems and the leadership of each saw unification as a process that they could harness in order to bolster their respective positions (Phillips, 2008: 48; Blumi, 2009: 4).

Agreement on unification was reached between the ruling party of the YAR, the General People's Congress (GPC), led by 'Ali 'Abdallah Salih, and the ruling party of the PDRY, the Yemen Socialist Party (YSP), led by 'Ali Salim al-Baydh. Blumi suggests that the well-educated socialists of the south believed that unification with the politically unsophisticated North could secure them immunity from challenge in the future. The formal power-sharing agreement gave the YSP key portfolios in future government such as the prime minister, ministry of defence and foreign minister (Carapico, 1998: 137; Blumi, 2009: 6). 'Ali 'Abdallah Salih became president of the new republic.

Unity was declared on 22 May 1990 and 'ushered in Yemen's most liberal, most political civic opening' (Carapico, 1998: 135–136). There was an 'unprecedented' relaxation of security, political, financial and legal controls; legal-constitutional guarantees of personal, press and political freedom. The initial power-sharing agreement divided posts in the Presidential Council, the Council of Ministers and Parliament more or less equally between the GPC and the YSP leaving 'unusual scope' for third parties to become politically involved (Carapico, 1998: 136). A new constitution, which was adopted after a nationwide referendum in 1991, enshrined voting and candidacy rights to all Yemeni citizens, equality before the law, a democratic political system and the independence of the judiciary. A new press law of 1990 guaranteed the right to freedom of expression, the press and access to information, leading to a huge increase in the number of publications in the newly unified state. Political and electoral laws led to the establishment of a range of political parties (some forty-five in all, twenty-one of which contested elections in 1993), while the removal of restrictions on meeting and organizing freely paved the way for a proliferation of grassroots organizations of all kinds (Carapico, 1998: 138–140; Phillips, 2008: 49–50). However, most of the apparatus of the two precursor states remained intact. For example, the process of integrating two army commands was left undone. Trade unions, which formed part of the power base of the YSP, and tribal militias loyal to Salih were left largely untouched. 'This meant that two different societies still existed with two completely different patronage networks in operation' (Blumi, 2009: 8) and the very different motivations for entering into union on the part of the leaders of the GPC and YSP made tensions between them inevitable.

The first parliamentary elections in the new Republic of Yemen were held in April 1993 after several postponements. In the elections it was the traditional leadership of the former YAR in the north that emerged victorious. The General

Civil society in contemporary Yemen   145

People's Congress won 145 seats in the 301-seat parliament. The former ruling party of the PDRY, the YSP, was the big loser, coming third in the elections, behind a newcomer, the Islamist *Islah* party, which had been established by a coalition of religious elements in the GPC, conservative businessmen and moderate and hardline Islamists.[3] The elections established the dominance of the GPC, and of the northern political elite generally, in post-unification political life.

Despite the popularity of the unification project nationally, the period from 1991 to 1994 was characterized by violence, instability and tensions between the GPC and the YSP, as well as demands for greater decentralization of power and autonomy for the South, in the face of what many saw as the increasing dominance of the GPC and its allies (Schwedler, 2006: 61–62). The expulsion in 1991 of 800,000 Yemeni workers from Saudi Arabia, following Yemen's failure to support an international military campaign against Saddam Hussein in Kuwait, added to these tensions, as did labour unrest and a wave of political assassinations.

Civil war broke out in April 1994 and saw the entry by what had been the army of the YAR into the territory of what had been the PDRY in response to the declaration of the Yemen Democratic Republic (YDR) in the South. The war lasted only two months and resulted not only in defeat for the forces associated with the YSP but also 'destroyed much of the buoyancy surrounding the idea of unity, and, by extension, democratization' (Phillips, 2008: 58). Most of the leaders of the breakaway republic fled the country. In its aftermath, the GPC cracked down on what were seen to be secessionist elements in the YSP and retracted some of the progressive reforms that had followed unification, in a series of constitutional amendments that were passed by a special committee without a public referendum. These amendments abolished the Presidential Council and strengthened the powers of the president. The amended constitution created an appointed Constitutional Council, allowed the president to appoint the prime minister, act as Head of the Supreme Judicial Council and issue laws by decree when parliament was not in session (Carapico, 1998: 57; Phillips, 2008: 59–60).

The period since the end of the Cold War has seen the consolidation of GPC control and that of President Salih. Although Salih lifted the state of emergency that had been declared in July 1994, there was no restoration of the 'privileges and tolerances established during the four-year liberal interlude' (Carapico, 1998: 188). Elections in 1997 were boycotted by the YSP and led to a substantial victory for the GPC which won 188 seats to Islah's 56 (Schwedler, 2002: 51). Despite the YSP boycott, the elections were generally seen as relatively free and fair. Nonetheless, the dominance of the ruling party since 1994 has led Day to conclude that 'the GPC has become virtually synonymous with the state' (Day, 2006: 134).

However, along with the consolidation of GPC rule, there have been some paradoxical political developments. While presidential elections in 1999 were won by Salih, in a manner all too reminiscent of other Arab states, with 96.3 per cent of the vote, the post Cold War period has also seen the establishment and

146   *V. Durac*

survival of an unlikely coalition between the two major opposition parties, the YSP and Islah. The so-called Joint Meetings Party (JMP) represents the institutionalization of a form of cooperation between Islamists and leftists seen elsewhere in the region but rarely as long-lived as in Yemen.[4] The JMP came into existence in 2002 when Islah and the YSP joined with three smaller parties to establish a joint opposition to the GPC.[5] Despite the attempts by the regime to prise the coalition apart, it has evolved in the direction of becoming 'a credible and formidable' opposition force (Burrowes and Kasper, 2007: 268). In the parliamentary elections of April 2003, the GPC won 225 seats, Islah 46 and the YSP seven. But, the high point of this alliance was the nomination by the JMP of an alternative, Faisal Bin Shamlan, to the candidacy of Salih in presidential elections in 2006. Despite a vitriolic campaign against Bin Shamlan, in the course of which he was linked to al-Qa'eda, he secured nearly 22 per cent of the official vote (Longley, 2007: 245; Day, 2008: 426).

However, contemporary Yemen faces severe challenges, challenges which some characterize as existential in nature. These stem from serious economic underperformance in the face of widespread poverty and poor educational and health infrastructure, rapidly increasing population levels, declining natural resources, in the form of oil and water, and the threat from radical Islamist forces. In some of the bleakest (or alarmist) analyses, this incendiary combination holds out the prospect of Yemen joining the ranks of 'failed' states. Yemen is one of the poorest countries in the Middle East, with a per capita GDP of US$930, has low levels of literacy and of primary, secondary and tertiary enrolment in education, and ranks 153 out of 177 countries in the UN's Human Development Index. Yemen is also faced with diminishing oil and freshwater reserves. While Yemen's oil industry is not significant by global standards, it has formed the basis of up to 90 per cent of export earnings and 75 per cent of the national budget. However, as output from its two major oilfields declines, the World Bank predicts that state revenues from oil and gas sales will fall to zero by 2017 (Johnsen, 2006; Hill, 2008: 7). Similarly dramatic predictions have been made regarding fresh water sources – if current usage patterns continue, then major urban centres face very significant shortages within the next twenty years. To this, some commentators have added the threat from radical Islamists, Yemen having long been associated with al-Qa'eda and violent 'jihadist' activities.[6] These difficulties are compounded by persistent unrest in Saada in northern Yemen, where a rebellion began in 2004 under the leadership of a Zaydi Shi'a leader, Badr al-Din al-Houthi, and which has been revived more recently since his death, as well as the re-emergence of southern grievances expressed in the form of public protests on a mass scale.[7] Anti-regime sentiment became even more widespread in early 2011 when street protests against the regime gradually spread to Yemen's major cities, drawing in a wide range of opposition forces to challenge Salih's continued grip on power.[8]

Civil society in Yemen

It is in this context that civil society operates in Yemen. However, while the substantial increase in the number of Yemeni CSOs and the range of activities which they undertake may be traceable to the political opening that followed unification (and to the desire on the part of the regime to represent Yemen as a democratizing state to the outside world), the history of civil society activism in the country goes considerably further back. Indeed, Yemeni civil society was the subject of one of the first country-specific book-length studies – Sheila Carapico's definitive text *Civil Society in Yemen: The Political Economy of Activism* which was first published in 1998. Labour unions were formed in colonial Aden around 1947. The Aden Trades Union Conference was formed in March 1956 (Carapico, 1998: 92). Association life in Aden culminated in the formation of cultural clubs, independent presses, labour and political parties, rural movements and local self-help groups. But, despite the role that such organizations played in the anti-colonial struggle, the PDRY regime, which followed the British departure from Aden, suppressed civil society until its dissolution in 1990 (Clark, 2003: 118). In northern Yemen, civil society played an important role in the removal of the former Imam in 1962 which paved the way for the establishment of the new republic (Clark, 2003: 118). In the YAR, local associations dealing with social welfare issues emerged, the most significant of which were the Local Development Associations (LDAs). However, these were viewed with suspicion by the state and were ultimately brought under state control.

The post-unification constitution of the Republic of Yemen, as amended in 1994, following the civil war, guaranteed freedom of association as well as the right to form associations.[9] Enabling legislation for associations was enacted in 1994 and in 1998 for cooperatives. The laws governing associations were updated in the Associations Law of 2001 which has been described as 'one of the least restrictive NGO laws in the region' (USAID, 2007). In drafting the law, the government consulted with NGOs and accepted some of their demands which included a request that there should be no requirement for prior government approval for receipt of foreign funding (USAID, 2007). The law provides for a straightforward process of registration for NGOs. On receipt of an application, the Ministry of Pensions and Social Affairs has one month in which to accept or reject the application. If the application is not processed within this time, it is deemed to have been accepted in law (Article 9). In the event that an application is rejected, a written statement of the grounds for the rejection must be sent to the applicant(s) and posted on the Bulletin Board of the Ministry (Article 10). Provision is also made for an appeals process if the application is rejected. However, despite its liberal, enabling tone, the law also includes quite sweeping penalty provisions. Article 68 (2) sets out a punishment of imprisonment for up to one year or a fine of up to 100,000 Yemeni riyals for a number of offences, including undertaking activities that are 'in excess of the purposes for which the association or foundation was established'. However, as USAID points out, the environment in which Yemeni CSOs operate is not wholly comprehended by an analysis of

148   *V. Durac*

legal texts – the political level is all important. The government proclaims itself to be supportive of a vibrant civil society – the official view is that civil society is a trusted partner in the development of Yemen, which is also consistent with the government's interest in being perceived internationally as tolerant and democratic. However, there is still widespread official distrust of CSOs that are seen as meddling in politics (USAID, 2007). This is a claim borne out in the views of CSO activists in Yemen.

The 2001 law certainly had the effect of facilitating the easy registration of CSOs. The numbers of registered CSOs grew from a few hundred in the early 1990s to 3,150 in 2002 to over 5,600 in 2007 (USAID, 2007).[10] The Ministry of Social Affairs and Labour, which now deals with registration, currently lists 5,632 CSOs, about half of which are in Sana'a. They range from small, one-person organizations to very large-scale operations. However, the apparently large numbers are misleading and only a fraction of these are active – estimates range from a few hundred to a thousand.

The 2007 USAID assessment of the civil society sector in Yemen suggests that its growth in scale has been due to a number of factors, including poverty, population growth and the increasing inability of the state to provide essential services (USAID, 2007). In light of this, it is not surprising that the vast majority of CSOs (as is the case elsewhere in the Middle East) are service-oriented and charity-based while advocacy and politically oriented groups are very much a novelty, and only a small number of them are effective. Yemeni CSOs, whether service-oriented or not, vary widely in terms of capacity, institutional strength or weakness, and relationship with the government. Most are weak and lack capacity, but a number are very well-organized and resourced. What is notable is the extent to which the most successful service-oriented organizations in the country enjoy close links with the government. The Charitable Society for Social Welfare is perhaps the best resourced CSO in the country. The Society was founded in 1990 and has close links with the *Islah* political party (it is also known as the *Islah* Charitable Society). However, it has an independent administrative system and rejects claims that it is affiliated with the party.[11] It is the most successful humanitarian CSO in the country and one of the few active in every governorate in Yemen (Clark, 2003: 123–126). Currently it has over 700 employees and 12,000 volunteers and, despite its undoubted links with the *Islah* party, works closely with the Ministries of Health and Social Affairs, UN agencies in Yemen and other CSOs in a range of fields.[12] The Yemen Women's Union was established in 1990, although precursor organizations existed both in Aden and the YAR. The YWU has twenty-two branches across the country, 165 centres and many more village-level committees. It has twenty-one employees and claims to have 'thousands' of volunteers.[13] The YWU works on issues of literacy, training, education and poverty reduction and has 'quite broad acceptance'.[14] Like CSSW, it works closely with government – the chairwoman of the organization is a former diplomat and describes its relationship with the government as 'very good' – if it does not have a good relationship with government, then it will not be heard.[15] The

Civil society in contemporary Yemen 149

extent to which the most effective service-oriented CSOs are interlinked with the Yemeni government is illustrated by two further examples. The Social Fund for Development, which was established in 1997, developed and implemented 3,500 projects with a total cost of around $260 million, benefiting nearly seven million people and providing about 8,000 jobs in its first six years of existence (Al-Arhabi, 2004). While the SFD has won praise for its efficiency and reach, its Managing Director, Abdulkarim Al-Arhabi, is also the the Deputy Prime Minister for Economic Affairs and Minister of Planning and International Cooperation, while the Chairman of the Board of Directors is the Prime Minister.[16] Despite the undoubtedly successful record of the organization and its reputation for getting things done, this clearly is not a non-governmental organization in any save the most technical sense of the term. Finally, one of the largest 'CSOs' in the country, the Al-Salih foundation, is headed up by the president's son, Ahmad Ali Abdullah Salih.

Advocacy and politically oriented groups are a small minority of CSOs in Yemen. They work in the areas of human rights protection, civic and political participation, freedom of expression and accountable government (USAID, 2007). These organizations tend to have much more ambiguous relationships with government. However, as with the larger service-oriented CSOs, the necessity to maintain relations with the government, despite engaging in activities critical of it, is a consistent theme. Groups like HOOD (National Organization for Defending Rights and Freedoms), the Media Women's Forum and the Yemen Polling Center occupy an ambiguous zone in Yemeni civil society. HOOD was established in 1998 and is based in Sana'a, but is active in fourteen other provinces. Its main objectives are: monitoring human rights violations; providing advice and assistance to those directly affected; and working for legal reform. It has also worked on media freedoms, trade union rights and the provision of assistance to Yemeni detainees in Guantanamo Bay. Its activists are lawyers, journalists and parliamentarians for the most part. Its activities place it at odds with the government but it seeks to keep lines of communication open and has met with the Secretary-General of the GPC. The ambiguous nature of the relationship can be seen in the fact that the authorities have refused to renew its licence while it receives invitations to official events.[17] The Media Women's Forum (MWF), which is one of the most high-profile advocacy CSOs in Yemen, was established in Sana'a in 2004 and is dedicated to upholding the principles, standards and values of human rights and working for gender equality in the media. As well as its advocacy work, the MWF is involved in an extensive range of activities including media training for women, conferences on gender and the media, and the establishment of a database of women journalists. The activities of the organization have brought it into controversy in Yemen where gender inequality is deeply entrenched (Cooke, 2008). The chairwoman of the organization has been subjected to attack in the pro-government press and has been threatened with prosecution.[18] However, like many other more politically oriented CSOs in Yemen, the organization claims to have good relations with the government and its chairperson has met several times with the president (this

150   *V. Durac*

despite describing him as an 'enemy' in a newspaper interview in April 2008).[19] The Yemen Polling Center (YPC) was established in 2005 to carry out surveys and opinion polls on issues such as political elites, bribery and citizen participation in political life. As with most other organizations working in what are seen as sensitive areas, the YPC adopts a very cautious public profile. It carefully describes its work as a contribution to the building of 'a free, open and democratic society' in Yemen by bringing together researchers, journalists and newspaper editors and characterizes Yemen as 'an emerging democratic country'.[20] Its concern to maintain good relations with the government is evident in the fact that the Deputy Minister for Human Rights sits on its Board of Trustees.

Civil society and the state

It is clear from the most cursory analysis that the proliferation of CSOs in Yemen since unification has had very limited impact on the political system in the country. The simplistic argument, that growth in the civil society sector will lead to democratic political change, is not supported by any available evidence. Instead, the character of Yemeni CSOs and the context within which they operate suggest very different conclusions.

Civil society in Yemen suffers from severe limitations which prevent it from playing a significant role in the politics of the country. These stem from the interrelationship between the character of CSOs in Yemen and the social, economic and political environment that they inhabit. In the first instance, there are problems of capacity – Phillips cites the regime's unwillingness to rely on outright oppression of opposition groups and activists, preferring instead to allow organizations to 'run out of steam' due to lack of capacity (Phillips, 2008: 116). All but the very largest CSOs lack capacity to build themselves into sustainable organizations and have limited absorptive capacity. Many are dependent on one individual, typically the founder of the organization, or, at best, a few members (USAID, 2007). Lack of capacity was identified consistently in interviews with civil society activists and others in Yemen as a barrier to effectiveness.[21] The Friedrich Ebert Stiftung (FES) in Yemen rated the capacity of CSOs at 'two out of ten' as compared with 'zero out of ten' a decade ago.[22] The undemocratic nature of many CSOs and lack of cooperation and coordination between them also prevents their effective functioning (Phillips, 2008: 122).[23]

The large numbers of CSOs (if only on paper) signals the degree of fragmentation of civil society in Yemen. Such large numbers prevent the emergence of a smaller number of more coherent actors with more coherent agenda to press against the government. Lack of resources at all levels has particular consequences for civil society, increasing, as it does, economic dependence on government and outside sources, and expanding the scope for the regime to 'buy off' or co-opt critical civil society activists and organizations through financial inducements. Phillips cites the view of a Board member of a long-standing political NGO that all opposition activists in Yemen make a deal with the government, except for a few idealists who are unsuccessful as a result (Phillips, 2008: 130).

Civil society in contemporary Yemen 151

For more politically oriented civil society activists, a range of other challenges have to be faced. Despite the appearance of an open and plural space for activism, the existence of 'red-lines' has been identified. These include the role of the president, the regime's relationship with the United States and the response to the Houthi rebellion in Saada. For those who cross the line, and despite regime reticence to resort to outright repression, the consequences are serious. Members of the Yemeni press who have criticized the regime have been subjected to brutal attacks, abductions and imprisonment (International Press Institute, 2007). With this implicit threat in mind, government offers of 'assistance' may be difficult to turn down, since the alternative to having minimal political impact may be to have none at all (Phillips, 2008: 130).[24]

Finally, for many political civil society activists there is the dilemma that any challenge that weakens the regime may pave the way for an alternative that is seen as less preferable. Fear of further Islamist successes prompts many to opt for an incremental approach to political change in Yemen that offers effective support to the regime. Despite her opposition to much that the regime is doing, Rahma Hugaira of the Media Women's Forum offered unambiguous support to the government because it represented a better option than an alternative dominated by conservative Islamists who find the work of the MWF deeply problematic.[25]

The result of lack of capacity, limited resources and competition between CSOs for those resources, and government control strategies, has been the emergence of a civil society sector that lacks autonomy from the state. The most effective CSOs are those with the closest connections to the regime, especially in the area of service-provision. For advocacy and more politically oriented organizations, the dominance of the regime over the public sphere, its use of co-optation or repression as circumstances require, and the fear for many of the consequences of any destabilization of the status quo, significantly limit the potential impact of their efforts.

Further evidence of the ineffectiveness of Yemeni civil society in promoting democratic political change is yielded by an analysis of the 2011 protest movement which emerged, like its counterparts elsewhere, from outside established centres of political activity, not least as an expression of frustration with the absence of movement in the direction of political reform in the country.[26]

Conclusion

The case of Yemeni civil society supports a number of conclusions. It is clear that the potential contribution which civil society can make to democratic political change in the Middle East has been greatly overstated. This is not an endorsement of the claim that civil society is *ipso faco* alien to the region on religious or cultural grounds. However, where civil society is under-resourced, lacking in capacity and penetrated by the state, its potential to contribute to democratic political reform is severely circumscribed. In fact, under these circumstances, the existence of an apparently vigorous civil society (measured

152 *V. Durac*

crudely in terms of the number of CSOs in operation) may have the paradoxical effect of lending support to authoritarian regimes, who derive political and economic benefits from the apparent presence of a plural and lively associational sector, without facing any significant political challenge from that sector. This echoes findings from other contexts in the Middle East. Wiktorowicz has discussed the ways in which regime control of civil society in Jordan circumscribes the activities of CSOs and renders them limited in the promotion of democracy while offering the regime benefits through the receipt of international aid by organizations controlled by the regime (Wiktorowicz, 2002: 89). As Jamal observes, the political context within which civic associations operate is key to whether or not they are likely to promote democratic political change (Jamal, 2007: 9). In the Middle East, organizations that are critical of undemocratic regimes face restrictions if not outright disbandment while those that are supportive enjoy rights and privileges denied to others. The result is that where the survival of such organizations is tied to regime endorsement then civil society 'can and does reinforce existing political regimes and not democracy per se' (Jamal, 2007: 9–10). This is linked to the broader point, which has been made by Schlumberger, that political liberalization in the Middle East is not a process initiated as a result of pressure from below, nor does it invariably lead in a democratic direction. Instead it is better understood as a survival strategy of regimes (Schlumberger, 2000: 118).

Following on from this, it becomes clear that the model of the relationship between civil society and democratic political change which is derived from the experience of Latin America and Eastern Europe over twenty years ago is entirely inappropriate to the Middle East and merely leads to the creation of expectations that cannot be fulfilled. It is precisely because civil society in the Middle East lacks autonomy from the state, is characterized by close linkages with the state, and operates within a framework largely defined by that state that it is unlikely to challenge entrenched authoritarian structures. Indeed, in the case of Yemen, overarching political change is rarely a primary concern of civil society organizations in the region which are, for the most part, concerned with meeting the array of social, educational and other issues that flow from the enormous problems that the country faces. In engaging with these problems, it is, in fact, inevitable that civil society actors will seek to cooperate with and gain influence over a state which despite its weakness remains by far the most powerful actor in the system. The dependence of Yemeni civil society organizations on the state stems from the antecedent realities of Yemeni political and social life, characterized by permeable relations between political parties, civic activists and Islamic actors and the state, as well as a blurring of political and ideological dividing lines. In this sort of context, closer engagement with the state, as opposed to confrontation, is most likely to serve the interests of those organizations, even if this means offering nothing but disappointment to those outside observers who are fixated on the democratizing potential of civil society.

Civil society in contemporary Yemen 153

Notes

1 In a similar vein, Edwards suggests that the liberal conception of civil society is now dominant: 'It is Alexis de Tocqueville's ghost that wanders through the corridors of the World Bank, not that of Habermas or Hegel' (2004: 10).
2 See also Sayyid (1993). For a very different perspective on this, see Harik (1994). At p. 50, Harik argues that the democratic character of civil society, while important, 'is not a precondition for political democracy'.
3 For a detailed study of the *Islah* party, see Schwedler (2006).
4 See Schwedler and Clarke (2006).
5 For a detailed account of the process whereby the JMP came into existence, and the ideological shifts underlying this, see Browers (2007).
6 One interviewee in Sana'a, speaking off the record, expressed the view explicitly that 'Yemen is facing collapse' in the face of severe challenges that were not being addressed in any effective fashion. Interview with civil society activist, Sana'a, March 2008.
7 On the Houthi rebellion, see Phillips (2008: 71–72) and Glosemeyer (2004). For more on Southern discontent, see Day (2008) and Longley and Al-Iryani (2008).
8 See, for example, International Crisis Group (2011).
9 Article 57 of the Constitution states:

> In as much as it is not contrary to the Constitution, the citizens may organize themselves along political, professional and union lines. They have the right to form associations in scientific, cultural, social and national organizations in a way that serves the goals of the Constitution. The state shall guarantee these rights, and shall take the necessary measures to enable citizens to exercise them. The state shall guarantee freedom for the political, trade, cultural, scientific and social organizations.

10 According to Carapico, at the time of unification in 1990, there were 250 agricultural societies and cooperatives, forty-eight consumer associations, twenty-one craft societies, nineteen fishermen's associations and about one hundred housing cooperatives (Carapico, 1998: 154).
11 CSSW Secretary General, Abdul-Majeed Farhan, has stated that because of the name 'people think the society is completely affiliated with the party and adopts its policy. I can assure you that this is not right and the society is completely independent.... It has its own policies' (Al-Omari, 2008).
12 Interview with CSSW, Sana'a, 31 March 2008.
13 Interview with Ramzia Abbas Aleryani, Chairwoman of YWU, Sana'a, 30 March 2008.
14 Interview with Djoeke Adimi, First Secretary, Embassy of the Netherlands, Sana'a, 26 March 2008.
15 Interview with Ramzia Abbas Aleryani, Chairwoman of YWU, Sana'a, 30 March 2008.
16 The SFD is separate from the government, has its own budgets, 'can move faster than government and do lots of larger projects'. Interview with Djoeke Adimi, First Secretary, Embassy of the Netherlands, Sana'a, 26 March 2008.
17 Interview with Khalid Alanesi, Executive Director of HOOD, Sana'a, 30 March 2008.
18 Interview with Rahma Hugaira, Chairperson of Media Women's Forum, Sana'a, 31 March 2008.
19 See Al-Showthabi (2008).
20 Interview with Hafez al-Bukari, President of Yemen Polling Center, Sana'a, 29 March 2008.
21 For example, the lack of technical capacity, and of 'human, technical and other resources in the country' was identified as a major obstacle by Yasser Abdullah Mubarak, Good Governance Project Manager, Oxfam in an interview in Sana'a,

154 *V. Durac*

30 March 2008. Lack of capacity and the limited resources of NGOs were also identified as key issues by Abduallh Ahmad Al-Syari, Director of International Cooperation for Development/Progressio, in an interview in Sana'a, 29 March 2008. See also USAID (2007).

22 Interview with Felix Eikenber, Resident Representative, Freidrich Ebert Stiftung, Sana'a, 30 March 2008.

23 In an interview, Djoeke Adimi identified 'lack of transparency' as a common characteristic of NGOs in Yemen. She also commented on the lack of inter-NGO cooperation 'due to the limited pot of funding'. Interview with Djoeke Adimi, First Secretary, Embassy of the Netherlands, Sana'a, 26 March 2008.

24 Phillips argues that, while patron–client relationships abound in the Arab world, they are pervasive in Yemen because the bleak economic situation limits people's options for political independence (Phillips, 2008: 130).

25 Interview with Rahma Hugaira, Chairperson of Media Women's Forum, Sana'a, 31 March 2008. Similar views were expressed off the record, by other interviewees, one of whom identified the increased influence of conservative Islamists as contributing to existential challenges facing the country.

26 Hill and Nonneman argue that the political crisis in Yemen 'follows a simultaneous loss of faith in the legitimacy of the government, the established opposition and the parliamentary framework' (Nonneman and Hill, 2011). The 2011 protest movement which began as a grassroots response to corruption and the ineffectiveness of established political actors in Yemen was quickly marginalized as inter-elite competition and the efforts of the established opposition to hijack the movement gained traction. See Al-Sakkaf (2011) and Nonneman and Hill (2011).

Bibliography

Al-Arhabi, A. (2004). 'The Second International Roundtable on Managing for Development Results.' Available at www.mfdr.org/documents/sessions/Plenary4/Plenary4AbdulkarimAl-Arhabi.doc (accessed 17 February 2009).

Al-Omari, M. (2008). 'Interview with Islah Charitable Society Secretary General Dr. Abdul Majeed Farhan', *Yemen Post*. 17 March. Available at www.yemenpost.net/21/InvestigationAndInterview/20081.htm (accessed 28 February 2009).

Al-Sakkaf, N. (2011). 'The Politicization of Yemen's Youth Revolution', *Arab Reform Bulletin*, 27 April. Available at www.carnegieendowment.org/arb/?fa=show&article=43735 (accessed 16 May 2012).

Al-Showthabi, A. (2008). 'Interview with Yemen Women Media Forum Chairwoman Rahma Hugaira', *Yemen Post*. 21 April. Available at www.yemenpost.net/26/InvestigationAndInterview/20081.htm (accessed 2 April 2009).

Albrecht, H. (2005). 'How Can Opposition Support Authoritarianism? Lessons from Egypt', *Democratization*, 12(3), 378–397.

Albrecht, H. and Schlumberger, A. (2004). '"Waiting for Godot": Regime Change Without Democratization in the Middle East', *International Political Science Review*, 25(4), 371–392.

Alhamad, L. (2008). 'Formal and Informal Venues of Engagement', in Lust-Okar, E. and Zerhouni, S. (eds) *Political Participation in the Middle East*. London: Lynne Rienner Publishers.

Allen, C. (1997). 'Who Needs Civil Society?', *Review of African Political Economy*, 73, 329–337.

Arkoun, M. (2004). 'Locating Civil Society in Islamic Contexts', in Sajoo, A.B. (ed.) *Civil Society in the Muslim World: Contemporary Perspectives*. London: I.B. Tauris.

Civil society in contemporary Yemen 155

Berman, S. (1997). 'Civil Society and Political Institutionalization', *American Behavioral Scientist*, 40: 6562–6574.

Blumi, I. (2009). 'Unique Authoritarianism: Shifting Fortunes and the Malleability of the Salih Regime in Yemen, 1990-Present', *EUI Working Papers 2009/10*. Available at http://cadmus.eui.eu/dspace/handle/1814/10734 (accessed 5 March 2009).

Browers, M. (2004). 'Arab Liberalisms: Translating Civil Society, Prioritising Democracy', *Critical Review of International Social and Political Philosophy*, 7(1), 51–75.

Browers, M. (2007). 'Origins and Architects of Yemen's Joint Meeting Parties', *International Journal of Middle East Studies*, 39, 565–586.

Burrowes, R.D. and Kasper, C. (2007). 'The Salih Regime and the Need for a Credible Opposition', *Middle East Journal*, 61(2): 263–280.

Carapico, S. (1998). *Civil Society in Yemen: The Political Economy of Activism in Modern Arabia*, Cambridge: Cambridge University Press.

Carapico, S. (2000). 'NGOs, INGOs, GO-NGOs and DO-NGOs: Making Sense of Non-Governmental Organizations', *Middle East Report*, Spring (214), 12–15.

Chabal, P. and Daloz, J.P. (1999). *Africa Works: Disorder as Political Instrument*, Oxford: International African Institute in association with James Currey.

Clark, J. (2003). *Islam, Charity, and Activism: Middle-Class Networks and Social Welfare in Egypt, Jordan, and Yemen*, Bloomington: Indiana University Press.

Clark, J. (2004). 'Social Movement Theory and Patron–Clientelism: Islamic Social Institutions and the Middle Class in Egypt, Jordan, and Yemen', *Comparative Political Studies*, 37(8), 941–968.

Cooke, R. (2008). 'Is this the worst place on earth to be a woman?', *The Observer*, 11 May.

Day, S. (2006). 'Barriers to Federal Democracy in Iraq: Lessons from Yemen', *Middle East Policy*, 13(3), 121–139.

Day, S. (2008), 'Updating Yemeni National Unity: Could Lingering Regional Divisions Bring Down the Regime?' *Middle East Journal*, 62(3), 417–436.

Edwards, M. (2004). *Civil Society*, Cambridge: Polity.

Giner, S. (1995). 'Civil Society and Its Future', in Hall, J.A. (ed.) *Civil Society: Theory, History, Comparison*. Cambridge: Polity Press.

Glosemeyer, I. (2004). 'Local Conflict, Global Spin: An Uprising in the Yemeni Highlands', *Middle East Report*, 232, 44–46.

Harik, I. (1994). 'Pluralism in the Arab World', *Journal of Democracy*, 5(3), 43–56.

Hawthorne, A. (2004). 'Middle Eastern Democracy: Is Civil Society the Answer?', Carnegie Endowment for International Peace. Available at: www.carnegieendowment.org/publications/index.cfm?fa=view&id=1463 (accessed 5 April 2009).

Hill, G. (2008). 'Yemen: Fear of Failure', *Chatham House Briefing Paper*, available at www.chathamhouse.org.uk/publications/papers/download/-/id/677/file/12576_bp1108yemen.pdf (accessed 2 February 2009).

International Center for Not-for-Profit Law (ICLN) (2001). 'Yemen – Law Concerning Associations and Foundations (No. 1 of 2001) (2001) [English]'. Available at www.icnl.org/knowledge/library/dlogin.php?file=Yemen/yemen-101-en.pdf (accessed 1 February 2009).

International Crisis Group (2011). 'Popular Protest in North Africa and the Middle East (II): Yemen Between Reform and Revolution', *Middle East/North Africa Report* No. 102.

International Press Institute (2007). 'World Press Freedom Review: Yemen'. Available at www.freemedia.at/cms/ipi/freedom_detail.html?country=/KW0001/KW0004/KW0108/ (accessed 22 March 2009).

156   *V. Durac*

Ismael, T.Y. and Ismael, J.S. (1997). 'Civil Society in the Arab World: Historical Traces, Contemporary Vestiges', *Arab Studies Quarterly*, 19(1), 77–87.

Jamal, A. (2007). *Barriers to Democracy: The Other Side of Social Capital in Palestine and the Arab World*, Princeton: Princeton University Press.

Johnsen, G. (2006). 'Salih's Road to Reelection', *Middle East Report Online*. Available at www.merip.org/mero/mero011306.html (accessed 16 May 2012).

Kamrava, M. (2007). 'The Middle East's Democracy Deficit in Comparative Perspective', *Perspectives on Global Development and Technology*, 6(1), 189–213.

Kamrava, M. and Mora, F.O. (1998). 'Civil Society and Democratisation in Comparative Perspective: Latin America and the Middle East', *Third World Quarterly*, 19, 893–915.

Kelsay, J. (2002). 'Civil Society and Government in Islam', in Rosenblum, N.L. and Post, R.C. (eds) *Civil Society and Government*. Princeton and Oxford: Princeton University Press.

Longley, A. (2007). 'The High Water Mark of Islamist Politics? The Case of Yemen', *Middle East Journal*, 61(2), 240–260.

Longley, A. and Al-Iryani, A.G. (2008). 'Fighting Brushfires with Batons: An Analysis of the Political Crisis in South Yemen', *Middle East Institute Policy Brief*. Online. Available at www.mideasti.org/files/fighting-brushfires-batons-yemen.pdf (accessed 22 March 2009).

Mardin, S. (1995). 'Civil Society and Islam', in Hall, J.A. (ed.) *Civil Society: Theory, History, Comparisons*. Cambridge: Polity Press.

Moore, P. and Salloukh, B. (2007). 'Struggles Under Authoritarianism: Regimes, States, and Professional Associations in the Arab World', *International Journal of Middle East Studies*, 39(1), 53–76.

Nonneman, G. and Hill, G. (2011). 'Yemen, Saudi Arabia and the Gulf States: Elite Politics, Street Protests and Regional Diplomacy', *Chatham House Briefing Paper*, Middle East and North Africa Programme, MENAP BP 2011/01.

Norton, A.R. (1993). 'The Future of Civil Society in the Middle East', *The Middle East Journal*, 47(2), 205–216.

Phillips, S. (2006). 'Foreboding About the Future in Yemen', *Middle East Report Online*. 3 April. Available at http://merip.org/mero/mero040306.html (accessed 18 October 2008).

Phillips, S. (2008). *Yemen's Democracy Experiment in Regional Perspective: Patronage and Pluralized Authoritarianism*, New York: Palgrave Macmillan.

Rahman, M.A. (2002). 'The Politics of "Uncivil" Society in Egypt', *Review of African Political Economy*, 29(91), 21–35.

Rosenblum, N.L. and Post, R.C. (eds) (2002). *Civil Society and Government*, Princeton: Princeton University Press. Available at: http://press.princeton.edu/titles/7214.html (accessed 5 April 2009).

Sayyid, M.K. (1993). 'A Civil Society in Egypt?' *The Middle East Journal*, 47(2), 228–242.

Schlumberger, O. (2000). 'The Arab Middle East and the Question of Democratization: Some Critical Remarks', *Democratization*, 7(4), 104–132.

Schwedler, J. (2002). 'Yemen's Aborted Opening', *Journal of Democracy*, 13(4), 48–55.

Schwedler, J. (2006). *Faith in Moderation: Islamist Parties in Jordan and Yemen*, Cambridge: Cambridge University Press.

Schwedler, J. and Clarke, J. (2006). 'Islamist-Leftist Co-operation in the Arab World', *ISIM Newsletter*, 18 Autumn. Available at www.isim.nl/files/Review_18/ Review_18–10.pdf (accessed 16 March 2009).

UNFPA Yemen (2008). 'Yemen Times and UNFPA Organise Seminar on Rapid Analysis Results.' Available at http://yemen.unfpa.org/News/news117.htm (accessed 15 October 2008).

United States Agency for International Development (USAID) (2007). 'Yemen: Civil Society Sector Assessment.' Unpublished document.

Wiktorowicz, Q. (2000). 'Civil Society as Social Control: State Power in Jordan', *Comparative Politics*, 33(1), 43–61.

Wiktorowicz, Q. (2002). 'The Political Limits to Nongovernmental Organizations in Jordan', *World Development*, 30, 77–93.

Yom, S.L. (2005). 'Civil Society and Democratization in the Arab World', *Middle East Review of International Affairs*, 9(4), 14–33.

9 Relations between professional associations and the state in Jordan

Janine A. Clark

Introduction

In 2005, Jordan's Prime Minister proposed legislation that would have limited the opposition-led professional associations' (PAs') activities to purely professional ones, taken greater control of their financial and disciplinary matters, and amended their electoral system, among other initiatives. Any of these, if implemented, would have severely diminished the PAs' political and financial power and influence, and consequently, the oppositions' abilities to press political demands. The legislation, however, was never brought for a final vote in parliament, but the threat nevertheless worked. Despite the PAs' strength, as witnessed by their massive demonstrations and presumably public support, the PAs restrained themselves – undertaking fewer political activities and quieting their demands. Political activities have continued, but they are generally less provocative and, with some exceptions, even during the 2011 Arab Spring, not been aimed at inciting the street. The question is why. Given that the government did not follow through on its threat or on an early one in 1996 (Nevo, 2001) why did they dampen their activities? Conversely, if the PAs are so strong, why did the government retreat from the legislation? Finally, what can the freezing of the 2005 law tell us about state–society relations in Jordan and in authoritarian regimes of the Arab world in general?

The answer to the 2005 puzzle lies in understanding that opposition groups and the state are often engaged in a more mutually interdependent relationship than most studies of state–society relations in the Arab world would imply. As the prospects for democracy in the Arab world dimmed throughout the late 1990s and early 2000s, scholars progressively shifted their attention to explaining enduring authoritarianism (Albrecht and Schlumberger, 2004), focusing on the role of political institutions (Haklai, 2009; Lust-Okar, 2005), rents, and other 'survival strategies' or strategies of adaptation which authoritarian rulers employ in order to maintain their power (Bank, 2004; Lucas, 2004). In these studies, the state is treated as powerful, if not all-knowing, and opposition groups, while not considered pawns of the regime, are largely portrayed as responding to state-structured incentives and disincentives by cooperating with or by engaging in conflict with the regime. With few exceptions, these studies

I am indebted to Sami Hourani for his help with the research for this chapter.

Professional associations and the state in Jordan 159

focus almost exclusively on the political goals, strategies and activities of both the state and the opposition.

Yet, the notion that opposition actors within civil society play a solely political role is a false one. The dominant opposition groups in the Middle East, the Islamists, also are engaged in social and economic activities. As Islamist groups have come to dominate, through elections, a variety of civil society institutions, such as professional associations (PAs) and university student councils, they have had to deal both with audiences or clients who extend far beyond their political constituency and with the functional goals and the day-to-day working activities of these organizations. In the case of PAs, these would include professional licensing, for example. As demonstrated by the analysis of the relationships between the Islamist-dominated PAs in Jordan and the state, the functional goals and activities of both the state and these civil society organizations, the quotidian routines, partly dictate the relationship between state and oppositions. The Islamist opposition in Jordan's PAs needs the state in order to carry out the functional goals of the PAs and thereby also assure their own political popularity just as the state relies on the PAs, and by extension the Islamist opposition, to carry out the quasi-state functions that the PAs have been mandated to perform and to help ensure economic stability. The end result is a state that appears less autonomous than most studies of enduring authoritarianism imply and an opposition that is less conflictual than commonly portrayed.

A study of Jordan's PAs is particularly useful for understanding state–society relations in the Arab world. As in much of the region, Jordan's PAs historically have taken a leading role in pressuring for political reform (Longuenesse, 1990; Hourani, 2000; Kornbluth, 2002: Moore and Salloukh, 2007). The PAs, furthermore, are representative of PAs throughout the region in that the Islamist opposition has dominated the PAs since the late 1980s/early 1990s. However, in contrast to other Arab states (with the exception of Lebanon), Jordan's PAs are not part of a corporatist structure and have relatively few institutional ties to the state. Institutionally they cannot be considered functional agencies of the state. Jordan's PAs thus can be considered a "crucial" case study; evidence challenging the dominant literature and indicating an interdependent relationship between the opposition and the state in Jordan would indicate a similarly interdependent relationship in states with similar institutional structures or greater corporatist ties (Gerring, 2006: 49).

The literature

Studies of enduring authoritarianism in the Arab world largely focus on the central state's efforts at political domination. They tend to view the state and civil society primarily in conflictual terms, focusing "on the ways and means of Goliath's power," (El Ghobashy, 2008: 1604) specifically how authoritarian regimes structure relationships of control over the opposition and the institutions of the opposition. Recent scholarship has emphasized the significance of formal rules on the strategic calculations of political actors, and the manipulation of formal rules and institutions is increasingly seen as one of the innovations – in

160   *J.A. Clark*

concert with tried-and-true strategies of coercion, surveillance, patronage, corruption, and personalism – of "upgraded authoritarianism" in response to the "triple threat of globalization, markets, and democratization" (Heydemann, 2007: 3). Studies of Arab PAs are no exception and also tend to focus on top-down strategies of political control. State–PA relations are deemed to be marked by conflict or cooptation and, at best, portrayed as a dance in which the regime warns PAs when they near political red lines. In this scenario, conflict erupts when PAs ignore these warnings (Nevo, 2001).

Studies of Arab PAs, however, largely overlook the ways in which the quotidian activities of PAs shape their relations with the state (El Sayed, 1988; Fahmy, 1998). As Carrie Rosefsky Wickham (2002: 193) writes of the Islamist leadership in Egypt's PAs: "As the leaders of large, public institutions, Islamic Trend officials ha[ve] to cultivate and maintain relationships with government ministries, local government authorities, and public and private financial institutions." While state efforts at political control should not be underestimated, it is equally important to examine the day-to-day activities and interactions between the PAs, their constituencies and the state and how, as a result of these interactions, the state may rely upon and, indeed, need associations and the ways in which associations, even those dominated by opposition groups, such as Jordan's PAs, may nurture closer relations with state organizations, considering them beneficial or at least necessary.

Pete W. Moore and Bassel Salloukh (2007: 54) are two of a limited number of scholars who challenge the largely bivariate conceptualization of state–civil society relations. They conceptualize a continuum of PA–state interactions ranging from coordination to contestation, with coordination representing those interactions in which the state and groups borrow from each other the authority to do what they cannot do alone and contestation involving PA mobilization to block state policy or voice opposition as well as state action to mute that opposition. These different patterns of state intervention into PA life are determined by the political relevance of the respective historical social bases of the regime on the one hand and by the PAs on the other (2007: 55). In this view, Jordan's PAs represent "one of the clearest examples of contestation in the Arab world" (2007: 55), due to the nature of their social bases. However, they focus exclusively on PAs' political activities and not on their professional ones, overlooking the full scope and nature of state–PA relations.

Mona El Ghobashy (2008: 1596), examining Egypt, is one of the few scholars to examine both political and professional activities. Bemoaning the abovementioned focus on Goliath's power, she argues that institutional changes in Egypt have led to changes in the relationship between state agents and citizens. She argues that under Islamist leadership, PAs became new arenas for collective claim-making, transforming them into formalized and routinized sites of bargaining with state agents. This bargaining entails both concrete material benefits, such as pensions and health care plans, as well rules of governing associational autonomy and press freedoms (in the case of the Egyptian Press Syndicate). This approach situates professional activities in terms of state–societal relations, but

Professional associations and the state in Jordan   161

she focuses on legal mobilization in pursuit of various demands and not on the actual performance of these professional activities.[1] The day-to-day dealings between PAs and state organizations and state officials are neglected.

As will be shown below, the 2005 puzzle can only be made understandable using a lens that encompasses not only the political activities but also the functional activities of the PAs.

Strategies of state control

Despite political liberalization in Jordan since 1989, the King retains considerable powers. Jordan is a constitutional monarchy with a bicameral parliament – the upper and lower houses of the House of Representatives and the Senate, respectively, but the King is a "venue to himself as he stands above the state machinery" (Lucas, 2005: 22). He is the head of state; he appoints the Prime Minister, the cabinet, and the Senate, and convenes and adjourns the (elected) House of Representatives. The King orders elections, dissolves parliament, declares martial law, and approves and proclaims laws. The King is the commander-in-chief of the armed forces; he declares war and signs treaties. The elected House of Representatives has powers to approve, amend or reject legislation; but the House cannot initiate legislation. The House of Representatives has the right to call for and cast a vote of confidence in the King's appointed cabinet and to override the King's veto by a two-thirds majority on a joint session of the two houses; however, the joint session must be called by the monarchy-appointed PM. All laws must be ratified by the King and under certain circumstances the cabinet may also decree laws (which the King then ratifies if he so chooses). Finally, the judicial system is also firmly under the King's control – the King appoints judges by royal decree. Arab Spring reformists are demanding amendment of the constitutional articles that grant the King and the constitutional powers of the King have been a subject of great debate over the past one and a half years.

The Hashemite regime's ability to survive historically has been attributed not only through its ability to manipulate the vast executive and legislative powers granted to the King and his appointed cabinet in the Constitution but by two additional broad strategies. The first are the strategies employed to maintain support from key constituencies, namely the "tribes," and to a lesser extent, secular liberals, and the business community (Brand, 1994). Successive kings have collectively privileged Jordanians of Jordanian origin (often referred to as the tribes) as opposed to Jordanians of Palestinian descent since the early formation of the state (Nevo, 2001: 188–189). A tribal elite thus has been created as a result of key tribes being granted influential positions in the state apparatus and other tribes being preferentially hired into the army and civil service.[2]

The second broad strategy is the regime's attempts to weaken and divide the opposition. The regime has used a variety of tactics, including repression, direct and indirect co-optation, threatening restrictive legislation, and what can only be called "politics of distraction" – the endless barrage of royal initiatives that keep that press and opposition busy and distracted from more pressing issues or

162   *J.A. Clark*

fruitful activities. These initiatives would include the numerous (appointed) royal commissions aimed (in name at least) at democratic reform that provide the multiple advantages of securing support from pro-regime constituents, potentially co-opting the opposition, hindering the opposition's ability to unite and creating a whirlwind of activity with few results.

The divide and rule strategy can most clearly be seen in the state's historical privileging of the Muslim Brotherhood (MB) over other political trends. The MB was registered as a legal charitable society in 1945 under the patronage of King Abdullah I.[3] During the period of martial law (1957–1989), the MB's privileged relationship with the monarchy was solidified further as the state viewed the growth of the MB as an effective means for undermining the rise and popularity of pan-Arab nationalism in the 1950s and 1960s and of Palestinian political factions in the 1970s and, as a result, allowed it to operate freely while other parties were forced underground or abroad (Boulby, 1999).

In return for its protected status, the MB supported the monarchy politically. By-and-large, it refrained from criticizing the political structure or the legitimacy of the monarchy itself. Prior to the advent of democracy in 1989, MB leaders were rewarded for their loyalty and cooperation with positions in various governments, particularly the Ministry of Education and the *Awqaf*. In recognition of the MB's loyalty during Jordan's 1970–1971 Civil War, for example, King Hussein made Izhaq Farhan, a prominent MB, the Minister of Education for five consecutive cabinets, from October 1970 to November 1974. He was Minister of *Awqaf* in 1972 for approximately one year.[4]

The authoritarian regime in Jordan thus has structured relations of inclusion and exclusion with societal groups all the while ensuring that the King retains considerable political and economic powers – powers which even opposition groups cannot afford to ignore. The state thus serves as an important centripetal force – one that ensures that opposition groups and parties jockey for positions near the center.

Jordan's PAs as political and professional actors

Under pressure from urban professionals, the Jordanian cabinet created PAs to address their members' professional needs and defend their rights. The first generation of PAs was created in the early 1950s, a second in the 1960s and 1970s and a third wave in the 1990s, the most recent being in 1998 (Hourani, 2000). Today, there are 12 PAs[5] with a total of approximately 120,000 professional members.[6] Given monopoly of representation – a condition demanded by Jordan's professionals – the PAs essentially perform many of the state's functions. They have the legal and administrative responsibility of maintaining professional standards and discipline, invest their members' fees and manage members' social security, health insurance and retirement funds.

Unlike counterparts in corporatist systems, PAs in Jordan have a relatively great degree of autonomy. Each is governed by its own by-law issued by the Council of Ministers. That the PAs have been created by law and not by ordinance gives them freedom of action not available to other societies or even labor

Professional associations and the state in Jordan   163

unions for that matter as they cannot be dissolved by the government (Hamayil, 2000). PAs have enjoyed the right to elect their own boards, even during martial law. The government does not have the legal right to interfere in the council or presidential elections of the PAs. Furthermore, the PAs have the right to refer any of their members to an internal disciplinary council and to try them, suspend them from work for a certain period of time, and to delete their names from the associations without the intervention of any other authority with the exception of the Supreme Court.

In general, the by-laws of the PAs stipulate that their functions are purely professional; however, as there are no clear provisions regarding political activities, PAs interpret their roles quite liberally. For example, the by-laws of the Jordanian Engineers Association (JEA) state that the association's purpose is to "defend the interests and dignity [of] members and to do everything possible to achieve the professional goals of the JEA" (Hamayil, 2000: 87). A number of leaders interpret this to include political activities, arguing that the struggle for political freedoms is a prerequisite for building an effective association. Similarly, the JEA argues that its anti-normalization activities (aimed at preventing normalization of relations with Israel) defend the interests and dignity of its members.

Indeed, Jordan's PAs effectively have acted as institutions of the opposition throughout most of their history. As Hani Hourani (2000: 59) argues, the absence of political parties for extended periods of time prior to 1989, the freezing of parliamentary life from 1974 to 1983 and the restrictions on civil society all boosted the political role of Jordan's PAs. Thus, the PAs historically have filled a political vacuum in Jordan. Just as significantly, the PAs historically have focused on regional issues, and particularly the issues related to the Arab–Israeli crisis, and to a lesser extent on domestic issues. As early as the 1960s, the PAs coordinated various elements of civil society in collective efforts to press opposition demands. During martial law, the PAs created an umbrella for the banned political parties and organizations. Consequently, the regime used coercive measures and threats to limit the activities of the PAs to purely professional ones in attempts to control the PAs. In 1988, the late King Hussein issued a royal directive to the PM that the PAs be confined to their professional role and refrain from political activities (Hourani, 2000: 42).

Since 1989, the political role of the PAs has increased, largely because political parties in Jordan continue to be weak and ineffective (Lust-Okar, 2001). The PAs brought thousands to the street in opposition to the 1994 Jordanian-Israeli peace accord. They also played a prominent role in the creation of the National Committee for the Cancellation of the Israeli Trade Fair, which brought Jordanian centrist political figures for the first time into a coalition with leftists and Islamists (Schwedler, 2005). The Committee's four-day boycott gathered over 3,000 protesters and successfully discouraged virtually any Jordanian participation at the January 1997 Israeli trade and industrial fair that was held outside Amman. They have continued organizing protests against Jordanian foreign policies regarding Israel, the US and Iraq.

164   *J.A. Clark*

Prior to the Arab Spring, six of Jordan's 12 PAs were considered highly politicized: the JEA; Jordanian Medical Association; Jordanian Dentists Association; Jordanian Bar Associations; Jordanian Nurses and Midwives Associations; Jordanian Agricultural Engineers Association.[7] Historically, these PAs have been dominated politically by one of two trends: an alliance of leftists and nationalists or the Islamists. The leftists and nationalists run in the PA elections on a Green List while the Islamists run on a White List. While the Green List won the majority of seats in PA elections and dominated the associations throughout the 1980s (with the Islamists having only limited representation in the JEA, the Bar Association and the Medical Association), in the early 1990s, the Islamists began asserting their political strength and dominating the elected boards of the PAs. Islamists (predominantly the MB) now largely control the boards of the JEA, Medical Association (JMA), Agricultural Engineers Association, the Pharmacists Association and the Nurses and Midwives Association (Hamayil, 2000).

Due to their political activities, government interference in PAs' activities has increased since 1989. Security forces stormed the PAC, arrested PA leaders and refused to recognize election results.[8] In 1996 and then 2005, the government introduced legislation to limit the activities of the PAs.[9] In 1996, a year after King Hussein personally expressed concerns regarding both the political activities of the PAs and the fact that membership in the PAs is a precondition for all professionals to work in their designated profession, the (appointed) upper house tabled a proposal that the Higher Council for Interpretation of the Constitution examine the constitutionality of the PAs' laws. The legislation proposed to curb the political activities of the PAs and to eliminate mandatory membership. The Prime Minister did not support the proposed legislation and it did not reach the lower house of parliament for vote.

Similarly, on March 6, 2005, the cabinet proposed legislation which, if passed, would have affected PAs' funds, activities and elections.[10] The proposed legislation authorized the Audit Bureau to inspect associations' financial records in order to ensure that their funds are used only for professional activities and for the updating of professional standards and to ensure that these funds are solely distributed in Jordan (and not in the West Bank or Gaza). It similarly limited the topics of discussion at any PA meetings, councils and committee meetings exclusively to professional matters. PAs also were required to obtain prior written approval from the Interior Ministry in order to hold a public gathering or meeting. The proposed law also stipulated that disciplinary matters would be removed from the PA activities. In place of the PAs' disciplinary councils, a council comprised of one judge, one government-appointed PA member and one PA-appointed member, both with over 20 years of experience would be formed to address all disciplinary matters. The disciplinary board would have the authority to punish and suspend members from the practice of their professional for a variety of vague, ill-defined infractions.

In terms of PA elections, the law stipulated that the PAs establish branches in the governorates throughout Jordan (and sever all ties with their branches in the Palestinian territories). These branches would then elect what the proposed law

Professional associations and the state in Jordan 165

termed "intermediary commissions" which in turn would elect the president and board members of each PA – thus taking electoral power away from the General Assembly. Furthermore, these elections would be held according to one-man-one-vote (as in the national elections) and not according to the list system as is practiced presently. Finally, the proposed law called for new elections within three months of the law's sanctioning by Royal Decree. During these three months, a temporary administration would be formed to oversee the PAs' functioning and to help the PAs "straighten their policies."[11]

While the proposed law was originally tagged as urgent when it was sent to the lower house of parliament, MPs voted against granting it urgent status (as requested by the cabinet). They instead referred it to the legal committee of the lower house.[12] Several prime ministers later, the law remains frozen but not withdrawn.

Understanding the puzzle: state and PA interdependence

This chapter contends that we cannot understand why the law was frozen or why the PAs responded by subduing their activities without placing the law within the larger context of professional obligations of the PAs and the consequent interactions and mutually beneficial relationship between the PAs and the state. State strategies of control must be understood within this larger context of interdependence.[13] As Bassam Hadadeen, Minister of Parliament in 2005 and current Member of Parliament (MP) stated, the relationship between the PAs and the state is based on mutual benefits.[14] Maen NSour, Director General of Jordan's Social Security Corporation (SSC) agrees that the relationship between the PAs and the state is an interdependent one.[15] As Jumana Ghnaimat of *Al-Ghad* newspaper elaborates, the relationship between the PAs and the state may look oppositional but in reality the two are on very good terms; they are quite compatible with each other – their relationship is based on mutual interests and benefits.[16]

Certainly, one explanation for the freezing of the law is that the PAs, as important oppositional voices and what some regard as Jordan's only democratic and transparent entities,[17] were simply too strong; that MPs bowed to the pressure of their protests in the run-up to the vote in Parliament. As stated above, however, this explanation does not address why the PAs subsequently subdued their political activities. Other explanations include the argument that the proposed legislation was drafted and passed by the Upper House in too hasty a manner and that the Lower House responded by granting the proposed legislation greater time for reflection.[18] This explanation, of course, explains why the proposed legislation was sent to the legal committee but cannot explain why it was frozen.

It also could be argued that the state withdrew the controversial legislation[19] as part of a larger strategy to maintain popularity,[20] wherein it initiates unpopular legislation with the aim of freezing or amending it later in order to ensure support for the government.[21] However, this approach not only assumes that the state is a rational unitary actor but that the population would not continue to be

166   *J.A. Clark*

angry that the law was proposed in the first place, even after it was frozen. It further begs the question if the freezing of the law was to gain popular support, why was the law not completely withdrawn?

Similarly, other analysts were noted in the press as being skeptical of the intent of the law since each of the three concerned parties – the government, the Lower House and the PAs – achieved what analysts termed a "temporary triumph."[22] By sending the proposed law to its legal committee, the Lower House took a stance in favor of democracy and granted all parties concerned the opportunity to discuss and amend the law. Indeed, in the weeks and months following the Lower House's decision not to vote immediately on the legislation, there were a series of meetings between the PAs and the MPs and between MPs and cabinet ministers – with all parties calling for suggestions, reservations and cooperation.[23] However, this explanation appears convincing in hindsight, but for the state to be able to predict the actions and reactions of the state, the elected MPs and the PAs and to accurately craft legislation and plans based on these predictions would have been a significant feat.

Rather, the explanation for the freezing of the 2005 law requires situating the event within a broader context, one which examines the professional role of professional associations and their significance for the professional classes, the state and the Islamists. At the broadest level, PAs represent Jordan's social elite – the professional middle class whose growth and development is vital to the country's economic and political future. Changes to the role and responsibilities of the PAs would be highly disruptive to the stability of the state. In the context of a weak parliament and even weaker parties, the PAs fulfill the middle class's professional and political aspirations.[24] As political scientist, Mohammad al-Momani, stated, the PAs comprise highly educated people both in terms of quantity and quality; they are a tool for change, and herein lies the biggest pressure on the state.[25] Political analyst, Hani Hourani, concurs: the state needs the PAs because they comprise the middle class and, consequently, are a source of social and economic stability for the country.[26] Furthermore, many PA members work for state institutions, including the military.[27] Also as a consequence of mandatory membership, a significant proportion of the PA members are Jordanians of Transjordanian descent and the state would be unwilling to undermine this segment of society.[28] By virtue of their social base, the educations and status of their members, and the indispensible roles their members play within the state, society and economy, the state relies upon and needs the PAs.

The importance of the PAs to Jordan's economy includes also their extensive professional responsibilities. As stated above, PAs are responsible for the licensing of all professions and also for disciplinary matters, education and training.[29] As Wael Saqqa, former President of the JEA (and President in 2005) stated, the PAs shoulder a lot of responsibilities on behalf of the government. First of all, the PAs have a big role in regulating the professions. This saves the state time, effort and money in planning, regulating the professions and in creating an authority that represents professionals and which professionals trust.[30] Quite simply, the state needs the PAs to organize an army of professionals and their work.[31] The PAs fulfill roles that the state cannot do on its own.[32] Indeed, the ministries' drafting of regulations and laws is regularly done in coordination with the PAs.[33]

As a result of the PAs' professional roles, the PAs also are convenient pressure valves for the government and the state. Individual PAs are responsible for decisions regarding salary raises (minimum wage) for various professional fields, such as doctors and engineers. They are also responsible for setting the prices of fees for professional services. Ultimately, this means that the PAs and not the state receive the brunt of public resentment when fees are raised or salary increases denied.[34]

Indeed, as will be discussed in greater detail below, the law was originally proposed in order to safeguard and enhance the economic role and performance of the PAs. Triggered by the blacklisting of engineer, Raed Qaqish, from the JEA after he participated in a television interview with an Israeli official (Qaqish did not meet with the Israeli but was interviewed by satellite), various MPs demanded that the PA elections laws be changed in order to prevent the use of PAs as political tools by political parties, namely the IAF.[35] The law was then proposed by the Minister of Internal Affairs at the time, Samir Habashneh; according to MPs, however, Habashneh significantly strengthened the proposed law to add a variety of limitations on the PAs' role and activities.[36] The essential aim stayed the same though – to limit IAF access to the PAs and to strengthen the PAs as professional institutions.

However, the economic role of the PAs extends beyond the functions stated above. Indeed, the interdependence of the PAs and the state can be clearly seen in the PAs', particularly the JEA's, provision of pensions and other services. As Izzeddien Kanakriyyeh, Secretary General at the Ministry of Finance stated, the PAs not only offer good services but save the government substantial effort.[37] Conversely, the state is the biggest employer and investor, and PAs, as professional bodies, need the state to employ their members and to invest its money.[38] Consequently, the proposed legislations' threat of supervision by the Audit Bureau elicited concern within the PAs as professional institutions worried about the services they provide their members and also within the Islamist leadership worried about their ability to maintain votes. The Islamist leadership within the PAs has much to lose should the PAs be undermined. At a very minimum, it would lose an important soapbox from which it can legally and vocally publicize its message (and potentially recruit members). Just as importantly, Islamists' ability to provide services would be negatively affected. This would potentially result in them losing votes in PA elections or, more accurately, losing more votes. As Ghnaimat stated, the PAs under IAF leadership must be cautious in the degree to which they pressure the government as they, the IAF, would be the ones to suffer first should their ability to provide pensions to their members be eliminated. These services are what give them their social support.[39]

Social security in Jordan is provided by the Social Security Corporation (SSC) under the Ministry of Labour. Membership in the SSC is obligatory for all Jordanians employed in the public, military and private sectors[40] with the exception of

168   *J.A. Clark*

small companies with fewer than five employees.[41] The SSC presently has 920,000 members and in 2010 paid out more than 38 million JD for pensions.[42] Covering old age and disability pensions, and soon extending its services to include maternity and health insurance,[43] SCC is the main umbrella organization and the major support for Jordanian people.

However, as of yet, the SSC has not been able to provide full or adequate coverage to all Jordanians, including Jordanian professionals. At present, in terms of pensions, only approximately 50 percent of the Jordanian labor force is covered.[44] The gap in coverage is largely due to the fact that small enterprises are not as of yet fully covered – a significant proportion of professionals are self-employed and do not, as of yet, qualify. In addition, as stated above, short-term benefits, such as sickness, maternity and unemployment benefits, are still not implemented. This leaves the approximately 50 percent of Jordanian workers and their families without any income support in case of the occurrence of old age, invalidity or death and leaves all Jordanian workers without any financial support in case of the occurrence of one of the above short-term contingencies.[45] Furthermore, the SSC's financial future is not stable: reports estimate that the SSC's revenues and expenditures will reach a break-even point as early as 2017 and that it will not be able to meet its financial obligations to its subscribers in 2038.[46]

Thus, PAs' services, and particularly those of the JEA, fulfill an important function for Jordan's professionals. Indeed, as the current MP and former Deputy Prime Minister and former Minister of Trade and Industry, Mohammad Haliqa, stated, while the economic role of the PAs is relatively limited in that their economic activities are not on a national level, they support their members and improve their living conditions.[47] Over the years, the PAs have acquired hundreds of millions of JDs through investment. Membership fees are invested and reinvested and used for members' social security, pension, health insurance and savings funds. The PAs also buy vast tracts of land and then divide the plots and resell them to their members at a highly competitive rate. While admittedly the JEA has by far the most extensive coverage as compared to other PAs, stopping these forms of assistance would ultimately produce a large "crack in the wall of Jordanian society."[48] Given that the membership of the PAs is estimated as high as 150,000 members and that the average household size is five people, an extremely large number of Jordanians depend partially or fully upon the PAs.[49] Saqqa estimates that 20 percent of Jordanian society benefits from the services provided by the PAs.[50] As he summarizes, the PAs

> take care of members at all levels, be economic or social. We give them health care, housing, zero-interest loans of all sorts, education, marriage and what have you.... We also support the national economy by so many projects in all fields, especially real estate and industry.... The professional associations are the professional arm of a strong society and economy. Only a stupid government would weaken such an institution.[51]

Professional associations and the state in Jordan 169

The JEA has by far the largest resources and provides the most services of any PA; an examination of the enormity of its finances, investments and services is instructive in demonstrating how this one PA contributes to the economic well-being of the countries' professionals and their families.[52] The JEA provides eight main services: (1) a pension fund for members and beneficiaries; (2) a social insurance fund which provides pension and compensations for members in case of disability or death; (3) a cooperation fund (TAKAFUL) which provides grants in case of death or permanent disability; (4) a savings and financing fund that provides incentives for members to save and provides interest-free loans; (5) a health care fund which provides medical treatment for members and families; (6) a marriage loan (30,000 JD) for members, to be repaid free of interest over 40 monthly installments; (7) a loan for financing education of members' children (1,000 JD repaid free of interest over ten months; the loan can be repeated five times); and (8) free health care for inpatients covering members paying all their due contributions plus spouse and youngest child.

All members pay annual membership fees of approximately 40 JD. According to a report on the JEA's pension fund, 30,000 JEA members contribute to the pension fund and 45,000 contribute to the social insurance fund – these members pay these contributions above and beyond their annual membership fees. There are four pension plans, ranging from 200 JD to 600 JD per month; social insurance premiums are 20 JD annually (calculated at 50 percent of membership fees).[53]

The JEA invests its resources into four different portfolios: (1) equities though participation in various companies in Jordan; (2) real estate; (3) loans and financing to JEA pension fund contributors to finance the purchase of housing and other essential commodities; and (4) deposits in Islamic banks. In 2006, the greatest share went to loans and finance (45 percent), with 31 percent in real estate, 23 percent in equities and 1 percent in bank deposits. The object of the loan and financing portfolio is not only to enable members to afford housing, apartments, land plots and other essential needs, but to generate investment income for the JEA (thus increasing financing to the pension fund) and to stimulate the local economy by providing money for commercial transactions between JEA members and traders and sellers. Thus, the JEA views its activities as part of an important three-way relationship between it, the local market and the engineer/member. The JEA activates the local market through investment and in return receives "financial and moral support" from the local market. The JEA offers engineers/members loans and finance and in return receives engineers' loyalty. And engineers/members purchase from the local market and in return receive attractive commodity prices.

According to the report, the JEA's net asset value at the end of 2006 was 126.6 million JD.[54] Its rate of return on total investment was 10 percent. In recent years, the JEA investment performance – rate of investment (ROI) – has been two to four times that of similar funds in Jordan and the region. Its total revenue for 2006 was 22.8 million JD and its total investment income for 2006 was 12 million JD. In terms of expenses, it distributed 5.35 million JD in pension expenses in 2006 alone. That same year, the JEA expended 26.1 million JD in loans and financing to 2,148 members.

170   *J.A. Clark*

Certainly, in many cases, the SSC provides a greater portion of a professional's pension and benefits, particularly if the professional is not an engineer as there is significant variance between the PAs.[55] Nadia Rawabdeh of the Pension Department at the SSC argues that every medical doctor, engineer and other professional is a member of the SSC and primarily depends on SSC pensions rather than PA pensions largely because PA pensions pay less. According to her, most professionals register for the highest pension salaries in the SSC and the lowest pension salaries in the PAs (presumably to receive some benefits from their obligatory membership fees).[56] Nsour agrees and states that if the PA stopped providing pensions, most of the PA beneficiaries would not be affected as they have the SSC.[57]

However, for many professionals (even those who are not self-employed), these assessments simply do not hold. The maximum pension a member can receive from the SSC is 75 percent of the average salary in the last two years of work. Yet public sector employees, which include a significant number of doctors and engineers, are paid extremely low salaries, often as little as 500 JD or 600 JD per month even after significant years in the work force.[58] This wage is considered so low that repeated governments have made efforts to stem the flow of doctors out of public hospitals and into private hospitals in Jordan and abroad. According to the SSC website (accessed in 2011), a public servant employee earning approximately this amount, with a wife and three underage children, and retiring at the mandatory age for males at 60 would receive 404.659 JD per month.[59] This amount is not significantly higher than the minimum monthly PA pension of 200 JD per month; in some cases the SSC monthly pension salary may be lower than the PAs', depending for which PA pension plan the professional registered. Furthermore, the cost of living in 2006 (the most recent available Household Income and Expenditures Survey by the Jordanian Department of Statistics) places the average monthly expenditure of each Jordanian family at 629.166 JD[60] – and the compounded inflation rate between 2006 and 2010 was 24.5 percent.[61] At least for engineers working in the public sector, the PA pension is a necessity.

The very strength of the PAs' pension and services further points to the interdependence between the PAs and the state. As Hadadeen states, the PA cannot play the economic strength card against the government as any threat to its economic services will affect the PAs' – specifically the IAF's – social base and interests.[62] Studies indicate that PA members do not vote strictly along political lines; rather, members vote for their leadership based both on professional and political grounds. Islamist candidates cannot count on members sympathetic to the Islamist political trend to carry them into power. In his study of PAs, Hamayil found that between 1985 and 1995, 47.5 percent of candidates ran for elections on both a professional and political platform while 43.7 percent ran on a purely professional basis (Hamayil, 2000: 63–64). When Hamayil broke this analysis down to the various associations, he found that the JEA represented the approximate average of the associations with 47.6 percent of the candidates nominating themselves on a professional and political basis and 47.6 percent on a purely professional basis (Hamayil, 2000; Clark, 2010).

Professional associations and the state in Jordan 171

Abdullah Al-Ghosheh, an independent leftist, illustrates this point. He ran on a White/Islamist List in 2003 elections for Architects (a sector of the JEA). He then chose to run on a Green (nationalist/leftist) List in 2006. In both elections, he achieved the second highest number of votes and served on the architects' board. Names and people count – not just the political trend of the list or party. Voters expect professional services (Clark, 2004).

The significance of professional services to Islamist popularity and strength must also be put into context of declining PA-membership participation and electoral turnout. Despite the important role the PAs, with the Islamists at the helm, have played in Jordanian politics, analyses of voting turnouts in the PAs indicate that the actual number of those who are paying their dues and voting in PA elections has been consistently declining. Thus, the number of professionals actually voting for the Islamists is not as great as it would first appear. Islamist weakness in the PAs helps explain their response to the proposed law. They simply cannot afford to lose more votes as a result of any potential decline in professional services.

For example, the JEA commands approximately 40,000 engineers (Hamayil, 2000). However, when we look at the JEA membership and the number of members paying annual dues between 1975 and 1995, we see a decline in dues-paying members that has become particularly acute since 1989. In 1975, the percentage of dues-paying members was 60.8 percent. In 1985, the percentage of dues-paying members had dropped to 54.9 percent. In 1995, only 49.3 percent of the membership paid their dues (Hamayil, 2000). So great are the numbers of members who do not pay their fees that many councils do not even suspend their members for non-payment (Hamayil, 2000).

Declining participation rates in its general assembly meetings exacerbate the JEA's declining membership. Some PAs have participation rates of over 75 percent, but the Islamist-controlled JEA has a participation rate that hovers between 50 percent and 52 percent in PA elections (Hamayil, 2000: 80). The rate drops even lower when we examine the turnout at the JEA's general assemblies – to as low as 2.5 percent. As Hussein Abu Rumman (2000: 90) observes, this means that the percentage of participants in the general assembly meetings of the JEA regularly can be less than 1 percent.

The same can be said about the JEA's electoral turnout. In its 2006 elections, Saqqa won the presidency by a landslide – according to the press. Upon closer examination, however, the turnout rate was so low that Saqqa actually only received approximately 2,000 votes from approximately 25,000 eligible voters. His only opponent received 100 votes.[63] Based on these trends, the Islamist leadership simply cannot afford any legislation that would hinder its ability to win the PA elections either by eliminating mandatory membership, as proposed in 1996, or altering the electoral laws or inspecting their financial resources, as proposed in 2005.

Declining PA membership participation can be attributed largely to Islamists' focus on political issues at the perceived expense of professional issues.[64] While little research has been conducted on the topic, Hourani argues that Islamists

172   *J.A. Clark*

have been unable to solve a number of problems, such as issues dealing with the internal structures of PAs, as a result of their focus on political issues (Hourani, 2000: 60). Similarly, Hussein Abu Rumman states that the confrontation between the government and the PAs has diverted the PAs from a necessary discussion as to their appropriate role, including the degree to which they should be political forums.[65] Indeed, the growing political role of the PAs, including their choice of tactics, is not without its dissenters. PAs have organized a significant number of professional activities in tandem with their political activities, but a growing number of members and newly accredited (primarily non-Islamist) professionals in particular feel that the professional role of the PAs is being neglected for the sake of the political.[66] Al-Momani agrees: as a result of their political activism, the PAs are not handling their professional responsibilities well.[67]

Related to the appropriate role of the PAs is the issue of practices that "do not agree with the law or stand near the edge" such as the blacklists of normalizers (which placed the lives of those on the list at risk) and the penalizing of professionals, such as Qaqish, who make contact with Israel by dismissal from the PA. With posting of the blacklists, the PAC's anti-normalization activities lost considerable support both within and without the PAs as members questioned the choice of tactics and whether or not they were indeed in the best interests of the membership. The decline in PA membership activity can be attributed to the blacklists, the number of falsely printed names on the lists, and the violence that surrounded them. Finally, there is a small but growing debate within the PAs as to whether or not membership should be compulsory. Hussein Abu Rumman (2000) states that another growing

> trend has emerged within the professional associations which believes that compulsory membership runs counter to the principles of human rights, and that this obligation is largely responsible for the enlargement of the associations' political role and for the retreat from democracy inside them.

These internal divisions as a result of Islamist neglect of the professional role of the PAs have all contributed to decreasing participation in PA elections and, ultimately, to relatively low numbers of votes for the Islamists.

This tension is somewhat paralleled at the national level where Islamists lost a considerable number of seats in the 2007 elections partially as a result of their focus on foreign policy concerns as opposed to domestic economic concerns (such as services).[68] In the 2007 national elections, the IAF (the political party of the MB) lost significant seats as compared to previous national elections, including seats in what traditionally are MB strongholds. While government corruption cannot be discounted in explaining these losses, the MB/IAF also must be held responsible. Analysts such as Mohammad Abu Rumman (2008: 63) argue that the MB/IAF's loss is due to its "extreme inflexibility in [its] foreign policy platform and the shallowness of [its] policy toward internal affairs."

Professional associations and the state in Jordan 173

Mohammad Abu Rumman's study (2008) of the IAF's official statements and declarations demonstrates that of the 38 declarations posted on the IAF website in 2007, 13 addressed issues pertaining to the relationship between the Islamic movement and the state, eight concerned Palestine, and six concerned political reform; only three concerned social topics and one economics. Furthermore, declarations dealing with social and economic issues remain consistently at the bottom of the IAF's list of priorities over the last several years. As Mohammad Abu Rumman summarizes, out of the total of 208 declarations made in 2005–2006, 9 dealt with the economic situation and seven with social issues. The overwhelming majority of declarations were concerned with regional Arab affairs (60), political reform issues (44), the Palestinian cause (31), normalization (29) and the relationship with the state (26). If we calculate all declarations on regional issues (combining Arab affairs, the Palestinian cause and normalization), we find that 58 percent of the IAF declarations pertain to foreign affairs in the region. Only 4.3 percent dealt with the economic situation and 3.36 percent with social issues.

Surveys confirm that Jordanians are most concerned with economic issues. The 2007 poll conducted by the Jordan Center for Social Research (JCSR) found that the three national priorities of Jordanians are all economic in nature: the rising cost of living, unemployment and poverty.[69] The poll found that 48.8 percent of Jordanians believe that the rising cost of living is the most important problem facing Jordan. When asked specifically about the most important political problem requiring the government's immediate attention, only 7.3 percent stated the Palestinian issue – an issue of paramount concern to the MB/IAF. The University of Jordan's Center for Strategic Studies (CSS) 2005 poll found similar results. When respondents were asked to determine the five most important problems facing Jordan, number one in terms of priority for treatment was poverty and unemployment (54 percent of respondents in 2005). The Palestinian issue was ranked as number one by only 8.9 percent of respondents.[70]

On a final note, the Islamists would be wary of and concerned with any negative changes to the financial situation of the PAs, as these would impact their ability to dispense patronage to members and supporters. PAs are powerful, economic tools, and whoever controls the purse strings can bestow favors. Indeed, a second tier that financially benefits from those in power has developed around the PA services and investments. Businesses benefit as the Islamist-dominated PAs source out their expenses, for example, printing expenses or hotel and restaurant expenses associated with hosting a conference.[71] There is a large ring of MB supporters and voters who benefit from patronage bestowed through these means.[72]

Thus, despite political tensions with the regime, Islamists have a vested interest in maintaining good relations with the regime and in responding to the regime's threat – even if the law was only frozen. The Islamist movement as a political movement may have real ideological and political differences with the regime; the Islamists as head of a functional organization (the PAs) have very real reasons for subduing their activities.[73]

The freezing of the law

The freezing of the 2005 law thus makes sense when seen in the larger context of state–society interdependence. As Hourani states, the implementation of the 2005 law would have been disastrous for Jordan. The PAs would be divided between each other and within each profession, thus weakening their unity and their ability to be effective; there would have been social-economic instability as a result of the economic role the PAs are playing, and the government would not have been able to take on the economic burden the PAs are presently handling. In addition to this, the country's biggest organized civil society organization would have been morally weakened. Young professionals would have been less inclined to participate in politics. Just as importantly, had the law passed, Islamist activists may have established their own organizations or become more active in party politics, and, as a consequence, present a bigger (and less contained) political threat to the state.[74] It is little wonder that numerous MPs stated that an order to freeze the law came from above – from the General Intelligence Directorate (GID) potentially at the behest of the Royal Court. Through informal channels, MPs were informed of the dangers of the law and requested not to let it pass. Once it was sent to the legal committee, it consequently never made it back to the light of day.

These same informal channels exist between the state (and the GID in particular) and the PAs (including those which the Islamists dominate). The PA leadership speaks of being invited to relatively frequent meetings requested by the GID where PA activities are discussed. That the state adopts an approach that relies, when possible, more on persuasion and negotiation is unsurprising in light of the "tricky" relationship between the state and the PAs particularly where Islamists are at the helm. As one analyst stated, rather than deliver a knock-out blow, it is better for the state – given its interdependent relationship with the PAs – to win points throughout the game and attempt to contain the Islamist leadership.

For its part, the Islamists also eschew confronting the state, preferring to safeguard the important role the PAs play for the IAF, recognizing the dependence of the PAs and thereby the party on the state. It is little wonder that PA activities became more subdued after the freezing of the 2005 law – there are fewer anti-normalization activities, the PAs are more reserved politically and they are not working as closely with political parties.[75] Seen in light of this interdependence, it is also understandable that the PAs did not initiate the 2011 uprisings in Jordan[76] and, most recently, the PA Complex refused to host a planning conference conducted by the March 24th movement in order to plan a demonstration for July 15, 2011.[77]

Conclusion

By focusing on the functional goals and activities of both the state and the PAs, this chapter demonstrates an important face of state-opposition relations in

Professional associations and the state in Jordan 175

authoritarian regimes – their functional interdependence. Interdependence does not mean equality as the state holds the upper hand in this relationship by its mere control of the legislative organs. However, as demonstrated above, having the upper hand also does not mean that it is easy for the state to take legal action against the PAs. As Zayyan Zawaneh, economic and political analyst and former advisor to the Central Bank of Jordan, the Ministry of Finance and the IMF argues, any threat from the government towards the PAs' economic or social construction is perceived as a threat to every member inside the PA. Every member will stand out and defend the PAs' rights. This makes PAs a stronger body than the government itself.[78] Thus, we find the actions of the state may be tempered or even reversed by the needs and dictates of the functions of the state. Relations of confrontation, coordination and co-optation may mark the political relationship between states and civil society in the Arab world, however, a deeper look at the ongoing functional concerns and activities indicates that state–PA relations are far more interdependent and, therefore, ambiguous than studies indicate. The state and PAs – even when dominated by the opposition – need each other. This indicates a more limited ability of authoritarian elites to "maximize their relative autonomy from society's less supportive sectors" than depicted in studies of upgraded authoritarianism (Pierret and Selvik, 2009).

Shining a light on the functional relationship between the PAs and the state reveals a more ambiguous relationship between the state and the opposition and a more divided opposition.[79] Political and functional goals and activities may require different relations between state and society; they may simultaneously require a politically oppositional stance and activities, yet functional cooperation. These potentially different dictates must be weighed and balanced by both the state and the PAs and go a long way towards explaining policy reversals.

Yet, it is not the case that the opposition must simply walk a fine line between functionally cooperating with the state while maintaining an oppositional stance in the eyes of their followers (Rosefsky Wickham, 2002: 193–194, 200–202, 212). In the PAs, Islamists are charged with conducting, maintaining and improving professional activities and services and PA members weigh these functional goals just as importantly, and perhaps more importantly, than the political agenda that the Islamists bring with them to the table. Decisions over which activities to pursue or not have real, and sometimes negative, consequences for the internal unity of the Islamists and of the PAs and for the support for the Islamists. Indeed, this ambiguity calls the Islamist strategy of penetrating core political institutions into question.

Notes

1 In her study of the MB in Egypt, Rosefsky Wickham also mentions the PAs' professional activities and dealings with state ministers, however, her focus is on the degree to which the Islamists have maintained their oppositional status in the eyes of their followers (Rosefsky Wickham, 2002: 193–194, 200–202, 212).

2 Asha'ir (large clans or tribes; 'ashi'ra, singular) are socially constructed units with social, economic and political functions. As Brand states, the 'ashira is an important

176   *J.A. Clark*

basis of affiliation and a source of prestige and patronage in Jordan and plays a central role in the identity of many Jordanians (Brand, 1995: 48). While during the early years of the monarchy there was an attempt, despite the biased recruitment of Jordanians into the military, to balance the representation of Jordanians and Palestinians into the state (with Palestinians receiving important positions in the civil service and municipalities), the privileging of Jordanians of Jordanian descent became more entrenched following the civil war of 1970–1971.

3 The Jordanian branch of the MB was established in 1945 by Abdul Latif Abu Qura, a wealthy merchant who came into contact with the Egyptian Brotherhood when he visited Palestine in the late 1930s. In the 1940s, Abu Qura visited the founder of the Muslim Brotherhood in Egypt, Hassan al-Banna, and returned to Jordan with two Egyptian MBs who were assigned to assist him in establishing the MB in Jordan.

4 A waqf (pl. awqaf) is a religious endowment, often in the form of land. The revenues of the waqf are to be used for charitable or religious purposes.

5 There are also two professional societies which have fewer powers.

6 Estimates vary from 95,000 to 150,000.

7 Since 1989, the JEA and the JMA, along with the Jordanian Bar Association, have become extremely active politically, particularly in activities resisting normalization with Israel.

8 The JEA's 2002 elections were suspended and not held until 2003.

9 In 1988 and 1989, there were also attempts to limit PA political activities. See Houran (2000: 44).

10 *Al-Sharq al-Awsat*, March 7, 2005. www.aawsat.com/details.asp?article=286709&iss ueno=9596.

11 *The Star*, March 10–16, 2005.

12 *The Jordan Times*, March 14, 2005.

13 Although it could not be verified, one political analyst claimed that the state is so dependent upon the PAs that the PAs have at times threatened the state that they will dissolve these various funds should the state proceed with the action under discussion. Jamil Abu Bakr. Interview with author. Amman. March 23, 2008.

14 Interview with Research Assistant on behalf of author. Amman. July 17, 2011.

15 Interview with Research Assistant on behalf of author. Amman. July 19, 2011.

16 Interview with Research Assistant on behalf of author. Amman. July 21, 2011.

17 Mamdouh al-Abbadi. MP. Interview with Research Assistant on behalf of author. Amman. July 21, 2011.

18 *The Star*, March 10–16, 2005.

19 Included in this larger campaign would be, for example, the proposed NGO law that involved far greater restrictions upon NGOs.

20 Noor Khamaisee. Political Analyst. Interview with author. Amman. March 22, 2008.

21 Noor Khamaisee. Political Analyst. Interview with author. Amman. March 22, 2008.

22 *The Star*, March 17–23, 2005.

23 As part of their initial response, the PAs conducted numerous large rallies in front of the PA complex. In addition, several MPs spoke out against the proposed law.

24 Jamil Nimri. Political Analyst. Interview with author. Amman. March 20, 2008.

25 Interview with Research Assistant on behalf of author. Amman. July 20, 2011.

26 Interview with Research Assistant on behalf of author. Amman. July 14, 2011.

27 Mohammad al-Momani. Political Scientist. Yarmouk University, Jordan. Interview with Research Assistant on behalf of author. Amman. July 20, 2011; Hani Hourani. Political Analyst. Interview with Research Assistant on behalf of author. Amman. July 14, 2011.

28 Furthermore, observers argued that forcing the law through parliament, where members of parliament (MPs), from the professional middle class – including Jordanians of Jordanian descent – would be unwilling to pass the law, would involve a potentially embarrassing showdown for the King – one he presumably would want to

Professional associations and the state in Jordan　177

avoid. Mohammed Sweidan. Political Analyst. Interview with author. Amman. March 20, 2008.

29 This range of activities would affect all ministries that are affiliated with the PAs, such as the Ministry of Health or the Ministry of Public Works and Housing (to which the JEA is attached), to name just two. Noor Khamaisee. Political Analyst. Interview with author. Amman. March 22, 2008; Mohammed Sweidan. Political Analyst. Interview with author. Amman. March 20, 2008.

30 Wael Saqqa, President of the JEA. Interview with Research Assistant on behalf of author. Amman. June 24, 2010.

31 Noor Khamaisee. Political Analyst. Interview with author. Amman. March 22, 2008.

32 Hani Hourani. Political Analyst. Interview with Research Assistant on behalf of author. Amman. 14 July 2011.

33 Izzeddien Kanakriyyeh, Secretary General, Ministry of Finance. Interview with Research Assistant on behalf of author. Amman. June 24 2010. A broad spectrum of ministers would have reservations regarding the proposed law for fear that it would undermine the PAs' ability to license and maintain professional standards. Jamil Nimri. Political Analyst. Interview with Author. Amman. March 20 2008.

34 Noor Khamaisee. Political Analyst. Interview with Author. Amman. March 22 2008.

35 Bassam Hadadeen. MP. Interview with Research Assistant on behalf of author. Amman. July 17, 2011; Raed Qaqish. Former MP. Interview by Research Assistant on behalf of author. Amman. July 18, 2011; Zayyan Zawaneh, Economic and Political Analyst, Former Advisor at the Central Bank of Jordan, the Ministry of Finance and the IMF. Interview by Research Assistant on behalf of author. Amman. July 21, 2011.

36 The Prime Minister at the time was Faisal Al Fayez.

37 Interview with Research Assistant on behalf of author. Amman. June 24, 2010.

38 Noor Khamaisee. Political Analyst. Interview with author. Amman. March 22, 2008.

39 Interview with Research Assistant on behalf of author. Amman. July 21, 2011.

40 The SSC took over the civil pension system in 1995 and the military pension system in 2003. These two systems exist only for those members enrolled in it prior to the respective deadlines.

41 With the passing of a new law in 2010, the SSC is now in the process of expanding its services to enterprises under five persons. *Jordan Times*, April 10, 2011.

42 Nadia Rawabdeh. Pension Department. Social Security Corporation. Interview with Research Assistant on behalf of author. Amman. July 19, 2011.

43 International Labour Office, *Decent Work Country Programme, Jordan*, Unpublished Report. August 2006, p. 12; Rawabdeh. Interview with Research Assistant on behalf of author. Amman. July 19, 2011.

44 *Jordan Times*, April 10, 2011.

45 International Labour Office, *Decent Work Country Programme, Jordan*, Unpublished Report. August 2006, p. 12.

46 *Jordan Times*, June 21, 2009; Jawad Hadid, Chairman, The Social Security Investment Commission, Social Security Corporation, *Management of Public Pension Funds The Jordanian Experience*. Unpublished Report. June 9, 2003.

47 Interview with Research Assistant on behalf of author. Amman. July 19, 2011.

48 Issa Hamdan. Elected JEA Board Member. Interview with author. Amman. March 22, 2008.

49 Issa Hamdan. Elected JEA Board Member. Interview with author. Amman. March 22, 2008.

50 Wael Saqqa, President of the JEA. Interview with Research Assistant on behalf of author. Amman. June 24, 2010. Saqqa further argued that without the help of the PAs, the middle class would disappear in Jordan.

51 Wael Saqqa, President of the JEA. Interview with Research Assistant on behalf of author. Amman. June 24, 2010.

178 *J.A. Clark*

52 This section is based on Mohammad Sartawi (CEO Sartawi Consulting) and Mohammad Nofal (Director, Pension and Social Insurance Funds, JEA), "Investment of Private Pension Funds: The Case of the Jordan Engineers Association (JEA)," unpublished paper presented at the 11th Regional Pension and Social Insurance Conference, May 29–31, 2007, Amman, Jordan.
53 The majority of members belong to the plan requiring a payment of 600 JD per month.
54 See also *The Jordan Times*, March 8, 2005.
55 The JEA's successes do not represent all PAs. Mohammad Haliqa, MP. Interview with Research Assistant on behalf of author. Amman. July 19, 2011.
56 Interview with Research Assistant on behalf of Author. Amman. July 19, 2011.
57 Interview with Research Assistant on behalf of author. Amman. July 19, 2011.
58 Until recently, a General Practitioner appointed by the ministry to a public hospital begins with a monthly salary of 350–400 JD. In late 2010, this was raised to 500 JD. *Jordan Times*, September 1, 2010.
59 www.ssc.gov.jo/english/pages.
    php?menu_id=14&local_type=0&local_id=0&local_details=0&local_
    details1=0&localsite_branchname=SSC.
60 www.dos.gov.jo and see *Jordan Times*, September 27, 2007.
61 www.dos.gov.jo/dos_home_e/main/jorfig/2010_e/jor_f_e.htm.
62 Interview with Research Assistant on behalf of author. Amman. July 17, 2011.
63 Abdullah al-Ghosheh. Elected JEA Board Member. Interview with author. Amman. May 24, 2006.
64 These debates and their resultant divisions within the PAs are largely masked behind the Islamist majorities. Their depth cannot be ascertained.
65 Hussein Abu Rumman, "Case Study 7: The Problem of the Political and Professional Roles in the Professional Associations" unpublished paper available online, Al-Urdun al-Jadid Research Center.
66 Abdullah al-Ghosheh, Elected JEA Board Member. Interview with author, Amman, May 24, 2006; Qaqish. Interview with Research Assistant on behalf of author. Amman. July 18, 2011. See Hamzeh (1996: 185); Hourani and Schwedler (1997: 278); Nevo (2001): 177–178).
67 Interview with Research Assistant on behalf of author. Amman. July 20, 2011. There is variance between PAs with some PAs, such as the Medical Association, conducting more professional activities than others. Mamdouh Al-Abbadi. MP. Interview by Research Assistant on behalf of author. Amman. July 21, 2011.
68 The IAF boycotted the 2010 parliamentary elections.
69 Jordan Center for Social Research (JCSR), "Democratic Transformation and Political Reform in Jordan," National Public Opinion Poll no. 5, October 21, 2007.
70 Center for Strategic Studies (CSS), University of Jordan, "Democracy in Jordan," 2005 Poll, September 2005, Amman.
71 Abdullah al-Ghosheh. Elected JEA Board Member. Interview with author, Amman, March 13, 2005.
72 For greater details on the MB and patronage, see Clark (forthcoming).
73 A final influential factor in determining Islamist response to the frozen law also was the larger political context and, according to interviewees, the Islamists' belief over time that there was a high likelihood that the regime would follow through on (or unfreeze) the legislation. The year 2006 witnessed the government taking aim at several institutions with the stated goal of eliminating corruption. One of these institutions was the MB's charity, the Islamic Center Charity Association (ICCS). While this would not have been a factor in 2005 (when the PAs initially engaged in sit-ins and actively lobbied to have the proposed law removed), the PAs' less provocative political stance shortly after the law was sent to the legal committee and throughout the following year can be placed within the context of the regime's assault on the

ICCS. In 2006, the ICCS's elected board was suspended and since that time a government-appointed committee has run the central administration of the ICCS. This background would have weighed heavily on the Islamist leadership of the PAs – threats can become reality.

74 Interview with Research Assistant on behalf of author. Amman. July 14, 2011.
75 Hourani. Interview with Research Assistant on behalf of author. Amman. July 14, 2011.
76 Hadadeen. Interview with Research Assistant on behalf of author. Amman. July 17, 2011.
77 Hourani. Interview with Research Assistant on behalf of author. Amman. July 14, 2011; Qaqish. Interview with Research Assistant on behalf of author. Amman. July 18, 2011.
78 Interview with Research Assistant on behalf of author. Amman. July 21. 2011.
79 Pierrot and Selvik similarly note Islamists' ambiguous relations with the regime in Syria. In their study of the private charities run by the al-Zayd movement, they argue that the Syria regime and the Islamist opposition are engaged in an increasingly interdependent relationship as the state relies on the Islamist charities – who are funded and supported by largely anti-regime Islamists – to provide for the needs of the poor while the Islamists depend on state privileges to carry out their activities. Ibid.

References

Abu Rumman, H. (2008) "Internal democracy in the professional associations: realities and prospects for the future," in Warwick Knowles (ed.) *Professional Associations and the Challenges of Democratic Transformation in Jordan*, Amman: Al-Urdun Al-Jadid Research Center.

Albrecht, H. and Schlumberger, O. (2004) " 'Waiting for Godot': Regime change without democratization in the Middle East," *International Political Science Review*, 25: 371–392.

Bank, A. (2004) "Rents, cooptation and economized discourse: three dimensions of political rule in Jordan, Morocco and Syria," *Journal of Mediterranean Studies*, 14: 155–179.

Boulby, M. (1999) *The Muslim Brotherhood and the Kings of Jordan*, Atlanta, GA: Scholars Press.

Brand, L. (1994) *Jordan's Inter-Arab Relations: The Political Economy of Alliance Making*, New York: Columbia University Press.

Brand, L. (1995) "Palestinians and Jordanians: a crisis of identity," *Journal of Palestinian Studies*, 24: 46–72.

Clark, J. (2004) *Islam, Charity and Activism: Middle Class Networks and Social Welfare in Egypt, Jordan and Yemen*, Bloomington: University of Indiana Press.

Clark, J. (2010) "Questioning power, mobilization and strategies of the Islamist opposition: how strong is the Muslim Brotherhood in Jordan?," in Holger Albrecht (ed.) *Contentious Politics in the Middle East*, Florida: Florida University Press.

Clark, J. (forthcoming) "Patronage, prestige and power: the ICCS within the Muslim Brotherhood," in Samer Shehata (ed.), *Islamist Politics in the Middle East: Contemporary Trajectories* (forthcoming).

El Ghobashy, M. (2008) "Constitutional contention in contemporary Egypt," *American Behavioural Scientist*, 51: 1590–1610.

El Sayed, M. (1988) "Professional associations and national integration in the Arab

180   *J.A. Clark*

world, with special reference to lawyers associations," in Adeed Dawsha and William Zartman (eds.) *Beyond Coercion*, Kent: Croom Helm.

Fahmy, N. (1998) "The performance of the Muslim Brotherhood in the Egyptian Sindacates: an alternative formula for reform?" *Middle East Journal*, 52: 551–562.

Gerring, J. (2006) *Case-study Research: Principles and Practices*, New York: Oxford University Press.

Haklai, O. (2009) "Authoritarianism and Islamic movements in the Middle East: research and theory-building in the twenty-first century," *International Studies Review*, 11: 27–45.

Hamayil, U.K. (2000) "Institutional characteristics of the Jordanian professional associations," in Warwick Knowles (ed.) *Professional Associations and the Challenges of Democratic Transformation in Jordan*, Amman: Al-Urdun Al-Jadid Research Center.

Hamzeh, Z. (1996) "The role of professional associations in Jordan's democratic experiment (1989–1993)," in Hourani and Hussein Abu Rumman (eds) *The Democratic Process in Jordan ... Where To?* Amman: Al-Urdun al-Jadid Research Center.

Heydemann, S. (2007) "Upgrading authoritarianism in the Arab world," The Brookings Institution, *Analysis Paper*, 13, pp. 1–37. Available at www.brookings.edu/~/media/Files/rc/papers/2007/10arabworld/10arabworld.pdf (last accessed 2007).

Hourani, H. and Schwedler, J. (eds) *Islamic Movements in Jordan*, Amman: Al-Urdun Al-Jadid Research Center.

Hourani, H. (2000) "The development of the political role of the professional associations: a historical survey 1950–1989," in Warwick Knowles (ed.) *Professional Associations and the Challenges of Democratic Transformation in Jordan*, Amman: Al-Urdun Al-Jadid Research Center.

Kornbluth, D. (2002) "Jordan and the anti-normalization campaign, 1994–2001," *Terrorism and Political Violence*, 14: 80–108.

Longuenesse, E. (1990) "Ingenieurs et marché de l'emploi en Jordanie," in Elisabeth Longuenesse (ed.) *Batisseurs et Bureaucrates: ingenieurs et societé au Maghreb et au Moyen Orient*, Lyon: Maison de l'Orient Mediterranéen.

Lucas, R. (2004) "Monarchical authoritarianism: survival and political liberalization in a Middle Eastern regime type," *International Journal of Middle East Studies*, 36: 103–119.

Lucas, R. (2005) *Institutions and Politics in the Survival of Jordan*, Albany: State University of New York Press.

Lust-Okar, E. (2001) "The decline of Jordanian political parties: myth or reality," *International Journal of Middle East Studies*, 33: 545–569.

Lust-Okar, E. (2005) *Structuring Conflict in the Arab World: Incumbents, Opponents and Institutions*, Cambridge: Cambridge University Press.

Moore, P. and Salloukh, B. (2007) "Struggles under authoritarianism: regimes, states and Pas in the Arab world," *International Journal of Middle East Studies*, 39: 53–76.

Nevo, J. (2001) "Changing identities in Jordan," *Israel Affairs*, 9: 169–184.

Pierret, T and Selvik, K. (2009) "Limits of authoritarian upgrading in Syria: private welfare, Islamic charities and the rise of the Zayd movement," *International Journal of Middle East Studies*, 41: 595–614.

Rosefsky Wickham, C. (2002) *Mobilising Islam*, New York: Columbia University Press.

Schwedler, J. (2005) "Cop rock: protest, identity, and dancing riot police in Jordan," *Social Movement Studies*, 4: 155–175.

10 An 'activist diaspora' as a response to authoritarianism in Myanmar

The role of transnational activism in promoting political reform

Adam Simpson

Introduction

On a remote stretch of the Salween River, between the proposed Dar Gwin and Wei Gyi hydropower dam sites and where it forms the border between Thailand and Myanmar (Burma),[1] sits the Ei Tu Hta camp for ethnic Karen internally displaced peoples (IDPs) in Karen National Union (KNU) controlled Myanmar. The family of Hsiplopo, the leader of this camp, live three hours walk away but he is unable to visit them because the *tatmadaw*, the Myanmar military with which the KNU has been engaged in the world's longest running civil war, have camps that are only two hours walk away. The camp is also built on steep hillsides, denuding the forest cover in the limited area available, and is unable to grow its own rice, relying instead on regular donations from the UN and other NGOs shipped upriver by longtail boat.[2] This type of human and environmental insecurity colours the daily existence of both the Karen people in this camp and many other ethnic minorities in Myanmar. Nevertheless, despite these conditions, Hsiplopo's commitment to a campaign against the proposed nearby dams is resolute: 'We don't want dams ... the military cannot build the dams because the KNU will not let them while the people do not want them.'[3]

This stance reflects the opposition to the dams of many environmental activists and groups who inhabit the nebulous and dangerous borderlands regions of eastern Myanmar. It also represents a form of activated citizenship although the concept of citizenship for ethnic minorities in Myanmar is itself problematic as their relationship to the Myanmar state is often little more than one of oppression and conflict. Despite the civil conflict in these areas, and perhaps because of it, these activists often operate beyond the remit of the tatmadaw undertaking perilous work with the KNU to promote human and environmental security for ethnic minorities. As an activist from the Karen Environmental and Social Action Network (KESAN) explains: 'KESAN's programs are in the KNU area [in Myanmar] so we have a close relationship with the KNU leaders.'[4] It can be difficult for environmental activists in the North, for whom this precarious

182   *A. Simpson*

existence is entirely foreign, to fully comprehend the existential struggle that dictates much environmental activism in the South, particularly under authoritarian regimes such as that of Myanmar, which has been dominated by the military since 1962. As a result, many Northern environment movements, and the American environment movement in particular, have been historically apolitical with the issues of 'human health, shelter, and food security' traditionally absent from their agendas (Doyle 2005, 26).

This lack of political analysis on the issues of central importance to survival in the South and the movements they spawn is also reflected within many academic writings on environmental politics. Despite an increased focus on the environment in the last two decades, most approaches to environmental politics still examine predominantly ecological issues or regulatory regimes and focus particularly on the affluent states of the North (Howes 2005; Kutting 2000; Paehlke and Torgerson 2005). Although there has been increased attention on environmental movements in recent years, much of the material also focuses primarily on movements within the North (Carter 2007; Doherty 2002; Doyle 2000; Dryzek *et al.* 2003; Gottlieb 2005; Hutton and Connors 1999; Rootes 2007; Sandler and Pezzullo 2007; Shabecoff 1993). There has been some analysis of environment movements in the South (Doherty 2006; Doherty and Doyle 2006; Doyle 2005; Duffy 2006; Dwivedi 1997, 2001), and various studies of transnational activism more generally (della Porta *et al.* 2006; Eschle and Maiguashca 2005; Keck and Sikkink 1998; Reitan 2007; Routledge *et al.* 2006; Rupert 2000), but only limited studies on how authoritarianism in the South specifically impacts on environmental activism (Doyle and Simpson 2006) or policy (Fredriksson and Wollscheid 2007). There are numerous studies that examine civil society under authoritarianism more broadly but these tend to focus on more traditional and formalised civil society organisations (Jamal 2007; Liverani 2008; Sater 2007). This chapter adds to this literature by delving more deeply into environmental politics under the military in Myanmar and examines the transnational campaigns against several proposed hydroelectric dams on the Salween River in eastern Myanmar. As transnational projects these dams are being undertaken by governments and transnational corporations (TNCs) but, as with most large energy projects in Myanmar, they are designed to export most of their electricity to either Thailand or China.

Despite national elections in November 2010 that returned Myanmar to nominally civilian rule the 2008 constitution, on which the elections were based, provides for a continuing central role for the military in the country's governance (Holliday 2008). Although the election process was flawed, fraudulent and tightly controlled, with many generals from the former military regime, the State Peace and Development Council (SPDC),[5] merely stepping out of their uniforms to take up senior positions in the new government, there is little doubt that incremental change towards civilian rule is occurring and the potential for political discourse in Myanmar may well improve over time. While many exiled or human rights groups rightly point out that civil conflict and human rights abuses, particularly in the eastern border regions, continue,[6] some analysts, such as the

Transnational activism in Myanmar 183

former International Labour Organization (ILO) Liaison Officer in Myanmar, Richard Horsey, are more optimistic about the 'new level of scrutiny' (Horsey 2011, 4) that has accompanied the new parliament. The current Liaison Officer, Steve Marshall, who is possibly more intimately involved with the new government than any other Westerner likewise argues that 'there is no doubt that the political landscape has changed'.[7]

This top down political change has accompanied a less visible but nonetheless significant increase in domestic civil society activism in recent years and particularly since Cyclone Nargis in 2008 (Sabandar 2010; South 2004). The main beneficiaries of this opening have been humanitarian NGOs that have focused on emergency relief to natural disasters such as Nargis and Cyclone Giri in 2010,[8] but there has also been increased activity by environmental groups and NGOs. These groups, as with all those actors who wish to avoid sanction or imprisonment in Myanmar, engage in a certain amount of self-censorship to avoid overtly political critiques of the government but there is increasing space available for pursuing third sector environmental governance. This increased domestic activism has improved the prospects of collaboration between domestic and exiled groups with prominent domestic environmentalists running trainings on the border or in Thailand for exiled groups such as KESAN.[9] Regardless of recent changes, however, after five decades of authoritarian rule the local environmental movement remains embryonic with significant limitations in experience and expertise. It has, therefore, been the transnational environment movement occupying Myanmar's borderlands that has provided the most fertile and important outlet for environmental activism and governance of large-scale hydropower projects in Myanmar.[10]

This case study therefore suggests that, whereas hybrid regimes offer domestic spaces for political competition and therefore foster domestic civil society (Diamond 2002; Jayasuriya and Rodan 2007; Levitsky and Way 2002), traditional authoritarian regimes such as that which has afflicted Myanmar are more likely to create an *activist diaspora*, a dynamic transnational community of expatriates who engage in environmental activism in borderland regions or neighbouring countries. As this case study demonstrates, an activist diaspora tends to transcend ethnic divisions and therefore provides a multi-ethnic cohesion which is often absent from the broader exile community. As 'divide and conquer' has been one of the tatmadaw's main strategies in neutralising opposition by ethnic minorities, Myanmar's activist diaspora may contribute to more potent domestic social movements that promote democracy, human rights and environmental security in Myanmar.

Environmental politics in Myanmar

Myanmar, more than most other countries, epitomises the interdependence of human and environmental security (Barnett 2001; Doyle and Risely 2008). The blatant disregard for human rights and rapacious exploitation of the country's environment and natural resources by successive military dominated regimes has

184   *A. Simpson*

had dire implications for human and environmental security and prompted significant transnational civil society activism. Despite the 2010 election the US State Department's human rights report for that year suggested that little improvement had been achieved in Myanmar:

> Government security forces were responsible for extrajudicial killings, custodial deaths, disappearances, rape, and torture. The government detained civic activists indefinitely and without charges. In addition regime-sponsored mass-member organizations engaged in harassment and abuse of human rights and prodemocracy activists. The government abused prisoners and detainees ... and imprisoned citizens arbitrarily for political motives. The army continued its attacks on ethnic minority villagers, resulting in deaths, forced relocation, and other serious abuses. The government routinely infringed on citizens' privacy and restricted freedom of speech, press, assembly, association, religion, and movement. The government did not allow domestic human rights nongovernmental organizations (NGOs) to function independently, and international NGOs encountered a difficult environment.
>
> (US Department of State 2011, 1)

Likewise the Myanmar government and its select few business associates have pursued large-scale development projects with little concern for the environmental consequences. In Myanmar's early decades during the period of 'the Burmese road to socialism', state authoritarianism and incompetence depleted ecosystems while running down the economy. With a precipitous fall in foreign aid leaving the economy on the verge of collapse following the crackdown in 1988 the military offered attractive incentives for foreign investment through its *Union of Myanmar Foreign Investment Law*. This created a market economy that opened the door to joint ventures with foreign companies that were interested in exploiting Myanmar's natural resources, resulting in a variety of transnational energy projects (Lintner 1990, 165; MacLean 2003, 16; McCarthy 2000, 235; Myat Thein 2004, 123). In the subsequent two decades the energy sector, including hydropower, was the primary recipient of FDI and accounted for more than 98 per cent of all foreign investment in Myanmar for the 2006–2007 fiscal year.

McCarthy argues that particularly since the SPDC military junta came to power in 1988 there has been a 'hard sell' of the country's natural resources with no evidence of this money being redistributed among Myanmar people nor any evidence of long term planning guiding foreign investment projects being approved by the Myanmar Investment Commission (MIC) (McCarthy 2000, 260–261). Other studies have also demonstrated that development projects in Myanmar have not benefited the majority of the Myanmar people with environmental problems linked inextricably to human rights abuses, particularly of ethnic minorities (Skidmore and Wilson 2007). Despite the daily restrictions on the general population it is these ethnic minorities in Myanmar's mountainous border regions, including the Karen, Shan, Kachin and Mon, who have been the particular targets of repression (Fink 2008; Khin Zaw Win 2010; Lintner 1999; Smith 1999; South 2009).

Transnational activism in Myanmar 185

The multiplicity of individual security challenges facing the people of Myanmar means it is extremely difficult to differentiate between those that are linked to 'the environment' and those that aren't as rampant logging and environmental destruction together with a total lack of environmental impact assessment (EIA) in the country are intrinsically linked to non-democratic governance and authoritarian military rule. A national environmental law to establish environmental institutions and standards has stood dormant since being drafted with UN assistance in 2005/6 and even if this law is passed during the current parliament it is unlikely to be promulgated, according to Win Myo Thu, an influential domestic environmentalist, until its final year in 2014.[11] The government's failings combined in its inadequate response to Cyclone Nargis in May 2008 that killed 140,000 people, destroyed 800,000 houses and left millions of Irrawaddy delta residents homeless and facing disease and malnutrition. While some authors argued that the governance of the relief-and-recovery process led by the Association of Southeast Asian Nations (ASEAN) was 'good and strong' (Sabandar 2010, 202) others argued that the government's response was characterised by its hallmark 'policy incompetence, neglect and brutality' (Vicary 2010, 208). Aid delivery eventually improved under the ASEAN-led Tripartite Core Group but the government's immediate response to the disaster was to hold up visa applications for foreign journalists and aid workers and deny entry to Western aid deliveries, leading to a massive build-up of food, medicine and disaster response expertise in Bangkok in the crucial early days following the event (Fink 2009, 108–110; Larkin 2010, 8–10; Vicary 2010, 214–218).

The role of the state has also been particularly central to the insecurity faced by Myanmar's ethnic minorities, both through assaults on their person and on their environment through the *four cuts* campaign that aims to restrict insurgents' access to food, funds, intelligence and recruits (Smith 1999). Displaced ethnic communities, whose crops have been burned and who have been forced from their homes by the military, are obliged to engage in environmentally destructive practices such as 'slash and burn' or 'shifting agriculture' cultivation methods rather than their more sustainable and traditional rotational techniques, and their constant movement may result in unsustainable rates of harvest for timber and non-timber products, such as bamboo and rattan (Doyle and Simpson 2006, 756). These peoples therefore face challenges to their human security, whether considered from a narrow (political violence by the state), or broad (freedom from want), school perspective (Kerr 2007, 95).

Although restrictions are most severe in the ethnic minority areas open dissent against the government is not tolerated throughout Myanmar and an independent civil society critical of the state is embryonic. By the end of the 1990s Steinberg contended that the regime had

> attempted to divide the opposition, both ethnic and political, and ... eliminated all vestiges of civil society in Burma ... independent NGOs do not exist beyond village temple societies.
>
> (Steinberg 1998, 275)

186   *A. Simpson*

A few years later South argued that this view was overly pessimistic with his research from the early 2000s finding that various civil society actors were re-emerging in both conflict zones and ceasefire or government controlled areas (South 2004, 244–249). Although domestic civil society activism has increased significantly in recent years it is from an extremely low base and the limited outlets for social mobilisation are unlikely to represent a threat to the military ruling class (Brownlee 2007, 217–218). The absence of both media freedom and the opportunity for public protest in Myanmar limits outlets for dissent although, despite steep penalties, attempts to block access to internet sites are not always effective. Nevertheless, barriers to the free flow of information into Myanmar and a stifled media mean that Myanmar's borders are more than mere speed bumps for the transnational sharing of activist strategies, tactics and philosophies (Doyle and Simpson 2006, 758).

The authoritarian security apparatus in Myanmar usually ensures that public displays of dissent are quickly extinguished but in September 2007, for the first time since 1988, widespread opposition to the regime overflowed onto the streets across the country before being brutally suppressed by security forces and pro-military militias (AFP 2007; *BBC News* 2007b; ICG 2008). In August the SPDC had announced enormous increases in fuel prices that increased the cost of living and transport, further reducing already precarious human security for the peoples of Myanmar. Compressed natural gas, which is used by public buses, was reportedly increased 500 per cent (DPA 2007; Human Rights Watch 2007). Myanmar exports vast amounts of natural gas to Thailand through the Yadana and Yetagun pipelines, which could have otherwise been used to maintain lower gas prices (Simpson 2007). Initially the protests were led by Buddhist monks, with attacks on lay activists thought to be more likely than on the revered *sangha*. A brutal crackdown nonetheless ensued including the close range murder of a Japanese journalist by the military caught on video during the protests (*Times Online* 2007). The Myanmar state media announced that nine people had been killed in the crackdown but foreign ambassadors and observers suggested the death toll could have been 'many multiples of that' with hundreds of monks also detained and ransacked monasteries littered with 'pools of blood' (*BBC News* 2007a).

Despite the military's brutal suppression of the protests activists employed certain globalising technologies which the regime had difficulty in containing. One group used its listserve to email out a link to a *MySpace* video of the violent arrest of activist Suu Suu Nway, which was viewed over 14,000 times in a week (Aye Mi San 2007b). The same site showed a video of veteran activist Min Ko Naing making a democracy speech to a large crowd of people before his rearrest (Aye Mi San 2007a). In another exemplar of the twenty-first century globalisation of information-sharing the *Wikipedia* site for the protests was set up on 21 September, only three days after the protests commenced (*Wikipedia* 2008). Although this speed of publication would now be considered almost lackadaisical, with the social media, *Twitter* and *Facebook*, having revolutionised citizen activism once again during the 2011 Jasmine Revolutions, it allowed for the rapid distribution of information on the protests. At their height on 29 September, however, the

Transnational activism in Myanmar   187

military took the extraordinary step of shutting down all international links to the internet and temporarily suspending most mobile phone services throughout the country (Ball 2008, 78; Chowdhury 2008, 13).[12] Despite such heavy-handed attempts at control, these technologies remain crucial in their ability to expedite communication linkages between activists within Myanmar and those in exile.

Building an activist diaspora

As a result of restrictions and multiple insecurities at home activists from Myanmar often remove themselves from the military's sphere of influence, either to the 'liberated areas' independent of tatmadaw control such as Ei Tu Hta IDP camp at the border with Thailand on the Salween River, or, where possible, to less authoritarian neighbouring countries to facilitate their operations. These activists become the transnational agents who undertake the campaigns against large-scale development projects in Myanmar. These activists may be in the environmental movement but their concerns are related directly to human rights abuses and they experience a parallel process to one described by O'Kane for women in the area:

> for those trapped in the unsettled and ambiguous Burma-Thailand borderland space, distinctions between public/private, politics/survival, mother/ activist, freedom fighter/illegal alien collapsed and become inseparable experiences. The collapse and/or significant restructuring of how these binary categories of relations are lived in the transversal spaces resulted in transformations in [their] political awareness.
>
> (O'Kane 2005, 15)

Hsiplopo, the Ei Tu Hta camp leader, epitomises this complexity. Having grown up in Yangon he joined the KNU in 1973 and thereafter lived in the forest and the camps along the Thai-Myanmar border. His multiple identities change over time and have included KNU member, father, husband, camp leader, and IDP and anti-dam activist. This experience echoes the arguments of Kaiser and Nikiforova that,

> [b]orderlands are not marginalized spaces ... but rather ... central nodes of power where place and identity across a multiplicity of geographical scales are made and unmade.
>
> (Kaiser and Nikiforova 2006, 940)

It is these displaced communities of these borderlands that have been most vocal against the Salween Dams in Myanmar. These struggles parallel the opposition against the Narmada and Tehri Dams of India, where Vandana Shiva notes local communities do not just struggle to preserve their homeland, they struggle against the destruction of entire civilisations and ways of life (Shiva 1989, 189). Despite the dangers these activists often re-enter Myanmar incognito to undertake research for NGOs that are based outside Myanmar's borders.[13]

188 *A. Simpson*

These activists create networks between displaced communities inside Myanmar and the exiles across the border. Some of these networks were initiated by Dr Cynthia Maung, a Karen doctor who founded the Mae Tao Clinic (MTC) in the border town of Mae Sot after being driven into exile in Thailand after the 1988 protests (Cynthia Maung 2008).[14] Mae Sot is now the busiest entry port for Myanmar migrants and refugees and has become a crucial centre of operations for exiled NGOs (Smith and Piya Pangsapa 2008, 202). Although the MTC is based in Mae Sot and provides health services and education to refugees in Thailand it also provides these services covertly for IDPs in Myanmar itself through Back Pack Health Worker Teams (BPHWT).[15] Its activities within Myanmar are characteristic of Cleary's assertion that organisations in the South, and particularly under authoritarian regimes, are more often service providers than simply lobby groups (Cleary 1997). Although initiated to provide emergency food relief and medical assistance the programme has also been supplemented by a longer term Community Development Programme that focuses on developing self-reliance within displaced communities by encouraging participatory decision making and community needs assessment. The programme started in Karen State, then moved on to Karenni, Mon, Shan, Kachin and now Chin and Arakan States, covering many of the border states that host transnational energy projects. The underground movement that these efforts developed provides ready-made networks for other NGOs and groups to use to undertake research and activism over the projects.

The exodus from Myanmar to other countries to escape authoritarian repression, particularly following the 1988 crackdown, has resulted in what can be considered an *activist diaspora*. The inclusive domain of the term 'diaspora' has, at times, been stretched to render it almost meaningless with academic literature on, for example, liberal or queer diaspora leading Brubaker to argue that '[i]f everyone is diasporic, then no one is distinctively so' (Brubaker 2005, 3). Myanmar's expatriate activists, however, fulfil not only traditional aspects of the term based on dislocation or 'the dispersal of a people from [their] original homeland' (Butler 2001, 189), but also on what Sökefeld argues are

> imagined transnational communities [each of which is a] transnationally dispersed collectivity that distinguishes itself by clear self-imaginations as community.
>
> (Sökefeld 2006, 267)

Additionally, his focus on social movement theory and forms of mobilisation dovetails with the concept of an activist diasporic community. This concept, deriving as it does from a largely progressive and democratic activist community, also avoids the pitfalls that Anthias considers afflicts some diasporic communities, such as a lack of trans-ethnic solidarity and gender awareness (Anthias 1998). It is true that there remains significant friction between some ethnic communities of Myanmar but this is largely absent in the environmental activist

Transnational activism in Myanmar   189

community examined, resulting in a more unified and effective voice. Indeed a long-time Myanmar activist from the North observed its development:

> When I first came to the Thai-Burmese border region with [my organisation][16] in 1994 I noticed that political parties and ethnic armies were driving the opposition but it now seems that NGOs and civil society are making the running.[17]

An activist diaspora is created when activists leave their local authoritarian environments for transnational settings, creating transnational networks of exiled activists. In the case of Myanmar expatriate activists escaping authoritarianism are distributed throughout the world but are particularly active in the Thai-Myanmar border region, which is the focus of this chapter. This activist diaspora, despite the potential difficulties it poses for activists with regards to language difficulties and sometimes precarious citizenship status, also provides many opportunities. Training that would otherwise not be accessible at home is often made available by aid agencies or human rights groups. Improved accessibility to other transnational activists and the media in cosmopolitan environments also creates opportunities for developing activist strategies and tactics and facilitating communication of messages to a wider audience, particularly through increased proficiency in English. In addition, in the case of Myanmar most activists don't actively petition the Myanmar regime directly as their experience suggests there is little to be gained. They therefore focus their energies primarily on transnational activities and facilitate linkages and communication with other transnational activists, based predominantly in Thailand, that help convey their campaigns on cross-border energy projects in Myanmar to a more spatially dispersed transnational audience.

While it is well established that the Myanmar regime, as with other authoritarian regimes, suppresses opposition and dissent at home (Brownlee 2007; ICG 2008; Lintner 1999; Smith 1999; South 2009), it actually appears to stimulate transnational linkages and activism through the activist diaspora, indicating that authoritarian regimes may actually be stimulating the growth of transnational activism by creating nodes and networks of activists encircling the regimes. While there appears to be an inverse relationship between authoritarianism and activism at a local level, with more authoritarian regimes resulting in less local activism, there also appears to be a direct relationship between local authoritarianism and activism at the transnational level, with more authoritarianism resulting in greater transnational activism.

As a consequence of civil conflict between the Myanmar military and insurgent ethnic groups, Myanmar's borderlands are particularly important in the development of the activist diaspora and other transnational networks, particularly as the boundaries between Myanmar's insurgent groups and activists can sometimes be blurred. Insurgent groups often specifically target border regions for their 'intrinsic, tactical and material importance' (Acuto 2008, 33), which are in a continuous state of flux:

190   *A. Simpson*

Numbers of border arrivals and crossings fluctuate in relation to military operations, economic deterioration inside Burma and the continued possibility of sanctuary in Thailand. Each location has its own historical, cultural and geographical characteristics and people's semi-permanence there has complicated and re-constituted the borderlands in various political, social, economic, cultural and environmental ways. In this way Burmese political opposition groups have also become established components on this complex human milieu.

(O'Kane 2005, 14–15)

Similarly, in Myanmar's western border regions adjoining Bangladesh and India refugees and insurgents populate both sides of the mountainous borders although expatriate activists tend to congregate in the major cities of Bangladesh and India. These borders and the populations in the surrounding regions are, therefore, relatively 'fuzzy' rather than hard and well defined (Chaturvedi 2003; Christiansen *et al.* 2000; Gleditsch *et al.* 2006). Borderlands are 'grey zones' that, particularly in times of conflict, acquire several meanings beyond that of mere legal boundaries (Acuto 2008, 32), and are in themselves central to the forming of identity, being

central nodes where the intersections of power, place and identity are made visible. As both zones of contestation and spaces of becoming, borderlands are fundamental sites in the multiscalar reconfiguration of the sociospatial imaginary, and far from disappearing in a borderless world, their number and significance are increasing markedly ... in the increasingly fragmented, ruptured place-identities of contemporary timespace.

(Kaiser and Nikiforova 2006, 952)

The Thai–Myanmar border area epitomises these 'zones of contestation'. Due to authoritarian rule and precarious livelihoods in Myanmar environmental campaigns are leavened with concerns over democratisation and human rights and the complexity on Myanmar's periphery provides a compelling case study on the impacts of authoritarianism on multiscalar civil society activism.

The campaign against the Salween Dams

The main case study for this chapter is a set of proposed hydroelectric dams on the Salween River in Myanmar including the Wei Gyi and Dagwin Dams along the Thai border, the Hat Gyi (or Hutgyi) Dam in Karen State and the Tasang Dam in Shan State (see Figure 10.1). The dams are at various early stages of their development but all face campaigns over the issues of environmental degradation and military repression of ethnic minorities that have accompanied other transnational energy projects in Myanmar (Simpson 2008). One of the main beneficiaries of electricity will be the Electricity Generating Authority of Thailand (EGAT) while water will be diverted from Myanmar into Thailand's

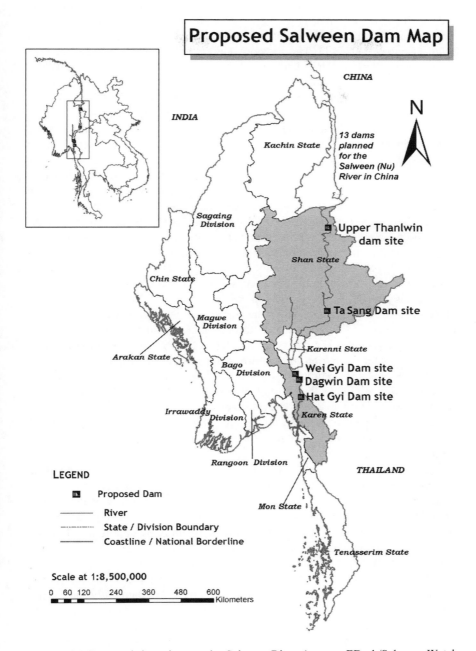

Figure 10.1 Proposed dam sites on the Salween River (source: EDesk/Salween Watch 2007).

192   A. Simpson

Bhumiphol and Sirikit reservoirs (Piya Pangsapa and Smith 2008, 493). In June 2006 China's largest hydropower company Sinohydro Corporation agreed to partner EGAT and build the $1 billion 1,200 MW Hat Gyi Dam Project (Corben 2006; Osborne 2007, 11). The previous December Myanmar's Department of Hydroelectric Power (DHP) had signed a MoU with EGAT for the 'development, ownership and operation' of the Hat Gyi Hydropower Project (EGAT and DHP 2005).[18] In April 2006 the Thai construction company MDX Group formed a $6 billion joint venture with (DHP) to build the 7,110 MW Tasang power plant and in March 2007 China's state-owned Gezhouba Group announced that it had won a contract for the diversion tunnel as part of the dam construction (AP 2006; Sapawa 2007).

The campaigns against these projects are representative of broader campaigns by activists and ethnic minorities against environmental devastation and political repression in Myanmar. The Hat Gyi Dam, slated as the first dam to be built, reflects these issues, being in an area still prone to civil conflict between the KNU and the tatmadaw. Despite attempts to continue work on the Hat Gyi Dam security is still tenuous in the region with EGAT suspending the project in September 2007 following negative publicity from NGOs and the media after two employees died from wounds associated with the civil conflict. Ethnic conflict in the area has already displaced 500,000 ethnic Karen, with 140,000 refugees registered in Thai refugee camps along the border (Corben 2007). Various estimates suggest between 75,000 and 100,000 further ethnic minorities will be displaced by the Hat Gyi and other dams (DPA 2006; McLeod 2007; Pianporn Deetes 2007). In a pattern common to most transnational energy projects in Myanmar the impacts on local communities are often detrimental while the benefits are accrued further afield. As the World Commission on Dams (2000) made clear it is always the marginalised who are most adversely impacted by large dams with a World Bank funded ecologist arguing 'many large dams exacerbate poverty by damaging the fisheries and wetlands on which the poorest people depend most' (Pearce 2006, 10).

The Salween River passes through Shan, Karenni and Karen states in Myanmar before emptying into the Gulf of Martaban at Mawlamyine (Moulmein) in Mon State. The proposed Salween Dams therefore precipitated a multi-ethnic dimension to the campaign, similar in nature to the campaign against the Shwe Gas Pipeline in Myanmar which provided a unifying opportunity to bring together Arakanese, Burman – from central Myanmar – and Shan activists (Simpson 2008).[19] As an indicator of this emerging multi-ethnic cooperation Sai Sai, the Shan coordinator of Salween Watch and Burma Rivers Network (BRN) – two of the coalitions campaigning against the Salween Dams – began attending meetings with the Arakanese-dominated Shwe Gas Movement in Chiang Mai from 2008, indicating increased cross-campaign cooperation as well.[20]

Environmental groups had been aware of the proposed Salween Dam projects in Myanmar since the 1990s,[21] but it wasn't until 2003 that the campaigns began to reach beyond the activist networks. In December 2003 the *Bangkok Post*, whose environmental writers were networked with Salween activists, ran a

Transnational activism in Myanmar 193

prominent front page story with the headline 'China plans 13 dams on Salween' (Kultida Samabuddhi and Yuthana Praiwan 2003).[22] Although concentrating on the upper Salween in China (the Nujiang or Nu River), it also drew widespread attention to the impending Salween Dam projects in Myanmar and became the first of many articles on the topic.

Facilitating local activism in Myanmar is difficult as activists face problems of access to communities in the Salween region due to the authoritarian rule of the Myanmar military. Nevertheless, the issues relating to the Salween Dams and, indeed, dams throughout Myanmar resulted in a sprawling network of groups and umbrella organisations producing a plethora of websites and detailed reports. Following the experience of previous campaigns, environmental groups involved with the Salween campaign were aware of the need for creating networks early on between local communities and activists to harness local knowledge but access to the areas was always a problem. Recent technologies such as the internet, mobile phones and desktop publishing have resulted in greater coordination and publicity for a wider transnational audience but direct contact with local communities in Myanmar often still requires face-to-face communication, resulting in high-level security risks for activists.

As a central organisation within the Salween campaign the Karenni Development Research Group (KDRG) is a coalition of nine Karenni civil society organisations and a member of both Salween Watch and Burma Rivers Network (BRN). It undertakes research within Karenni State in Myanmar, which it has published transnationally (KDRG 2006), but faces extreme difficulties organising any public activities in the region and its research is undertaken incognito. The manifold problems for activists and local communities in this region are set out by Aung Ngyeh, a Karenni activist with the KDRG and BRN:

> [The] people inside Burma, they didn't know about the plans of dam construction on the Salween. Therefore, the first thing that we have to do inside Burma is to raise awareness of dam's construction.... To organise public action inside Burma, it's very hard as Burmese people [are] subjected to living under [an] oppressive regime. Most dam construction plans are located in ethnic lands ... where long run civil war [is] found. So, the villagers who are staying in those dam construction sites have suffered from various kinds of human rights abuse for long time and they have to struggle for their [survival]. The people who will be affected from the dams ... have to live in their own lands as internally displaced person [IDPs]. Their lives is full of risks and ... their lives can be destroyed [at any time] so they have to hide in deep jungle for their safety. So when, we have tried to deliver the messages of dam construction plans to [them], we have also faced difficulty to [reach] them.[23]

Large-scale relocation in Karenni State near the Salween River has occurred since 1996, the year when 212 villages in an area thought to be sympathetic to the Karenni National Progressive Party (KNPP) were relocated as the area became progressively militarised (KDRG 2006, 15). According to the Shan Sapawa Environmental Organization (Sapawa) this also occurred upstream in Shan State, in a pattern common along the Salween, where, as part of a wider anti-insurgency campaign, 60,000 villagers from areas adjoining the Tasang Dam site and flood zone were relocated in 1996 (Sapawa 2006, 20–24). Sapawa is the first Shan organisation dedicated to the preservation of the environment in Shan State and it has been particularly active over the Tasang Dam project. Two of the Shan founders of Sapawa, Sai Sai and Khin Nanda, were graduates of the 2001 EarthRights Burma School for activists run by EarthRights International (ERI), an NGO founded by Karen exile Ka Hsaw Wa.[24] Sai Sai became the Sapawa spokesperson and worked with ERI between 2001 and 2003 and later, as a coordinator, with Salween Watch and the BRN.[25] Despite undertaking research on the Myanmar side of the border Sapawa, as with KDRG, has been unable to organise significant public activities in the Salween region.[26] In contrast the Myanmar military, as part of its public relations campaign, forced over 400 villagers, many of whom have worked on projects as forced labour, to attend the official launch of the Tasang Dam in March 2007 with Thai construction company MDX and high-ranking Myanmar military officials (Sapawa 2007).

Downriver from both Shan and Karenni States the Salween River forms part of the border with Thailand in Karen State, the sites for both the Wei Gyi and Dar Gwin Dams (see Figure 10.2), with the Hat Gyi Dam further downriver

Figure 10.2 The Salween River in the dry season between the Wei Gyi and Dar Gwin Dam Sites (source: author).

Transnational activism in Myanmar 195

entirely within Karen State (KDRG 2006, viii; KRW 2004; Salween Watch n.d.). Displacement has also been rampant within Karen State with the Karen founder and director of the Karen Environmental and Social Action Network (KESAN), who grew up near the Wei Gyi Dam site, moving downriver with his family each time there was an attack by the tatmadaw until they finally left Myanmar permanently in 1995 after the fall of Manerplaw.[27]

The proximity to Thailand has, however, made organising some actions possible on the river. Karen Rivers Watch (KRW), a coalition of Karen organisations formed in June 2003, organises protests with activists and villagers along the river near the dam sites for the International Day of Action Against Dams on 14 March every year (Cho 2008; KRW 2007; Saw Karen 2007). The events have transnational elements but there is also a large local component with local activists raising local awareness about the projects through the dissemination of knowledge, which is intended to empower villagers (see Figure 10.3).[28] As an activist with KRW and Karen Office of Relief and Development (KORD) noted: 'we ask local villagers to share their feelings and knowledge; we mobilise the community from the Karen side'.[29]

Nevertheless, although these actions have occurred inside the official borders of Myanmar the locations where they have taken place can be defined as politically fuzzy to the extent that they are not part of Myanmar totally controlled by the Myanmar military or government. Giddens argues that in Weber's definition of a state the territorial element of a claim to a monopoly of violence over a given territory may be 'quite ill-defined' and that this 'claim' may well be contested (Giddens 1987, 18–19). The areas where protests have taken place are areas of Karen State largely controlled by the KNU, like the area surrounding Ei Tu Hta IDP Camp, considered by the ethnic Karen as 'liberated areas', contesting the Myanmar military's claim of sovereignty over the area.[30] Absolute control over these areas may be fluid but security considerations are paramount with activists reticent to discuss the location of the protests to avoid recriminations. An ERI activist suggested that the protests happened at 'safe areas for ... activists and villagers',[31] while a KESAN activist later disclosed the location on condition it not be divulged.[32] The protests inside Myanmar are, therefore, not undertaken to appeal to the military regime that controls most of the country. Indeed they would probably be violently suppressed. Rather, they are undertaken in areas over which the military has little influence, for both local peoples and an international audience, which may change over time according to military operations making it difficult for activists to predict locations far in advance.

Due to the tenuous control by the Myanmar military in many of these regions the dams may provide a potentially valuable role for the tatmadaw in the repression of insurgent groups. Once the dams are built the reservoirs behind the dams will flood large areas that provide either shelter or transit zones for insurgent groups. Around the Tasang Dam the Shan State Army South (SSAS) still has sporadic battles with the Myanmar military while the Dar Gwin, Wei Gyi and Hat Gyi sites provide security for the KNU and are also the busiest routes for Karen refugees fleeing Myanmar into Thailand (KHRG 2007, 38–39). The Wei

Figure 10.3 Anti-dam poster by Karen River Watch at Ei Tu Hta IDP Camp in KNU-held Myanmar (source: author).

Transnational activism in Myanmar 197

Gyi Dam will also flood most of Karenni State's two river valleys that lie upstream where the KNPP is active (Kusnetz 2008). One Northern activist with extensive experience in the region argues that as a result of these projects ethnic IDPs in these areas are effectively 'held hostage' by the Myanmar military in the negotiations between themselves, ethnic insurgents and the Thai state.[33]

The Hat Gyi Dam has been slated as the first Salween Dam to be constructed in Karen State being the only one out of the lower three dams to be entirely within Myanmar's borders and therefore lowering the level of external scrutiny (Noam 2008; Pianporn Deetes 2007; Tunya Sukpanich 2007). While security is generally more tenuous for activists deeper in Myanmar there are also tatmadaw garrisons on the Myanmar side of the river near the Dar Gwin and Wei Gyi Dam site (KRW 2004, 13), and in February 2008 ten tatmadaw soldiers were injured after being shot by Karen insurgents while crossing the river along the border (Saw Yan Naing 2008).[34] The attack occurred near Ei Htu Tar IDP Camp on the Myanmar side and the villages of Mae Sam Laep and Ban Ta Tar Fung on the Thai side where local villagers oppose the dams.[35] It was less than a month later when the villagers gathered on the river near the Wei Gyi Dam site secured by the KNU for their protest. Although there was little confidence that the protests would influence the Myanmar government Karen villagers on the Thai side also felt a sense of powerlessness in relation to the Thai government:

> if the govt wants to build [the dams] it will as we are only poor people but, still, we and other villages send ... representatives to meetings in Mae Hong Son, Chiang Mai and Bangkok.[36]

Despite the increased opportunities for public participation in the political process in Thailand compared with Myanmar it is not without its authoritarian characteristics (Simpson 2004, 32).

On the Myanmar side of the border the protests at insecure sites are the only outlet for Myanmar villagers to voice their concerns over the dam projects. As with other projects in Myanmar there has been no formal public participation in the Salween Dam projects. Initially, under the Thaksin government in September 2006, a senior official from EGAT announced that it would not be undertaking EIAs for the projects at all (Markar 2006; Piyaporn Wongruang 2006). In November 2006, however, following the coup that ousted Thaksin and intense public pressure in Thailand, Chulalongkorn University's Environmental Research Institute was commissioned by EGAT to conduct an EIA for the Hat Gyi Dam. It was not a transparent procedure, however, as public participation was not to be part of the process and the report was to remain confidential with only EGAT having disclosure rights (Pianporn Deetes 2007; Tunya Sukpanich 2007). According to an activist with KESAN the EIA was finished in December 2008 with the group endeavouring to get access to it through the *Freedom of Information Act.*[37]

Security in the Hat Gyi area was tenuous, however, and in May 2006 an EGAT geologist lost his leg to a mine while surveying the area and, according to

198   *A. Simpson*

later reports, died from his wounds (KRW 2006; KRW and SEARIN 2006; Kultida Samabuddhi 2006; Tunya Sukpanich 2007). In response to this and ongoing concerns Thailand's Human Rights Commission recommended that the Hat Gyi Dam be abandoned (*Watershed* 2007). In July 2007 30 EGAT engineers and other workers began a three-month feasibility study of the Hat Gyi Dam but encountered opposition from local Karen villagers. According to one activist the immediate area is a *brown* area,[38] largely controlled by the DKBA, which generally supports the tatmadaw, but contested by the KNU.[39] As another activist put it, 'the DKBA have the upper hand but the KNU can go in anytime'.[40]

Nevertheless the KNU controls much of the area to the east towards the border and, as a result of opposition among villagers, has banned the EGAT team from the reservoir site, a position KRW supported: 'The KNU will reach a decision based on the interests of the people ... [they] should listen to the people and work with them to stop these dam projects because they will have a long term impact' (Cho 2007).

After talks with EGAT in the border town of Mae Sot the KNU later relented and gave the team permission to conduct a two-day survey but the KNU and local villagers remained opposed to the dam project (Saw Yan Naing 2007). In September 2007 another EGAT employee surveying the Hat Gyi site died from an artillery shell and the remaining 42 EGAT staff were evacuated to Thailand (AP 2007; TNA 2007). No one took responsibility for the attack but it highlighted that these are highly insecure sites for major projects. As an activist from ERI pointed out, 'even if [the tatmadaw] crush the KNU [in the Wei Gyi and Hat Gyi area] they will melt into the forest and continue their fight'.[41] Another activist noted that even if the tatmadaw controlled the area it would always be easy for insurgent groups to covertly take in a hand-held RPG.[42] The role of the KNU in these negotiations highlighted that in these dam projects, where official channels of public participation are effectively closed, it is largely through a militant insurgent group that local villagers and activists are able to influence the development project.

While security considerations for ethnic Karen communities in the region become part of the precarious daily existence both inside Myanmar and sometimes in the Thai-Myanmar borderlands they are entirely foreign to the Northern activists who are only practiced in organising protests in their own countries.[43] While intelligence agencies in the North have been known to target environmental groups and security responses to protests have been over-exuberant, activists generally have civil liberty protections unheard of for ethnic minority communities in Myanmar. As a result, in contrast to many environment movements in the North, the focus of these protests in Myanmar is one of simply survival for the communities.

Transnational activism – creating an activist diapsora

Due to the restrictions on local activism inside Myanmar the transnational aspects of the campaign against the Salween Dams took on a much greater

Transnational activism in Myanmar 199

significance. The exodus of activists from Myanmar-proper since the 1988 protests and a series of subsequent environmental campaigns assisted in the development of Myanmar's activist diaspora, which provided ready made activist networks for the transnational Salween campaign. A key element of this activity was the formation of transnational coalitions that pooled their resources and formed strong organisational ties. While the transnational campaign emphasised the universal human rights of the affected ethnic minority communities in Myanmar the campaign also promoted their culturally specific identity. This cultural particularism extended into the ecological realm where the importance of indigenous knowledge of biodiversity was highlighted (KESAN 2008).

The transnational Salween Dams campaign demonstrated the depth and vitality of the Myanmar activist diaspora, particularly within Thailand and the Thai-Myanmar borderlands. Salween Watch, Karen Rivers Watch and Burma Rivers Network were all formed in the last decade as coalitions of smaller environmental groups to oppose large dams in Myanmar. They are staffed primarily by expatriate ethnic minority communities of Myanmar and operate mainly from Chiang Mai and towns in the Thai–Myanmar borderlands. These three organisations are all actually coalitions, rather than networks, with even the Burma River Network noting on its website that

> [t]he new *coalition* ... is comprised of [ten] civil society groups representing communities from different regions of Burma being impacted by at least 20 large dams planned by the military regime [emphasis added].
>
> (Burma Rivers Network 2007)

There is a relative paucity of studies on the nature of coalitions in the literature on environmental activism although some studies have demonstrated their growing importance in transnational campaigns (Bandy and Smith 2005; Carter 2007, 162). Yanacopulos has argued, however, that coalitions afford economies of scale (Yanacopulos 2005a, 259), and the anti-dam, or pro-river, coalitions of Myanmar have worked effectively by pooling their minimal resources and exploiting the growing availability of inexpensive communications technologies. They have all worked closely with ERI, although ERI has maintained a low profile in the campaign, preferring ethnic organisations to drive the operation.[44] The Salween Watch coalition was formed in February 1999, drawing in activists such as Sai Sai and Pipob Udomittipong who had previously worked for ERI (Salween Watch 2007).[45]

Karen Rivers Watch (KRW), a coalition of Karen organisations including Chiang Mai-based KESAN, and the Mae Sariang-based NGOs, Karen Office of Relief and Development (KORD) and Karen Women's Organization (KWO), undertook protest actions along the Salween River in Karen State although it is largely based in Thailand (KRW 2007; Saw Karen 2007). KORD was formed a decade earlier and brought expertise to KRW in both emergency relief and community development. KORD's director, Nay Tha Blay, argued that it took this two pronged approach in both its fieldwork – 'we give them fish but we also

200   *A. Simpson*

teach them to fish' – and also in the development of both local and international networks.[46]

Burma Rivers Network (BRN) was formed more recently in May 2007 and brought together organisations working across Myanmar with its mission being to

> protect the health of river ecosystems and sustain biodiversity, and to protect the rights and livelihoods of communities affected and potentially affected by destructive large-scale river development.
>
> (Burma Rivers Network 2007)

The pooled expertise from the various component organisations was particularly useful in the launch of the comprehensive BRN website in January 2009 which examined dam issues related to six rivers (Burma Rivers Network 2009). Despite the assertion from Yanacopulos that coalitions 'have broader strategic aims than single-issue thematically focused networks' (Yanacopulos 2005b, 95), these coalitions are relatively specific in their aims, although with different geographic foci. The secretary and coordinator of BRN, Aung Ngyeh, outlined the rationale for the formation of the BRN when other, more localised, coalitions such as Salween Watch already existed:

> The plans of dam construction are not only found on Salween River but the plans are also found on the other rivers in other ethnic lands such as Kachin, Arakan, Chin. Therefore, it's very important to have a network group of Burmese civil society organizations which are working on environmental issues. At a result, initiated by Salween Watch, Burma Rivers Network (BRN) is formed to carry our advocacy campaigns against dam construction inside Burma.[47]

These coalitions have made particular attempts to create networks with activists and NGOs in China who oppose dams on the Nu River in Yunnan Province.

The emergence of affordable desktop publishing has allowed many ethnic minority groups to publish professional reports on the dams and their potential impacts to maintain their campaign's momentum. Most reports have been published in English in Thailand and aimed at transnational audiences but some have also been published in Burmese and ethnic languages such as Karen, with the aim of importing them into Myanmar covertly and disseminating them within communities.

The first of these professional reports appeared in 2004 in which KRW and Salween Watch provided the first detailed analysis on the plans for the Salween. KRW published *Damming at Gunpoint*, written mainly by Law Plah Min (KRW 2004),[48] while Salween Watch co-authored *Salween Under Threat* with the Southeast Asia Rivers Information Network (Salween Watch and SEARIN 2004; SEARIN 2007), which both argued that environmental damage and human rights abuses would flow from construction of the dams. In *Damming at Gunpoint* the dams are regarded as projects that will cause oppression of Karen communities while providing huge revenues for the Myanmar military:

> It can be seen that the regime's plans to exploit the water resources in the Salween River, by building dams and selling hydropower to Thailand, fit into its ongoing strategy of subjugating the ethnic areas and exploiting the natural resources there.
>
> (KRW 2004, 10)

Salween Under Threat provides a central rationale for the transnationalisation of the campaign. Not only are TNCs and governments from various countries involved with the projects but activists from outside Myanmar have more chance of voicing their opposition without violent retribution and are better able to influence their governments:

> There is an urgent need for people to speak out, as local potentially-affected people face dangers in they choose to protest ... because dissidence is met with fierce and often fatal retaliation. Those who are able to express concerns, including indigenous communities and international NGOs working outside of Burma, should therefore challenge these projects. This challenge is likely to appeal to the deepest conscience of [foreign] governments, financial institutions, the Thai public and concerned parties from the US, Japan, and Europe.
>
> (Salween Watch and SEARIN 2004, 12–13)

The vulnerable political and social environment in which these communities live ensures that the focus of these reports is on issues of human rights and social justice in Myanmar rather than simply ecological issues, while still emphasising nonviolent solutions: '[Salween Watch] and BRN, have practiced nonviolent means as we thought that we can achieve our activities eventually by practicing [nonviolence]'.[49]

As a result the organisations' reports analyse the projected damage to forest and wetland ecosystems along the Salween, but the effects are couched largely in terms of the adverse impacts on livelihoods of riverine communities (Salween Watch and SEARIN 2004, 15–22). When dealing with ecological issues, however, there is also a focus on the importance of indigenous knowledge. In *Khoe Kay: Biodiversity in Peril*, a report by KESAN on the biodiversity of the western side of the Salween River at the Wei Gyi Dam site in Myanmar, the anonymous primary author makes connections between their Western university scientific knowledge and their indigenous heritage:

> Because many plants are toxic to humans, the local people need to know the species well before using them. Local species identification methods are based on humans' five senses.... Since I was young my parents have taught me how to identify plants and animals so I can survive in the forest. They

202   A. Simpson

taught me to make a fire when there is not lighter by using bamboo chits or stones, and how to extract water from plants. . . . This knowledge is important and useful ... when travelling deep in the forest.

(KESAN 2008, 5)

While written by a Karen team and extolling the virtues of indigenous knowledge the report's centrality to the transnational campaign is emphasised by it being only available in English and therefore inaccessible to most Karen communities in Myanmar.

The vulnerability of these communities to ecological crises is emphasised in the response of BRN to Cyclone Nargis, in which it argued that the military regime's energy policies together with its forest and mangrove destruction would only exacerbate climate change and its impacts (Burma Rivers Network 2008). Even nominally ecological concerns in the campaign are, however, infused with implicit democratising perspectives. In the first paragraph of *Khoe Kay* the aim of the report is stated: 'to document and expose the severe threats faced by this stretch of the Salween, both from large dams and ongoing militarization' (KESAN 2008, 6). More focus is, however, given to specific human rights concerns such as the impact on internally displaced peoples (IDPs) in the Salween region as a result of both clearing the reservoir zone and through village relocations forced by the military as part of its *four cuts* campaign against insurgents (KRW 2004, 42).

The two 2004 Salween publications provided the stimulus for various other groups to publish reports on their particular areas of interest (KRW 2004; Salween Watch and SEARIN 2004). In 2006 the Karenni Development Research Group (KDRG) published *Dammed by Burma's Generals*, drawing parallels between the proposed Salween Dams and the experience of Karenni communities impacted by the Mobye Dam and the Lawpita Hydropower Project in the west of their state (KDRG 2006).[50] In the same year the Shan Sapawa Environmental Organization (Sapawa) published *Warning Signs*, examining development in the upper reaches of the Salween in Shan State (Sapawa 2006).

At the other end of the Salween River, Mon State hosts the Salween delta so the exiled Mon Youth Progressive Organization (MYPO) has its office in Sangkhalaburi in Karnchanaburi Province, near where Mon State borders Thailand. The office was raided by the Thai police in 2002 when Thaksin Shinawatra's government was putting all Myanmar NGOs under pressure but it continued operations and in 2007 published a report entitled *In the Balance* that called for a halt to investments in the Salween Dams (MYPO 2007). Although these individual reports are important, more critical for the campaign, according to Aung Ngyeh, are the networks that grow out of parallel campaigns, such as that against the Myitsone Dam on the Irrawaddy River in Kachin State.[51] These networks are sometimes facilitated by relatively well resourced North-South organisations such as ERI but often personal relationships in expatriate communities provide the links that connect organisations, even if assistance is also provided by Northern funders such as the Open Society Foundation.[52]

Transnational activism in Myanmar 203

As well as published reports there are a number of websites dedicated to the campaign against the Salween Dams and listserves are regularly used to keep activists and interested people around the world informed of recent events (Salween Watch 2007; SEARIN 2007). As Reitan notes in her study of Jubilee 2000 these forms of electronic activism can create multiple forms of information diffusion that stimulate growth of transnational networks (Reitan 2007, 80). This provides further evidence that confirms Castells' assertion that environmental movements employ these new communications technologies as mobilising and organising tools (Castells 2003, 187). Saiz sees such developments particularly positively, using the technologies of globalisation to provide the possibility of thinking and acting locally and globally at the same time (Saiz 2005, 163–164). Most groups in the Salween campaign have therefore ensured a prominent online presence but, as della Porta and Diani find in other cases, many who have signed up for the listserve are already either part of the campaign or have other links to activists in the campaigns (della Porta and Diani 2006, 133).

The ability to tap into global communications and networks – access that is strictly limited in Myanmar – has been an important determinant in the development of transnational activism for exiles from Myanmar. In the Thai-Myanmar border region this has often resulted in the movement out of the jungles, villages and refugee camps to towns and cities where this access can be expedited. The environmental activism of these exiled communities can be generalised from O'Kane's study:

> Intersections between globalisation processes and women's activism occur in border locations via INGOs, communication technologies and resources attracted to the borderlands for economic, political, military and humanitarian reasons.
>
> (O'Kane 2005, 20)

O'Kane's findings are particularly relevant for women activists such as those who attend the EarthRights Burma School in Chiang Mai, which sets aside half its positions for women as well as ensuring a diversity of ethnicities.[53] As a graduate herself Khin Nanda, the School Training Coordinator, noted that although it was initially difficult to fill the eight women positions the demand had gradually increased until applications outstripped the positions available.[54] She further argued that this sort of empowerment had challenged established norms within ethnic communities, which were often conservative, with respect to the promotion of women into prominent or influential roles.

As a result of the influx into the Thai-Myanmar border region Myanmar exiles inhabit many of the Thai towns along the border roads such as Mae Sot and Mae Sariang with a vast congregation of activists in Chiang Mai. In addition to the publications and online activities, therefore, the congregation of Myanmar exiles in this borderlands region also provides a conduit for transnational actors from outside the region to become involved. Unfortunately for NGOs in the region, however, the conduit also operates in the reverse direction. Many

204   A. Simpson

Myanmar exiles on the Thai side of the border are awaiting resettlement in third countries and this can act as a 'brain drain' for NGOs. Throughout 2007–8 this exodus was particularly acute with NGOs losing up to half their staff with highly trained activists being resettled in Northern countries such as the US, Canada and Australia. Although this could present an ideal opportunity for transnational-ising the campaigns, in reality the difficulty in refugees finding work and adapt-ing to their new lives often means they lose touch with the campaigns.[55]

Most of the international protests against TNCs' involvement in the Salween Dams were organised through a network of online activists although as della Porti and Diani note, these virtual networks operate best when initiated by real social linkages of the sort described above (della Porta and Diani 2006, 133). In their study of a similar campaign against a mine in Peru Haarstad and Fløysand argue that the same connections existed, specifically

> the way in which resistance strategies against the agenda of a multinational corporation were enhanced by, or were even dependent upon, the processes of globalization.
>
> (Haarstad and Fløysand 2007, 304)

These results are consistent with evidence drawn from broader environment and justice movements that the internet has revolutionised movement development and tactics (Curran 2006, 75; Doherty 2002, 172; Eschle 2005, 21; Klein 2001). While these technologies can be used for activism and seeking out alternative media perspectives, high internet penetration in a society does not necessarily reflect greater activism or social awareness. As Lewis notes in his examination of the internet in Southeast Asia, Thais are much less comfortable with the English language than their neighbours in Malaysia and Singapore and, partially as a result, much of the internet use in Thailand is for game playing rather than engaging in activism or searching out alternative media (Lewis 2006, 115). With limited English literacy in Thailand the campaigns face difficulties in the Thai language press, which, although relatively open compared with neighbouring countries, rarely covers the transnational campaigns in Myanmar that are fea-tured in the English language press:

> Thais depend on vernacular dailies for the news about Burma. But neither the high-circulation papers nor the specialist dailies print much Burma news. When they do, however, it is usually negative [and] not supported by concrete evidence.
>
> (Wandee Suntivutimetee 2003)

Despite these obstacles Thai environment groups such as TERRA have played key roles in supporting exiled Myanmar activists in the Salween campaign (TERRA 2008).[56]

Regardless of the benefits of forming coalitions there are also great advan-tages to these transnational contacts remaining as loose networks rather than

Transnational activism in Myanmar   205

becoming a single organisation with a central authority. These sort of networks, often 'greatly facilitated by the internet, can ... enable relationships to develop that are more flexible than traditional hierarchies' (Routledge 2003, 335). Keck and Sikkink argue that the motivations to form these transnational advocacy networks are primarily shared principled ideas or values (Keck and Sikkink 1998, 30), which in this case are founded on justice and the protection of human rights and the environment in Myanmar. International organisations engaging in the Salween campaign, such as International Rivers, may be focused on the health of rivers but like the Myanmar activist diaspora their support is also couched in the terms of justice for riverine inhabitants (International Rivers 2007).

Conclusion

Through an examination of a case study of the campaigns against the Salween Dams in Myanmar this chapter finds that the extent of *local* or *transnational* activism in environmental campaigns against projects can be linked to the degree of authoritarianism of the political regime in the home country where the projects occur. The evidence from this case study suggests four interrelated conclusions regarding the relationship between the extent of activism and the nature of political regimes in the South. First, there appears to be a *direct* relationship between authoritarianism and the extent of human rights abuses and environmental destruction linked to development projects, particularly transnational energy projects, in the South. Under traditional authoritarian regimes, such as in Myanmar, these adverse impacts are therefore likely to be greater than under democratic or hybrid regimes. Second, there is an *inverse* relationship between authoritarianism and the ability of local activists to voice their concerns through protest and various media, with increasing authoritarianism resulting in fewer outlets for dissent.

Third, these local restrictions under traditional authoritarian regimes increase the importance of developing transnational networks and coalitions to undertake transnational campaigns. These regimes are therefore likely to stimulate the creation of activist diasporas comprised of expatriates who engage in activism transnationally from outside their home country. Activists leave their local authoritarian environments for transnational settings, creating transnational networks of exiled activists. In the case of Myanmar expatriate activists escaping authoritarianism under the Myanmar military are distributed throughout the world but particularly active in Thailand and the 'liberated area' of the Thai-Myanmar border region, beyond the reach of Myanmar's military.

This activist diaspora, despite the difficulties it poses for activists, also provides opportunities. Training that would not be accessible in local settings may be available. Improved accessibility to other transnational activists and the media in cosmopolitan environments also creates opportunities for developing activist strategies and tactics and facilitating communication of messages to a wider audience, particularly through increased proficiency in English, the lingua franca of transnational activism and media. In addition, in the case of Myanmar most

206   *A. Simpson*

activists don't petition the Myanmar regime directly as previous experience demonstrates they are unlikely to influence its policies and decision-making processes. They therefore focus their energies primarily on transnational activities, hoping to influence international businesses, governments or publics to support their cause. Although in countries such as China they face severe impediments to changing the behaviour of these various actors this form of activated citizenship has still experienced limited success in delaying progress on construction of the Salween Dams. The transnational networks that contribute to the development of this activist diaspora may also form under more liberal or competitive regimes but the greater opportunities and outlets for dissent at home generally focus activists into local modalities.

Fourth, the evidence therefore suggests a distinctive relationship between the level of authoritarian governance and the predominance of local or transnational activism under authoritarian regimes. There appears to be an *inverse* relationship between the level of authoritarian governance and the level of *local* activism but a *direct* relationship between the level of authoritarian governance and the level of *transnational* activism, with increasing authoritarianism resulting in greater transnational activism.

This relationship arises because although the desire to express dissent increases as authoritarianism increases, so do the personal costs from expressing that dissent. If there are few sites of competition such as in a traditional authoritarian regime local protests are limited as increasing repression results in the costs of activism becoming too great in terms of personal sacrifice. In Myanmar the regime has been traditional authoritarian for much of the time since 1962 resulting in minimal local activism. Public displays of defiance are therefore extremely rare and when this has occurred, such as during 1988 or 2007, it has resulted in a violent and brutal response from the military that has eventually suppressed dissenting voices. This authoritarianism, while suppressing opposition at home, actually appears to stimulate transnational linkages and activism through the activist diaspora, indicating that authoritarian regimes may actually be fuelling the growth of transnational social movements in the South by expanding transnational networks of activists.

While authoritarian governance tends to impact on the level of activism this chapter finds that, in conjunction with precarious living conditions, it also impacts on the issues focused upon by environment movements in the South. The campaign against the Salween Dams tended to focus on issues of human rights and social justice and was therefore emancipatory in its outlook. Ecological issues were also significant but not of primary importance above and beyond other issues. Nevertheless, achieving justice for communities, primarily for ethnic minorities in Myanmar, was intimately linked to issues of ecological health. In general, however, traditional authoritarian rule and more precarious living conditions result in a greater focus on human rights and justice. As Doherty notes, environmental struggles in the South are often 'struggles for democracy and against the unequal distribution of power' (Doherty 2007, 80). Environmental organisations and movements in the South therefore see no conflict in pursuing human rights in conjunction with environmental justice. As a result of these concerns, democracy and justice are key philosophies and practices within these movements.

Activists in these movements also perceive, sometimes through their experience in violent conflict, that nonviolent activism is the only likely path to achieving their goals. Although nonviolence takes a pre-eminent role in the environmental campaigns the repression faced by ethnic minorities in Myanmar means that exiled activists often remain networked to ethnic minority insurgent groups within Myanmar as they are seen as the only institutions both willing and able to provide protection and security for ethnic minorities.

In conclusion, although Myanmar's activist diaspora is simply comprised of those Myanmar exiles engaged in the transnational environmental activism described above its multi-ethnic character, and its emphasis on cooperation across ethnic boundaries, sets it apart from much of the exiled community, which is still riven by ethnic friction. The increasing level of cooperation between ethnic-based green groups over projects such as the Salween Dams highlights a level of cross-ethnic collaboration rarely seen either inside or outside Myanmar. Central to the long term success of the Myanmar military in maintaining control of Myanmar has been the promotion of divisive policies that have played ethnic minorities off against each other. Myanmar's 2008 Constitution provides for a continuing central role for the military in the country but by stimulating transnational activism that unites ethnic minorities the Myanmar military has created an effective international movement that promotes environmental justice and security for the long-suffering people of Myanmar.

Notes

1 Although many transnational activists and foreign governments still use the country name 'Burma' many activists within the country now use the officially recognised 'Myanmar'. As the name is unlikely to ever revert to Burma I have used Myanmar throughout this chapter.

2 Nay Tha Blay (2009, 7 January). *Interview with author*. Director of Karen Office of Relief and Development (KORD) and activist with Karen Rivers Watch (KRW). KORD Office, Mae Sariang, Thailand.

3 Hsiplopo (2009, 6 January). *Interview with author*. Ei Tu Hta Camp Leader/Chairman. Ei Tu Hta Camp, KNU controlled Myanmar on the Salween River.

4 Alex Shwe (2009, 8 January). *Interview with author*. Activist with KESAN (aka Ko Shwe). Chiang Mai, Thailand.

5 The SPDC was effectively in power from 1988 to 2011, although under the name State Law and Order Restoration Council (SLORC) in its early years. Between 1962 and 1988 Myanmar was ruled by General Ne Win through the Revolutionary Council and Burma Socialist Program Party (BSPP) (Charney 2009).

6 Human Rights Watch Staff (2011, 22 March). *Interview with author*. Washington DC; Open Society Foundation Staff (2011, 25 March) *Interview with author*. New York; US Campaign for Burma Staff (2011, 22 March). *Interview with author*. Washington DC.

7 ILO Liaison Officer (2011, 9 May). *Interview with author*. ILO Offices, Yangon, Myanmar.

208   *A. Simpson*

8 Bobby Maung (2011, 7 January). *Interview with author*. CEO, Network Activities Group (NAG). Yangon, Myanmar.
9 Win Myo Thu (2011, 5 January). *Interview with author*. MD and Founder, ECODEV. Yangon, Myanmar.
10 This book was going to press soon after the new 'civilian' government was formed in 2011 when it was still too early to discern the resultant impacts on domestic environmental activism. As a result, most of the research undertaken for this chapter analyses environment movements in the context of Myanmar's years under direct military rule. Updates on both the domestic and transnational implications of the reforms undertaken by the new government can be found in Simpson (2013a, 2013b).
11 Win Myo Thu (2011, 10 May). *Interview with author*. MD and Founder, ECODEV. Yangon, Myanmar.
12 The military was able to shut down these international links because since 1999 it has controlled the only two Internet Service Providers (ISPs) in the country. At the time the only other occasion in which similar action was taken was in Nepal in February 2005 when the now deposed King declared martial law, although since this time it has been repeated particularly throughout the Middle East and North Africa in several uprisings.
13 Ka Hsaw Wa (2004, 14 January). *Interview with author*. Co-Founder/Executive Director ERI. Chiang Mai, Thailand. Catherine (2005, 10 January). *Interview with author*. Pseudonym for Assistant Director, Southeast Asia Office of ERI. ERI Office, Chiang Mai, Thailand.
14 Cynthia Maung (2004, 18 January). *Interview with author*. Founder of Mae Tao Clinic. Mae Sot, Thailand.
15 In 2005 there were 70 Back Pack Teams in eastern Myanmar comprising three to four health workers each that also provided food support for IDPs, carrying 5 kg bags of rice deep into Myanmar. Patrick (2005, 11 January). *Interview with author*. Pseudonym for activist with Myanmar NGO based in Chiang Mai with Thai and foreign employees. Chiang Mai, Thailand.
16 Withheld on request for security reasons.
17 Patrick (2009, 2 January). *Interview with author*. Pseudonym for activist with Myanmar NGO with Thai and foreign employees. Chiang Mai, Thailand.
18 The Thai and Burmese governments had been attempting to keep their plans for the project concealed and the MoU was not made public. A copy of the MoU was later leaked to the journalist Richard Lloyd Parry and posted on *The Times* website (Parry 2006).
19 Phyo Phyo (2011, 7 January). *Interview with author*. Pseudonym for activist with Shwe Gas Movement. Yangon, Myanmar.
20 Jockai Khaing (2009, 2 January). *Interview with author*. Pseudonym for activist with Arakan Oil Watch. Chiang Mai, Thailand. Sai Sai (2009, 9 January). *Interview with author*. Co-founder of Sapawa and coordinator of Salween Watch and BRN. Chiang Mai, Thailand. Wong Aung (2009, 6 April). *Interview with author*. Global Coordinator, Shwe Gas Movement (SGM). Chiang Mai, Thailand.
21 Giannini, T. (2000, 22 January). *Interview with author*. Co-Founder ERI (now Lecturer in Law, Human Rights Program, Harvard Law School). Bangkok, Thailand.
22 Pipob Udomittipong (2004, 14 January). *Interview with author*. Activist with ERI. ERI Office, Chiang Mai, Thailand.
23 Aung Ngyeh (2007, 13 December). *Email to author*. Pseudonym for activist with KDRG and Coordinator of BRN. Mae Hong Song, Thailand.
24 Khin Nanda (2009, 4 April). *Interview with author*. Training Coordinator, EarthRights School Burma. At EarthRights School Burma, Northern Thailand.
25 Sai Sai (2009, 9 January). *Interview with author*. Chiang Mai, Thailand.
26 Sai Sai (2007, 17 December). *Email to author*. Chiang Mai, Thailand.
27 Paul Sein Twa (2009, 6 April). *Interview with author*. Director, KESAN. KESAN Office, On the Thai-Burmese border (location withheld).

Transnational activism in Myanmar 209

28 Aung Ngyeh (2007, 13 December). *Email to author*. Pseudonym for activist with KDRG and Coordinator of BRN. Mae Hong Song, Thailand.
29 Nay Tha Blay (2009, 7 January). *Interview with author*. Director of KORD and activist with KRW. KORD Office, Mae Sariang, Thailand.
30 Myint Thein (2004, 19 January). *Interview with author*. NLD-LA General Secretary and Burma Lawyers' Council (BLC) Founding Executive Council Member. BLC Office, Mae Sot, Thailand.
31 Chana Maung (2008, 25 March). *Email to author*. Team Leader, Southeast Asia Office, EarthRights International (ERI). Chiang Mai, Thailand.
32 M. Bergoffen (2009, 8 January). *Interview with author*. Lawyer with KESAN. Chiang Mai, Thailand.
33 S. Green (2009, 6 April). *Interview with author*. Pseudonym for Activist with KESAN (formerly with E-Desk/Images Asia). KESAN Office, on the Thai-Burmese border (location witheld).
34 Pipob Udomittipong (2004, 14 January). *Interview with author*. Activist with ERI. ERI Office, Chiang Mai, Thailand.
35 Hsiplopo (2009, 6 January). *Interview with author*. Ei Tu Hta Camp Leader/Chairman, KNU Member. Ei Tu Hta Camp, KNU controlled Myanmar on the Salween River; Junatoo (2009, 6 January). *Interview with author*. Volunteer nurse from Mae La Refugee Camp. Ei Tu Hta Camp, KNU controlled Myanmar on the Salween River.
36 Sanchai (2009, 6 January). *Interview with author*. Activist and wife of village deputy chairman. Ban Ta Tar Fung, Salween River, Thailand.
37 Alex Shwe (2009, 8 January). *Interview with author*. Activist with KESAN (aka Ko Shwe). Chiang Mai, Thailand.
38 The tatmadaw divides Myanmar into 'white' areas, which are under complete military control, 'brown' areas, which are essentially under control but where resistance forces can occasionally penetrate, and 'black' areas, where there is regular armed resistance activity.
39 Alex Shwe (2009, 8 January). *Interview with author*. Activist with KESAN (aka Ko Shwe). Chiang Mai, Thailand.
40 Naing Htoo (2009, 9 January). *Interview with author*. Programme Coordinator, EarthRights International (ERI). ERI Office, Chiang Mai, Thailand.
41 Ibid.
42 Ka Hsaw Wa (2009, 9 January). *Interview with author*. Co-Founder/Executive Director ERI. ERI Office, Chiang Mai, Thailand.
43 Ka Hsaw Wa (2004, 14 January). *Interview with author*. Co-Founder/Executive Director ERI. Chiang Mai, Thailand; K. Redford (2004, 15 January). *Interview with author*. Co-Founder/Director ERI. ERI Office, Chiang Mai, Thailand.
44 K. Redford (2009, 9 January). *Interview with author*. Chiang Mai, Thailand. Sai Sai (2008, 18 March). *Email to author*. Chiang Mai, Thailand.
45 Pipob Udomittipong (2005, 3 January). *Interview with author*. Chiang Mai, Thailand; Sai Sai (2009, 9 January). *Interview with author*. Chiang Mai, Thailand.
46 Nay Tha Blay (2009, 7 January). *Interview with author*. Director of Karen Office of Relief and Development (KORD) and activist with KRW. KORD Office, Mae Sariang, Thailand.
47 Aung Ngyeh (2007, 13 December). *Email to author*. Pseudonym for activist with KDRG and Coordinator of BRN. Mae Hong Song, Thailand.
48 Paw Wah (2008, 18 March). *Email to author*. Activist with KRW. Chiang Mai, Thailand.
49 Aung Ngyeh (2007, 13 December). *Email to author*. Pseudonym for activist with KDRG and Coordinator of BRN. Mae Hong Song, Thailand.
50 This project was also examined in a publication by graduates of ERI's Earth Rights School (Earth Rights School of Burma 2008, 81–97).

210   *A. Simpson*

51 Aung Ngyeh (2007, 13 December). *Email to author*. Pseudonym for activist with KDRG and Coordinator of BRN. Mae Hong Song, Thailand.
52 Open Society Foundation Staff (2011, 25 March) *Interview with author*. New York.
53 During a visit to the school in April 2009 the author met with students of diverse ethnicities including Kachin, Chin, Karen, Karenni, Shan, Mon and Arakanese.
54 Khin Nanda (2009, 4 April). *Interview with author*. Training Coordinator, EarthRights School Burma. At EarthRights School Burma, Chiang Mai, Thailand.
55 Alex Shwe (2009, 8 January). *Interview with author*. Activist with KESAN (aka Ko Shwe). Chiang Mai, Thailand. C. Browning (2009, 8 January). *Interview with author*. Activist with KESAN (former AusAID volunteer). Chiang Mai, Thailand. P. Rogers (2009, 5 January). *Interview with author*. Co-founder, Drug and Alcohol Recovery and Education (DARE) Network. Mae Sariang, Thailand.
56 Premrudee Daoroung (2011, 13 May). *Interview with author*. Co-director TERRA. Bangkok.

References

In keeping with the format of other writings on this region Thai and Burmese authors are listed by their first names rather than surnames as this is often the name by which they are commonly known.

Acuto, M. (2008). 'Edges of the conflict: A three-fold conceptualization of national borders.' *Borderlands*, 7(1). www.borderlands.net.au/vol. 7no1_2008/acuto_edges. htm. Accessed: 18 June 2008.
AFP (2007, 23 August). 'Protesters continue to defy Burmese junta.' *ABC News*. www. abc.net.au/news/stories/2007/08/23/2013678.htm. Accessed: 24 August 2007.
Anthias, F. (1998). 'Evaluating "diaspora": Beyond ethnicity.' *Sociology*, 32(3): 557–580.
AP (2006, 4 April). 'Myanmar, Thailand sign US$6 billion hydropower plant agreement.' *Associated Press (AP)*.
AP (2007, 4 September). 'Thai hydro project workers evacuated from Myanmar after shelling kills 1.' *International Herald Tribune (Associated Press)*.
Aye Mi San (2007a). *88 Student Leader Min Ko Naing Speech*. http://vids.myspace.com/ index.cfm?fuseaction=vids.individual&VideoID=15374254. Updated: 9 August. Accessed: 6 September 2007.
Aye Mi San (2007b). *Arrest of Suu Suu Nway and Protesters*. http://vids.myspace.com/ index.cfm?fuseaction=vids.individual&VideoID=16956884. Updated: 29 August. Accessed: 6 September 2007.
Ball, J. (ed.) (2008). *Come Rain or Shine: A Personal Account of Burma, the 2007 Uprising and Cyclone Nargis* (Chiang Mai: Mizzima News Agency).
Bandy, J. and J. Smith (eds) (2005). *Coalitions across Borders: Transnational Protest and the Neoliberal Order* (Lanham, Maryland and Oxford: Rowman and Littlefield).
Barnett, J. (2001). *The Meaning of Environmental Security: Ecological Politics and Policy in the New Security Era* (New York: Zed Books).
BBC News (2007a, 28 September). 'Soldiers break up Burma protests.' http://news.bbc. co.uk/2/hi/asia-pacific/7017496.stm. Accessed: 4 June 2008.
BBC News (2007b, 23 August). 'Burma activists protest over fuel.' http://news.bbc.co. uk/2/hi/asia-pacific/6959724.stm. Accessed: 4 June 2008.
Brownlee, J. (2007). *Authoritarianism in an Age of Democratization* (New York: Cambridge University Press).

Transnational activism in Myanmar 211

Brubaker, R. (2005). 'The "diaspora" diaspora.' *Ethnic and Racial Studies*, 28(1): 1–19.

Burma Rivers Network (2007). *Press Release: Dam-Affected Communities Unite to form Burma Rivers Network* (Burma Rivers Network (BRN)). 5 June. www.ksdf.org/read. asp?title=Dam-affected communities unite to form Burma Rivers Network&CatId=Pub lications&id=24. Accessed: 14 April 2008.

Burma Rivers Network (2008). *Press Release: Nature's Wake-Up Call to Burma* (Chiang Mai: Burma Rivers Network). 7 May 2008.

Burma Rivers Network (2009). *Burma Rivers Network*. Chiang Mai. www.burmariver-snetwork.org/. Updated: 19 February. Accessed: 23 February 2009.

Butler, K. D. (2001). 'Defining diaspora, refining a discourse.' *Diaspora*, 10(2): 189–219.

Carter, N. (2007). *The Politics of the Environment: Ideas, Activism, Policy*. Second edition (Cambridge: Cambridge University Press).

Castells, M. (2003). *The Power of Identity*. Second edition (Oxford: Blackwell Publishing).

Charney, M. W. (2009). *A History of Modern Burma* (Cambridge: Cambridge University Press).

Chaturvedi, S. (2003). *Geopolitics of India's Cultural Diversity: Conceptualization and Contestations*. GERM (Groupe d'Etudes et de Recherches sur les Mondialisations). www.mondialisations.org/php/public/art.php?id=11963&lan=EN. Updated: 31 May. Accessed: 24 August 2007.

Cho, V. (2007, 23 August). 'Thai EGAT team discuss dam project with KNU.' *The Irrawaddy*. www.irrawaddy.org/article.php?art_id=8327. Accessed: 19 December 2007.

Cho, V. (2008, 14 March). 'Ban the dam, say activists.' *The Irrawaddy*. www.irrawaddy. org/article.php?art_id=10888. Accessed: 17 March 2008.

Chowdhury, M. (2008). *The Role of the Internet in Burma's Saffron Revolution* (Internet and Democracy Project, Berkman Center for Internet and Society, Harvard University, Cambridge, Massachusetts). 28 September. http://cyber.law.harvard.edu/sites/cyber. law.harvard.edu/files/Chowdhury_Role_of_the_Internet_in_Burmas_Saffron_Revolution_0.pdf. Accessed: 8 October 2008.

Christiansen, T., F. Petito and B. Tonra (2000). 'Fuzzy politics around fuzzy borders: The European Union's "near abroad".' *Cooperation and Conflict*, 35(4): 389–415.

Cleary, S. (1997). *The Role of NGOs under Authoritarian Political Systems* (London: Macmillan).

Corben, R. (2006, 11 July). 'Chinese-Thai-Burmese dam projects raise humanitarian, environmental concerns.' *VOA.com (Voice of America)*. www.voanews.com/english/ archive/2006–07/2006–07–11-voa10.cfm?CFID=29441064&CFTOKEN=71678385. Accessed: 24 August 2006.

Corben, R. (2007, 28 February). 'Salween dams would displace thousands, activist warns.' *The Irrawaddy*. www.irrawaddy.org/article.php?art_id=6775. Accessed: 15 March 2008.

Curran, G. (2006). *21st Century Dissent: Anarchism, Anti-Globalization and Environmentalism* (Basingstoke, Hampshire: Palgrave Macmillan).

Cynthia Maung (2008). *Mae Tao Clinic*. Mae Sot, Thailand. www.maetaoclinic.org/. Accessed: 15 April 2008.

della Porta, D. and M. Diani (2006). *Social Movements: An Introduction*. 2nd edition (Malden, MA: Blackwell).

della Porta, D., M. Andretta, L. Mosca and H. Reiter (2006). *Globalization from Below: Transnational Activists and Protest Networks* (Minneapolis and London: University of Minnesota Press).

212 A. Simpson

Diamond, L. (2002). 'Elections without democracy: Thinking about hybrid regimes.' *Journal of Democracy*. April, 13(2): 21–35.

Doherty, B. (2002). *Ideas and Actions in the Green Movement* (London and New York: Routledge).

Doherty, B. (2006). 'Friends of the Earth International: Negotiating a transnational identity.' *Environmental Politics*. November, 15(5): 860–880.

Doherty, B. (2007). 'Environmental movements.' in C. Okereke (ed.) *The Politics of the Environment: A Survey* (London and New York, Routledge).

Doherty, B. and T. Doyle (2006). 'Beyond borders: Transnational politics, social movements and modern environmentalisms.' *Environmental Politics*. November, 15(5): 697–712.

Doyle, T. (2000). *Green Power: The Environment Movement in Australia* (Sydney: UNSW Press).

Doyle, T. (2005). *Environmental Movements in Majority and Minority Worlds* (New Brunswick, New Jersey and London: Rutgers University Press).

Doyle, T. and M. Risely (eds) (2008). *Crucible for Survival: Environmental Security and Justice in the Indian Ocean Region* (New Brunswick, New Jersey and London: Rutgers University Press).

Doyle, T. and A. Simpson (2006). 'Traversing more than speed bumps: Green politics under authoritarian regimes in Burma and Iran.' *Environmental Politics*. November, 15(5): 750–767.

DPA (2006, 28 February). 'Villagers want end of Salween dams.' *Bangkok Post (Deutsche Presse-Agentur GmbH)*. www.bangkokpost.com/breaking_news/breakingnews.php?id=117124. Accessed: 30 March 2007.

DPA (2007, 24 August). 'New protests, arrests in Burma.' *Bangkok Post*. www.bangkokpost.net/topstories/topstories.php?id=121062. Accessed: 24 August 2007.

Dryzek, J. S., D. Downes, C. Hunold, D. Schlosberg and H.-K. Hernes (2003). *Green States and Social Movements: Environmentalism in the United States, United Kingdom, Germany and Norway* (New York: Oxford University Press).

Duffy, R. (2006). 'Non-governmental organisations and governance states: The impact of transnational environmental management networks in Madagasacar.' *Environmental Politics*. November, 15(5): 731–749.

Dwivedi, R. (1997). *People's Movements in Environmental Politics: A Critical Analysis of the Narmada Bachao Andolan in India* (The Hague: Institute of Social Studies).

Dwivedi, R. (2001). 'Environmental movements in the global South: Outline of a critique of the "livelihood" approach', in P. Hamel, H. Lustiger-Thaler, J. N. Pieterse and S. Roseneil (eds), *Globalization and Social Movements* (Basingstoke and New York: Palgrave).

Earth Rights School of Burma (2008). *Gaining Ground: Earth Rights Abuses in Burma Exposed* (Chiang Mai: EarthRights International). July. www.earthrights.org/files/Reports/Gaining Ground – ERSB 2008.pdf. Accessed: 10 September 2008.

EGAT and DHP (2005). *Memorandum of Agreement* (EGAT, Department of Hydroelectric Power, Union of Myanmar). December. http://timesonline.typepad.com/times_tokyo_weblog/2006/03/documents_on_th.html – more. Accessed: 29 March 2006.

Eschle, C. (2005). 'Constructing "the anti-globalisation movement"', in C. Eschle and B. Maiguashca (eds), *Critical Theories, International Relations and 'the Anti-Globalisation Movement': The Politics of Global Resistance* (London and New York: Routledge).

Eschle, C. and B. Maiguashca (eds) (2005). *Critical Theories, International Relations*

Transnational activism in Myanmar 213

and *'the Anti-Globalisation Movement': The Politics of Global Resistance.* (London and New York: Routledge).

Fink, C. (2008). 'Militarization in Burma's ethnic states: Causes and consequences.' *Contemporary Politics.* December, 14(4): 447–462.

Fink, C. (2009). *Living Silence in Burma: Surviving under Military Rule.* Second edition (London and New York: Zed Books).

Fredriksson, P. G. and J. R. Wollscheid (2007). 'Democratic institutions versus autocratic regimes: The case of environmental policy.' *Public Choice.* March, 130(3–4): 381–393.

Giddens, A. (1987). *The Nation-State and Violence* (Berkeley and Los Angeles: University of California Press).

Gleditsch, N. P., K. Furlong, H. Hegre, B. Lacina and T. Owen (2006). 'Conflicts over shared rivers: Resource scarcity or fuzzy boundaries?' *Political Geography.* May, 25(4): 361–382.

Gottlieb, R. (2005). *Forcing the Spring: The Transformation of the American Environmental Movement.* Revised and updated edition (Washington, DC: Island Press).

Haarstad, H. and A. Fløysand (2007). 'Globalization and the power of rescaled narratives: A case of opposition to mining in Tambogrande, Peru.' *Political Geography.* March, 26(3): 289–308.

Holliday, I. (2008). 'Voting and violence in Myanmar: Nation building for a transition to democracy.' *Asian Survey*, 48(6): 1038–1058.

Horsey, R. (2011). *The Initial Functioning of the Myanmar Legislatures* (New York: Conflict Prevention and Peace Forum). 17 May.

Howes, M. (2005). *Politics and the Environment: Risk and the Role of Government and Industry* (St Leonards, NSW: Allen & Unwin).

Human Rights Watch (2007). *Burma: Arbitrary Detention of Protesters* (New York: Human Rights Watch (HRW)). 22 August. http://hrw.org/english/docs/2007/08/22/burma16718.htm. Accessed: 30 August 2007.

Hutton, D. and L. Connors (1999). *A History of the Australian Environment Movement* (Cambridge and Melbourne: Cambridge University Press).

ICG (2008). *Burma/Myanmar: After the Crackdown* (Brussels: International Crisis Group (ICG)). 31 January. Asia Report No. 144. www.crisisgroup.org/library/documents/asia/burma_myanmar/144_burma_myanmar___after_the_crackdown.pdf. Accessed: 1 February 2008.

International Rivers (2007). *Burma's Salween Dams Threaten Over Half a Million Lives Downstream.* International Rivers (formerly International Rivers Network (IRN)). http://internationalrivers.org/en/southeast-asia/burmas-salween-dams-threaten-over-half-million-lives-downstream. Accessed: 1 February 2008.

Jamal, A. A. (2007). *Barriers to Democracy: The Other Side of Social Capital in Palestine and the Arab World* (Princeton, New Jersey: Princeton University Press).

Jayasuriya, K. and G. Rodan (2007). 'Beyond hybrid regimes: More participation, less contestation in Southeast Asia.' *Democratization.* December, 14(5): 773–794.

Kaiser, R. and E. Nikiforova (2006). 'Borderland spaces of identification and dis/location: Multiscalar narratives and enactments of Seto identity and place in the Estonian-Russian borderlands.' *Ethnic and Racial Studies.* September, 29(5): 928–958.

KDRG (2006). *Dammed by Burma's Generals* (Karenni Development Research Group (KDRG)). March. www.salweenwatch.org/images/stories/downloads/publications/dammed-eng.pdf. Accessed: 19 May 2012.

Keck, M. E. and K. Sikkink (1998). *Activists Beyond Borders: Advocacy Networks in International Politics* (Ithaca and London: Cornell University Press).

214   *A. Simpson*

Kerr, P. (2007). 'Human security', in A. Collins (ed.) *Contemporary Security Studies* (Oxford: Oxford University Press).

KESAN (2008). *Khoe Kay: Biodiversity in Peril* (Chiang Mai: Karen Environmental and Social Action Network (KESAN), Wanida Press). July. www.salweenwatch.org/images/stories/downloads/brn/2008_009_24_khoekay.pdf. Accessed: 1 October 2008.

Khin Zaw Win (2010). '2010 and the unfinished task of nation-building', in N. Cheesman, M. Skidmore and T. Wilson (eds), *Ruling Myanmar: From Cyclone Nargis to National Elections* (Singapore, Institute of Southeast Asian Studies).

KHRG (2007). *Development by Decree: The Politics of Poverty and Control in Karen State* (Karen Human Rights Group (KHRG)). April. www.khrg.org/khrg2007/khrg0701.pdf. Accessed: 25 March 2008.

Klein, N. (2001). 'Farewell to "The End of History": Organization and vision in anti-corporate movements', in L. Panitch and C. Leys (eds), *Socialist Register 2002: A World of Contradictions* (London: Merlin Press).

KRW (2004). *Damming at Gunpoint: Burma Army Atrocities Pave the Way for Salween Dams in Karen State* (Kawthoolei, Burma: Karen Rivers Watch (KRW)). November. www.freewebs.com/krw_reports/Dam english1.pdf. Accessed: 18 April 2006.

KRW (2006). *Joint Statement on the International Day of Action Against Dams for Water and Life*. Karen River Watch (KRW). www.salweenwatch.org/news/march282006–30.php – 1. Updated: 16 March. Accessed: 11 May 2006.

KRW (2007). *Karen Rivers Watch*. Karen Rivers Watch (KRW). www.karenriverwatch.net/. Updated: 24 March. Accessed: 22 October 2007.

KRW and SEARIN (2006). *Joint Statement on the International Day of Action Against Dams for Water and Life* (Karen Rivers Watch (KRW) and Southeast Asia Rivers Network (SEARIN)). 16 March. www.salweenwatch.org/news/march282006–30.php – 1. Accessed: 11 May 2006.

Kultida Samabuddhi (2006, 5 May). 'New call to scrap dams after geologist loses leg.' *Bangkok Post*. www.bangkokpost.net/News/05May2006_news10.php. Accessed: 5 May 2006.

Kultida Samabuddhi and Yuthana Praiwan (2003, 18 December). 'China plans 13 dams on Salween.' *Bangkok Post*. 1.

Kusnetz, N. (2008, 8 June). 'Burma dams would flood rebel territories.' *San Francisco Chronicle*. A-4. www.sfgate.com/cgi-bin/article.cgi?f=/c/a/2008/06/08/MNIM10GJUC.DTL. Accessed: 10 June 2008.

Kutting, G. (2000). *Environment, Society and International Relations: Towards More Effective International Environmental Agreements* (London and New York: Routledge).

Larkin, E. (2010). *Everything is Broken: A Tale of Catastrophe in Burma* (New York: Penguin Press).

Levitsky, S. and L. A. Way (2002). 'The rise of competitive authoritarianism.' *Journal of Democracy*, 13(2): 51–65.

Lewis, G. (2006). *Virtual Thailand: The Media and Cultural Politics in Thailand, Malaysia and Singapore* (London and New York: Routledge).

Lintner, B. (1990). *Outrage: Burma's Struggle for Democracy*. 2nd edition (London and Bangkok: White Lotus).

Lintner, B. (1999). *Burma in Revolt: Opium and Insurgency since 1948*. Second edition (Chiang Mai: Silkworm).

Liverani, A. (2008). *Civil Society in Algeria: The Political Functions of Associational Life* (London and New York: Routledge).

Transnational activism in Myanmar 215

MacLean, K. (2003). *Capitalizing on Conflict: How Logging and Mining Contribute to Environmental Destruction in Burma* (Thailand: EarthRights International & Karen Environmental & Social Action Network).

Markar, M. M. (2006, 29 September). 'Dams on Salween: Test for Burmese, Thai juntas.' *IPS/IFEJ*. www.ipsnews.net/news.asp?idnews=34935. Accessed: 1 November 2006.

McCarthy, S. (2000). 'Ten years of chaos in Burma: Foreign investment and economic liberalization under the SLORC-SPDC, 1988 to 1998.' *Pacific Affairs*, 73(2): 233–262.

McLeod, G. (2007, 8 July). 'Atrocity before the deluge.' *Bangkok Post*. www.bangkok-post.com/topstories/topstories.php?id=119986. Accessed: 17 August 2007.

Myat Thein (2004). *Economic Development of Myanmar* (Singapore: Institute of Southeast Asian Studies).

MYPO (2007). *In the Balance: Salween Dams Threaten Downstream Communities in Burma* (Mon Youth Progressive Organization (MYPO)). www.salweenwatch.org/downloads/IntheBalance.pdf. Accessed: 3 August 2007.

Noam, Z. (2008, 14 March 2008). 'Damming Salween needs proper study first.' *Bangkok Post*. www.bangkokpost.com/140308_News/14Mar2008_news20.php. Accessed: 17 March 2008.

O'Kane, M. (2005). *Borderlands and Women: Transversal Political Agency on the Burma-Thailand Border* (Victoria, Australia: Monash University Press).

Osborne, M. (2007). *The Water Politics of China and Southeast Asia II: Rivers, Dams, Cargo Boats and the Environment* (Sydney: Lowy Institute for International Policy). May. www.lowyinstitute.org/. Accessed: 10 May 2007.

Paehlke, R. and D. Torgerson (eds) (2005). *Managing Leviathan: Environmental Politics and the Administrative State*. Second edition (Peterborough, Ontario: Broadview Press).

Parry, R. L. (2006, 22 March). 'Sold down the river: Tribe's home to be a valley of the dammed.' *Times Online*. www.timesonline.co.uk/tol/news/world/asia/article743880.ece. Accessed: 18 February 2008.

Pearce, F. (2006). 'Mega-dams back on the agenda.' *New Scientist*. 16 September, 191(2569).

Pianporn Deetes (2007, 28 February). 'The invisible costs of the Salween dam project.' *The Nation*. Bangkok. http://nationmultimedia.com/2007/02/28/opinion/opinion_30028089.php. Accessed: 30 March 2007.

Piya Pangsapa and M. J. Smith (2008). 'Political economy of Southeast Asian borderlands: Migration, environment, and developing country firms.' *Journal of Contemporary Asia*, 38(4): 485–514.

Piyaporn Wongruang (2006, 4 September). 'Salween dam project "likely to go ahead without study".' *Bangkok Post*.

Reitan, R. (2007). *Global Activism* (London and New York: Routledge).

Rootes, C. (ed.) (2007). *Environmental Protest in Western Europe*. Updated paperback edition (Oxford: Oxford University Press).

Routledge, P. (2003). 'Convergence space: Process geographies of grassroots globalization networks.' *Transactions of the Institute of British Geographers*, 28(3): 333–349.

Routledge, P., C. Nativel and A. Cumbers (2006). 'Entangled logics and grassroots imaginaries of Global Justice Networks.' *Environmental Politics*. November, 15(5): 839–859.

Rupert, M. (2000). *Ideologies of Globalization: Contending Visions of a New World Order* (London: Routledge).

Sabandar, W. (2010). 'Cyclone Nargis and ASEAN: A window for more meaningful

216   *A. Simpson*

development cooperation in Myanmar', in N. Cheesman, M. Skidmore and T. Wilson (eds), *Ruling Myanmar: From Cyclone Nargis to National Elections* (Singapore: Institute of Southeast Asian Studies).

Saiz, A. V. (2005). 'Globalisation, cosmopolitanism and ecological citizenship.' *Environmental Politics*, 14(2): 163–178.

Salween Watch (2007). *Salween Watch: Threatened Peoples, Threatened River.* Salween Watch. Chiang Mai. www.salweenwatch.org/index.html. Updated: 21 November. Accessed: 14 December 2007.

Salween Watch (n.d.). *Proposed Salween Dams.* Salween Watch. Chiang Mai. www.salweenwatch.org/maps/dam_site_on_river.html. Accessed: 14 December 2007.

Salween Watch and SEARIN (2004). *The Salween Under Threat* (Salween Watch and Southeast Asia Rivers Network (SEARIN)). September. www.salweenwatch.org/downloads/UnderThreat.pdf. Accessed: 21 February 2007.

Sandler, R. D. and P. C. Pezzullo (2007). *Environmental Justice and Environmentalism: The Social Justice Challenge to the Environmental Movement* (Cambridge, MA: MIT Press).

Sapawa (2006). *Warning Signs: An Update on Plans to Dam the Salween in Burma's Shan State* (Chiang Mai: Shan Sapawa Environmental Organization (Sapawa)). www.salweenwatch.org/downloads/warning sign.pdf. Accessed: 30 November 2007.

Sapawa (2007). *Press Release: 400 Villagers Forced to Attend 'Celebration' by Thai MDX to Launch Construction of Tasang Dam on the Salween River in Shan State* (Chiang Mai: Shan Sapawa Environmental Organization (Sapawa)). 29 March. www.salweenwatch.org/March29_SAPAWA_PressRelease_Eng.html. Accessed: 14 December 2007.

Sater, J. (2007). *Civil Society and Political Change in Morocco* (London and New York: Routledge).

Saw Karen (2007). 'Karen communities keep watch.' *Salween Watch Newsletter.* August, 1(1): 5. www.salweenwatch.org/downloads/Salween Watch_Vol 1 August 2007–1 FINAL.pdf. Accessed: 22 October 2007.

Saw Yan Naing (2007, 29 August). 'KNU allows EGAT to survey Salween River dam site.' *The Irrawaddy.* www.irrawaddy.org/article.php?art_id=8416. Accessed: 30 August 2007.

Saw Yan Naing (2008, 4 March). 'Mae Hong Son businessmen unhappy with border closure.' *The Irrawaddy.* www.irrawaddy.org/article.php?art_id=10695. Accessed: 27 March 2008.

SEARIN (2007). *The Salween River (Nu Jiang).* Southeast Asia Rivers Network (SEARIN). www.searin.org/salween_en.htm. Updated: 11 July. Accessed: 10 August 2007.

Shabecoff, P. (1993). *A Fierce Green Fire: The American Environmental Movement* (New York: Hill and Wang).

Shiva, V. (1989). *Staying Alive: Women, Ecology and Development* (London and New Jersey: Zed Books).

Simpson, A. (2004). 'Gas pipelines and green politics in South and Southeast Asia.' *Social Alternatives.* December, 23(4): 29–36.

Simpson, A. (2007). 'The environment-energy security nexus: Critical analysis of an energy "love triangle" in Southeast Asia.' *Third World Quarterly.* April, 28(3): 539–554.

Simpson, A. (2008). 'Gas pipelines and security in South and Southeast Asia: A critical perspective', in T. Doyle and M. Risely (eds), *Crucible for Survival: Environmental*

Transnational activism in Myanmar 217

Security and Justice in the Indian Ocean Region (New Brunswick, New Jersey and London: Rutgers University Press): 210–227.

Simpson, A. (2013a). *Energy, Governance and Security in Thailand and Myanmar (Burma): A Critical Approach to Environmental Politics in the South* (Farnham: Ashgate).

Simpson, A. (2013b). 'Market building and risk under a regime in transition: The Asian Development Bank in Myanmar (Burma)', in T. Carroll and D. Jarvis (eds) *The Politics of Marketising Asia* (Basingstoke and New York: Palgrave Macmillan).

Skidmore, M. and T. Wilson (2007). *Myanmar: The State, Community and the Environment* (Canberra: ACT Asia Pacific Press, ANU).

Smith, M. (1999). *Burma: Insurgency and the Politics of Ethnicity.* 2nd edition (London: Zed Books).

Smith, M. J. and Piya Pangsapa (2008). *Environment and Citizenship: Integrating Justice, Responsibility and Civic Engagement* (London and New York: Zed Books).

Sökefeld, M. (2006). 'Mobilizing in transnational space: A social movement approach to the formation of diaspora.' *Global Networks*, 6(3): 265–284.

South, A. (2004). 'Political transition in Myanmar: A new model for democratization.' *Contemporary Southeast Asia*, 26(2): 233–255.

South, A. (2009). *Ethnic Politics in Burma: States of Conflict* (London and New York: Routledge).

Steinberg, D. I. (1998). 'The road to political recovery', in R. I. Rotberg (ed.) *Burma: Prospects for a Democratic Future* (Washington, DC and Cambridge, MA: Brookings Institution Press, World Peace Foundation and Harvard Institute for International Development).

TERRA (2008). *Salween River.* Towards Ecological Recovery and Regional Alliance (TERRA) and Foundation for Ecological Recovery (FER). www.terraper.org/key_issues_view.php?id=6. Updated: 16 January. Accessed: 1 February 2008.

Times Online (2007, 28 September). 'Video shows Japanese journalist Kenji Nagai "being shot deliberately".' www.timesonline.co.uk/tol/news/world/asia/article2550369.ece. Accessed: 20 March 2008.

TNA (2007, 5 September). 'Thai dam project in Burma suspended.' *Bangkok Post (Thai News Agency).* www.bangkokpost.net/topstories/topstories.php?id=121362. Accessed: 5 September 2007.

Tunya Sukpanich (2007, 11 November). 'Salween on a precipice.' *Bangkok Post.* www.bangkokpost.net/. Accessed: 19 December 2007.

US Department of State (2011). *2010 Country Reports on Human Rights Practices: Burma* (Washington DC: Bureau of Democracy, Human Rights, and Labor, US Department of State). 8 April. www.state.gov/documents/organization/160450.pdf. Accessed: 10 June 2011.

Vicary, A. (2010). 'The relief and reconstruction programme following Cyclone Nargis: A review of SPDC policy', in N. Cheesman, M. Skidmore and T. Wilson (eds), *Ruling Myanmar: From Cyclone Nargis to National Elections* (Singapore: Institute of Southeast Asian Studies).

Wandee Suntivutimetee (2003, 1 October). 'Burma in the Thai Press.' *The Irrawaddy.* www.irrawaddy.org/article.php?art_id=3132. Accessed: 25 September 2008.

Watershed (2007, March–October). 'Thailand's Human Rights Commission recommends Hutgyi dam be shelved.' www.terraper.org/pic_water/WS12_2_web.pdf. Accessed: 17 March 2008.

WCD (2000). *Dams and Development: A New Framework for Decision Making* (World

218   *A. Simpson*

Commission on Dams (WCD). London: Earthscan). 16 November. www.dams.org/report/. Accessed: 18 December 2006.

Wikipedia (2008, 1 June). '2007 Burmese anti-government protests.' http://en.wikipedia.org/wiki/2007_Burmese_anti-government_protests. Accessed: 5 June 2008.

Yanacopulos, H. (2005a). 'Patterns of governance: The rise of transnational coalitions of NGOs.' *Global Society*. July, 19(3): 247–266.

Yanacopulos, H. (2005b). 'The strategies that bind: NGO coalitions and their influence.' *Global Networks*, 5(1): 93–110.

11 Civil society in the digital age: how the Internet changes state–society relations in authoritarian regimes

The case of Cuba

Bert Hoffmann

Introduction

The experiences of democratization in Latin America and Eastern Europe in the 1980s and early 1990s brought attention to the forces of civil society as key actors in the demise of authoritarian rule (O'Donnell and Schmitter 1986; Cohen and Arato 1992; Bernhard 1993; Linz and Stepan 1996). More recent literature questions the inherently pro-democratic character of civil society activism (Warren 2000; Armony 2004; Jamal 2007). In both lines of argument, societal associations or social movements are at the core of the inquiry. However, Hirschman's category of "voice," which encompasses as much articulation of discontent as it does actions of protest (Hirschman 1970), reminds us that for civil society activism to evolve, something fundamental is necessary: an arena in which voices can be raised and heard and in which government and society interact. The question of civil society, thus, is intrinsically linked to the conditions, contours, limitations and possibilities of communication, media and the public sphere.

Ever since the term "Facebook revolution" (Smith 2011) was coined for the social mobilizations that led to the downfall of the Mubarak regime in Egypt, this link between communication, civil society activism and democratization has received great media attention. However, most of this attention focused on the mobilizing potential of the digital media at the moment of rupture. This chapter takes a contemporary perspective as it seeks to contribute to our understanding of the Internet's impact on civil society dynamics in a non-pluralist context through a diachronic comparison. Based on an empirical study of the Cuban case, the argument is as follows. Prior to the entry of the Internet, the civil society debate centered around the quest for higher degrees of autonomy for associations and institutions within the framework of the state-socialist regime. In contrast, the new media enabled the emergence of a new, less state-dependent type of public sphere; as a consequence, the civil society debate has become increasingly centered on the assertion of individual citizenship rights within and

220   *B. Hoffman*

vis-à-vis the state. The reformist civil society quest of the pre-Internet period failed in part because of its character as behind-the-scenes-struggle, shielded from public view, which impeded a broader mobilization of protest when the state decided to rein in the incipient push for civil society. In contrast, the current drive for civil society indeed finds strong public repercussion; for its democratizing potential to come to fruition, the crucial fault-line is to connect web-based voice to public debate and social action in the country's physical off-line environment.

By taking Cuba as object of empirical analysis, this study selects a case with a particularly thorough form of authoritarian hold over the public sphere: a formal monopoly of the Cuban state on mass media, established in the historic experience of twentieth-century state-socialism and upheld even two decades after the fall of the Berlin Wall. At the same time, Cuba is strongly exposed to transnational influences and a transnational articulation of voice, due to a large number of emigrant and diaspora communities that remain highly attached to their country of origin (Fernández 2005).

The approach chosen to analyze the impact of the Internet on state–society relations is through a diachronic comparison of the Cuban development in two distinct periods: the pre-Internet period, i.e., Cuba in the early to mid 1990s, when the Cold War alignment had already become history but web-based technologies did not yet have a major presence on the island; and more than a decade later, since the mid to late 2000s, when web-based media had made their entry on the island.

Formal data on Internet access and use are scarce and unreliable. For 2009, the Cuban Ministry of Informatics and Communications gives the figure of 1,450,000 Cubans, or 12.7 percent, as "Internet users" (ONE 2009)[1] without specifying the precise uses this number includes. The figure certainly should not be mistaken for access to the World Wide Web, which remains severely restricted. Instead, the figure most probably includes all Cubans with some kind of (even if only sporadic) access to closed domestic networks or with access to e-mail services. At the same time accounts are shared and, as for other goods and services, also Internet access has a black market side that escapes official statistics. Moreover, Internet content "travels" by USB stick also to many who do not have access themselves.

For both these periods, the study relies on the analysis of numerous primary documents, as well as newspapers and secondary literature. In the case of the post-Internet phase, in addition to the above, documents published on the web have been a primary source of analysis. While some authors link issues of civil society and Internet voice merely to the political opposition, this chapter does not limit its focus to this divide but analyzes as much societal actors working within the established institutions of the socialist state as well as those outside of it. In both periods under scrutiny field trips to the island were undertaken in which actors from a broad range of positions were interviewed. While these interviews are not cited directly due to political sensitivities, they provide an invaluable background for the trends described.

Civil society in the digital age 221

Following this introduction, I will briefly discuss the role of civil society and public sphere under authoritarian regimes, and locate the Cuban case study in this context. I will then analyze the civil society debate as it evolved in Cuba in the early to mid 1990s, which focused on the quest for associational autonomy as a means of pluralization within the state-socialist framework. Next, I sketch Cuba's late and reluctant acceptance of the Internet and the state's efforts to maintain a maximum of control. I then turn to the different ways in which societal actors have since come to use digital and web-based media to raise their voice and claim participation as one of their rights of citizenship. The chapter concludes with a discussion of the democratizing potential of these new civil society dynamics.

Public sphere under authoritarian regimes: locating the Cuban case

Authoritarian regimes of whatever brand include in their repertoire mechanisms of control, along with the manipulation, co-optation and restriction of media and the public sphere. Therefore, if we use the concept of the public sphere, it is inevitably distant from the Habermasian ideal type of discourse and deliberation in democratic polities (Habermas 1962). However, a number of studies on Iran (Semati 2008) and China (Calhoun 1994) and on Arab publics (Lynch 2006) have labeled the public sphere concept also relevant for authoritarian political contexts, offering a much lighter definition of the public sphere as "active arguments before an audience about issues of shared concern" (Lynch 2006: 32). In this sense, non-democratic polities can be understood to have public spheres "with adjectives" – restricted, precarious, incipient, weak, etc.

The forms and degree of the limits various authoritarian regimes impose on the public articulation of voice vary, but no matter which regime is in question, the regime's reach is largely limited to the territorial boundaries of the nation-state in which it exercises power. As traditional media, too, were bound to the nation-state, widening the public sphere hence needed to be thought of as an "opening," "thaw," "decompression" or "liberalization" of the regime (e.g., O'Donnnell and Schmitter 1986: 26).

The Internet era forces us to rethink this understanding. The inherently transborder character of web-based communication and media technologies challenges established "filters" to access and patterns of regulation in any state. However, our thesis is that the political impact is all the stronger the more a state is at odds with political pluralism and the more it relies on control over media and the public sphere in the national arena.

Cuba certainly has been such a case ever since the early years after the 1959 Cuban Revolution, when the government of Fidel Castro adopted socialism as the country's political model. While the regime survived the collapse of Soviet-style socialism in Eastern Europe, it was reluctant to take up Internet-based technologies. The island became the last of all Latin American countries to join the Internet, having done so as recently as 1996 (Valdés 1997). Since then, computer

222   B. Hoffman

use and digital communication technologies have spread, but controlling and limiting access to the Internet and web-based media has been a crucial concern for state authorities.

The Cuban Revolution of 1959 redefined state–society relations. Most existing civil society organizations were either disbanded or transformed (and new ones created) according to a mold in which loyalty and subordination to the revolutionary leadership were a *conditio sine qua non*.[2] With the so-called "process of institutionalization" in the 1970s, state–society relations were formally modeled in Marxist-Leninist fashion: the Constitution of 1976 defined the Communist Party as the "highest leading force of society and of the state, which organizes and guides the common effort" (República de Cuba 1992 §5) and declared as the mission of "the social and mass organizations … the edification, consolidation and defense of the socialist society" (República de Cuba 1992 §7). Freedom of speech and of press was limited, by constitutional prescription, "in keeping with the objectives of socialist society" (República de Cuba 1992 §53). To this end, Article 52 of the Cuban Constitution effectively establishes a monopoly on mass media: "Material conditions for the exercise of that right are provided by the fact that the press, radio, television, cinema, and other mass media are state or social property and can never be private property."

Organizational activities that remained (at least partially) outside of these parameters were few and narrowly restricted; arguably, the most important one being the Catholic Church, which maintained a nationwide and legally recognized institutional infrastructure that included media for internal circulation (Armony and Crahan 2007).[3]

In the charismatic brand of socialism that characterized post-1959 Cuba and set it apart from the standard Eastern European model (Hoffmann 2008), formal prescriptions like the constitutional provisions on the media were complemented with declarations by the charismatic leader, Fidel Castro, which carried no less practical weight. The key statements on the margins for voice were his so-called "words to the intellectuals" from 1961, which provided the following maxim: "Within the Revolution, everything. Against the Revolution, nothing."[4] This sentence, repeated ad infinitum ever since, acquired law-like status and left ample discretion for the power-holders to define at every instance what was "within" and what was "against" the revolution. Aside from media, a central and related concern was on public space. In the dualism of Cuba's charismatic brand of socialism, formal restrictions on the freedom of assembly also found their informal equivalent in the slogan "The street is Fidel's!",[5] a code the state invoked to justify the prohibition or repression of protesting voices in public. The severe limits imposed on public voices contrasted with an often surprising level of tolerance towards criticism voiced in private – an ambivalence which led Cubans to paraphrase Fidel's 1961 words as "Under the roof, everything. In the street, nothing."[6]

Civil society in the 1990s: the quest for associational autonomy and its limits

After the regime collapses in Eastern Europe and the demise of the Soviet Union in 1991, a profound economic, social and ideological crisis in Cuba ensued, one that called into question the viability of state–society relations as they had developed in the three decades since 1959. Internationally, civil society had gone from a buzzword in academia to a resounding career path in international and development politics. In particular, the role ascribed to civil society in bringing down state-socialism in Eastern Europe (Havel 1978; Cohen and Arato 1992) provided the background for the concept being taken up by U.S. policy towards Cuba, which in the early 1990s publicly adopted "the fostering of Cuba's civil society" as a "second track" next to economic sanctions to bring about regime change in Havana.

These political overtones notwithstanding, it was within the official intellectual institutions on the island that in the mid 1990s, the term "civil society" became the focus of a key debate about the country's course (Gray and Kapcia 2008). As the concept of civil society stresses some degree of autonomy from the "political society" (state, parties, parliaments, etc.) (e.g., Fernández 1993: 99), in a state-socialist country this conception invariably raises the question about the role of state and party and the margins of associational autonomy within such a framework. This debate about civil society within state-socialism marked a new discussion not only for Cuba, but also internationally.

An article by Rafael Hernández from Havana's Center for American Studies (CEA) initiated the Cuban civil society debate in 1994. In it, he underscored the Marxist ideological credentials of the term claiming its tradition in the writings of Hegel, Marx and Gramsci and argued for "the necessity and usefulness [of applying] the concept to the analysis of current problems in Cuba" (Hernández 1994: 30).[7] Hernández argued that both civil society and the socialist state are "organic segments of the socialist system," which are interconnected and mutually reinforcing (ibid.: 31). Moreover, the distinction between civil society and the state should be of great practical importance for Cuba because "the dynamics of civil society have been overshadowed by a strong politicization of social relations and institutions in Cuba" (ibid.: 30). This indirect call for a de-politicization of social relations provides the signpost for the ensuing debate: reclaiming greater autonomy of the social sphere and its organizations and institutions from the state.

The background of this argument is the deep economic crisis that has plagued Cuba since the demise of its socialist allies overseas in 1989/90 and the consequences of that crisis for Cuban society – above all, the bitter divide between the depressed *peso* economy and the emergent enclaves of "dollarized" sectors in tourism and joint ventures, and the rapidly growing role of illegal and legal market mechanisms.[8] Hernández (ibid.: 30) writes:

> The problems the Cuban society is facing cannot be contained within the limits of an economic analysis. Both the causes and the consequences of the

224   *B. Hoffman*

crisis transcend this dimension. However, even within this narrow framework it is obvious that "the realm of economic relations" in Cuba has changed.... It now comprises phenomena such as the informal economy, which is characterized by the growth of independent work and the black market, as well as the rise of new forms of labor in the mixed sector of the new, markedly differentiated, economy.

The concept of civil society suggested by Hernández is thus framed as primarily a response to the increasing differentiation of Cuban society, resulting from the economic crisis. Other contributions pushed the Cuban civil society debate further. Most importantly, Hugo Azcuy, one of Hernández's colleagues at the CEA, wrote of the "necessity for more plural *expressions* in Cuban society," (Azcuy 1995: 105, emphasis in original) for which the concept of civil society "should not only be used as an instrument of analysis, but also as a *project*" (Azcuy 1995: 105, emphasis in original). This idea of civil society as a project of socialist renewal hence became a leitmotif of Cuba's intellectual reform discourse in the mid 1990s. Azcuy (1995: 108) posits "the strengthening of Cuban civil society and its necessary autonomy within the framework of the revolutionary project of which it understands itself to be a part" as its frame of reference.[9]

If state authorities feared civil society as a potential loss of power, in the following text contribution Hernández is explicit in reversing this logic. The activation of civil society is meant precisely to come to the rescue of a socialist state whose needs for "new forms of legitimacy" in order to secure regime stability are acknowledged:

> As the sphere in which the tensions and conflicts facing the state are enacted, it is in the interest of and the responsibility of the state to search within civil society for new forms of legitimacy and arenas of consensus.... Without the consensus of civil society, not only will the legitimacy of the government suffer damage, but also the stability of the system itself.
>
> (Hernández 1996: 88)

In terms of audience, the reach of this debate was limited. It mostly moved within academic or intellectual institutions, with the Center for American Studies (CEA) as the epicentre,[10] and journals, including *Temas* magazine, directed by Hernández, became the key forums of the debate. The civil society discourse hardly ever found reflections in the state-controlled mass media. However, there was an empirical side to this debate which was played out in the tug-of-war about the redefinition of the nature of societal associations and their relation to the state. The economic crisis had not only led to a heterogenization of society, but had also left established institutions in cultural, social or academic fields cash-strapped, as the money from the state coffers dried up. As a consequence, a search for new funding possibilities began. While also playing well to members' aspirations of more autonomy from the state, the label "non-governmental organization" (NGO)

Civil society in the digital age 225

promised to be the key for access to donor money from international development actors, both private and public.

In the early 1990s, this label gradually began to encompass associations with remarkable differences. At least two types must be discerned: for one, institutions and organizations that had been created by the socialist state in past decades and that now were "re-labeled" NGOs. This encompasses professional associations like the writers' union UNEAC, which posed as an NGO even though its president was a member of the Politburo, and research centers that had been founded by the Communist Party's Central Committee. Even official "mass organizations"[11] into which nearly every Cuban is organized began to pass themselves off as NGOs, a process that reached its climax with the participation of the women's organization FMC, led by Raúl Castro's wife Vilma Espín, as an NGO at the United Nations Women's Summit in Beijing in 1995.

Given their origin and institutional subordination to the Party and the state, there is much reason to see these re-labeled NGOs as *neo-* rather than as *non*-governmental organizations.[12] Nevertheless, also within many of these organizations, this semantic shift of emphasis came as part of an unspoken tug-of-war about the relative degrees of autonomy from the central state apparatus.

The quest for associational autonomy was even more visible in the second category of new organizations that sprung up as NGOs in the 1990s within a broad spectrum of cultural, social and ecological activities. None of these, however, was awarded official recognition without safeguarding mechanisms for state control. These safeguarding mechanisms had an institutional and a personal side: all registered NGOs were formally "assigned" to a state institution, and they were usually led by persons who were judged to have given sufficient proof of their political loyalty. At times, they overlapped. For example, the ecological NGO "ProNaturaleza" was founded in 1993 mainly by senior bureaucrats and scientists from the Ministry of Science, Technology and Environment; it was assigned to the ministry, and at the beginning also had its offices in the very same building as the ministry.

Also, to a much lesser extent, new grassroots organizations sprung up. By and large, the more distance they kept from the political establishment, the more informal they remained. A case in point was the Action Group for the Free Choice of Sexual Orientation (GALEES), which attracted international attention when in 1995 it unfolded a huge rainbow flag, the symbol of the gay movement, in front of the state leadership during the May 1 Parade. GALEES was never officially recognized; after a few years of existence, it was dissolved.

Whether the initiatives were top-down or bottom-up, or something in between, these struggles about autonomy and recognition were played out behind the scenes. They became public only by accident, or through cases of individuals breaking with the established discipline and offering insights into processes otherwise shielded from public view or debate.

The latter was the case in what had arguably become the most prominent of the new Cuban NGOs, the "Foundation Pablo Milanés," founded by the Cuban singer of that name in 1993. This NGO was largely meant to formalize and

226   B. Hoffman

expand activities in support of young Cuban artists, which Pablo Milanés had already been sponsoring individually with the foreign-exchange earnings from his international music contracts. While Milanés had a conflicted trajectory under the revolution, including suffering ugly sanctions in the 1970s, he more than once affirmed his unconditional loyalty to Fidel and the revolutionary process, and was regarded as a reliable showcase artist for the government's international projection. But despite its impressive success in the acquisition of international funds, Milanés's foundation was short-lived, disbanding only two years after its creation. In 1995, Milanés, in an unusual act of civil disobedience, publicly lamented the constant curtailment of the foundation's autonomy by the state body to which it was assigned, the Ministry of Culture, and declared the project closed. The time and place of Milanés's protest, however, underscores how much this going public was the exception in a context that demanded keeping conflicts behind closed doors: Milanés called the international press to Havana airport, making his statements minutes before boarding a plane for a prolonged stay outside of the country. Cuban media did not echo any of it, and the news was left to spread through word-of-mouth communication.

This inability to communicate struggles for associational autonomy to a wider audience left the concept of civil society as a project for pluralization within Cuban socialism defenceless, when in 1996 the state leadership decided to cut it short. The medium was a Politburo report read by Raúl Castro (1996), Fidel's brother and then head of Cuba's Armed Forces, at the V. Plenum of the CP Central Committee, which was broadly covered as front-page news in all Cuban media. In it, the state leadership decries the notion of "civil society" as part of the "ideological subversion" to which some in Cuba had presumably fallen victim. The charges were worded harshly, as the civil society debate was described as a "Trojan Horse [that] intends to promote the division and subversion of the country" (Castro 1996: 6ff.) and its proponents as a "fifth column of the enemy."[13] The report explicitly referred to the "bitter experience with the Center for American Studies." In its wake, the CEA's director was dismissed, and after a painful investigation process, all senior researchers were transferred to other institutions (Hoffmann 1997).

Given the government's firm grip on the public sphere, no public voice of protest on the island against the Politburo's heavy-handed measure was able to reach a broader audience.[14] While *Temas* magazine managed to survive, neither it nor any other publication could continue the debate on associational autonomy as frankly as before. On the level of associations, many continued to work in their respective fields, albeit within narrowed margins of action. While the term "NGO" has not been banned entirely, it is disliked. Many of the "re-labeled NGOs" were oriented to switch into reverse and to proudly emphasize, rather than hide, their association to the Party and to state institutions.

The conception of civil society as a project of pluralization from within the state-socialist order failed in part because it was unable to access a sufficiently wide public sphere. According to Hirschman, who distinguishes between "vertical voice" (expressions of protest against superiors) and "horizontal voice"

Civil society in the digital age 227

(communication among peers), "horizontal voice is a necessary precondition for the mobilization of vertical voice" (Hirschman 1986: 82). In Cuba, aside from the structural obstacles on horizontal communication, such as poor telecommunications or fear of being spied on, it was the non-public character of the struggles for associational autonomy that impeded horizontal voice to develop in a way that would have allowed for the mobilization of vertical voice when the state decided to rein in the incipient civil society project.

Enter the Internet: the public sphere in transnational times

As the Cuban state's approach to the public sphere is based on the state monopoly over mass media, any media beyond the reach of the nation-state's authority signify a political challenge. The classic forms of cross-border media outreach by radio and TV, of which the U.S.-funded Radio and TV Martí programs sent from Florida are typical exponents, have long been a political battlefield. The Cuban government has dispensed considerable energy and resources to jam transmissions to the island.

The case of the Internet is different, however, since it is transnational by its very structure. It does not require special outreach efforts by the sender to reach a cross-border audience; quite to the contrary, once connected to the network, it requires filtering or censorship efforts to keep undesired information out.

The Cuban government has been all too aware of the political challenges the new media imply. However, in a protracted process, the island finally joined the Internet in 1996, as the last country in the American hemisphere to do so. It is often overlooked that joining the Internet was almost simultaneous to the Politburo's crackdown on the civil society debate. The decision-making process was thorny as important segments of Cuba's ruling circles saw the Internet primarily as a political threat and as "a weapon of war" of the United States (Sánchez Villaverde 1995). Fidel Castro himself warned at a public rally on August 5, 1995, that the United States government "speak[s] of 'information highways' ... which they want to impose on the world, through propaganda and the manipulation of human mentality" (cited in ibid.: 39).

Connecting to the Internet, hence, was an eminently political decision.[15] Of crucial importance was the example of China, which had joined the Internet with a full IP connection three years earlier. The Chinese experience showed that Internet access was (at least in the short or medium term) compatible with communist party rule (Press *et al.* 1999; Kalathil and Boas 2003). Moreover, the Beijing government was also willing to share with Cuba its technological and administrative know-how for minimizing the Internet's potentially destabilizing effects.

Nevertheless, Cuba's leadership opted for a hard-handed domestic political move to show that Internet connection would not lead Cuba down the perilous path of eventual regime change. Washington's Cuba strategy, as encoded in the so-called "Torricelli Law"[16] of 1992, combined tightening the economic embargo with a "track two" strategy of increasing communication – notably, exempting

228   B. Hoffman

telecommunications and Internet access from the trade sanctions. The declared motive was thus to foster pluralist civil society structures as seeds of democratization. If Havana was to accept the challenge of increased communication, it did so only after crushing the incipient debate about civil society as a project of reform. Cuban authorities announced the decision to join the Internet only a month after Raúl Castro read the crushing Politburo report.[17]

Law decree 209 of 1996, "Access from the Republic of Cuba to Information Networks of Global Reach,"[18] sets out the government's basic approach in dealing with the new information and communication technologies: introduce them in controlled form in order to minimize their negative effects. To achieve this, Internet access will, according to the decree, be employed "according to the interests of Cuba, giving priority to juridical persons or institutions that are of greater relevance to the life and development of the country." In other words, Internet access is principally for official institutions and state companies, not for individual users.

On this premise, the state has expanded the development and diffusion of the digital technologies on the island. Access in official institutions is limited and controlled. Many institutions' computers have access only to domestic Cuban networks, but not to the World Wide Web. International e-mail communication, however, has become widely permitted. Moreover, all legitimate users have to sign declarations not to "misuse" the technology for accessing "anti-Cuban" content – interpretation of this is of course left to the discretion of the authorities. Cuban users are well aware that Internet use at institutional access points can be monitored. Finally, as the state maintains a monopoly on Internet service providers, it can use different technological means to block or sabotage specific sites. As Kalathil and Boas (2001) concluded in their study, the Cuban government was able to exert considerable control over the political impact of the Internet through reactive and proactive measures.

However, this did not resolve the key contradiction between the inherently transnational character of web-based media and a nation-state-based media monopoly, nor could it prevent the spread and use of such media. Despite a restrictive context, a decade later the new web-based media have become a firm presence in Cuba and an ever more important channel of information, communication and articulation.

Before we turn to this, a brief word should be said regarding the political context: In July 2006, Fidel Castro fell so seriously ill that he delegated – temporarily, as was stressed initially – his positions at the helm of the state, the Party and the armed forces to his younger brother Raúl Castro, who had been his deputy in all these offices over the past decades (Hoffmann 2009). In February 2008, Raúl also formally became Fidel's successor as Cuban head of state. While this gradual succession process became a display of political stability, it remained fraught with ambiguity. By all available evidence, Fidel Castro continues to retain an important informal role with considerable veto power, and Raúl Castro's initial promise to transform the regime into a more institution-based type of socialism so far remains largely unfulfilled.

Civil society in the digital age 229

Asserting citizenship: the public sphere and civil society in the Internet era

While the new digital, web-based media share common characteristics, at this point we need to break down the analysis into different, albeit interconnected, types of media use based on the Internet. To this end, I will single out three different ways in which societal actors have come to use the digital and web-based media to raise voices and claim public space and citizenship rights: first, the use of digital recordings posted on the World Wide Web to reach an audience for cultural activities that are not promoted by the state's official institutions, as well as to provide global transparency for events that occur behind closed doors; second, e-mail as perhaps the most widely used of the web-based media in Cuba, which in particular facilitates horizontal voice and the decentralized circulation of information; and third, the growing number of blogs by Cuban citizens, a phenomenon which in recent years has become a key political battlefield about the possibilities and limitations of Cuba's public sphere.

The web as audience: bypassing institutions, creating transparency

Aside from e-mail communication and the medium of blogs, two more elements shall be discussed to analyze the impact of the digital technologies on Cuba's public sphere and civil society action: the web's function as a provider of (1) an audience for cultural activities that bypasses the filter of the established cultural production modes and distribution outlets, and (2) an audience and transparency for what otherwise would have remained behind closed doors or within the confines of those physically present. For both, aside from the Internet itself, the diffusion of low-cost, small-sized technologies for digital audio and video recording has been crucial.

In the past, Cuban artists had a fundamental dependence on the state's infrastructure for the production and circulation of their work. While Cuba's cultural institutions offered varying degrees of flexibility and tolerance over time, the limits of what was possible were constantly negotiated. Artists who failed or refused to adapt to the exigencies of the state found themselves cut off from most artistic circuits, and a continuous stream of intellectuals opted to go into exile.

Dependence on the state's material infrastructure was probably greatest in film-making, as much in the resources needed to produce films as in access to cinemas or television to show them. Even though the film institute, ICAIC, is considered a bastion of the liberal tendencies within Cuba's cultural scene, in the 1990s, the taboo-breaking film *Alicia en el pueblo de Maravillas*, while filmed with the ICAIC's support, was banned from cinema screens after only three showings.

A decade later, new forms of film-making emerged. Based on digital cameras and personal computers, a series of shorts and documentaries have been filmed entirely outside the official structures of production. No less important was the distribution side: while the films were not shown by Cuban cinemas or TV, they were passed around on CDs (where they reached at least part of their domestic audience), and they made their way onto YouTube, where they instantly were accessible to a global audience. The most emblematic films became a series of shorts by Eduardo del Llano, one of the authors of the *Alicia* film a decade earlier. Del Llano's ten-minute *Monte Rouge*, for instance, is a biting satire in which state security officials promote a more "participatory" form of eavesdropping, by asking the citizens themselves to choose the place to install microphones in their home. Del Llano submitted this film to the national film festival, where it was rejected. This, however, did not prevent the artist from reaching his audience: thousands on the island have seen the ten-minute movie on digital copies on their computers or DVD players, and on YouTube, the movie shows more than 50,000 viewers in one year.[19]

Similarly, in music, alternative diffusion via the web has become a standard feature for critical rap singers, such as "Los Aldeanos" or "Hermanos de Causa," or for iconoclastic rock bands such as "Porno para Ricardo."[20]

In this type of web-based outreach to a global audience, the contrast to the 1990s is clearly visible. Artists are not as inevitably focused on the struggle to stretch the limits of the permissible within their respective institutional affiliation as before, as the new digital media allow them to circumvent – at least to a considerable degree – the state institutions' filters and censorship and find alternative outlets.

A key feature of the tug-of-war over associational autonomy in the 1990s was the fact that it was largely played out behind the scenes, "under roof" and shielded from public view. The opposite phenomenon has emerged in the 2000s, sometimes labeled "videostroika" (Venegas 2010: 178): Time and again, non-public debates in closed circuits have been given public exposure through unauthorized audio or video recordings, often made with cell-phone technologies. Such was the case when, in early 2008, National Assembly President Ricardo Alarcón held a meeting with students at the Cuban Informatics University, a prestige project of the government. Meant to be a closed-door meeting, a video recording was leaked to BBC and put on YouTube, showing students confronting the veteran Cuban leader with highly critical questions.[21] As a result, it received worldwide attention. This in turn had repercussions in Cuba, and – despite the restrictions on Internet access – USB sticks and word-of-mouth propaganda made the civic courage of the questioning students rapidly known.

Similarly, recordings brought to public knowledge a tumultuous meeting of Party leaders with dissatisfied employees in the hard-currency sector of the economy, and student protests at the Cuban Arts Institute, which otherwise few but those physically present would have heard about. In all these cases, while the digital technologies provided the physical means, it was civic voice in the non-virtual world that was filmed and given public exposure, as much as it required citizens' action to record the proceedings and see to their distribution.

Civil society in the digital age 231

E-mails as "non-institutional press": from horizontal to vertical voice

While not reaching as broad a coverage as in most other Latin American countries (ITU 2009) the use of e-mail has become a standard feature for many Cubans, and most particularly so among the young, urbanized professional sectors. While less frequently, also for wider sectors of the population the ties to emigrated relatives are a major driver for e-mail communication needs (even if access to computers is far from quotidian). Hence, e-mail has greatly increased horizontal communication among Cubans, as well as between Cubans living on the island and those residing in other countries.

Recalling Hirschman's distinction, the use of e-mail in Cuba provides excellent evidence of how horizontal voice can lead to the mobilization of vertical voice. In Cuba, the ground-breaking case was the so-called "*polémica intelectual*" (debate of the intellectuals) or, as others call it, "*la guerrita de los correos electrónicos*" ("little e-mail war") at the beginning of 2007. This brought a medium into the spotlight of Cuban public life that enabled a dynamic of horizontal voice hitherto unknown in a media regime of vertical communication. The dividing line between mass and individual media blurred just as much as the accustomed division between one-to-many media (radio, TV, newspapers, etc.) in the public sphere and one-to-one communication (telephone, letters, etc.), traditionally thought of as pertaining to the private sphere.

The initial impulse that triggered the *polémica* was a program on state TV featuring Luis Pavón, the most notorious figure of Cuba's dogmatic and intolerant cultural policy of the 1970s, known as the "*quinquenio gris*" (the "gray five years"). While the state never allowed an open debate about this period, its eventual end had been sealed by the dismissal of its leading exponents by the end of the 1970s. The experience of the 1970s, however, had been so traumatic that the sudden reappearance of its figurehead cadres on state television in 2007 sent shockwaves through the intellectual community. However, now this shock was no longer absorbed individually or discussed only in closed-door meetings, but became a collective, e-mail-based articulation of protest.

When a young writer, Jorge Ángel Pérez, sent an e-mail expressing his disgust about the TV appearance to a number of colleagues, he kicked off a flood of e-mails, written and received mostly by intellectuals residing in Cuba. Participants in this e-mail debate were senior writers and artists as well as little-known students or cadres of state institutions – including Mariela Castro, the daughter of Raúl Castro. It is important to note that all these interventions were made not in the name of some institution or organization, but individually – "*a título personal*." As a consequence, beyond the issue at stake, the *polémica* was also about something more general: the legitimacy of individual participation in a public debate of public affairs – not resulting from an institutional position or organizational mandate, but as a citizen's right.

The state leadership eventually declared the TV appearances to have been mere accidents, and withdrew the notorious cadres from television. However, by

232   B. Hoffman

that time, the e-mail *polémica* had already evolved well beyond the event that triggered it and called for a critical public discussion of Cuba's "gray years." After weeks in which e-mail communication had been the principal media, the official writers' union, UNEAC, opened some semi-public space for a controlled discussion within the "under roof" circuits of the institution, while restricting spillovers into a broader public debate. The by-invitation-only debate at the UNEAC head offices on January 30, 2007 became emblematic of the official containment strategy, as a group of mostly younger intellectuals gathered outside the building, demanding, unsuccessfully, entry into and participation in the discussions. Among those left outside, this experience underscored the need for an open debate without official institutions being the gatekeepers authorizing or excluding speakers and audience.

In the months after the initial assembly, the UNEAC organized a series of topical debates on the cultural policy of the 1970s. While these were marked by rather frank discussion, participation was limited to a small audience of intellectuals, without Cuba's mass media providing significant echoes of it or taking the issues to a broader audience. However, the closed-door meeting unintentionally gave birth to an independent blogger movement in Cuba that since has risen to great public prominence. In the wake of the UNEAC meeting, one of those left outside, then little-known 32-year-old philologist Yoani Sánchez, circulated an e-mail, concluding: "We need many more debates than this, and we will not continue to wait until they invite us to participate" (Sánchez 2007). She went from words to deeds by pioneering the first independent blog written from within Cuba, called "Generation Y" (www.desdecuba.com/generaciony). (I will address the phenomenon of blogging in the following section.)

As to e-mail, the impact of the *polémica* was so strong that e-mail received official recognition as a new medium in what seemed to signal a new approach in the state's media policy. When Raúl Castro took over from Fidel in 2006, he issued a call for debate and self-criticism (Castro 2006a, 2006b). Eliades Acosta, who in 2007 was promoted to the important position of director of the cultural department of the Communist Party's Central Committee, took up this call in an interview in which he strongly criticized the inertia of the official press. But while this had happened before, Acosta entered new territory when he explicitly spoke of "this great non-institutional press – e-mails, which have come to stay." Moreover, he not only acknowledged the existence of this "non-institutional press" but also praised them as proof of "a healthy activation of the civic spirit of the Cubans" (Cubarte 2007).

The explicit emphasis on "civic spirit" is in line with the reassertion of citizenship displayed by the authors of the e-mail debate; but it is remarkable for an interpretation emanating from the Communist Party leadership, which over the past five decades stressed collective rather than individual political articulation, and which associated "civic virtues" with the bourgeois past that needed to be overcome rather than with the socialist future that needed to be constructed. However, Acosta's novel take did not carry the day in the upper echelons of Cuba's government. The interview, which had been published exclusively on the

Civil society in the digital age 233

Cuban Ministry of Culture's website,[22] was taken down the very next day. Half a year later, Acosta had to resign his position altogether.

E-mail communication, however, did indeed come to stay as part of Cuba's public sphere. There have been numerous examples since, where e-mail has been used to spread voices of dissatisfaction to peers. On different occasions, intellectuals such as literary critic Desiderio Navarro and actors Luis Alberto García and Armando Tomey, have circulated letters critical of official policies, primarily via e-mail.[23] For instance, Armando Tomey's "open letter" starts out protesting a specific deterioration of his conditions to eventually address broader political issues and to call "to give participation to everybody!" (Tomey 2009). Again, the recourse to the condition of citizen becomes explicit, as he continues that he "like[s] so much the expression by [Ecuador's left-wing President Rafael] Correa, who called his revolution a 'Citizens' Revolution'" (ibid.). In the circulation of this letter, horizontal voice and vertical voice work in tandem, creating a public space of civic critique and debate beyond the narrow constraints of the state monopoly over mass media.

New kids on the blog: citizen journalism to activate citizenship rights

If blogs – that is, websites run by individuals with diary-like entries of information and personal comment – have experienced a worldwide boom, this is largely due to their ability to empower individuals as "senders" in a global media world. Blogs do not require great technological or financial resources, and they have a unique capacity to circumvent the traditional gatekeeper function of established media (Neuberger 2006). In a country where this gatekeeper function takes the form of a state monopoly by a single-party regime, such an ability to circumvent media filters challenges the state's grip on the public sphere.

In Cuba, blogging was, as we have seen above, directly born out of the constraints on public debate in the physical world. Moreover, it had to overcome the constraints on access to the web, and of the Cuban state's monopoly on Internet provider services (Hoffmann 2004: 215–219). So, pioneering blogger Yoani Sánchez had her blog set up on a server outside of the island. Because she (as most everybody on the island) is not legally able to have domestic Internet access, she needs to post from public-access sites, such as in international hotels, by uploading her writings from USB sticks. In fact, Sánchez speaks of herself as a "blind blogger," as she often publishes on the web without actually being able to access her blog on the Internet.

Initially, Yoani's blog passed below the radar of state censors not familiar with the medium and underestimating its potential impact. Even the author herself did not anticipate the attention it would draw; for her, the blog was originally somewhat of a "personal exorcism, a therapy to fight the apathy and frustration, to reflect things that were part of my reality but were not acknowledged in the press, or on the radio or on TV."[24] However, it is precisely the Cuban state's tight control over the media which serves as a political magnifying

234   B. Hoffman

glass when even seemingly minor articulations of voice escape its control. From a personal exorcism by a young unknown, Yoani Sánchez's blog was propelled to international fame in no time. In April 2008, one year after the blog's launch, Sánchez was awarded the prestigious Ortega y Gasset prize in the category of digital journalism, an award soon followed by many others. This international recognition, combined with the state's outspoken hostility against her, made her a prominent public figure within Cuba. Even though few on the island can regularly access her blog, Sánchez's initiative was contagious, and a growing number of independent bloggers identifying themselves as "citizen journalists" (Celaya González 2009a) have sprung up. (A good number of them are grouped under the platforms www.desdecuba.com and www.vocescubanas.com.)

The state's reaction to the emerging independent "blogosphere" was twofold. On the repressive side, Sánchez and other unauthorized bloggers have been portrayed as mercenaries of the revolution's enemies – access from within the island to a number of blogs' websites has been technically blocked and Sánchez has been repeatedly denied permission to leave the island to receive awards or speak at conferences. Another blogger reports that, after unveiling her pseudonym, she was informed that her husband would be dismissed from his workplace if she continued her blog (Celaya González 2009b).

At the same time, however, the state also embraced the new medium as a means to counter the ideological challenge. In line with the so-called "Operation Truth," in which Cuba's Informatics University (UCI) is commissioned with the task to counter "anti-Cuban" content on the Internet, a number of official blogs emerged as top-down initiatives that take on the guise of non-state sites or individualized blogs to gain credibility in its outreach to an international public.[25] This embrace of the Internet goes so far that Fidel Castro's regular opinion pieces – the so-called "Reflections by Compañero [Comrade] Fidel" – have come to be often first published in the website "CubaDebate" (www.cubadebate. cu), leading some to call Fidel "Cuba's Supreme Blogger" (Balboa 2009).[26]

However, blogs have spread and become fashionable to a much wider spectrum of students, professionals and intellectuals within Cuba. Many have started personal blogs with diverse contents and backgrounds. This part of the blogosphere is closest to the debates about autonomy within the state-dependent institutions in the 1990s. While some bloggers declare that they see themselves in the revolutionary trenches against the enemy's propaganda war,[27] others explore the margins for debate. Around Cuban ex-diplomat Pedro Campos, a so-called "Socialismo Participativo y Democrático" group emerged, which criticizes the Cuban government "from the left" in the name of a more participative socialist project.[28] But also, numerous other individuals from within Cuba's official institutions have started up personal blogs. According to its own data, no less than 170 members of the official journalists' union, UPEC, run some type of blog (www.upec.cu/blogueros/directorio_blogs.html).

In the blogosphere, the spaces for pluralism are wider than in Cuba's traditional media, but they remain dependent on the state's goodwill. Time and again, the lines of the politically permissible have been marked by sanctions against

Civil society in the digital age 235

those who "went too far." Such was the case when the author of the blog "El Último Swing" (www.ultimoswing.wordpress.com), while identifying with the revolutionary project, provided an irreverent account of the for-Party-faithful-only showings of videos explaining the ouster of top Party cadres Carlos Lage and Felipe Pérez Roque in mid 2009 (Salas 2009). The author was called to discipline, relocated from his university workplace, and the blog remained largely discontinued. While the conflict was never an object of public discussion, the solidarity shown in the comments section of his critical blog post reflects the pressures he evidently suffered.

The dilemma of the state's acceptance of the medium of blogs has also been vividly illustrated by the first platform for blogs written with official consent, called "Bloggers Cuba" (www.bloggerscuba.com). Launched in November 2008, only one year later, the person who had been driving the project left, and while the blog entries remain conspicuously vague about the circumstances, it is again the comments section that gives a lively account of the pressures and tensions that accompanied the experience of a medium inevitably linked to the individual articulation of voice within a political context based on top-down mass media and low levels of tolerance for political dissent.[29]

From voice via web to civil society action?

Cubans from different social backgrounds and divergent political positions have come to use the new media in forms that bypass the filters and controls established in the traditional mass media. While the Cuban state, as typical for authoritarian regimes, continues to construct a polarized foe–friend dichotomy, with the new web-based articulations, the line of distinction between those raising voices "from within" and those "from without" the system has become blurred. This is a direct consequence of the new media's character as many-to-many media, which is inherently at odds with the top-down logic of the traditional, vertical media so central to the Cuban state's media monopoly. Although the political content and ultimate aims may vary widely, all those who use e-mail or blogs to voice their personal views are, by the very fact of using these media, advocating a right to participate in the public sphere individually and beyond the state monopoly on mass media, and without their writings having to be approved by editors-in-chief or program directors. Hence, using citizen media becomes a civic action in itself, a part of a more self-assertive civic attitude vis-à-vis the state – to borrow Holston's (2008) expression, an "insurgent citizenship" claiming its communication rights. Recalling McLuhan, here, indeed, the medium is the message.

However, in yet other ways the web-empowered voice is translating into what should be conceived of as civil society action in an authoritarian context. One way in which this has occurred has been through its loudspeaker function. The preceding sections have highlighted some of the moments where non-state, web-based media brought to light civic action that otherwise would have passed unnoticed, leading to new social dynamics: an emblematic case is the "*polémica*

236   B. Hoffman

intelectual" sparked by an individual critical comment sent via e-mail and leading to an institutional response by the official writers' union and a mobilization for participation around its main office.

A second effect refers to the development of the collective identity of actors empowered by digital media. The mentioned movement of critical rap singers whose increased autonomy vis-à-vis the state relies on the use of digital media can be understood – as Geoffray (2010) convincingly shows – as a "new modus of non-conventional collective action" within an authoritarian context. Similarly, the bloggers are not only isolated individuals posting their voices on the web, but they have developed an informal sense of collectivity as an "independent blogger movement," as difficult to ignore as to demarcate precisely.

A third aspect is the bloggers' direct interaction with actors in the physical, non-virtual spaces of Cuban society. Emblematic have been incidents protagonized by, again, Yoani Sánchez. A case in point is her encounter with Mariela Castro, Raúl Castro's daughter. In a public conference, Mariela Castro, in her function as head of Cuba's National Center for Sexual Education, presented the state's new approach of maximum tolerance towards different sexual orientations. In the Q&A session that followed, Sánchez raised the question of when such tolerance would also be granted towards different political orientations. In this encounter the Cuban president's daughter gave an evasive, yet friendly answer; however, when the blogger later posted a video of this on the web, Mariela Castro had to retract, writing a highly offensive text decrying Sánchez's intervention as a counter-revolutionary provocation.[30] Other similar actions include the bloggers' public appearance in an arts performance in the Havana Biennial in 2008, and the participation, in spite of officials denying the bloggers entry, at an "*último jueves*" debate event organized by *Temas* magazine.[31]

A fourth element is organization. Yoani Sánchez has not only become Cuba's most prominent blogger but also the epicentre of its diffusion. While state security intervened against a first bloggers' meeting in October, Sánchez established a home-grown "blogger academy" with regular meetings teaching the necessary skills and providing spaces for debate, and even holding an independent "blogger award" contest called "Isla Virtual."[32] Despite its informal organizational setting, this can be understood as an association-in-the-making of civil society.

A fifth element is connecting with other social actors on the island. Beyond organizing with fellow bloggers, Yoani Sánchez and the group of friends around her have developed strong links to critical groups within the Catholic Church such as "Convivencia" led by Dagoberto Valdés, as well as to some imprisoned dissidents and to the "Ladies in White," an organization created by the wives and mothers of political prisoners pressing for their release. When in 2010, forced into action by hunger-striking dissidents, the government negotiated the release of 52 imprisoned dissidents, Yoani Sánchez's blog and Twitter feeds mobilized international attention, and she, herself, became an actor in the negotiated resolution. The moment the Church-mediated agreement with the government reached Sánchez, she and some of the "Ladies in White" went to the hospital to persuade hunger-striker Guillermo Fariñas – in a highly critical state

Civil society in the digital age 237

of health after 134 days without food – to suspend his fast even before the actual release had started.

At the same time, dissenting groups from the margins of Cuba's cultural sphere, such as the critical academics of the Cátedra Haydee Santamaría or the grassroots cultural activists of OMNI Zona Franca,[33] not only became involved in establishing their own articulation through the web, but also turned publicly against the restrictions and repression suffered by themselves and by the bloggers. After Yoani Sánchez suffered a brief kidnapping by plain-clothes security agents, and her husband, journalist Reynaldo Escobar, was rudely harassed by an organized street mob, on November 6, 2009, the Omni Zona Franca collective staged a public "No more violence!" street demonstration[34] – under the guise of a cultural performance, but unequivocal in its message, and an open challenge to a system which for half a century has been adamant in not allowing independent mobilizations on the streets.

Conclusions

A precondition for civil society activism to evolve is some degree of public sphere in which it can "breathe." The state monopoly on mass media, as exercised by the Cuban state, has been a particularly thorough form of authoritarian control over the national public sphere. The comparative empirical analysis of civil society dynamics in the 1990s and in the 2000s has shown the notable impact of the digital, web-based media on the contours of the public sphere and has also demonstrated that this, in turn, impacts the activities, conception and organizational forms of societal actors.

In the pre-Internet period, within a very much restricted public sphere, the civil society debate largely focused on behind-the-scenes struggles for increased autonomy of associational life within the state-socialist framework (e.g., Azcuy 1995). In contrast, a decade later we witness the emergence of a self-assertive "citizenship from below," which demands, and to some degree *enacts* (empowered by digital and web-based technologies), a widening of the public sphere and a greater degree of citizen autonomy from the state, leading to a different type of civil society activity. While this "insurgent citizenship" – to borrow Holston's (2008) expression – defies the socialist regime's traditional design of state–society relations, its effect on democratization depends on the extent to which web-based voice is able to connect with off-line public debate and social action.

However, the initial question – that of whether civil society activism fosters processes of regime change – does not have a clear-cut answer. While regime opponents see the struggles over Internet access, blogs and e-mails as a *pars pro toto* for the civic liberties of liberal democracy, reformists from within the system argue the need for more participation and wider margins of debate, precisely because they are indispensable to regain legitimacy for the socialist project.

As of this writing, the government, it seems, has come to accept the fact that its media monopoly has become porous. The government's crucial concern is

238   *B. Hoffman*

containment: to minimize the domestic impact, to put brakes on the contagion effect, and, most importantly, to keep the pluralism of the web-based voice from spilling over into Cuba's non-virtual public sphere. This echoes the state's traditional "under the roof, everything – in the street, nothing" approach towards dissenting voices; on the web, as "under the roof," much may be tolerated, as long as it doesn't take to "the street," that is, combine with social action in the physical world.

The state's attitude towards leading blogger Yoani Sánchez exemplifies this policy. While her blog is de facto tolerated for the consumption of the outside world, domestic access to it is blocked. And when the blogger moved to social activism in the physical world in 2009, the regime reacted heavy-handedly, including using physical intimidation and orchestrating mobilizations of "enraged revolutionaries" against her and fellow bloggers. Similarly, those still working within and those dependent on official structures are admonished and told to keep their distance from those branded as "counter-revolutionaries."

However, as the chapter has shown, not only has the state media monopoly become porous, but so have the state's walls of containing web-based voice from spilling over into Cuban society. Some 15 years after Cuba joined the Internet, the web-based media not only represent a leak of voice to a globalized public, but they have led to a limited, yet important transformation of state–society relations. They empower a new reassertion of citizenship rights that challenge established rules, and they foster the emergence of new social actors and forms of action.

The case also shows that there is no automatism from such trends to a process of either gradual reform or radical regime change. The crucial fault-line remains the physical space on the island, where the costs for individual voice and collective action remain high. Just as much as in Egypt Facebook alone neither explains the discontent of large shares of the population nor why the army desisted from militarily cracking down on the Tahrir Square protest, also in Cuba for more large-scale political transformations to occur, a wider set of factors would need to combine, probably including frictions within the political elite or changes in the external constellation of allies and foes. But the expansion of voice, the reassertion of citizenship rights, and the web-based support for civic action in the physical world have already changed the contours of state–society relations. Once conditions arise – be it for a reform movement towards a more pluralist model of socialism or for an all-out regime change-type democratization process or anything in between – these transformations will undoubtedly shape the future process of political change.

Notes

1 These figures are also those reproduced by the International Telecommunications Union (ITU 2009).
2 For Cuban civil society prior to 1959, see Armony and Crahan (2007); on trade unions and the women's federation, see Mariféli Pérez-Stable (1994).
3 While the Afro-Cuban religions are more popular and encompass wide nets of social

Civil society in the digital age 239

relations, their weak institutionalization gives them a much less visible role in the national public arena.

4 Orig. "Dentro de la Revolución, todo. Contra la Revolución, nada."
5 Orig. "La calle es de Fidel!"
6 Orig. "Bajo techo, todo. En la calle, nada."
7 Even at this early point, political resistance against the use of the term became evident. When published in the journal of the official Cuban writers' association, UNEAC, it was prefaced by a "Letter to the Editor" in which a member of the association reprimands Hernández for his "imprecise" use of the term which he identified with the counter-revolutionary strategy of the U.S. government.
8 Parallel to the debate on civil society, a similar debate evolved about increased autonomy for economic actors and resulting reform steps (see Carranza *et al.* 1995; for an overview see Hoffmann 1995, 1997).
9 This plea for greater autonomy of the social sphere also is the leitmotif of the volume edited by Haroldo Dilla (1996), whose articles cover such diverse topics as agrarian cooperatives, the participation of women and the generation gap in Cuba.
10 Aside from the cited Hernández and Azcuy, other CEA scholars that were key exponents in the debate were Haroldo Dilla and Juan Valdés Paz, and Julio Carranza and Pedro Monreal in the economic field.
11 This includes the Unity Trade Union (CTC), the Committees for the Defense of the Revolution (CDR), the small farmers' association ANAP, the women's organization FMC, the students' organization FEU and the pupils' organization FEEM and, for the youngest, the organization of the Young Pioneers.
12 This certainly is not an invention of Cuban socialism alone, but can be found in different forms in many countries, particularly throughout the so-called "Third World." In the jargon of the international development community, the ironic term "GONGO" (Government-Organized Non-governmental Organization) has been coined (see Koschützke 1994: 39).
13 Preceding the Politburo report, the party newspaper *Granma* had published a devastating article against the civil society concept by the director of the PCC's party academy, Valdés Vivó (1996). See also Hart Davalos (1996).
14 The Politburo-mandated, half-year-long process of intervention in the Center for American Studies, led by veteran hardliner José Ramón Balaguer, was entirely shielded from public view. Through undisclosed channels the internal documents of these proceedings were eventually leaked after the case was closed, and published in the U.S. (Giuliani 1998).
15 This process is described in detail in Valdés (1997), and Hoffmann (2004: 199–208).
16 Named after its author in the U.S. Congress, Robert Torricelli; the law's official name is: Cuban Democracy Act.
17 In fact, Cuba's first IP connection was not from Cuba to Canada, as initially announced, but a direct link from Cuba to the U.S. provided by the U.S. company Sprint, a deal made possible only under the provisions of the Torricelli law.
18 Official title: *Decreto No. 209: Del acceso desde la República de Cuba a redes informáticas de alcance global*; published in: Gazeta Oficial No. 27, September 13, 1996. Cf. also Press (1998); Valdés and Rivera (1999: 147f.).
19 www.youtube.com/results?search_type=&search_query=monte+rouge&aq=f (access: April 1, 2009). For an in-depth study of recent Cuban "street filmmaking" see Stock (2009).
20 "Porno para Ricardo," whose hard-hitting lyrics, to put it mildly, are more than explicit, is banned from public performance and radio, but video clips and recordings from concerts in private settings are circulating on the island and on the web, with YouTube showing scores of ten thousands of viewers www.youtube.com/results?search_type=&search_query=porno+para+ricardo&aq=f (access: April 1, 2009). When band leader Gorki Águila was arrested in 2008 on charges of "social

240 B. Hoffman

dangerousness," this, too, became a public issue on the web as the band as well as bloggers like Yoani Sánchez posted their "Free Gorki!" protests, mobilizing international solidarity. Gorki Águila was eventually ordered to pay a mere 30 USD fine for the lesser offense of public disorder.

21 Ravsberg (2008); for the video see www.youtube.com/watch?v=X_nMQD2xwJs.

22 www.cubarte.cu, November 22, 2009. However, copies of it circulated on the Internet on a number of sites (e.g., www.pacocol.org/es/Inicio/Archivo_de_noticias/Diciembre07/24.html).

23 In her blog "Generación Y," Yoani Sánchez (2009) lists these letters (and links to them), describing the phenomenon as a new "cartismo" – in a play of words, as the Spanish "*carta*" means as much "letter" as it does "charter."

24 Cited at http://cuba.blogspot.com/2008/05/yoani-snchez-denuncia-que-los.html (access: March 31, 2009).

25 An example is "Yohandry's weblog" (http://yohandry.wordpress.com), which was created as a state-sponsored response to Yoani Sánchez's "Generation Y" and which continuously spends much energy and space on denouncing Sánchez's blog and activities.

26 While the website describes "CubaDebate" as "a media of alternative information," it is directed by Randy Alonso, the senior news anchor of Cuba's state TV and a long-standing confidant of Fidel Castro. Surprisingly enough for a communist party's lead newspaper, *Granma* has been reproducing some of Fidel's "reflections" with the note "taken from CubaDebate," underscoring that the web, not the paper, was the *locus* of first publication of the reflections of the Party's general secretary (a post Fidel retains even after the handover of state leadership to his brother).

27 For example, the post titled "If they wage their war by blogs, then by blogs we will win it" in "Vladia's blog" (Si de "blogazos" es la guerra que se nos hace...); November 26, 2009 http://vladia.blogcip.cu/2009/11/26/si-de-blogazos-es-la-guerra-que-se-nos-hace/.

28 http://cubaspdboletin.blogspot.es/; see also: www.kaosenlared.net/noticia/cuba-boletin-socialismo-participativo-democratico-n-49.

29 Blog entry by David Chapet from December 24, 2009 communicating his decision to leave "Bloggers Cuba" and subsequent comments at www.bloggerscuba.com/post/felicidades/, including (December 30, 2009): "Thank you Chapet for opening a window in the wall! And congratulations for leaving, before BC [Bloggers Cuba] disappears or, what would be worse, becomes a caricature of itself." To which Chapet only replies "Thanks, brother."

30 The video of the encounter was posted at the Generation Y website on December 17, 2008 (www.desdecuba.com/generaciony/?m=200812); Mariela Castro's text was published on the CENESEX website but is no longer available online (see also www.cubaencuentro.com/es/cuba/noticias/mariela-castro-acusa-a-yoani-sanchez-de-recibir-honorarios-del-exterior-y-la-llama-gallita-e-insignificante-140046).

31 See entries in the Generation Y blog on March 30, April 2 and October 30, 2009 (www.desdecuba.com/generaciony).

32 http://knol.google.com/k/yoani-s%C3%A1nchez-8-promoci%C3%B3n-de-la-blogosfera-cubana#Academia_Blogger.

33 http://elblogdelacatedra.blogspot.com/; http://omnifestivalpoesiasinfin.blogspot.com/. For an in-depth study of both these groups as non-conventional modi of collective action, see Geoffray (2010).

34 For a video of the demonstration, see http://omnizonafrancaen.eltinterocolectivo.com/.

References

Armony, A. (2004) *The Dubious Link: Civic Engagement and Democratization*, Stanford: Standford University Press.

Armony, A. and M. Crahan (2007) *Does Civil Society Exist in Cuba?* Miami: Florida International University; Cuba Info Commissioned Report; http://cubainfo.fiu.edu/Documents/CrahanDoesCivilSocietyExistInCuba.pdf (accessed November 3, 2009).

Azcuy, H. (1995) "Estado y sociedad civil en Cuba," *Temas*, 4: 105–110.

Balboa, J. (2009) "Fidel, el bloguero mayor," *Proceso*. Mexico. www.proceso.com.mx/noticias_articulo.php?articulo=67420 (accessed April 12, 2009).

Bernhard, M. (1993) "Civil Society and Democratic Transition in East Central Europe," *Political Science Quarterly*, 108: 307–326.

Calhoun, C. (1994) *Neither Gods nor Emperors: Students and the Struggle for Democracy in China*, Berkeley: University of California Press.

Campos, P. (2008) *Cuba necesita un socialismo participativo y democrático. Propuestas programáticas.* www.kaosenlared.net/noticia/cuba-necesita-socialismo participativodemocratico-propuestas-programa (posted August 17, 2008, accessed January 23, 2009).

Carranza Valdés, J., P. Monreal and L. Gutiérrez (1995) *La restructuración de la economía cubana. Una propuesta para el debate*, La Habana: Editorial Ciencias Sociales.

Castro, R. (1996) Informe del Buró Político (en el V. Pleno del Comité Central del Partido, March 23, 1996), *Granma Internacional*, April 10, pp. 4–8.

Castro, R. (2006a) *Speech by the Second Secretary of the Central Committee of the Party, First Vice-President of the Councils of State and Ministers, Minister of the Revolutionary Armed Forces, Army General, Raúl Castro Ruz, at the Political Ceremony, Military Review and March of the Combatant People in Commemoration of the 50th Anniversary of the Landing of the Granma Yacht and the Day of the Revolutionary Armed Forces, and in Celebration of the 80th Birthday of the Commander-in-Chief, Fidel Castro Ruz, Given on December 2nd 2006*; cited from the English version at the Cuban Foreign Relations Ministry's homepage. www.cubaminrex.cu/English/50TH%20Aniversary/50anivi.htm (accessed July 24, 2007).

Castro, R. (2006b) "No Enemy Can Defeat Us," interview with Raúl Castro in *Granma*, August 18, 2006; English version cited from the Cuban Foreign Relations Ministry's homepage. www.cubaminrex.cu/English/The%20imperialism/No%20enemy%20can%20defeat%20us.htm (accessed July 24, 2007).

Celaya González, M. (2009a) *Periodismo ciudadano: un canal de la sociedad civil*, http://desdecuba.com/generaciony/?page_id=600 (accessed November 3, 2009).

Celaya González, M. (2009b) *Durmiendo con el enemigo*, http://desdecuba.com/sin_evasion/?p=146, published: February 17, 2009 (accessed November 3, 2009).

Cohen, J. and A. Arato (1992) *Civil Society and Political Theory*, Cambridge: MIT Press.

Crahan, M. and A. Armony (2007) "Rethinking Civil Society and Religion in Cuba," in Bert Hoffmann and Laurence Whitehead (eds.) *Debating Cuban Exceptionalism*, New York/London: Palgrave, pp. 139–163.

Cubarte (2007) *Entrevista a Eliades Acosta*, www.cubarte.cu, published: November 22, 2007 (accessed November 3, 2009).

Dähn, H. and J. Heise (eds.) (2003) *Staat und Kirchen in der DDR. Zum Stand der zeithistorischen und sozialwissenschaftlichen Forschung*, Frankfurt am Main: Peter Lang.

Dilla, H. (ed.) (1996) *La participación en Cuba y los retos del futuro*, La Habana: Ediciones CEA [Centro de Estudios sobre América].

242   *B. Hoffman*

Eckstein, S. (1994) *Back from the Future: Cuba under Castro*, Princeton: Princeton University Press.

Espinosa, J. C. (1996) "The 'Emergence' of Civil Society in Cuba," *The Journal of Latin American Affairs*, 4: 24–33.

Fernández, D. J. (1993) "Civil Society in Transition," in Cuban Research Institute (ed.) *Transition in Cuba: New Challenges for U.S. Policy*, Miami: Florida International University.

Fernández, D. J. (ed.) (2005) *Cuba Transnational*, Gainesville: University Press of Florida.

Geoffray, M. L. (2010) "Culture, politique et contestation á Cuba (1989–2009). Une sociologie politique des modes non conventionnels d'action collective en contexte autoritaire," PhD thesis at Sciences-Po, Paris.

Giuliani, M. (1998) *El Caso CEA: Intelectuales e Inquisidores en Cuba. ¿Perestroika en la Isla?*, Miami: Ediciones Universal.

Gray, A. and A. Kapcia (eds.) (2008) *The Changing Dynamic of Cuban Civil Society*, Gainesville: University Press of Florida.

Gunn, G. (1995) "Cuba's NGOs. Government Puppets or Seeds of Civil Society?" *Cuba Briefing Paper Series No. 7*, Washington D.C.: Center for Latin American Studies, Georgetown University.

Habermas, J. (1962) *Strukturwandel der Öffentlichkeit: Untersuchungen zu einer Kategorie der bürgerlichen Gesellschaft*. Neuwied: Luchterhand. [The Structural Transformation of the Public Sphere: An Inquiry into a Category of Bourgeois Society, Cambridge: Polity, 1989].

Havel, V. (orig. 1978) "The Power of the Powerless," reproduced in Vaclav Havel and John Keane (1985) *The Power of the Powerless: Citizens Against the State in Central-Eastern Europe*, New York: Palach Press, pp. 23–96.

Hart Dávalos, A. (1996) "Sociedad civil y Organizaciones No Gubernamentales," *Granma Internacional*, September 13, p. 3.

Hernández, R. (1994) "La sociedad civil y sus alrededores," *La Gaceta de Cuba*, No. 1/94, La Habana: Unión Nacional de Escritores y Artistas de Cuba, UNEAC, pp. 28–31.

Hernández, R. (1996) *Sobre la sociedad civil en Cuba*, in Haroldo Dilla (ed.) *La participación en Cuba y los retos del futuro*, La Habana: Ediciones CEA [Centro de Estudios sobre América], pp. 82–97.

Hernández, R. (1997) *Y sin embargo se mueve. Reordenamiento y Transición en Cuba Socialista*, Presentation at the seminar "Seguridad, Transiciones Post-Autoritarias y Cambio Social en El Caribe de la Post-Guerra Fría: Los casos de Cuba, Haití y República Dominicana"; March 14/15, 1997 at FLACSO, Santo Domingo (Dom. Rep.).

Herrero, S. (1996) "El 'Igualitarismo' en Cuba," *The Journal of Latin American Affairs*, 4(1): 11–15.

Hirschman, A. (1970) *Exit, Voice, and Loyalty: Responses to Decline in Firms, Organizations, and States*, Cambridge: Harvard University Press.

Hirschman, A. (1986) "Exit and Voice. An Expanding Sphere of Influence," in Albert O. Hirschman (ed.) *Rival Views of Market Society*, New York: Viking.

Hoffmann, B. (ed.) (1995) *Cuba. Apertura y reforma económica. Perfil de un debate*, Caracas: Editorial Nueva Sociedad.

Hoffmann, B. (1997) "Cuba – la reforma desde adentro que no fue," *Notas* No. 9, Frankfurt am Main: Vervuert, pp. 48–66.

Hoffmann, B. (2004) *The Politics of the Internet in Third World Development. Challenges*

Civil society in the digital age 243

in Contrasting Regimes with Case Studies of Costa Rica and Cuba, New York: Routledge.

Hoffmann, B. (2005) "How Do you Download Democracy? Potential and Limitations of the Internet for Advancing Citizens' Rights in the Third World: Lessons from Latin America," *International Politics and Society*, 3: 30–46.

Hoffmann, B. (2009) "Charismatic Authority and Leadership Change: Lessons from Cuba's Post-Fidel Succession," *International Political Science Review*, 30(3): 229–248.

Holston, J. (2008) *Insurgent Citizenship: Disjunctions of Democracy and Modernity in Brazil*, Princeton: Princeton University Press.

ITU [International Telecommunications Union] (2009) *Perfiles Estadísticos de la Sociedad de la Información 2009. Region América*, ITU: Geneva.

Jamal, A. (2007) *Barriers to Democracy*, Princeton: Princeton University Press.

Kalathil, S. and T. Boas (2001) "The Internet and State Control in Authoritarian Regimes: China, Cuba and the Counterrevolution," *First Monday* [Online], Volume 6, Number 8. www.firstmonday.org/issues/issue6_8/kalathil/ (accessed November 3, 2009).

Kalathil, S. and T. Boas (2003) *Open Networks, Closed Regimes: The Impact of the Internet on Authoritarian Rule*, Washington D.C.: Carnegie Endowment for International Peace.

Koschützke, A. (1994) "Die Lösung auf der Suche nach dem Problem: NGOs diesseits und jenseits des Staates," in Dietmar Dirmoser, Wolfgang Gabbert and Bert Hoffman (eds.) *Lateinamerika Analysen und Berichte 18: Jenseits des Staates*, Bad Honnef: Horlemann, pp. 39–64.

Lauzurique, R. (1996) "La Crisis Económica Cubana: Causas, Paliativos y Expectativas," *The Journal of Latin American Affairs*, 4(1): 16–23.

Linz, J. and A. Stepan (1996) *Problems of Democratic Transition and Consolidation: Southern Europe, South America, and Post-Communist Europe*, Baltimore: The Johns Hopkins University Press.

Lynch, M. (2006) *Voices of the New Arab Public: Iraq, al-Jazeera, and Middle East Politics Today*, New York: Columbia University Press.

López Vigil, M. (1997) "Sociedad Civil en Cuba. Diccionario urgente," *Envío* No. 184, Managua.

Malone, S. (1996) "Conflict, Coexistence and Cooperation. Church-State Relations in Cuba," *Georgetown University Cuba Briefing Paper Series* No. 9, Washington D.C.

Neuberger, C. (2006) "Weblogs verstehen. Über den Strukturwandel der Öffentlichkeit im Internet," in Arnold Picot and Tim Fischer (ed.) *Weblogs professionell*, Heidelberg dpunkt verlag, pp. 113–129.

O'Donnell, G. and P. Schmitter (1986) *Transitions from Authoritarian Rule. Tentative Conclusions about Uncertain Democracies*, Baltimore: The Johns Hopkins University Press.

Obra Nacional de la Buena Prensa (1995) *La voz de la Iglesia en Cuba*, Mexico.

ONE [Oficina Nacional de Estadística] (2009) "Anuario Estadístico de Cuba 2008," Edición 2009. www.one.cu/aec2008.htm (section 17 on information and communication technologies) (accessed November 3, 2009).

Pérez-Stable, M. (1994) *The Cuban Revolution: Origins, Course, Legacy*, Oxford: Oxford University Press.

Press, L. (1998) "The Internet in Cuba," *The Global Diffusion of the Internet Project. An Initial Inductive Study*, edited by the MOSAIC Group, http://som.csudh.edu/cis/lpress/devnat/nations/cuba/cubasy.htm (accessed November 3, 2009).

244   *B. Hoffman*

Press, L., W. Foster and S. Goodman (1999) "The Internet in China and India," *INET '99 Proceedings*, Internet Society. www.isoc.org/inet99/proceedings/3a/3a_3.htm (accessed November 3, 2009).

Puerta, R. (1996) *Sociedad Civil en Cuba*, Miami: Ed. Coordinadora Social Demócrata de Cuba.

Ravsberg, F. (2008) "Cuba: preguntas difíciles al gobierno," in *BBC Mundo.com*, http://news.bbc.co.uk/hi/spanish/latin_america/newsid_7227000/7227977.stm, published February 5, 2008 (accessed November 3, 2009).

República de Cuba (1992) *Constitución de la República de Cuba*. www.cuba.cu/gobierno/consti.htm (accessed November 3, 2009).

Salas, D. (2009) El video … (todos saben de qué se trata); blog post in: El Último Swing, June 24. http://ultimoswing.wordpress.com/2009/06/24/el-video%E2%80%A6-todos-saben-de-que-se-trata/ (accessed November 3, 2009).

Sánchez Villaverde, R. (1995) *La informatización de la sociedad: un arma de guerra del carril II*, La Habana: CID FAR.

Sánchez, Y. (2007) *Desde afuera. Pequeña crónica de lo que aconteció el 30 de enero afuera de la Casa de las Américas*. www.desdecuba.com/polemica/articulos/27_01.shtml (accessed November 3, 2009).

Sánchez, Y. (2009) "El nuevo cartismo," blog entry in *Generación Y*, October 3. www.desdecuba.com/generaciony/?p=2338 (accessed November 3, 2009).

Semati, M. (2008) *Media, Culture and Society in Iran: Living with Globalization and the Islamic State*, London: Routledge.

Smith, C. (2011) "Egypt's Facebook Revolution: Wael Ghonim Thanks the Social Network," *The Huffington Post*, February 11. www.huffingtonpost.com/2011/02/11/egypt-facebookrevolution-wael-ghonim_n_822078.html (accessed May 21, 2012).

Stock, A. M. (2009) *On Location in Cuba: Street Filmmaking During Times of Transition*, Chapel Hill: University of North Carolina Press.

Tomey, A. (2009) *Carta abierta de Armando Tomey*, e-mail circulation, reproduced as PDF at: www.desdecuba.com/reinaldoescobar/wp-content/uploads/2009/09/carta_tomey1.pdf (accessed December 22, 2009).

Valdés, N. (1997) "Cuba, the Internet, and U.S. Policy," *Cuba Briefing Paper Series* No. 13, Washington D.C.: Georgetown University, Center for Latin American Studies.

Valdés, N. and M. Rivera (1999) "The Political Economy of the Internet in Cuba," *Cuba in Transition* Vol. 9 (Association for the Study of the Cuban Economy [ASCE]), pp. 141–154. www.lanic.utexas.edu/la/cb/cuba/asce/cuba9/valdes.pdf (accessed November 3, 2009).

Valdés Vivó, R. (1996) "¿Sociedad civil o gato por liebre?," *Granma Internacional*, January 24, p. 3.

Venegas, C. (2010) *Digital Dilemmas: The State, the Individual, and Digital Media in Cuba*, New Brunswick: Rutgers University Press.

Warren, M. (2000) *Democracy and Association*, Princeton: Princeton University Press.

12 Reconsidering two myths about civil society

Evidence from Afghanistan

Kevin W. Gray

Introduction

In this chapter, I will adopt a type of immanent critique that asks how the terms 'civil society' and 'the public sphere' have come to be used by political scientists working on the Middle East and South Asia, and compare that to the actual theoretical development of the terms. I will argue that attempts to locate public spheres and civil society in the region have, in their rush to find areas of society that are functionally equivalent to the model of civil society in the literature, overlooked key components of the original theory. The two myths I identify are (1) that civil society does not serve a normative purpose (i.e., that it does not aid in the legitimation of government) and (2) that the way in which discourse occurs inside the public sphere and civil society is irrelevant.

Following a discussion of the origins of civil society inspired by critical theory, one which differs from the liberal tradition by rejecting an expansive reading of both civil society and the public sphere, I will try to develop an account of civil society that begins with the basic question: What it is that we expect civil society to do? I will proceed in two stages: first, I will take issue with the expansive understanding of civil society by developing a critique of contemporary work on the concept of civil society, by drawing on the sources of the revival of civil society discourse in the twentieth century. Second, I will use my own research on Afghanistan, and other research by other theorists whom I consider representative of the way theories of civil society have been applied to the region, to suggest additions that need to be made to the theoretical writings on the public sphere. I conclude by challenging the traditional way that civil society has been understood by researchers working on the Middle East and South Asia, and argue that they have ignored the role of discourse in the public sphere for legitimating government decisions.

Critical theory and the public sphere

The revival of interest in civil society can be traced to two specific problems. First, it can be traced to the revolutionary movements in Eastern Europe prior to 1989, whose leaders attempted to ascertain the conditions under which a civil

246   *K.W. Gray*

society might lead to a self-limiting anti-Stalinist revolution (Cohen and Arato, 1992). Second, it can be traced to the attempt by theorists to investigate the ways in which civil society might legitimate the political system in late capitalist society. It is with this second point (the first being largely irrelevant for my purposes) that I begin my attempt to theorize what it is we expect from civil society. Theorists working in this tradition trace their interest in civil society to two particular works on the public sphere published in the twentieth century: Hannah Arendt's *The Human Condition* (1958) and Jürgen Habermas' *The Structural Transformation of the Public Sphere* (1962[1991]).

In her work on the public sphere, Arendt took the Greek agora to be the *locus classicus* of public discourse. The agora exemplified the important properties that the public sphere must possess: in it, speakers come together in a public forum to discuss matters of common interest, outside the private sphere where there occurred the production of the necessities of survival, the subjects discussed in the public sphere do not belong to the private arena of the family but center on what are held to be matters of public interest. Obviously, Arendt's conception of the public sphere as an actual physical space where speakers can come together is too limited to account for the role of the media and discourse in modern society. Instead of conceiving of the public sphere as one arena in which all citizens participate in discourse, Habermas proposed to reinterpret the public sphere as an area of society composed of multiple loci of debate, whose members have access to a shared store of common knowledge.[1] The uniquely modern European bourgeois public sphere emerged out of changing economic and technological conditions at the beginning of the Industrial Revolution. Instead of debate occurring in the agora, the bourgeois public sphere arose out of the flow of information between traders and markets in different cities that occurred as capitalism developed. A public sphere could be said to exist, Habermas (1991: 2) argued, when actors were free to join and to participate in debates in public houses, cafes, etc. The new sites of debate, where literature, art, and later politics came to be argued over and perhaps legitimated, were the scores of coffee houses, open to members of the bourgeois class, that began to appear in the middle of the seventeenth century, first in London and later elsewhere (Habermas, 1991: 32–33).

From this perspective, the existence of the regions that are open to all participants in society depends on the growth of the capitalist system, which freed production from the feudal guild system and led instead to the capitalist realm of commodity exchange (Habermas, 1991: 3). What is important to the emergence of the public sphere is not that the state enacted laws to allow for civil associations to form, but that a realm of publicness came into existence because of the economic conditions that existed during the industrial revolution. For the public sphere to emerge in Europe, two decisive economics events were needed. First, the industrial revolution changed the nature of the family and the private realm of a family's's affairs. Activities once relegated to the household economy emerged into the public sphere: "economic activity … [came] to be oriented toward a commodity market that had expanded under public direction and supervision"

Reconsidering two myths about civil society 247

(Habermas, 1991: 19). For example, activities connected to mere survival (e.g., the production of food stuffs) which were formerly private, became elements of the capitalist system. Second, the demand for information about distant events led to the creation of a system of information exchange: "with the expansion of trade, merchants' market-oriented calculus required more frequent and more exact information about distant events" (Habermas, 1991: 18). Starting from the middle of the fourteenth century, mail services to carry information between towns and cities were established. These mail services, at first the exchange of private news-letters between merchants, led eventually to the establishment of journals and newspapers. News itself became a purchasable commodity.

It is important to note that, from this perspective, the public sphere does not merely supervene on the region of economic production separate from the state and the aristocracy, nor is it reducible to economics. The development of the capitalist system in Western Europe, Habermas argued, also created three important (contingent) social changes. First, inside the coffee shops traditional deference to rank and social class were abandoned, allowing for the strength of the best argument to determine the discussion. Second, the new form of public debate permitted a problematization of areas (e.g., politics) not previously open to discussion. Third, the process that gave rise to public culture meant that it was in principle impossible for the public sphere to become closed: any person, pro-vided they were literate, had access to the necessary materials to participate in public debate. Access to the public sphere was essentially the sort of commodity that could be purchased in the market place:

> readers, listeners, and spectators could avail themselves via the market of the objects that were subject to discussion. The issues discussed became 'general' not merely in their significance, but also in their accessibility: everyone had to *be able* to participate.
>
> (Habermas, 1991: 37)

Corresponding to these changes arose a general category of legal standing, sepa-rate from the aristocratic legal standing offered by estate and birth that "correspond[ed] to the fundamental parity amongst owners of commodities in the market and amongst educated individuals in the public sphere" (Habermas, 1991: 75). With the codification of civil law in Continental Europe, and within the framework of common law in Britain, a system of constitutional liberties became enshrined in law: freedom of opinion, speech, assembly and association, freedom to petition, equality of vote (for those eligible), etc.; within the intimate sphere, personal freedom, inviolability of the home, etc.; concerning transac-tions, equality before the law, protection of private property, etc. (Habermas, 1991: 83). Only the combination of a change in economic production, the emer-gence of new classes of producers and the changed nature of the autonomy of the individual produced the European bourgeois public sphere.

Of course, the public sphere is not identical to civil society, but it presents a broad outline, I believe, of what it is we should expect civil society to do. Civil

248   *K.W. Gray*

society is that space where citizens can come together to advocate for particular actions, to discuss government decisions and to challenge the legal order. A robust public sphere is required for civil society, as public debate provides the legitimation necessary for any model of democratic government.

There are, of course, other models of civil society. For instance, the Tocquevillian, the Gramscian, the liberal, etc. focus on the position of actors in society relative to the various spheres of production, the family, and the state, rather than on the question what it is we expect civil society to do. For Gramsci, civil society is merely a region of state hegemony, with little or no libratory potential; for de Tocqueville, conversely, civil society is the region where people resist the power of government. Problematically, such perspectives eviscerate the normative content of the theory, replacing a question of function with position. It is for that reason I prefer the Habermasian model of civil society, as it accords with the roles I believe that we expect the public sphere and civil society to perform in emerging democracies.

Criticism of the model

As we saw, critical theory claims that a series of economic and social changes were necessary for the emergence of the public sphere. Theorists critical of Habermas took issue with the changes that are supposedly required for civil society to emerge. Their criticism effectively boils down to two basic concerns. First, that Habermas' model is exclusionary, and second, that it is too culturally specific. The first objection is trivially true. When Kant discussed the role of public deliberation, he argued that only property-owning men of the bourgeois class (i.e., not members of the old aristocratic class) were sufficiently involved in the new capitalist economy to be admissible to the public sphere. Women, members of the proletariat, etc. were de facto excluded from the prevalent models of the public sphere. Habermas followed Kant and ignored the existence of alternative public spheres that existed contemporaneously to the bourgeois public sphere. First, authors have argued that there existed women's public spheres in nineteenth-century America and in salons in eighteenth-century France that did not exclude women in the same way as the bourgeois public spheres; second, that simultaneously to Habermas' bourgeois public sphere proletarian public spheres existed in Europe (Landes, 1988; Kluge and Negt, 1990; Ryan, 1992). In each case, theorists argued for the existence of simultaneous, multiple public spheres (i.e., non-bourgeois public spheres) that aided in legitimation.

Second, thinkers objected that the model of legitimation proposed by Habermas assumed the existence of a specifically European distinction between the public arena, the domestic arena, and the state. This is prominent in much recent scholarship on the Middle East and South Asia. First, in work on the Middle East and South Asia, one particular objection stands out: that Habermas focused too heavily on a certain understanding of public space that ignores the formation of public spheres in 'non-public,' domestic environments. Second, thinkers argue that public deliberation, like that in Habermas' public sphere, can occur in

Reconsidering two myths about civil society 249

the strong publics created by traditional tribal or governmental structures. Third, thinkers argue that changes in media technology have produced new public spheres that destroy traditional conceptions of publicity. I will take three examples from the literature to highlight these objections to Habermas' conception of the public and its role in legitimation.

First, in *Provincializing Europe*, Dipesh Chakrabarty (2000: 215) argues that because public spaces, in Bengali society under the British, were effectively colonial spaces, alternative civil spaces emerged in houses that allowed for something like the debate one would expect to occur in the public sphere. Chakrabarty (2000: 223–224) argues that the distinction made between public and private in Habermas' work depends on artificial Western categories of property and public space.

Second, Lisa Wedeen (2008), in her work on participatory politics in Yemen, argues that qat chews in Yemen function as spaces for the formation of democratic persons and for public deliberation even if they exist outside public spaces inside an authoritarian regime. Qat chews, occurring outside the European bourgeois context, are instead tied to hierarchical tribal decision-making processes that existed as part of the governing structures in society. If Wedeen (2008: 105) is correct, then spaces for opinion formation can exist because local governing authorities intervene to create them in "conditions fundamentally different from the ones Habermas identified as seminal in Western Europe." Wedeen (2008: 113) argues that qat chews satisfy the two main requirements of Habermas' theory: in them, citizens engage in critical discussion, and they play a mediating role that legitimates government decisions. Inside qat chews, political consultations occur between elites and citizens engage in mediated discussions by exchanging information through the exchange of information about contemporary events (Wedeen, 2008: 114).

Third, other writers have recently attempted to locate the existence of a transnational Islamic public sphere beyond the control of authoritarian governments. They argue that the spread of communication technology in the twentieth century created a transnational public with access to common information that changed the relationship between governments and their citizens while simultaneously changing the location of the public. With its advent, authoritarian regimes have been forced to justify their actions in response to criticism raised in *fora* beyond their control (Salvatore and Eickelman, 2004: 9). Moreover, the structure of the internet possesses (at least superficially) characteristics similar to the classical public sphere. It offers readily accessible material and allows for open dialogue while circumventing national authority (Anderson and Gonzalez-Quinjano, 2004: 53). Simultaneously, mass emigration has created diasporic publics, the existence of which has made it even more difficult for governments to censor discourse (Anderson and Gonzalez-Quinjano, 2004: 66). In sum, the argument being made is not that Habermas' model of legitimation through discourse is deficient, but instead that the distinction between private and public is too narrowly conceived, that the distinction between public and government is overly exclusionary, or that new technology requires changes to the model.

250   *K.W. Gray*

I think this point is worth stressing: the argument made by these theorists is not that we should eliminate the claim that legitimation occurs through discourse, but that the place of discourse in society has been conceived of too narrowly. In other words, these theorists have *not* shown that we require an expensive reading of the scope of the public sphere, but that we need to allow, in our theory of civil society, for other spaces of discourse within a public sphere whose goal is legitimation. The result of these criticisms has been the wholesale expansion of the public sphere beyond what any critical theorist ever intended, with unfortunate results.

The complicated relationship of the public sphere to civil society

Central to civil society's role in legitimating the state has to be the role the public sphere plays in controlling the economy and the government (Cohen and Arato, 1992: 411). However, the relationship between civil society and the public sphere requires modulating the structure of the public sphere somewhat to take into account the role that associations play in the modern world. Unlike in Habermas' early work, where the public sphere was assumed to be composed merely of individuals, contemporary work has tended to view organizations as inheritors of the role individuals might otherwise play in legitimating state decisions and in opinion formation. This modulation of the theory captures the important insight that there are multiple public spheres (what Fraser calls weak micro-publics) that contest, advocate for, and legitimate government decisions (Fraser, 1990: 74). These public spheres are composed of civil society actors, who act independently of state and economy to form a realm of contestatory politics.

However, the criticism of public sphere theory which I discussed above has, in my view, led to a tendency to expand the definition of civil society to include any organization that is involved in policy discussion, and has tended to obscure the importance of democratic deliberation as a key component of civil society. Theorists have seemed to say: if the public sphere has been defined too narrowly, then why not define any group that is involved in discussing, criticizing, or suggesting government policy as a civil society organization? I believe, on the contrary that, to paraphrase Vickie Langohr (2004), there has been too much emphasis placed on civil society and not enough on politics. Political scientists and policymakers have tended to adopt a field-of-dreams approach to civil society: if you build it, a democratic polity will emerge.

The failure to theorize properly what it is civil society should do has been reflected in the difficulty in defining which actors comprise civil society. This is manifested in two ways. First, in the literature on authoritarian regimes in the Middle East and South Asia, there has been an unfortunate tendency to assume that, because democratic polities do not exist, civil society can function in only one of two ways. For example, in his work on Moroccan civil society, James Sater is often guilty of assuming that civil society can serve only one of two

Reconsidering two myths about civil society 251

tasks: either it is a region of society opposed to the state (it contests state power), or it is a region of state hegemony (à la Gramsci) where the state can advance its own power through civil associations (Sater, 2007). Similarly, John L. Esposito (2003: 87), in his work on political Islam, argues that neo-Islamist parties are important not because they encourage legitimation through discourse, but because they encourage the lower and middle classes to become involved in politics and to contest state power. In so doing, he ignores the role civil society plays in opinion formation, preferring instead to focus on the role of neo-Islamist groups in challenging state hegemony. In both cases, civil society actors are assumed to either be means to change in government or an extension of the state's power. Such an approach may make sense in the context of authoritarian states, where questions of legitimation may realistically be put on the back-burner while actors agitate for greater political freedom; they do nothing however to explain what it is that we want civil society to accomplish or to explain why the term is analytically useful (Kamali, 2005).

The first myth, therefore, that we should abandon is that civil society is composed of any actors that are (even nominally) not part of the state or the economy. Second, too often the tendency in the literature has been to treat civil society merely as a region of society that is, in some marginal way, not directly part of the government bureaucracy (sometimes even including political parties) and not part of the private household (where the household is understood in the most minimalist way possible), with little or no attention paid to what we actually expect civil society to accomplish. This was the critique I advanced above of the liberal model of civil society. Very little work of which I am aware has focused on the actual nature of discourse in civil society. To embrace this myth is to argue, contrary to the account I presented, that deliberation does not matter in civil society and to argue that legitimation is irrelevant to our definition. This process of discounting deliberation has other deleterious effects. After all, if you are blind to deliberation, then you are de facto blind to its pathologies.

However, if the legitimating role to be played by civil society has been a *lacuna* in contemporary empirical work in political science, it is not the case that it has been ignored by all political theorists. Beginning with the assumption that civil society must not merely allow for the aggregation of individual preferences, but instead should encourage dialogue to aid in opinion formation, in their *Civil Society and Political Theory*, Jean Cohen and Andrew Arato (1992) discuss the necessary properties that civil society must possess for open communication to take place. Cohen and Arato argue that if we are prepared to take seriously the idea that discourse, rather than power, should aid in the legitimation of society, then discourse in civil society must possess four qualities. Civil society should possess: (1) appropriate conditions of plurality (including the presence of a variety of groups); (2) conditions of publicity (the presence of institutions of culture and communication); (3) a concept of privacy (a delineation between the domain of individual self-development and moral choice, and the necessary political norms for the ordering of society); and (4) legal structures, including positive law, that protects the rights of the individual (Cohen and Arato, 1992: 346).

252 K.W. Gray

Cohen and Arato's discourse-theoretic formulation of civil society has the advantage of capturing some of the more important insights about what it is we expect civil society to do: namely, to encourage democratic debate rather than merely to act in opposition to, or in concert with, the state's wishes. Their work also points to a series of weaknesses in other work on civil society – a tendency to ignore the conditions that would allow for civil society to function. I believe that Cohen and Arato provide a useful corrective to the attempts to enlarge the definition of civil society at the expense of the requirement that civil society legitimate government by allowing all to participate in politics

Continuing my attempt to diagnose the pathologies of literature on civil society, I wish to ask: Would the presence of all four conditions, outlined by Cohen and Arato, be sufficient to guarantee a functioning civil society, or are there other social conditions that must be satisfied? Since much recent work on civil society has eviscerated the concept of civil society of its normative components, preferring to focus instead on the relationship of civil society organizations to state, there is little scholarship of which I am aware that has studied the ways in which discourse occurs inside civil society between individuals, or between individuals and the state.

In Habermas' work, civil society was conceived of as a region of individuals coming together to debate policy. Legitimation occurred through processes of argument that involved the exchange of reasons and ethical claims rather than the assertion of interest positions. I showed above how this concept has been criticized as being the expansion of the patriarchal bourgeois household into a model of public discourse (only some people are allowed to participate), and therefore has been assumed to be exclusionary (Cohen and Arato, 1992: 216). On that telling, this model suffers from the deficiency of assuming the universality of European bourgeois patriarchal relations. This manifests itself in two ways: first, membership conditions in the public sphere are overly exclusionary, excluding women, the proletariat, etc. from deliberation. Nonetheless, I believe that problem can easily be fixed by relaxing membership conditions within the theory of the public sphere or by introducing group actors (civil society organization, etc.) who can help the subaltern gain access to public spheres. However, this is not the only way the model might be exclusionary. Not only does Habermas' model de facto exclude certain types of people, it may make assumptions about publicness and location that serve to systematically exclude certain types of public spheres that exist in other societies. For instance, Wedeen's discussion of qat chews and Chakrabarty's discussion of Bengali civil society both suggest that public sphere discourse can emerge in locations, such as inside private homes, that Habermas would have said were insufficiently public to be called part of civil society. Discussions of the internet's role of creating public spheres suggest that new technology leads to new public spheres in the Middle East and South Asia.

I believe that these theorists are guilty of assuming that any social structure where debate can occur is part of civil society or the public sphere if there are no direct vertical power relations. By this I mean that if a structure has no rigid

Reconsidering two myths about civil society 253

hierarchy, and if all are allowed to be present (if not heard), then a structure is sufficiently open to be part of civil society. There are a number of reasons why this attempt to extend the scope of the public sphere and, by extension, civil society goes too far. First, many of the groups that thinkers whom I discussed above classify as civil society organizations can better be classified as governmental or business organizations than NGOs properly speaking. These NGOs are, in Halliday's words, "self-righteous at best, elitist at worst" (cited in Challand, 2009: 29). They include so-called BINGOs (Business-influenced NGOs), RINGOs (Reactionary NGOs), and even GINGOs (Government-Influenced NGOs). It is not clear that we want to view these organizations as sources of legitimation inside society as their *raison d'être* is not to encourage dialogue so much as to advance state hegemony or the interests of economic actors. Second, attempts to develop or to reform civil society, in much of the developing world, are tied to a large international aid industry and, to a large extent, reflect the interests of these international actors. Participation in civil society often depends on an actor willing to toe the donor's line (Challand, 2009). Third, because these NGOs are often working in authoritarian political systems, they often have to enter into a pact with the state to depoliticize as part of a pact with the state to avoid entering into politics. If as a condition of functioning, NGOs are required to stay out of politics and engage only in the development of infrastructure, schools, hospitals, etc., then they cannot be said to be legitimating the state in the appropriate way.

Each one of these important critiques stresses the fact that there are often external checks on the actions of civil society actors: they are coerced into towing a specific line, either for or against the government. Moreover, I do not believe that the focus on external constrains exhaust potential pathologies that might emerge within civil society or that Cohen and Arato's four conditions exhaust the requirements for coercion-free discourse. Underlying their formulation of the conditions that would allow for civil society to emerge is an incomplete theorization, I believe, of how discourse in the public sphere needs to occur in order that it be appropriately legitimating.

My objection is that the expansion of civil society has not only tended to exaggerate the scope of civil society, but that there is almost no discussion of the literature of the difference between a rational and an empirical consensus. The concept of a Habermasian ideal speech situation and the grounding it provides to ethical discourse is largely ignored in the political theory literature. And yet, the concept of the ideal speech situation provides us with an important guide to what discourse requires. Foremost, there is, as I mentioned, no discussion of how agreement should be arrived at in civil society, nor is there a discussion of the distinction between rational as opposed to empirical consensus (the sort of consensus that might be tainted by power relations). Such considerations necessitate the sharing of reasons between individuals and groups in dialogue, and will-formation that is a result of dialogue (Cohen and Arato, 1992: 346). They presume the give and take of argumentation among equals. Rational consensus, conversely, is consensus brought about by structures of power, strategic action, unjust compromise, etc.

254   *K.W. Gray*

Returning to Wedeen's work (2008: 111) on civil society in Yemen, she identifies a number of important features of qat chews that, she believes, makes them de facto agents of legitimation in Yemeni civil society in the absence of electoral contestation. The sessions provide an opportunity to exchange information among community members, and to discuss recent mosque sermons that also form part of the discourse in civil society. Despite the fact that such sessions are indicative of flawed democratic practices by systematically excluding women, they allow for various members of society to exchange points of view (Wedeen, 2008: 121). However, it does not seem to me that listing the exclusion of women and the presence of overt hierarchies (e.g., seating arrangements in qat chews, which, to her credit, Wedeen mentions) exhausts the list of potential problems (Wedeen, 2008: 126). Wedeen fails to account for power dynamics at play inside these micro-publics. In the final section, I will discuss my own research as a way of illustrating this problem and will discuss pathologies of deliberation in Afghanistan.

What community organizations and democratic discourse in Afghanistan should tell us about deliberation

In my work on civil society in Afghanistan, I have been interested in whether or not discourse in the public arena acts in such a way as to enable civil society to serve its legitimating function. I will use that work as an example of some of the flaws in the attempt to generalize Habermas' theory. I will argue that even if Cohen and Arato's first four conditions were satisfied, they would not exhaust the requirements for coercion-free discourse.

I believe that it is helpful, in discussing pathologies of deliberation, to place those pathologies along a continuum of overt and covert exclusionary practices that manifest themselves in civil society. In the first instance, some people are overtly excluded from participating in civil society (as we saw women are in Yemeni qat chews). We see similar overt practices of exclusion, including gender segregation in contemporary institutions of Afghan civil society.

Unsurprising, there is strong gender segregation in traditional Afghan society. Gender segregation in Afghanistan does not entail that women have no means of influencing public debate (there are many ways in which they can). It does mean, however, that as a general proposition, in one analyst's words, Afghan society gives "patent ideological support to male authority over women in the public domain" (Harpviken *et al.*, 2002: 12). In public debate, women are expected to defer to men; all are supposed to defer to the elderly.

To the extent that women are included in public spheres, these spheres often exist as part of, not opposed to, prevailing norms of gender segregation, and may include spaces inside the home that are constituted exclusively by women. "The cultural norm of gender segregation, *purdah*, creates separate all-female forums and affects the strategy women and girls use to build networks for public influence in civil society" (Harpviken *et al.*, 2002: 12). Moreover, the work of women's NGOs is often severely hampered by overt social exclusion. For

Reconsidering two myths about civil society   255

instance, when women activists wish to make contact in other regions of the country, it is often the case that they need introduction through links based on kinship. In large segments of society, it is unacceptable for women to travel outside the community (and sometimes even the home) without the presence of men. The most radical example of this was the "infamous *mahram* decree of the Taliban" which focused on an unusually restrictive interpretation of the concept of guardianship and required women in public to be accompanied by a male relative (Harpviken *et al.*, 2002: 12).

Such overt processes of exclusion mirror what has been observed by other theorists in other regions. However, what interests me more than the overt processes of exclusion that attend civil society in the Middle East are the concomitant processes of covert exclusion. These include the systematic exclusion of some participants from speaking even if they are present, from having their arguments heard or from challenging the claims of participants who enjoy high social standing. For these reasons, several thinkers have argued that the idea of civil society has little or no applicability to the Arab Middle East, since the appropriate political freedoms and autonomy vis-à-vis the state and the individual are lacking (Bishara, 1996). For instance, Azmi Bishara, former Arab-Israeli politician and political scientist, argues that the lack of rights manifests itself in overt exclusionary processes designed to prevent individuals from participating in a fully vibrant public sphere. However, processes of covert exclusion, he argues, operate in Arab society that prevent individuals from acting as autonomous agents in a society that is prepared to accept that there are legitimate differences of opinions and ways to express them. While Bishara's understanding of the scope of civil society is very limited, he raises the important problems posed by social norms that prevent individuals from expressing themselves even if they have access to the institutions of civil society.

I believe that we can follow Bishara's critique and identify four covert exclusionary practices that operate inside civil society in the Middle East. First, in both informal and formal decision-making bodies, we see the voices of women ignored or silenced, even if women are present in those associations. Too often the emphasis has been on merely creating public space. NGOs working in the field and foreign governments funding their work often thought it enough to have institutions put into place where participants could interact; little thought was put into how the participants inside them should interact.

In recent work on democratic deliberation in Afghanistan, researchers have focused on public deliberation in two separate fora: first, inside traditional Shura (Islamic councils), and second, inside Village Organizations (VOs) and Community Development Councils (CDCs). Shura have a long history in Afghanistan. They have been used as dispute resolution mechanisms (sometimes with the mediation of local Imams) to solve disputes between neighboring tribes and communities (Haroon, 2007). VOs and CDCs were formed after the American invasion by granting agencies to serve as local advisory councils to oversee the dispersal of funds, particularly moneys coming from the National Solidarity Program (which granted US$200 to every household for infrastructure development). In many cases, they are not the weak publics Nancy Fraser speaks of, as

256   *K.W. Gray*

they are constituted by the national government or foreign aid organizations. However, they are useful settings to study public deliberation.

As one prominent Afghan research group, Afghanistan Research and Evaluation Unit (AREU), has pointed out, foreign NGOs in Afghanistan and foreign donors have often focused merely on quantifiable measures of access to Shuras, VOs, and CDCs in order to measure the success of their funding programs, and ignore whether or not these institutions are truly democratic and whether or not all groups have access to these councils. Too often, the symbolic participation of women in public institutions is seen as a measure of success. Tangible indicators such as the creation of physical space for women or the numbers of women present at public activities are used to demonstrate the achievement of gender equality (Wakefield and Bauer, 2005).

The hope in establishing VOs and CDCs was that they would be more inclusive. VOs tend to have female members whereas traditional Shuras tend to be composed, almost exclusively, of male elders. However, it is not clear that VOs and CDCs are any better at serving marginalized groups than older Shura. For example, AREU research in rural Samangan province showed that:

> [T]he NGO-established VO and the traditional Shura were markedly similar, both in terms of local power dynamics as well as notions of what benefits the VO could bring to the community. This situation suggests that there may not be much interest locally in changing the existing power dynamics to correspond with principles of participation and equity outlined in the NGO's mandate.
>
> (Wakefield and Bauer, 2005: 5)

Status relations in the community, jobs, relationships to prominent men, etc. color the degree to which reasons can be put forward, or someone can participate in a Shura. In other words, the ability to participate even in NGO-established Shuras depends on social rank and standing in a way not anticipated by NGOs working to establish civil society organizations.

In my own interviews with Afghan female parliamentarians, a common concern expressed to me is that while they are present in the parliament chamber, and are (occasionally) allowed to vote, their political positions seem to have little effect in rising above the din. Their discourse is largely ignored, they feel. In some cases the processes of exclusion are relatively overt – including male parliamentarians shouting "where is your head scarf?" or "you should feel shame" if the women are not seen as appropriately dressed.[2]

Similarly, in the January 2010 London Conference, according to Human Rights Watch, Afghan women

> were provided no official designation to feed into decisions nor negotiate conclusions. In an event that spanned an entire day and included more than 70 countries, only a single Afghan woman was included to speak as part of the official agenda, co-presenting the concerns of Afghan civil society.
>
> (HRW, 2010)

Reconsidering two myths about civil society 257

At a subsequent conference, the so-called June 2010 Consultative Peace Jirga, women were more successful at guaranteeing representation; 330 women, out of an estimated 1,600 people, participated in the conference (21 percent). However, statistics can be misleading. Several prominent women activists argued that they had been deliberately excluded from the jirga because they were too outspoken about women's rights prior to the assembly. Similarly, when "the jirga broke into 28 committees, with approximately 20 percent women's representation on each[,] [o]nly one woman acted as a committee chair, and very few women were given the chance to speak" (HRW, 2010). If the requirement is mere presence, then Afghanistan could be said to possess a fully inclusive public sphere. But in these cases, what we see is that being present is not a condition for a functioning civil society.

Second, a civil society institution must be the area of society where decisions are actually made. My earlier rejection of the state hegemonic and contestatory models of civil society hinged on their being distinct from power structures in society and able to make decisions on their own. In the case of gender, "[w] omen may be present at the table, but is this where decisions are made? Do those in the room have any authority to challenge decisions made if they do not agree with them?" (Wakefield and Bauer, 2005: 5). Only if the institutions possess the appropriate authority to make decisions and if these decisions are not made behind closed doors later (which is a concern that some Afghan parliamentarians have expressed to me) can a public sphere serve its function.

Third, gender norms created the apprehension that actors do not act sincerely in public debate. Women are often assumed to speak to an issue because of their gender, as members of minority religious and ethnic groups are assumed to be in favor of or opposed to an issue because they must necessarily be speaking as representatives of their gender. Men are assumed to vote one way because of their gender and women another. In the study by AREU, where researchers inter-viewed Afghan lawmakers:

> It was often stated by women that "men make the final decisions anyway because they are in the majority," implying a collective stance among men. Such a statement denotes not only a perception of relative powerlessness against a majority block, but also a perceived opposition between men and women. Thus, regardless of whether women do share interests on the basis of their gender, there is a general assumption that they ought to share these interests. There may well be differences between women, and between men, but essentially a strong gender divide between the interests of women and men is perceived, and this divide is seen (by some women at least) to deter-mine men's final authority in parliament.
>
> (Wordsworth, 2007: 7)

Women parliamentarians sometimes complain about being unable to participate because they cannot remain anonymous. This perhaps sounds unusual, given that the goal of encouraging female representation is to allow for women to be

258   K.W. Gray

present as women to address women's concerns. However, sometimes it is easier to make arguments if your background *is not known*. If you are always seen as a woman (or as a Shiite, or an Uzbek, or whatever), then people may ignore what you say (because you are speaking as a woman, a Shiite, or an Uzbek). In such cases, to have your argument heard, it is *better to hide* aspects of your identity.

Fourth, the norms of discourse demand relative independence in terms of the arguments that participants can make. Bishara thematizes this as the recognition of participants as autonomous agents free to make their own arguments and the broad social acceptance of a plurality of viewpoints. In my interviews with female parliamentarians in Afghanistan, several remarked that they are forced to frame their arguments in terms of Islam (even if it is the historical understanding of Islam they are going against) because "Islam is a common frame of reference" for all Afghans.

This is evidenced in recent debate over the age of marriage in Afghanistan. A recent law in Afghanistan (recently passed by parliament) proposed to raise the minimum age of marriage. Girls in parts of Afghanistan have traditionally married very young. The law would raise the minimum age of marriage and deny marriage licenses to couples when one party was under-age. Several male parliamentarians objected that this was un-Islamic and argued that the Prophet Mohammed married Aisha when she was seven years old.[3] Rather than argue that it was wrong to marry a seven-year-old or that a girl at that age could not consent or that the example of the Prophet was not relevant in the modern world (where continued schooling is important), the women argued that the example of the Prophet was inapplicable in this particular case. They argued that the Prophet merely assumed guardianship of Aisha when she was seven and that he only married her (or at least consummated the marriage) when she was much older.

The argument did seem to be effective (or at the very least provide a cover for men to vote for the law). The effectiveness of the argument aside, it points to another problem in discourse. There are certain third-rails in Afghan society that cannot be touched. The arguments that participants can put forward are constrained by these rules, which provide a discursive field in which participants must operate.

Conclusion

Following my discussion of the dynamics of public spheres in Afghanistan and elsewhere in the Middle East, I have suggested that we need to approach with caution the claims of researchers to have found a cornucopia of civic organizations that function as part of civil society. Instead, I have argued that function determines form with regard to civil society.

In general, there are two particular myths that are advanced: first, that any organizations that appear nominally independent of business and the government are part of civil society, and, second, that any dialogue encouraged by these structures is part of the public sphere. I have argued that this model is blind to the role of civil society and that the mere inclusion of members of the population

Reconsidering two myths about civil society 259

of different social status, religion, ethnicity, gender, etc. is insufficient to ensure that public deliberation can occur.

To Cohen and Arato's four conditions for the existence of civil society, I proposed to add four more of my own. First, the mere presence of all members of society in social structures is not enough to ensure a vibrant public sphere. Second, strong and weak publics must actually be places where decisions are made. Third, participants must be viewed as, and view others, as individuals who participate in discourse independent of specific social roles. Four, participants must not be able to rely on cultural mores to silence debate in the public sphere and to exclude the marginalized.

I began the chapter by investigating the relationship between civil society and the public sphere. In so doing, I challenged the broad definition of civil society that has been assumed in literature on democratization. In particular, I argued that the two dominant models of civil society (the state-hegemonic, and the contestatory) failed to capture the relationship between civil society and legitimation. Moreover, theorists have been blind, even in their rush to expand the public sphere, to power relations in civil society. Only a re-theoretization of the relationship between civil society and the public sphere could help us to identify pathologies of civil society in the region.

Notes

1 For this reason, it has become standard to refer to these organizations as micro-publics that, combined, form the public sphere.
2 All interviews with Afghan female parliamentarians occurred in Kabul in May 2010. My thanks to Dr. Bahar Jalali for helping to arrange these interviews and for her help with some translations. I have chosen not to name the parliamentarians interviewed for safety reasons.
3 Aisha's exact age is unclear but she was undoubtedly quite young by modern standards.

References

Anderson, J. and Y. Gonzalez-Quijano (2004) 'Technological mediation and the emergence of transnational Muslim publics' in Armando Salvatore and Dale Eickelman (eds.) *Public Islam and the Common Good*, Leiden: Brill.
Arendt, H. (1958) *The Human Condition*, Chicago: University of Chicago Press.
Bishara, A. (1996) *Democracy and Pluralism*, Ramallah: MUWATIN.
Chakrabarty, D. (2000) *Provincialising Europe: postcolonial thought and historical difference*, Princeton: Princeton University Press.
Challand, B. (2009) *Palestinian Civil Society: foreign donors and the power to promote and exclude*, London: Routledge.
Cohen, J. and A. Arato (1992) *Civil Society and Political Theory*, Cambridge: MIT Press.
Esposito, J. (2003) 'Islam and civil society' in John Esposito and Francois Burgat (eds.) *Modernising Islam*, Piscataway: University of Rutgers Press.
Fraser, N. (1990) 'Rethinking the public sphere: a contribution to the critique of actually existing democracy,' *Social Text*, 25/26.

260   *K.W. Gray*

Habermas, J. (1962[1991]) *The Structural Transformation of the Public Sphere*, Cambridge: Cambridge University Press.

Haroon, S. (2007) *Frontier of Faith: Islam in the Indo-Afghan borderland*, London: Hurst and Company.

Harpviken, K.B., A. Strand, and K. Ask (2002) *Afghanistan and Civil Society*, Peshawar and Bergen: The Norwegian Ministry of Foreign Affairs.

Human Rights Watch (2010) *The Ten Dollar Talib and Women's Rights*, Washington DC: HRW.

Kamali, M. (2005) *Multiple Modernities: civil society and Islam*, Liverpool: Liverpool University Press.

Kluge, A. and O. Negt (1990) *Offentlickeit und Erfahrung: Zur Organisationsanalyse von burgerlicher und proletariuscher Offentlickheit*, Frankfurt am Main: Suhrkamp.

Landes, J. (1988) *Women and the Public Sphere in the Age of the French Revolution*, Ithaca: Cornell University Press.

Langohr, V. (2004) 'Too much civil society, too little politics: the case of Egypt and the Arab liberalizers,' *Comparative Politics*, 36: 181–204.

Ryan, M. (1992) 'Gender and public access: women's politics in nineteenth-century America' in Craig Calhoun (ed.) *Habermas and the Public Sphere*, Cambridge: MIT Press.

Salvatore, A. and D. Eickelman (2004) 'Muslim publics' in Armando Salvatore and Dale Eickelman (eds.) *Public Islam and the Common Good*, Leiden: Brill.

Sater, J. (2007) *Civil Society and Political Change in Morocco*, London: Routledge.

Wakefield, S. and B. Bauer (2005) *A Place at the Table: women, men and decision-making authority*, Briefing Report, Afghan Research and Evaluation Unit, Kabul: AREU.

Wedeen, L. (2008) *Peripheral Visions: publics, power and performance in Yemen*, Chicago: University of Chicago Press.

Wordsworth, A. (2007) 'A matter of interests: gender and the politics of presence in Afghanistan's Wolesi Jirga,' Issue papers series, Kabul: AREU.

13 Conclusion

Francesco Cavatorta

Civil Society Activism under Authoritarian Rule: A Comparative Perspective provides readers with new theoretical and empirical insights into the relationship between civil society activism and authoritarian or liberal-authoritarian regimes. In the traditional literature on civil society, much is usually made of the supposed inextricable and almost natural linkage between civil society and democracy and democratization. Building on a growing literature attempting to problematize the inevitability of the link between civil activism and democracy or democratization, this volume offers a rather unique theoretical discussion about the meaning of civil society in addition to empirical evidence that illustrates how a more flexible definition of civil society can lead to a better understanding of how activism works under authoritarian or liberal-authoritarian constraints.

The definition of civil society that contributors used in this edited volume is very much a neutral one, along the lines of what has been suggested by Berman (1997, 2003) and Encarnacion (2006) and therefore it does not make any normative assumptions about the degree of 'goodness' of civil society activism in authoritarian and liberal-authoritarian settings. This approach to the study of civil society is not particularly innovative per se, but where the contributors make an important contribution to the literature is in the 'stretching' of the definition to include processes and actors that very rarely have been analysed. This 'stretching' of the definition has significant practical implications in terms of where to look for activism and what kind of activism to look for in non-democratic contexts. There are three specific areas where this stretched definition finds practical meaning.

First, the vast majority of contributors analyse forms of civil activism that go beyond formal hierarchical associations and organizations traditionally associated with civil society. What has emerged over the last decade and more recently with the outbreak of the Arab Spring is that traditional forms of associationalism no longer wholly define activism. Thus, focusing on groups that have a very clear hierarchical structure, a very well-defined leadership and legal status does not capture the dynamics that developed within society at large under authoritarian constraints. There is therefore the need to focus for instance on the activism of the individual, rehabilitating in some ways the figure of the dissenter who, in complete autonomy, decides to take up an issue and promotes it even under very difficult circumstances without having any linkage to routinized processes and organizations. This individual dissent, which seemed to be confined to intellectuals in the past, as Marlies Glasius describes in her contribution on political dissent in Eastern Europe and Latin America, can then find links through horizontal processes of connection with other like-minded individuals without having the necessity of setting up a formal organization. The multiplication of such forms of activism can then result in widespread civil activism that does not conform to the classic expectations of the literature on civil society, and this appears quite clearly in the contribution by Chomiak and Entelis for example when discussing non-hierarchical popular forms of engagement around football matches in Tunisia. In addition, this innovative understanding of activism permits the inclusion of non-traditional forms of expression such as the arts, a realm that authoritarian regimes have always attempted to control and direct in full knowledge that it can be the source of civil inspiration. The shift in focus from formal associations to horizontal and non-hierarchical forms is certainly greatly facilitated by new technologies, particularly social media. While it is important not to over-emphasize their role given that the Internet and social media are heavily policed by the authoritarian state in order to find out the different loci of dissent (Gladwell, 2010; Morozov, 2011), there is also no doubt that they constitute a significant development in terms of how society enters a dialogue with itself and with the institutions of the state, particularly in authoritarian contexts where other forms of expression and communications are closed off. While staying away from the assumption that social media have per se a democratizing potential as indicated in some quarters in the wake of the Arab uprisings, it is necessary to recognize that they are changing the way in which social mobilization, not necessarily linked to liberal or democratic demands, takes place. It is therefore in this new technological context that more diffuse, unstructured and non-hierarchical forms of association occur. Early studies of the Arab uprisings seem to confirm the validity of such a stretching out of the definition of civil society activism in so far as the expected civil society protagonists, namely human rights associations and politicized organizations, did not actually materialize at the helm of the protests, but simply followed the lead of movements that seemed to have appeared out of nothing as they existed only online prior to the early demonstrations (Aarts and Cavatorta, 2012). The contribution by Bert Hoffman on the Cuban case explores these issues extremely clearly and the Cuban case demonstrates how individual dissent can be a protagonist of civil activism once it migrates on-line, producing then process of linkages with other individuals with similar demands and issues. This on-line activism does not necessarily have to be successful in order to be important because it might take a long time to have a concrete effect on the political system and, paradoxically, does not even have to be about democratization as all sorts of issues that fall into the realm of society's interests can be discussed and tackled.

The second area in which the new theoretical understanding of civil society can be seen to have a rather potent application is the problematization of the

Conclusion 263

seemingly unquestioned assumption that activism in clearly non-political issues has, eventually, a positive spill-over effect on very political ones such as democratization and human rights. Looking at some of the cases under consideration in this volume, it emerges that at times this is indeed the case, but at others this is far from it. Adam Simpson provides a very convincing analysis as to how the focus on strictly environmental issues on the part of sectors of Burmese civil society, particularly on the part of those Burmese who live outside the country in the borderlands in Thailand, can and do over time transform into explicitly political demands for regime change and democratization. This is certainly facilitated by the very international nature of environmental activism and by the fact that the Burmese diaspora can express itself more freely, but there is another important element worth considering. In the Burmese case, the authoritarian state has been extremely reluctant to engage with such environmental issues and with the civil society representatives who have a profound interest in them. The case of Central Asia that Matteo Fumagalli explores in detail provides the opposite picture. Despite being potentially able to count on the support of foreign state entities, minorities tend to focus strictly on non-explicitly political issues such as language and cultural traditions without challenging in any way the authoritarian nature of the state in which they find themselves in as ethnic minorities. In this case civil society activism does not spill over into politics because such groups tend to be accommodating to the political system in so far as the state authorities engage with them or at least engage with some of their civil representatives. This means that where the state is also reasonably accommodating to specific non-political demands, civil society groups tend to look for voice and not choice, suggesting therefore that benefits can be obtained through engagement rather than confrontation and that being the privileged interlocutor matters more than guaranteeing equality of access to all associations and groups in society. Dynamics similar to the ones that Fumagalli describes are still in place for example in those countries of the Middle East and North Africa where authoritarianism has survived, precisely because the state seems to be more responsive to many non-political demands society is making and is able to pick interlocutors whose privileged links with state authorities allow them to operate, attain their objectives and augment social capital, much like Jamal (2007) had predicted. This is quite evident in the contributions that Janine Clark on Jordan and Vincent Durac on Yemen provide and that still retain considerable validity despite both countries having been, albeit to different degrees, rocked by the shockwaves of the Arab uprisings. The different outcomes that can be seen across different authoritarian cases on the assumption of the linkages and spill-over between non-political issues and explicitly political ones indicate that a multiplicity of potential roles are more suited to understand civil society activism.

The third area where a re-definition of the concept of civil society and civil activism becomes necessary is related to the public sphere. The assumption is that activism takes place in a relatively healthy public sphere, but this is quite a contradiction in authoritarian or liberal-authoritarian settings where the boundaries of the permissible within the public sphere and public debate are severely

264 F. Cavatorta

restricted and controlled. What does a healthy public sphere look like in an authoritarian regime? Traditionally, it is precisely the role assigned to civil society to enlarge the sphere of public and social engagement in authoritarian settings, but more modern and adaptable forms of authoritarian rule today (Heydemann, 2007) envisage the creation of rather unrestrained public spheres where legitimate and autonomous forms of civil society activism have to co-exist with state-sponsored forms of 'equally' civil activism rendering the challenge much more difficult than it might have been in the past. Within this public sphere it becomes much more complicated for external observers to precisely locate the kind of activism they are witnessing, as exemplified by the complexity of the Russian case examined in this edited collection. This complexity in identifying what one might label 'genuine civil society' has important policy-making repercussions in so far as building up civil society in authoritarian contexts is still one of the most preferred policies of the West-dominated international community.

This leads to the final point that this edited collection wishes to address. The rather pessimistic and highly complex picture of civil society activism in authoritarian and liberal-authoritarian settings corresponds certainly to the reality on the ground where civil activism does not alway provide the 'skills' to demand political democratization. As amply demonstrated, the traditional definition of civil society is no longer apt at understanding current dynamics whereby activism has to be looked for in *loci* that are outside the realm of formal associations and has to look at what the volume identifies as 'activated citizenship', which might not be necessarily pro-democratic. However, it is important to retain from this study that different outcomes are possible depending on the singular circumstances and that a classic role for civil society as agent of democratic political change can still occur, although not through the expected and traditional protagonists or processes.

References

Aarts, P. and F. Cavatorta (eds) (2012) *Civil Society in Syria and Iran: Activism in Authoritarian Contexts*, Boulder, CO: Lynne Rienner.

Berman, S. (1997) 'Civil Society and the Collapse of the Weimar Republic', *World Politics*, 47: 401–429.

Berman, S. (2003) 'Islamism, Revolution and Civil Society', *Perspectives on Politics*, 1: 257–272.

Encarnacion, O. (2006) 'Civil Society Reconsidered', *Comparative Politics*, 38: 357–376.

Gladwell, M. (2010) 'Why the Revolution Will Not Be Tweeted', *The New Yorker*, October 4: 42–49.

Heydemann, S. (2007) 'Upgrading Authoritarianism in the Arab World', The Brookings Institution, *Analysis Paper*, 13, pp. 1–37. Available at www.brookings.edu/~/media/Files/rc/papers/2007/10arabworld/10arabworld.pdf. Last accessed on 15April 2010.

Jamal, A. (2007) *Barriers to Democracy*, Princeton: Princeton University Press.

Morozov, E. (2011) *The Net Delusion: How Not to Liberate the World*, London: Allen Lane.

Index

Page numbers in *italics* denote tables, those in **bold** denote figures.

abono de familia 21
access, measures of 256
Acosta, Eliades 232–3
action, in art 67
Actions for Art Collective (CADA) (Chile) 65, 67
activated citizenship 2, 8–9, 181
activism: and associationalism 261–2; individual 261–2; politic al and non-political 263
activist diasporas 183, 188–9, 198–207; *see also* transnational activism
Acuto, M. 190
Aden 147; *see also* Yemen
advocacy, Yemen 149
aestheticism 68
Afghanistan 11; Community Development Councils (CDCs) 255–6; Consultative Peace Jirga 257; context and overview 245; deliberation 254–8; exclusion 254–5; gender segregation 254–5; marriage 258; measures of access 256; public sphere 254–8; Shura 255–6; status relations 256; summary and conclusions 258–9; Village Organizations (VOs) 255–6; women's participation 256–8
Afghanistan Research and Evaluation Unit (AREU) 256, 257
agora 246
Akaev, Askar 98
Al-Ghosheh, Abdullah 171
al-Momani, Mohammed 166, 172
Al-Mouatin 81
Allen, C. 138
Amenta, Edwin 29
amoral familism 13

anarchists, Portugal and Spain 19–20
anonymity 257–8
Anthias, F. 188
Arab spring, as democratization 4
Arab world, 'awakening of civil society' 1
Arato, Andrew 251–2, 253
Arendt, Hannah 37, 52, 137, 246
Arkoun, M. 140
art: confrontational 64–5; context and overview 57–8; as critical reflection 63–5; cultural policies 59–61; exasperation 67; exposing violence 65–6; instead of politics 68; as instrument of the political 58–63; marginality in 67–8; as means of expression 68–9; against the political 63–4; poverty in 67; as reflection of political 61; as refuge 68–9; repression 60; roles performed 58; summary and conclusions 69–70; use of body 66–8; *see also* Ceauçescu regime; Chile; Pinochet regime; Romania
art and politics, field of study 57–8
artists, as witnesses 63
arts 262
aspirations, dissident writing 48–9, 53
Association of South East Asian Nations 185
associational autonomy 223–7, 230
associationalism, and activism 261–2
associations, hierarchical 9
Associations Law (Yemen) 147
associative democracy 137–8
atomization 38–9, 52, 60
Aung Ngyeh 193, 200, 202
authoritarian backlash, Central Asia 95–6
authoritarian corporatism 111–12

266 *Index*

authoritarian regimes, liberalized 3
authoritarian systems: behavioural
repertoires 221; corporate-
authoritarianism 76; destructive
aspirations 37; institutions and support
6–7; motivation 51–2; reforms 2; state
and non-state actors 112; state-society
relations 4–8; variations in 2, 5–6; *see
also* Afghanistan; Central Asia; Chile;
Cuba; Jordan; Myanmar; Portugal and
Spain; Romania; Russian Federation;
Tunisia; Uzbeks; Yemen
authoritarianism: reinforced by civil
society activism 3–4; South America 36;
weakening 1
auto-totality 79
autonomy, associational 223–7, 230
Avanzada 65
Azcuy, Hugo 224

Bachelard, Gaston 73
Baikalsk pulp and paper mill 126
Banfield, Edward C. 13
bargaining 160–1
Batyov, Kadyrjan 101, 102–3
Bauer, B. 256
Bayat, Asef 78
Ben Ali regime, as paradoxical 75–7
Ben Ali, Zine El Abidine 73, 79
Benda, Vaclav 38–9, 41, 43, 48
Berkeley, California 74
Berman, S. 139–40, 261
Bin Shamlan, Faisal 146
Bishara, Azmi 255, 258
blacklisting 172
Bloggers Cuba 235
blogging, Cuba 233–5, 236, 238
Blumi, I. 144
Boas, T. 228
body, in art 66–8
Bone, Rudolph 66–7
borderlands 187, 189–90, 203–4
Borges, George Luis 13
boundaries, fuzzy 9
Bourguiba, Habib 75–6, 82
Bourguiba regime 75–7
Brandys, Kazimierz 38, 46
Brătescu, Geta 67
Brazil, conceptions of democracy 50–1
Bretton Woods institutions 137
Brigada Muralista Ramona Parra 64–5
Browers, M. 140–1
Brunner, J.J. 63
Burma Rivers Network 199, 200, 202

Burmese diaspora 9, 187–90, 198–205,
263; *see also* Myanmar

Caetano, Marcello 22
café culture, Tunisia 84
capitalism, and social change 247
Carapico, Sheila 142, 144, 147
Cardoso, Fernando Henrique 36, 37, 49, 50
Cârneci, M. 62
Carothers, T. 4
Castells, Manuel 28, 203
Castro, Fidel 222
Castro, Mariela 236
Castro, Raúl 226, 232
Catholic Church: Cuba 222, 236–7;
welfare role 21
caudillismo 36
Ceauçescu, Nicolae 57
Ceauçescu regime: cultural policies 60;
economic policies 60; use of art 58–9
censorship 60, 80–1
Center for American Studies (Cuba) 224,
226
Central Asia 9, 263; authoritarian backlash
95–6; context and overview 94–5; data
sources 96; ethnic politics 97–8;
opposition politics 96; shift in focus of
civil society 95; structure of ethnic
politics 99; summary and conclusions
107–8; Uzbek activism and ethno-
politics 99–107; Uzbek ethnic cultural
organizations 100–3; *see also* ethnic
minority politics
"Centre of Ethnic Culture" (Krasnodar)
122
Chabal, P. 138
Chakrabarty, Dipesh 249, 252
Charitable Society for Social Welfare
(Yemen) 148
Charter 77 41, 44–5
Chatterjee, Partha 18
Chile: centralization of power 59;
feminists 50; mass culture 61; politics of
art 62–3; popular music 62; television
62–3; transition to democracy 57; *see
also* art; dissident writing; Pinochet
regime
China, Internet 227
choice 263
Chomiak, Laryssa 10, 262
cinema, Romania 62
Cioroianu, A. 61–2
citizenship: from below 9; changing vision
of 16; defining 15–16; everyday

Index 267

citizenship 15–18; insurgent citizenship 18, 26
civil activism, theoretical conceptualizations 1
civil society: approaches to study 261; defining 14, 261; and democracy 138–40; and democratization 3–8; as distinct from civil society organizations 139; expectations 152; as ideologically loaded 137–8; Middle East 140–3; models of 246–8; necessary properties 251, 259; as neutral 3; as political space 15; as prerequisite of democratization 14–15; and public sphere 250–4; and regime change 139; rethinking 8–11; revival of interest 245–6; theoretical diversity 136–7
civil society activism, Myanmar 186–7
Civil Society and Political Theory (Cohen and Arato) 251–2
Civil Society in Yemen: The Political Economy of Activism 147
civil society organizations: as distinct from civil society 139; governmental or business organizations 253; Middle East 141; registration, Yemen 147–8; *see also* NGOs
Clark, Janine 9, 10, 263
Cleary, S. 188
coalitions, transnational activism 199–200
codification of law 247
coffee shops 247
Cohen, Jean 251–2, 253
collective identity 236
colour revolutions 53, 95–6
commonality 16
communication technology, public sphere 249
Community Development Councils (CDCs), Afghanistan 255–6
Community Development Programme (Myanmar) 188
constructivist dictatorships 37–8
Consultative Peace Jirga (Afghanistan) 257
Contardo, O. 63
corporate-authoritarianism, Tunisia 76
counter-culture, Tunisia 76–7
critical theory, and public sphere 245–8
Cuba 8–9, 10–11, 262; blogging 233–5, 236, 238; Catholic Church 222, 236–7; civil society in 1990s 223–7; conceptions of civil society 223–4; constitution 222; context and overview

219–21; control of Internet 221–2, 228; e-mail 231–3; effects of Castro's ill-health 228; film-making 229–30; Internet use 220; joining Internet 227–8; mass media 222; media as political challenge 227, 238; music 230; NGOs 224–6; Operation Truth 234; *polémica intelectual* 231–2, 235–6; process of institutionalization 222; public space 222; state control strategies 225; state-society relations 222; summary and conclusions 237–8; voice to action 235–7
Cuban revolution 222
Cultural Centre of Uzbeks of Tajikistan 100
cultural policies 59–61
culture of citizenship 140
Cyclone Nargis 185, 202

Daloz, J.P. 138
Dammed by Burma's Generals 202
Damming at Gunpoint 200–1
dams 192; *see also* Myanmar; Salween Dams
de Rivera, Primo 25
debate, polarization of 5
Del Llano, Eduardo 230
deliberation 254–8
della Porta, D. 203, 204
democracy: associative democracy 137–8; and civil society 138–40; and civil society activism 1–2; dissident writing 48–9; sustainability 53; versions 50–1
democratic criteria 4
democratic deliberation 250
democratic institutionalism, models 59
democratic practices, dissident writing 50–1
democratization 219; and civil society 3–8; and civil society activism 1–2; empirical evidence 5; timing of 47–8; transition paradigm 4
dependency theory 46
determinism 14
developmentalism: and housing 25–6; Portugal and Spain 21–2
Dewey, John 137
Diago, Alejandro 40–1
Diamond, Larry 8
Diani, M. 203, 204
diasporas: activist 183; Burmese *see* Burmese diaspora ; public spheres 249; use of term 188

268 *Index*

dictatorship, as obscuring term 36
dictatorships: atomization 38–9;
  constructivist 37–8; ideology 37–8;
  nature of 36; realist 37
Dienstbier, Jiri 43, 49, 51
disability, Russian Federation 117–18,
  123–5
discursive power 78
dissent: individual 262; Myanmar 186
dissident writing: appeal to law 44–5, 52;
  aspirations 48–9, 53; atomization 38–9;
  constructivist dictatorships 37–8;
  context and overview 34–5; democratic
  practices 50–1; features of proto-civil
  society 39–44; human rights 44–5, 52;
  on independence 43; and international
  community 45–6; internationalism
  52–3; living in the truth 40–1; non-
  violence 42–3; on organizational forms
  43–4; plurality 41–2; realist
  dictatorships 37; self-identification
  46–7; solidarity 39–40; sources 35–6;
  Soviet Union 78; strategies and
  aspirations 44–51, 53; summary and
  conclusions 51–3; timing of
  democratization 47–8; Tunisia 86;
  understanding regimes 36–9
divided soul 79
Doherty, B. 206
Dorfman, Ariel 37–8, 39, 41, 43, 45, 46, 47
Downey, Juan 65
Dragomir, Lucia 68
Durac, Vincent 9, 263

e-mail, Cuba 231–3
Eastern Europe 3, 262; *see also* dissident
  writing
economic activity, public sphere 246–7
Economic Houses (Portugal) 25
Edwards, M. 136–7
Egypt 160
Ei Tu Hta camp (Myanmar) 181, 187
El Ghobashy, Mona 159, 160–1
elections: Myanmar 182; Portugal and
  Spain 14; Yemen 144–5
Electricity Generating Authority of
  Thailand (EGAT) 190, 192, 197, 198
Eltit, Diamela 64, 66
Encarnacion, O. 261
Entelis, John P. 10, 262
Environmental Impact Assessments:
  Myanmar 185; Russian Federation
  126–7; Salween Dams 197
environmental law, violation 126–7

environmental policy, Russian Federation
  114, 115, 116, 118, 119, 126–9
environmental politics: academic literature
  182; Myanmar 183–7, 263
"Escena de Avanzada" 65
Esposito, John L. 251
ethnic cultural organizations 100–3
ethnic divisions, authoritarian systems 7
ethnic minorities, Myanmar 185
ethnic minority politics: data sources 96;
  spaces of engagement 96; summary and
  conclusions 107–8; Uzbek activism and
  ethno-politics 99–107; Uzbek ethnic
  cultural organizations 100–3; *see also*
  Central Asia
ethnic policy: Krasnodar 121–2; Russian
  Federation 113, 114, 115, 118, 119;
  Stavropol 120, 122
ethnic politics: Central Asia 97–8;
  structure 99
everyday citizenship 15–18
exasperation, in art 67
exclusion 252, 254–5
expectations, of civil society 152
experts, Uzbeks 106
expression, non-traditional 262

Facebook 85
family wage complement 21
Fariñas, Guillermo 236–7
feminists, Chile 50
film-making, Cuba 229–30
Flondor, Constantin 67
Fløysand, A. 204
football, as means of expression 81, 82–6
Foucault, Michel 83
Foundation Pablo Milanés (Cuba) 225–6
Franco dictatorship 20
Frankfurter School 39
Fraser, Nancy 255
free speech, football stadiums 83
fuel, Myanmar 186
Fumagalli, Matteo 9, 263

Garcia, M. 63
Garcia, Soledad 22
Garreton, Manuel Antonio 48, 50–1
gender inequality, Yemen 149–50
gender segregation, Afghanistan 254–5
Geoffray, M.L. 236
Ghalyun, Burhan 141
Ghnaimat, Jumana 165, 167
Giddens, Anthony 195
Gilberg, Trond 58

Index 269

Giner, S. 136
Glasius, Marlies 262
global communication, Myanmar 203
globalization, and resistance 204
government controlled NGOs (GONGOs)
142
Gramsci, Antonio 53, 137
grassroots organizations, Cuba 225
Gray, Kevin 11
Grigorescu, Ion 66, 67

Haarstad, H. 204
Habermas, Jürgen 78, 137, 221, 246–7,
252; critiques of 248–50
Hadadeen, Bassam 165, 170
Haliqa, Mohammad 168
Hamayil, U.K. 163, 164, 170, 171
Harpviken, K.B. 254–5
Hashemite regime 161–2
Hat Gyi Dam 192, 197–8
Havel, Vaclav 36, 38, 39, 40–1, 42, 43, 45,
48, 49, 50, 73, 79–80
Hawthorne, A. 142–3
Hegel, Georg 137
Hernández, Rafael 223–4
Hidden Transcripts (Scott) 78–9
hierarchical associations 9
Hirschman, A. 219, 226–7
Hoffman, Bert 8–9, 10–11, 262
Holston, James 16, 18, 235, 237
HOOD (National Organization for
Defending Rights and Freedoms)
(Yemen) 149
horizontal voice 8–9, 226–7, 231
Horsey, Richard 183
Hourani, Hani 163, 166, 171–2, 174
housing: allocation 25, 27; and morality
25; Portugal and Spain 24–9; and social
rights 26; underinvestment in 26
Housing for Poor Families (Portugal) 25
Hsiplopo 181, 187
human rights: dissident writing 44–5, 52;
Myanmar 182–3, 184; Yemen 149
Human Rights Watch 256, 257
hybrid regimes 3

Iberian Dictatorships: historiography 18;
legitimacy 22; *see also* Portugal and
Spain
identities: collective 236; national
identities 78; political identities 77–8
identity, concealment 257–8
ideology, dictatorships 37–8
"Imbunches" (Parra) 65

"In prison" (Grigorescu) 67
In the Balance 202
incongruity, of practice and belief 79
independence: dissident writing 43;
relative 52
India, opposition to dams 187
individual activism 261–2
individual, discursive power 78
industrial revolution, effects of 246–7
Instituto Nacional de Vivienda (Spain) 25
insurgent citizenship 18, 26, 235, 237
insurgents, Myanmar 189–90
integration into world economy,
authoritarian systems 7
interdependence: state and opposition 158;
state and professional associations
165–73, 174–5
international community, and dissident
writing 45–6
International Covenant of Civil and
Political Rights (ICCPR) 44
International Covenant on Economic and
Social Rights (ICESCR) 44
International Day of Action Against Dams
195
internationalism, dissident writing 52–3
Internet 8–9, 204–5, 262; blogging 233–5;
China 227; civil society activism 186–7;
e-mail 231–3; film-making 229–30;
music 230; public sphere 249, 252;
summary and conclusions 237–8; voice
to action 235–7; web as audience
229–30; *see also* Cuba
Iran, soccer 85
Irkutsk 126, 127–9; *see also* Russian
Federation
Islam, public sphere 249
Islamic societies 140–3
Islamist groups: Middle East 159; political
power 172–3; professional associations
(PAs) 164, 171–2

Jamal, A. 152
Jasmine Revolution 81
John Paul II 46
Johnston, Hank 78
Joint Meetings Party (JMP) 146
Jones Luong, Pauline 97–8, 108
Jordan 9, 10, 263; context and overview
158–9; economic concerns 173; general
Intelligence Directorate (GID) 174;
pensions 170; social security 167–8, 170;
state control strategies 161–2, 164–5; *see
also* professional associations (PAs)

270 *Index*

Jordan Center for Social Research, poll, 2007 173
Jordanian Engineers Association (JEA) 168–9, 171
journalism, Tunisia 86
July Theses (Romania) 59

Kaiser, R. 187, 190
Kalathil, S. 228
Kamrava, M. 139
Kanakriyyeh, Izzeddien 167
Kant, Immanuel 248
Karen Environmental and Social Action Network (KESAN) 181
Karen National Union (KNU) 181, 198
Karen Office of Relief and Development (KORD) 200
Karen Rivers Watch (KRW) 195
Karenni Development Research Group 193
Kawtharani, Wajid 140–1
Kazakhstan 97
Kelsay, J. 140
Khakim, Mirzo 106–7
Khin Nanda 203
Khoe Kay: Biodiversity in Peril 201–2
King, S. 76
Konrad, Gyorgy 37, 39, 40, 41, 42, 46–7, 49, 50
Krasnodar: environmental policy 126, 127, 128–9; ethnic policy 121–2; *see also* Russian Federation
Kubba, Laith 1
Kuper, Simon 85
Kyrgyzstan 97–8; party system 99; Uzbek politics 102; *see also* Uzbeks

Ladies in White (Cuba) 236–7
Langohr, Vickie 250
Latin America 3, 262
law: appeal to 44–5, 52; codification of 247
Law of Associations (Spain) 27
Law of Social Security (Spain) 21
leadership, NGOs 118, 125
Leal, António da Silva 22
legal standing 247
legislation, Yemen 144
legitimacy 6–7; and civil society 251; Iberian Dictatorships 22; and public sphere 250
legitimation, process of 252
Leppe, Carlos 66
Lewis, G. 204
L'Expression (Tunisia) 80–1

Li, L. 81
liberalization, political 11
liberalized authoritarian regimes 3, 4
Linz, J. 112
Lipset, S.M. 14
literature, as critical reflection 68
living in the truth 40–1
local activism, Myanmar 193

Madres de la Plaza de Mayo 40–1, 44–5
Mae Sot 188
Mae Tao Clinic 188
mail services 247
Malefakis, Edward 20
Mangalia Theses (Romania) 59
manpower, NGOs 117–18
"Map of Chile" (Downey) 65
Mardin, S. 140
Margins and Institutions (Richard) 65
marriage, Afghanistan 258
Marshall, Steve 183
Marx, Karl 137
mass media, Cuba 222
Maung, Cynthia 188
McCarthy, S. 184
McMann, K.M. 107–8
media, as political challenge 227, 238
Media Women' Forum (Yemen) 149–59
merchant guilds 140
Michnik, Adam 37, 47
Middle East: academic literature 159–61; civil society 140–3; exclusion 255; Islamist groups 159
Milanés, Pablo 226
minimum wage, Spain 21
Mitchell, Don 74
mockery 80
modernization: and housing 25–6; Portugal and Spain 21–2; ways of study 17
Monte Rouge (Del Llano) 230
Moore, Pete W. 142, 159
Mora, F.O. 139
morality, and housing 25
Morocco 74
Moulian, T. 61
music, Cuba 230
Muslim Brotherhood (MB) 162
Myanmar 188–9, 263; activist diaspora 187–90; borderlands 189–90, 203–4; civil society activism 186–7; Community Development Programme 188; constitution 182; context and overview 181–3; dams 181, 182; dissent 186; ecological crises 202; elections

182; environmental coalitions 199–200; environmental politics 183–7; ethnic minorities 185; foreign investment 184; fuel 186; global communication 203; human rights 182–3, 184; insurgents 189–90; local activism 193; networks 188; NGOs 203–4; political change 183; relocation and displacement 193–4, 195; repression 195–7; Salween Dams 190–8, **191**; summary and conclusions 205–7; websites 203; zones of contestation 190; *see also* Burmese diaspora

National Committee for the Cancellation of the Israeli Trade Fair 163
National Cultural Centre (UNCC) (Kyrgizstan) 100, 101, 102
national identity 78; Portugal and Spain 20; Tunisia 81–6
National Solidarity Program (Afghanistan) 255
nationalist intellectuals, Uzbeks 105–6
Nay Tha Blay 199–200
Negash, G. 57, 63
neighbourhood associations, Portugal and Spain 27–8
neo-liberalism 137–8
neo-Tocquevillian literature 74
networks 204–5; Myanmar 188, 202; virtual *see* technology
news, as commodity 247
NGOs: Cuba 224–6; governmental or business organizations 253; leadership 118; Middle East 141; Myanmar 188, 203–4; in popular uprisings 94; resources 117–19; *see also* civil society organizations; Russian Federation
Nikiforova, E. 187, 190
Nižnij Novgorod 124–5; *see also* Russian Federation
non-movements 78–9
non-violence 42–3
Norton, A.R. 139
Nsour, Maen 165, 170

O'Brien, Kevin J. 18, 81
Ochsenius, Carlos 69
O'Kane, M. 187, 190, 203
Omni Zona Franca (Cuba) 237
online opposition 204; *see also* technology
Operation Truth (Cuba) 235
opposition groups, portrayal 158–9
opposition politics, Central Asia 96
opposition, public space 78

oppositional activity 78
organizational forms, dissident writing 43–4
Osh conflict 98

Pais, Sidónio 25
Parra, Catalina 65
Parra, Marco Antonio de la 43
party system, Central Asia 99
pensions, Jordan 170
people, relationship with state 16–17
Pereirinha, José António 21
performance, resistance and opposition 78
Perjovschi, Lia 67
Perm 123–5; *see also* Russian Federation
Phillips, S. 150, 151
Pinochet regime 37–8, 39, 43, 45, 47, 57, 58, 60
Pintilie, I. 66–7
plurality 41–2
polarization, of debate 5
polémica intelectual (Cuba) 231–2, 235–6
political expression, alternative forms 78
political identities: alternative forms 87–8; formation 81–6; and sport 84–6; Tunisia 77–8
political Islam 76–7
political liberalization 11
political parties, Yemen 144–5
political space 15
political systems, Central Asia 99
politics: art against 63–4; reflected by art 61
politics of the art 61
'politics of the governed' 18
popular music, Chile 62
popular uprisings 94
Portugal and Spain: allocation of housing 25, 27; changing nature of citizenship 19–24; context and overview 13–15; developmentalism 21–2; dictatorships 20–2; elections 14; everyday citizenship 15–18; expansion of governmentality 17; housing 24–9; loss of global power 19; mobilization of urban poor 27–8; modernization 21–2; national identity 20; neighbourhood associations 27–8; segmented welfare 22; social insurance 19; social rights 17–18, 19; 'special regimes' 22; state building 25–6; summary and conclusions 29; urbanization 19, 24; welfare 21–4
positive normative connotations, of civil society 4–5

272   *Index*

Post, R.C. 136, 139, 141
poverty, in art 67
power, and resistance 83
press: Uzbeks 106–7; Yemen 144, 151
Prisoner Without a Name, Cell Without a Number (Timerman) 39
professional associations (PAs) 10; academic literature 159–61; bargaining 160–1; context and overview 158–9; creation and status 162–3; dubious legality 172; economic importance 166–7, 168–9; freezing of law 174; government interference 164; interdependence with state 165–73; Islamist groups 164, 171–2; Islamist leadership 167; membership 171–2; as political and professional actors 162–5, 172, 175; and political parties 167; resources 168–9, 173; services 169; as social elite 165; summary and conclusions 174–5; *see also* Jordan
protected housing (Spain) 25
proto-civil society, features of 39–44
Provincializing Europe (Chakrabarty) 249
public space: closure 60–1, 67–8; Cuba 222; definition and contestation 73–4; photographs of state leaders 79; resistance and opposition 78; *see also* art; dissident writing; Tunisia
public sphere 10–11; access to 247; Afghanistan 254–8; Arendt on 246; and civil society 250–4; communication technology 249; and critical theory 245–8; critiques of Habermas 248–50; exclusionary 252; Habermas on 246; Islam 249; re-defining civil society and activism 263–4; and transnationalism 227–8; use of term 221; women 248; *see also* Internet
Putin, Vladimir 111
Putnam, Robert 74, 84–5

Qaqish, Raed 167
qat chews 249, 252

Rahman, M.A. 137–8
Rawabdeh, Nadia 170
realist dictatorships 37
regime change, and civil society 139
Reitan, R. 203
relations, state and non-state actors 112
relationships, states and peoples 16–17
relative, independence 52
religious divisions, authoritarian systems 7

resistance: art 63; and globalization 204; and power 83; public space 78; rightful resistance 18, 24, 27, 81; Tunisia 80
resources: NGOs 117–19; state actors 118
revolutions: colour revolutions 53, 95; Cuba 222; Portugal 28
Richard, Nelly 65
rightful resistance 18, 24, 27, 81
riots, Kyrgyzstan 98
Rivera, A. 69
role, of civil society 1, 2
roles, performed by art 58
Romania: centralization of power 58; cinema 62; mass culture 61; politics of art 61–2; transition to democracy 57; *see also* art; Ceauçescu regime
Rosefsky Wickham, Carrie 159
Rosenblum, N.L. 136, 139, 141
Rosenfeld, Lottie 67–8
Rumman, Hussein Abu 171, 172
Rumman, Mohammad Abu 172–3
Russian Federation: case studies, actors 114–15; case studies, interests 115–16; case studies, issues 113–14; case studies, overview 112–13; case studies, resources 117–19; context and overview 111–13; disability 117–18, 123–5; Environmental Impact Assessments 126–8; environmental law 126–7; environmental policy 114, 115, 116, 118, 119, 126–9; ethnic policy 113, 114, 115, 118, 119, 120–2; negotiations between state and non-state actors 119–29; NGOs, legislation 111; public chamber 111; regional public chambers 124, 125; social policy 113, 114, 115–16, 118, 119, 123–5; summary and conclusions 129

Sabirov, Davron 100
Sai Sai 194
Saiz, A.V. 203
Salazar dictatorship 20
Salih, 'Ali 'Abdallah 144, 145, 146
Salloukh, B. 142, 159
Salween Dams 190–8, **191**; Environmental Impact Assessments 197; environmental reports 200–2; extension of campaign 192–3; multi-ethnic opposition 192; opposition poster **196**; repression 195–7; transnational activism 198–205
Salween River **194**
Salween Under Threat 201

Sánchez, Yoani 232, 233–4, 236–7, 238
Saqqa, Wael 166, 168, 171
Sater, James 250–1
Sattarov, Qurbon 100
Scott, James 78–9
self-censorship 183
self-identification, dissident writing 46–7
"Self-portrait before the parade"
  (Újvárossy) 66
"Self-portrait chestnut" (Bone) 66–7
"Self portrait toward white" (Brătescu) 67
semi-democracies 2
Shan Sapawa Environmental Organization
  194
Shiva, Vandana 187
Shura, Afghanistan 255–6
Simecka, Milan 43
Simpson, Adam 9, 263
Skocpol, T. 29
Slyomovics, Susan 74
soccer 262; Iran 85; as means of
  expression 81, 82–6
social boundaries, transgression 85–6
social divisions, authoritarian systems 7
Social Fund for Development (Yemen)
  149
social insurance, Portugal and Spain 19, 21
social media 186–7, 262
social non-movements 78–9
social policy, Russian Federation 113, 114,
  115–16, 118, 119, 123–5
social rights: and housing 26; Portugal and
  Spain 17–18, 19
social security, Jordan 167–8, 170
Society of Uzbeks (Kyrgizstan) 100, 101
Society of Uzbeks (Tajikistan) 100
Sökefeld, M. 188
solidarity 39–40
Solidarity 41, 44
South, A. 186
South America 36; see also dissident
  writing
Soviet Union, dissident writing 78
space: ethnic minority politics 96; political
  see political space; soccer fans 82–4; see
  also identities; soccer
spaces of contestation 10
Spanish Second Republic 20
"Speaking exercise/My mouth"
  (Grigorescu) 66
'special regimes,' Portugal and Spain 22
speech, in art 66–7
sport, and political identities 84–5
stakeholders, and state 111–12

Stanszkis, Jadwiga 44
state: control of civil society 141–2; and
  stakeholders 111–12
state actions, and everyday lives 17
state actors, resources 118
state and non-state actors 119–29; see also
  Russian Federation
state building, Portugal and Spain 25–6
state–civil society relations 159
state–society relations: authoritarian
  systems 4–8; Cuba 222
states, relationship with people 16–17
status relations 256
Stavropol 120–1, 122; see also Russian
  Federation
Steinberg, D.I. 185
stereotypes 106
strategies and aspirations, dissident writing
  44–51, 53
sub-Saharan Africa 138
survival strategies, authoritarian systems
  7–8
sustainability 53, 126

Tajikistan 97, 99; see also Uzbeks
talk, as oppositional activity 78
Taman Peninsula 126, 127
tatmadaw 181, 183, 187, 192, 195, 197,
  198
technology, and activism 193, 200, 203
television, Chile 62–3
terror, as control 61
Thailand 204; see also Myanmar
The Human Condition (Arendt) 246
"The Power of the Powerless" (Havel) 79
The Structural Transformation of the
  Public Sphere (Habermas) 246–7
theatre 69
Tilly, Charles 15, 24
Timerman, Jacobo 37, 39, 41, 42, 45–6
timing, of democratization 47–8
Tomey, Armando 233
Torres, R. 62
Torricelli Law 227–8
"Toward white" (Brătescu) 67
training, activist diasporas 188–9
transition paradigm, democratization 4
transnational activism 189, 198–205; see
  also activist diaspora; activist
  diasporas
transnationalism, and public sphere
  227–8
trust networks 24
Tulip revolution 102–3

274 Index

Tunisia 10; café culture 84; constitutional amendment 76; contesting space 77–81; context and overview 73–4; corporate-authoritarianism 76; dissident writing 86; images of Ben Ali 79; Islamic counter-culture 76–7; journalism 86; location of public spaces 85; paradox 75–7; political identities 77–8; political identity formation 81–6; press 80–1; public space 73–4; resistance and contention 80; soccer 81, 82–6, 262; soccer and state 83–4; state-led development 82; summary and conclusions 86–7
Turkmenistan 97

Újvárossy, Lászlo 66
ulama 140
underinvestment, in housing 26
Union of Myanmar Foreign Investment Law 184
United States, Cuba strategy 227–8
University of Jordan Center for Strategic Studies (CSS), poll, 2005 173
upgrading, of authoritarianism 2
urban poor, mobilization of 27–8
urbanization, Portugal and Spain 19, 24
US Department of State 184
Uzbek politics, Kyrgyzstan 102
Uzbek women 104–5
Uzbekistan 97
Uzbeks: activism and ethno-politics 99–107; Cultural Centre of Uzbeks of Tajikistan 100; differences between organizations 101; ethnic cultural organizations 100–3; experts 106; National-Cultural Centre (UNCC) 100, 101, 102; nationalist intellectuals 105; political representation 99; press 106–7; Society of Uzbeks (Kyrgizstan) 100; Society of Uzbeks (Tajikistan) 100–1; summary and conclusions 107–8; views of ethnic cultural organizations *103*, 103–4; voice 103–7

Vargha, Janos 46
Vasxheiyi, Judit 48
vertical power relations 252–3
vertical voice 226–7, 231
videology 62
videostroika 230
Village Organizations (VOs), Afghanistan 255–6

violence, exposure through art 65–6
"Viuda" (CADA) 66
voice 8–9, 219, 231–3, 263; to action 235–7; Uzbeks 103–7; vertical and horizontal 226–7, 231; vs. choice 10

Wakefield, S. 256
Wandee Suntivutimetee 204
Warning Signs 202
Washington Consensus 137
websites, transnational activism 203
Wedeen, Lisa 78, 249, 252, 253
Weffort, Francisco 39–40, 42, 45, 48–9
Weinthal, E. 108
welfare, Portugal and Spain 21–4
Whitebrook, M. 61
Wiktorowicz, Q. 139, 141, 142, 152
women: activists 203; gender inequality, Yemen 149–50; Myanmar 187; participation, Afghanistan 256–8; public sphere 248; at soccer matches 85–6; Uzbeks 104–5
world economy, authoritarian systems 7
writing; *see also* dissident writing
writing, resistance and opposition 78

Yanacopoulos, H. 199, 200
Yemen 9, 249, 263; advocacy 149; challenges to 146; civil society 147–50; civil society and the state 150–1; civil society organizations 148–9; civil war 145; constitution 144, 145, 147; context and overview 135–6; creation of Republic 143–4; elections 144–5; gender inequality 149–50; history of civil society activism 147; instability 145; legislation 144, 147; limitations on civil society 150; oppression 151; party system 145–6; political identities 78; post-Cold War 145–6; power-sharing 144; pre-unification 144; press 144, 151; qat chews 252, 254; resources 150; summary and conclusions 151–2; *see also* Aden
Yemen Polling Forum 149, 150
Yemen Women's Union 148
Yo'ldasheva, Aziza 104–5
Yom, S.L. 141

Zawaneh, Zayyan 175
zones of contestation 190

Taylor & Francis
eBooks
FOR LIBRARIES

ORDER YOUR FREE 30 DAY INSTITUTIONAL TRIAL TODAY!

Over 23,000 eBook titles in the Humanities, Social Sciences, STM and Law from some of the world's leading imprints.

Choose from a range of subject packages or create your own!

Benefits for you
- ▶ Free MARC records
- ▶ COUNTER-compliant usage statistics
- ▶ Flexible purchase and pricing options

Benefits for your user
- ▶ Off-site, anytime access via Athens or referring URL
- ▶ Print or copy pages or chapters
- ▶ Full content search
- ▶ Bookmark, highlight and annotate text
- ▶ Access to thousands of pages of quality research at the click of a button

For more information, pricing enquiries or to order a free trial, contact your local online sales team.

UK and Rest of World: **online.sales@tandf.co.uk**
US, Canada and Latin America:
e-reference@taylorandfrancis.com

www.ebooksubscriptions.com

A flexible and dynamic resource for teaching, learning and research.